B-17 FORTRESS
B-29 SUPERFORTRESS
——— AT WAR ———

B-17 FORTRESS
B-29 SUPERFORTRESS
— AT WAR —

ROGER A FREEMAN
DAVID A ANDERTON

This title first published by Ian Allan
as 2 separate volumes
B-29 Superfortress at War © David A. Anderton 1978
B-17 Fortress at War © Roger A. Freeman 1977

This edition published 1996 by The Promotional Reprint Company Ltd,
Kiln House, 210 New Kings Road, London SW6 4NZ
exclusively for Bookmart Limited, Desford Road, Enderby,
Leicester LE9 5AD and Book Sales Inc. in New York.

ISBN 1 85648 356 8

Printed and bound in Hong Kong

CONTENTS

Introduction

The history of the most famous of all United States military aircraft, the Boeing B-17 Fortress, has been substantially documented. In fact, a likely reaction to this work could be – *another* book on the Flying Fortress? However, the writer makes no excuse for subjecting the Fortress to further scrutiny, believing that some aspects have hitherto received scant attention.

The aim has been to present the aircraft as it was seen by those operating and maintaining it, explore its combat attributes and deficiencies and show why it became a legend. This has necessitated a wide search for former Fortress crew members who can accurately recall events rarely recorded in official records. The development and specification of the B-17, detailed in many earlier books, is only touched upon here where it is relevant to the 'Fortress at War'.

The book was inspired by the unfailing loyalty the writer has found that former air-crew have for this bomber. The writer too, must admit to a long-standing regard for the able Boeing which provided him with his most outstanding memory of World War 2. On the icy crystal clear morning of February 3, 1945, it was possible to see the contrailing of 25 formations, each of 30 to 40 aircraft, spread across some fifty miles of sky high above the flat East Anglian countryside – around a thousand Fortresses, all going to war.

Dedham 1976   Roger A. Freeman

Acknowledgements

In assembling material for this book a hundred people were consulted or assisted in some way, embracing nationals of ten different countries. A debt of gratitude is owed to them all who were so generous with their time.

Of the major contributors whose personal stories are recorded herein, 30 to 35 years after the event, only Colonel James Johnson still follows an air force career – being an electronics expert with a recent command in Europe. Brigadier-General Harold Bowman, Lieutenant Colonels Durward Fesmire, James Fletcher and John Minahan are all retired after lengthy USAF careers; John Minahan now administers an insurance agency in Germany.

Tom Danby is headmaster of a school at Wainfleet, England; Frank Furiga is in pharmaceuticals at Maple Heights, Ohio; Dan Knight is an accountant for an Orlando, Florida, construction company; George Parks retired in 1975 as a deputy in the Sheriff's office, Vallejo, California; Martin Goodman is a Los Angeles store manager while William Hess who lives at Houston, Texas is a writer and the acknowledged authority on American air aces.

Ben Phelper, a gifted portrait artist, resides at Hilltop Lakes, Texas. A great patriot, he heads the Watchdog Organisation. The Ball Gunner story is adapted from part of Ben's own book 'Shot Down', a unique record printed and illustrated by hand in a POW camp and reproduced facsimile. Gerald Dial farms the fertile soil of Lake City, Iowa; George Cuda married the landlord's daughter of his favourite pub and has a landscape gardening business at Bishop's Stortford, England, while Tom Wrigley is a chartered accountant at Boston – the English one. Bill Whitlow captains a DC-10 for National out of Miami, Florida.

Others whose help was no less valued are:

John Archer, Arthur Basham, C. Ellison Beck, Stan Bell, Roger Besecker, Cliff Bishop, Charles Bliss, Steve Birdsall, Serge Blandin, Alan Blue, Michael Bowyer, Ron Buxton, Vernon Burk, Robert Cavanagh, Paul Chryst, Walter Corsa, Larry Cummings, Tony Cushing, Arthur Evans, D. J. Evans, Stewart Evans, Michael Garbett, Michael Gibson, Werner Girbig, Brian Goulding, Joe Harlick, Ron Hartwell, Ted Hine, Lt Col Stephen Hinderliter, Harry Holmes, Ed Huntzinger, Vic Jenkins, Arey de Jong, John Jurkens, Dan Knight, Karl Kössler, Bernard Mallon, Vic Maslen, Ed Millson, Dr Karl Mistelle, Greg Moreira, James Mynatt, Lew Nalls, Cyril Norman, Pat O'Neil, Malcolm Osborn, Helge Paulsen, Geoff Pavey, Robert Pfeiffer, Alfred Price, John Rabbets, Kenn Rust, Herr Schubert, Seldon Smith, Charles Seymour, Danny Shalom, Dr Robert Simons, Bonnie Skloss, Don Smith, Vic Stachniewicz, John Stewart, Bob Sturges, Ralph Trout, Carl Vincent, Nellis Walter, Richard L. Ward, Denis White, Gordon Williams, Paul Williams, K. H. Woll and Gerrit Zwanenburg.

The Air Force Museum, Imperial War Museum, USAF Photographic Library, The Seattle Times, Albert F. Simpson Historical Research Center and Ministry of Defence also provided information.

On the production side Ian MacTaggart worked marvels with faded prints, the tedious job of proofing was aided by Ken Ranson and John Archer, Jean Freeman slaved at the typewriter, and the text had the benefit of Bruce Robertson's expertise in editorial matters.

To all these good people I extend my heartfelt thanks; without them there could have been no *Fortress At War*.

The Name that became Legend

The *Seattle Daily Times*, serving the area around the largest city of Washington State in the north-western corner of the United States, has always given a good measure of publicity to Boeing, the aircraft manufacturers, ultimately Seattle's major employer.

In 1935 Boeing, establishing themselves as a progressive force in the highly competitive and financially perilous business of aeroplane design and construction, were known to be working on the prototype of an advanced bomber; although the Company did its best to keep details secret. Final assembly took place in a hangar at Boeing Field, a few miles south-east of the city, and on the afternoon of July 16 the completed 4-engined aircraft, Boeing Model 299, was at last unveiled for public view.

A press photographer took pictures of the event and these, with details given by Boeing, arrived on the desk of Richard L. Williams, a member of the editorial staff. The laudatory copy prepared included the sentence: 'Ropes kept a throng of spectators from closely inspecting the fifteen-ton flying fortress, which made its first public appearance yesterday afternoon when it was rolled out of its hangar and its motors tested.' Williams noting the novel machine gun turrets jutting out from the streamlined metal body of the aircraft depicted in the photographs picked out as a caption heading the words – *15-TON FLYING FORTRESS*.

The title caught the attention of Boeing executives and Flying Fortress was later registered as a Company name for their Model 299, although in a rather different context, echoing the defensive posture of the nation and in line with the isolationist policy then pursued by the United States Government. The aircraft was ostensibly for long-range ocean patrol to protect America's coastline from a hostile fleet, although many officers of the Air Corps realised its offensive potential. But the Boeing was expensive and while a strong element within the Army Air Corps wanted the B-17 – the aircraft's official Army designation – the limited funds were largely invested in twin-engined competitors costing half as much. Thirteen Flying Fortresses were procured for trial purposes, becoming the pride of the Air Corps and the prime instruments in furthering a strategic bombing force. The YB-17s – designation of the test models – entered service during 1937 and were found to be as fast as some contemporary Air Corps fighters. With the installation of turbo-superchargers, permitting sub-stratospheric flight, an experimental model of the Flying Fortress was able to approach 300mph at 25 000 feet, at that time an extraordinary feat for such a big aircraft. This performance suggested that the Flying Fortress might elude fighter interception and outrange anti-aircraft artillery. With a new sophisticated bomb sight, achieving remark-

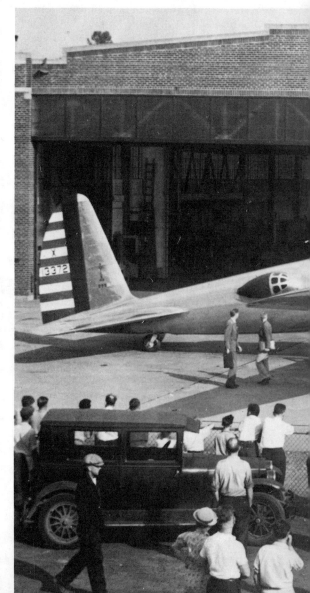

able accuracy even from great height, a new technique for daylight precision bombing emerged.

Political opposition to such a force of bombers was tempered by the Roosevelt administration's growing concern over the imperialistic aims of Japan in the Pacific and the domination of Europe by the Nazis. Not until late 1939, more than four years after the prototype's appearance, were the first true production versions of the Flying Fortress, the B-17B, obtained by the Air Corps; to be precise, just 50 days after World War 2 had erupted in Europe. And it was to be chiefly in Europe, in the hostile skies over Adolf Hitler's Third Reich that the Flying Fortress would become legendary.

In the United States services the short official designation B-17 was in common use for the aircraft, even when the abbreviated name Fortress was officially approved and in general use by the Allies. It was chiefly the Allied news media graphically promoting the Flying Fortress during the war years that made it seem the very embodiment of the American effort in the air. In later years Richard L. Williams became a senior editor with Time/Life publications, yet in all his distinguished career there can have been no other occasion when the choice of a simple heading for a new picture had such a profound effect.

Debit: The Model 299 outside the final assembly hangar on the afternoon of July 16th, 1935. Photographs taken on this occasion inspired the caption heading 15-TON FLYING FORTRESS that appeared in the 'Seattle Times' next day.

Too High

B-17C, 40-2076, in the
original British dress, takes
off on a proving flight from
Boeing Field, Seattle. In the
background is the hangar
from which the Model 299
was rolled out five and a
half years before.

'If we are at a loss for any aircraft of very long range and four-engine reliability it might be worth while to acquire a few of these bombers as a stop-gap. Without our own turrets – and I do not know if they could be fitted – the aircraft could operate only at night if opposed by modern fighters.' Thus Air Commodore Arthur Harris concluded his observations on the Boeing Flying Fortress in a report on military aircraft investigated during a visit to the United States in 1938. Harris – later the famous 'Bomber Harris' – was a member of a British Air Purchasing Commission party sent to view the American aircraft industry as a source of supply as the expansion of Nazi Germany threatened peace in Europe. Harris's report did not mince words in formal terms. It was pithy and to the point, laudatory about some aircraft and derisory on others. His observations on the Flying Fortress were tinged with scepticism: 'I have as yet failed to secure permission to look round inside this aircraft. From the outside it appears to be a fine piece of aircraft engineering. I saw it fly once, with apparently no load. It had a very bad take-off and stood up to a remarkably bad landing. The location and type of gun positions, in the shape of blisters on the hull, make it obvious that so far from being a "fortress" this aircraft is practically indefensible against any modern fighter.' Harris's further detailed criticism of the gun positions was scathing and the front cupola turret he

considered, 'More appropriately located in an amusement park than in a war aeroplane.'

Unlike most of the other aircraft inspected by the British party, the Flying Fortresses were on an Army Air Corps station. The request to see the four-engined bomber brought an afternoon visit to the 2nd Bomb Group at Langley Field, Virginia, the elite bombardment formation of the Air Corps, operating all but one of the first 13 Flying Fortresses. The exclusion of the British party from the bomber's interior was as much on political as security grounds. The 13 test models had been acquired only after much difficulty; factions within the Army and the Navy being still opposed to what they saw as an offensive weapon. The isolationist elements in Congress also viewed the aircraft with distaste and were not happy about its supposed defensive role. Criticism, from whatever quarter, was to be avoided and the Air Corps jealously guarded their hard-won prize. They were nonetheless mindful of the deficiencies highlighted in the YB-17s, particularly the armament, and both the USAAC and Boeing reviewed improvements that they hoped to incorporate in further orders.

In retrospect, Harris's appraisal was fair comment. The test model Flying Fortresses would have been highly vulnerable to attack by fighters of the types then going into service with the RAF and the Luftwaffe. British interest and activity was directed to obtaining

AN529 under guard at Squires Gate in April 1941, shortly after arrival in the UK. The temporary camouflage paint applied before leaving American (US Army olive drab to the upper surfaces and neutral gray to the lower) was the washable distemper type, and as can be seen much of this washed off during the trans-Atlantic trip. Both British and US crews were used for delivering Fortresses via Newfoundland to Prestwick.

other types of American military aircraft during the following two years but, with the fall of France and the critical situation that ensued during the summer of 1940 when Britain stood alone, positive interest in the Flying Fortress was revived. The political atmosphere in the USA had changed with the Administration's open support for the British cause and a huge expansion of America's own military forces was planned. Delivery of further Flying Fortresses, the new B-17B model during 1939-1940 followed by the much improved B-17C, had radically changed the position for the USAAC. Its doctrine of daylight strategic bombardment was no longer heresy. The RAF, while still critical of the bomber's armament and other equipment, was cognisant of the mode of attack propounded by the USAAC theorists; daylight precision attack from very high altitude where the effectiveness of enemy anti-aircraft fire and fighter interception would be minimised. The first few months of war had shown the RAF that, in general, heavy bombers were too vulnerable to enemy interception to operate effectively in daylight. The Air Corps concept offered a new approach for day operations and the RAF could not afford to neglect any possibility.

Approaches were made for the acquisition of new-model Flying Fortresses but the Air Corps were reluctant to lose precious bombers from their own expansion scheme or to risk their techniques being aborted by precipitate action which might bring repercussions on their own efforts to establish a strategic bombing force. The British met with a more sympathetic ear in the US Government. In late September 1940 Secretary of War Henry Stimson promised, among other things, to furnish the British with five Flying Fortresses. However, with an election pending, the US administration thought it wise to defer release due to 'political difficulties' but, with the November elections over, 20 B-17Cs were released to the RAF and allotted the serial numbers AN518-537.

These aircraft, having no self-sealing fuel tanks, were returned to Boeing for Goodrich self-seal units to be installed. As the B-17D model, then in production at Seattle, had priority for these tanks some delay resulted and the first four B-17Cs were not ready for movement to the UK until April 1941. Forced to part with some of their prized bombers, the USAAC then became anxious to advise in their use and assist in training RAF personnel. The RAF, while accepting all practical aid and politely acknowledging the Air Corps plans for employment, naturally preferred to operate using their own practical experience rather than adhere to Air Corps theory.

By early 1941 both the RAF and Luftwaffe had resorted to night operations for their medium and heavy bombers, generally leaving daylight operations to fast light bombers that stood a better chance of evading intercepting fighters, or operating in bad weather when extensive cloud gave protective cover. With the B-17C, named Fortress I in British service, RAF Bomber Command planners proposed to try a new approach in evading enemy opposition by the sheer altitude of the attack. At this time sub-stratospheric flight was rare and almost unknown in military operations. The turbo-superchargers on the Fortress's Cyclone engines enabled maximum performance to be obtained at 25 000 feet – 10 000 feet more than the normal operational altitude of British bombers at that time. However, to afford maximum protection, the RAF proposed to operate Fortresses as near to their combat-loaded ceiling as possible, an optimum of 32 000 feet eventually being considered as desirable. It was assumed that enemy fighters would have great difficulty reaching this altitude and locating the bomber, and the aircraft would be fairly safe from anti-aircraft fire. If the American high-altitude bomb sights proved their worth then targets could be hit with some measure of accuracy and such operations could be of inestimable value. This was basically the Army Air Corps concept with the exception that the RAF intended to operate at a much higher altitude –

The Famous: On June 6th, 1941 Prime Minister Winston Churchill visited RAF West Raynham, Norfolk, to review the latest RAF aircraft and equipment. USAAC officers Major James Walsh and Captain James Connally demonstrated a Fortress for him (believed to be the ill-fated AN522) and the scene was captured in this superb photograph.

some seven to ten thousand feet higher.

A special squadron, No 90, was re-formed to fly the Fortress Is in Bomber Command's No 2 Group which specialised in daylight operations. While squadron headquarters were at West Raynham, the aircraft were to be based on the nearby satellite airfield at Watton, a grass-surfaced field on the edge of a heathland area known as the Norfolk Breckland. The first Fortress* arrived at Watton on April 14 having flown into Ayr, Scotland that morning after an 8 hour 26 minute transatlantic flight. The aircraft was piloted by Major Walsh, an experienced Army Air Corps pilot, accompanied by two sergeant mechanics, Olsen and Benner. They assisted in training aircrew during No 90's formative stage, supplemented by other Air Corps personnel, but all in great secrecy as the US was ostensibly neutral.

Despite neutrality, the supply of war equipment to Britain under the Lend-Lease agreement was public governmental policy and great play was made of this by both British and American news agencies. The former in particular were anxious to impress upon the enemy how deeply America was involved with the hope that ultimately she would be drawn into the conflict. Although the Air Corps would have preferred not to have its concept of high altitude bombing with the Fortress put to the test by the RAF, many factions in the US administration were

anxious to bring the US aircraft industry to the forefront. No sooner had the first Fortress arrived than pressure was placed on Bomber Command to commit the aircraft to battle. Aware of the political implications of getting the vaunted Flying Fortress into battle, RAF Bomber Command decided to accept the bombers with a minimum amount of modification. Other aircraft types purchased from America were normally processed through Burtonwood, Lancashire, where standard British radio and signals equipment and identification lights were installed. It had also been intended to adapt the bomb racks to hold British bombs, but this was evidently abandoned with the availability of American 1100lb high explosive types in the UK.

Brigadier General Millard Harmon, a US observer of the air war in Europe, was acquainted with the initial Bomber Command opinions of the Fortress at this time. '. . . we are more than satisfied with performance, layout and crew comfort. The only point on which we are seriously doubtful is the efficiency of the defensive armament . . . experience will show.'

Training of the air crews was difficult to expedite due to the specialised nature of the Squadron's mission. The twenty crews had to be carefully selected to stand the physical demands of operating at what were then incredibly high altitudes. It was also desirable that none was over twenty-four years old and that all had operational experience on four-engined aircraft. Each man was required to undergo a test in the decompression chamber

Below: AN521 (which became 'K-King' in 90 Sqdn) seen here, in company with a Tomahawk and a Havoc at Northolt on June 21st, 1941, readied for an inspection by Sir Charles Portal, Chief of Air Staff, and General Cheney, US Air Attache, of US aircraft types supplied to Britain. This Fortress had been the first to arrive in the UK. An Airspeed Oxford can be seen landing in the background.

Bottom: All that was left of AN528, the first 'B-Baker' after it caught fire on dispersal at Polebrook. The fabric burnt from the large rudder highlights the B-17C's small amount of fin area in contrast to later model Fortresses. The bomber being refueled in the background is WP:G.

*Two aircraft made the crossing, the second flew to Burtonwood via Squires Gate for modifications.

at Farnborough, spending four hours at a simulated 32-36 000 feet. This was to eliminate those susceptible to 'bends' and 'chokes' – pains caused by bubbles in the blood and other body fluids and tissues resulting from the decreased barometric pressure at high altitude. The pains varied from dull aches in leg or arm joints to pains of crippling agony and the intensity varied with individuals. Chest constrictions or itching and pricking of the skin were other symptoms. Many men were eliminated through their susceptibility to bends and 60 per cent of the prospective crews were rejected on medical grounds.

Training in correct oxygen procedure was vital, for a failure in supply could produce anoxia – resulting in unconsciousness in a few minutes and death in ten at over 30 000 feet. Anoxia is an insidious condition in which a man is often unaware of the onset as the initial stages tend to make the victim elated and grossly overconfident. There would also be extreme cold during stratospheric flight with the risk of frostbite, so that electrically heated suits must be worn. In view of the physical hazards of operating at these altitudes, two RAF medical officers instructed and watched over the crews, often flying with them on training missions to observe the functioning of oxygen equipment. Such were the difficulties in assembling air crew meeting the stringent requirements that, at the end of its first month, the squadron could muster only three pilots and no complete crews. One of the three was the 'capable and energetic' Commanding Officer, Wing Commander J.

MacDougall, who now had a small team of American experts to help make the Squadron a viable unit. In addition to Major Walsh, two other US officers with B-17 piloting experience were on hand, three sergeant mechanics, Crawford a Boeing engineer and Franklyn Jones a Sperry technician.

By the end of the third week in May, 14 of the 20 Fortresses had reached Britain and five of these had been modified and delivered to 90 Squadron. Certain pro-British members of the US Government were impatient to see the Fortresses in action and Averell Harriman, the US Ambassador, explained to the British 'that the question of using the Flying Fortress operationally had become a political question of some importance', particularly as it had been well reported that these large bombers had been sent to Britain. Perhaps American interests did not appreciate the dilemma of priorities within the hard-pressed RAF but these proddings at a high level from both US and British sources did have the effect of accelerating supply and training. This brought further problems, not the least of which was the danger of flints on grass airfields piercing tyres of these heavy machines with disastrous consequences if this should occur on take-off. Because of this hazard at Watton an attempt had been made to operate from its nearby satellite at Bodney but one alarming landing was enough to convince Major Walsh and Wg Cdr MacDougall that the surface there was far too undulating for operating Fortresses safely. A move was made to Great Massingham where the surface seemed better,

Winston Churchill rubs an eye – in retrospect a suitable gesture in view of the misfortunes that befell the Fortress I – as he escorts Harry Hopkins, US Ambassador-at-large, on a review of US made aircraft at Northolt, July 20th, 1941. The Fortress is 'H-How', first of its kind to unload bombs on Germany, but thereafter relegated to training. The crew is that of Plt Off F. W. Sturmey, who would become the most distinguished in 90 Sqdn.

Top: Wg Cdr J. MacDougall starts No 2 on 'F-Freddie' for the raid on Brest, July 24th, 1941. Highly respected, MacDougall suffered physically at very high altitudes and received a new assignment three days after this raid. Sqn Ldr Webster took command of 90 Sqdn on the 29th.

Above: WP:F, AN530, thunders down the main runway at Polebrook for the July 24th operation. Camouflage scheme applied to the Fortresses at Burtonwood was specially devised for high altitude operations, with a special azure blue shade for the undersurfaces extending well up the fuselage sides and also being applied to the whole fin and rudder.

although regular inspections were carried out to locate stones. This was but a temporary move until Polebrook, the most advanced of the many new airfields in the area with hard surfaced runways, was available.

By mid-June nine Fortresses had been allocated to No 90 Squadron and high altitude training and practice bombing were in full swing. It was soon discovered that physiological problems were not the only ones at such heights. Taking the bombers up two miles beyond the altitude which the Air Corps considered the optimum for bombing (20 000 feet) brought mechanical and equipment difficulties. Extreme temperature change caused fractures in the welding of the engine exhaust flanges. The intricate turbo-supercharger controls became unduly sensitive and an unwitting abrupt control movement could cause the turbos to surge and cause disintegration of a turbine blower.

The Fortress was fitted with a Sperry autopilot system which could be controlled from the bomb sight, thus allowing the bomb aimer to fly flat turns while making adjustments to his sight on the bomb run. This too was hyper-sensitive at 30 000 feet and if the autopilot gyros were not synchronised before switching in the bomb sight, the aircraft would yaw violently placing tremendous strain on the fin and rudder. The extreme temperature changes in a climb or descent brought leaks and subsequently an ingress of

air to the hydraulic lines of the auto-pilot. It became necessary to bleed the system prior to take-off to ensure its function. Most of the systems were electrical and although normally trouble free, the intense cold and very low pressure made problems here too. However, reliance on electrics did keep the Fortress's interior cleaner than most of its hydraulic oil-soaked contemporaries and air crew could smoke in safety. The cigarette lighters installed in the cockpits of the earlier Air Corps B-17s however, were not in evidence. Another problem at 30 000 feet was the build-up of frost on the inner sides of windows restricting visibility and requiring dispersal by heated panels. Radio signals were weak at this altitude and further changes had to be made to the equipment.

Modification of the American oxygen system to take British regulators and masks had also to be effected. Oxygen masks were found to be uncomfortable and, if allowed to get damp on the ground tended to freeze up at high altitude. In fact, in an effort to eliminate moisture both oxygen masks and the electrically heated clothing were later kept in a specially heated building. Of all the technical troubles, however, the most persistent was the tendency of the Wright Cyclones to throw oil from the crankcase breathers. Mysteriously, the problem lay with individual engines for while one performed impeccably to 35 000 feet, another might throw oil at

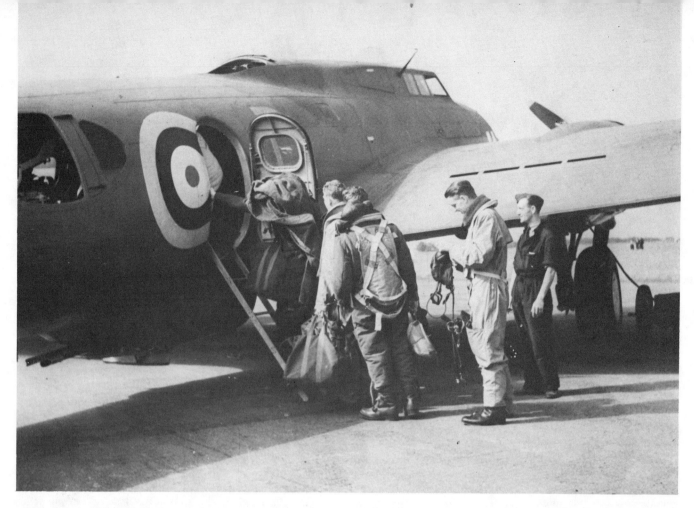

20 000 feet and the flow would grow alarmingly as altitude increased.

No 90 Squadron was unique in being trained for a new mode of bomb delivery. As such it was an experimental unit and its new experiences were at times fraught with danger. On the afternoon of June 22, Fortress AN522 was despatched from Massingham on a stratospheric training flight. At the controls were Flg Off J. Hawley and Lt Bradley, an experienced Air Corps B-17 pilot. In addition to the other three crew members – Sergeants Black, Garwood and Wills – the Fortress carried the squadron medical officer, Sqn Ldr Robson and a doctor from RAF Farnborough, Flt Lt Steward. The weather was fine with intermittent cloud patches which thickened as the flight proceeded and in some places cumulonimbus cloud boiled up to great heights. At 30 000 feet over Yorkshire the pilots were confronted with a cloud pile which they apparently tried unsuccessfully to climb over ending up in the thunderhead. Hailstones 'as large as golf balls' hurled into the open fuselage gun windows. In the grip of heavy ice accretion the pilots lost control and AN522 went into a terminal velocity dive. At around 25 000 feet the port wing was wrenched off and the fuselage broke in two aft of the wing, trapping Flt Lt Steward in the rear section. The tumbling tail section fell a further 12 000 feet before Steward was able to free himself and fall clear. He was the only man on the Fortress able to parachute to safety, landing not far from the wreckage at Catterick Bridge. Lt Bradley was the first airman of the US Army Air Force* to be killed on active service in World War 2.

Shortly after this distressing accident, No 90 Squadron moved its Fortresses to Polebrook. The tar on the runways was hardly dry and some facilities were uncompleted but the airfield was much more suitable for operating large and heavy bombers. Four of the RAF crews were now in an advanced state of training and, using the Sperry Mk 0-1 sight, bomb aimers had been able to achieve reasonable accuracy on the target range at Ashton. Drops had, however, only been made from up to 20 000 feet, considerably lower than the proposed altitude for attack. A crucial part of the USAAF technique for very high altitude bombing was the Norden sight. An extremely complex instrument that automatically computed many of the adjustments necessary for precise alignment on a target, the Norden was classified secret, so that the US Navy, who had developed it, would not countenance its release to the British. The Sperry sight was substituted for the Norden before delivery of the Fortresses and, while similarly a precision instrument, it demanded much greater skill in operating.

*US Army Air Corps became the US Army Air Force in June 1941.

Sqn Ldr A. D. MacLaren's crew boarding 'D-Dog', AN523, for the Brest operation of July 24th. This was the Fortress that was engaged in the epic battle with enemy fighters of August 16th. In this picture the two .50 guns can be seen projecting from the under emplacement.

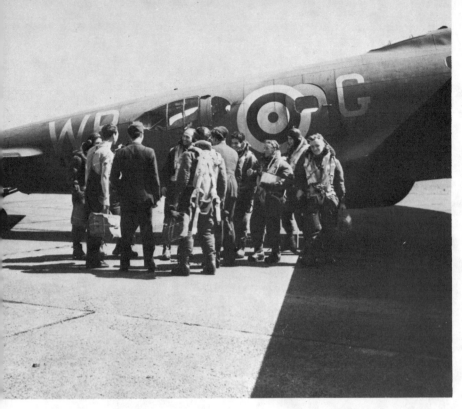

A 90 Sqdn aircrew discuss a training flight they have just completed in 'G-George'. On operational sorties the crew of seven consisted of two pilots, bomb-aimer/navigator, a fire controller (directing from the observation dome), wireless operator/top gunner, beam gunner and under gunner. A training crew – as in this picture – usually included an extra wo/gunner.

Maintenance difficulties also brought a high unserviceability rate, often reducing the bombers available to half. One evening after an engine check on Fortress *B-Baker*, her fitters commenced a test running. After priming No 2 engine, an attempt to start it brought a backfire and flames. Although the fire extinguisher button was pressed, the flames were not doused and in a matter of seconds the fire had spread to the wing. The station fire force was soon on the scene but efforts to contain the fire were in vain and *B-Baker* became a flaming mass beneath a black column of acrid smoke. The Court of Inquiry into this incident found an incorrect starting procedure had been used, partly as a result of ambiguous instructions in the manual – which was later amended.

Despite the limited experience of bomb aimers in using the Sperry sight, the political pressures from home and abroad to get the Fortress into battle precipitated the operational debut of the squadron. A prerequisite to any Fortress mission was clear weather and good visibility, a comparatively infrequent occurrence in North-West Europe. On July 8 the right conditions prevailed and three Fortresses were despatched from Polebrook to bomb the Wilhelmshaven naval base, some 400 miles distant. The plan was for the three aircraft to fly in loose formation and bomb individually from 30 000 feet, closing formation only if intercepted by enemy fighters. As there was more likelihood of interception after bombing, the Fortresses were to climb to an altitude of between 33 000 and 35 000 feet on the withdrawal. When setting out the formation was led by Wg Cdr MacDougall in *G-George* with Sqn Ldr MacLaren piloting

H-How and Plt Off Alex Mathieson in *C-Charlie* trailing. Wg Cdr MacDougall reached the target, but two of the four 1 100lb bombs could not be released and had to be brought back to base – moisture freezing in a solenoid was later diagnosed as the cause. To add to these troubles a turbo-supercharger collapsed on one engine with resultant loss of power. About a hundred miles out from the enemy coast, while still at 30 000 feet, two Me 109s were reported approaching the bomber but these did not open fire, neither did *G-George*'s gunners, whose vision was restricted by heavy frosting on windows. No more was seen of the fighters and *G-George* returned safely to Polebrook.

On the climb out all four engines of Sqn Ldr MacLaren's *H-How* began throwing oil from their crankcase breathers after the bomber had passed 23 000 feet, continuing as the climb proceeded. At 28 000 feet, concerned at the loss of oil, MacLaren decided to divert to attack a target of opportunity along the enemy coast before turning for home. The oil, trailing back from the engines, froze on the tailplane and elevators and built up to four inches thick in places. *H-How* began to vibrate and with such intensity that MacLaren feared his bomber was in danger of disintegrating. Attempting to stop the shaking, he first stalled the aircraft and then dived, but it made no difference. Such tremors were usually connected with engine trouble, so MacLaren shut down and feathered the propellers on each Cyclone in turn but there was no abatement. He then throttled back and started losing altitude; at approximately 18 000 feet the frozen oil started melting and by the time *H-How* was down to 16 000 feet the vibration had stopped.

Plt Off Mathieson in *C-Charlie* was able to proceed almost as planned, and although two of the bomber's engines threw a small amount of oil above 30 000 feet the bombs were dropped on the target area and Mathieson touched down at Polebrook 3¾ hours after take-off.

This initiation of the Fortress into action highlighted many problems. Freezing equipment and oil throwing had not been met in the low humidity environment in which B-17s generally flew in the USA. Over half the engines of the Squadron's Fortresses were now throwing excessive oil out of the crankcase breather at high altitudes, the phenomenon generally beginning in the neighbourhood of 27 000 feet. Prolonged loss could lower crankcase oil to a dangerous level and oil freezing on the tail surfaces could hazard control as had been highlighted in the maiden mission of *H-How*. In fact it was the only time *H-How* went to war. The behaviour of its engines made further high altitude sorties a dubious prospect and it was confined to training duties at lower levels. For *G-George* too, this was its only bombing sortie for, apart from the replacement to the turbo-super-charger, two of the engines showed signs of excessive discharge of oil from the breather. For subsequent operations Fortresses endowed with less troublesome 'power eggs' were selected and for four weeks only *C-Charlie*, *D-Dog* and *F-Freddie* could be employed. The oil trouble was thought to be faulty scavenging induced by humidity and cold and Wright engineers were hard put to find a solution.

Another difficulty was that of contrails which formed behind the aircraft at certain unpredictable levels in the upper atmosphere. As these immediately gave away the position and direction of the bomber to any hostile interceptors, the Fortress had either to climb higher or descend to get out of the contrail level. Frequently neither course was possible and the mission had to be abandoned. The inability to avoid 'trailing' was the reason for the failure of a prestige raid on Berlin attempted by the three Fortresses on July 23, the first bright clear day for two weeks that was really suitable. Clear skies allowed a run against the German battle-cruisers *Scharnhorst* and *Gneisenau* at Brest on the following day and against Emden's docks on the 26th. The various mechanical and environmental difficulties continued and the bombs dropped wide of the assigned aiming points. During the Brest raid it was noted that when a Fortress reached 28 000 feet, while flying over Cornwall, condensation trails began to form behind the aircraft. A height change of fifty feet either way saw the contrails disappear.

Another disturbing accident occurred on the afternoon of July 28. Flt Sgt Brook accompanied by Lt Hendricks, USAAF, was detailed for a training flight in *E-Easy*. A patchy overcast, estimated as eight/tenths cloud extended over Polebrook and *E-Easy* was seen to enter this at about 2 000 feet while climbing away from the airfield. After gaining an estimated 3 000 feet, and still in cloud, a change of engine note was heard by people on the ground and moments later *E-Easy* was seen to dive out of the clouds, the angle of descent increasing to near vertical. The right wing broke away a few hundred feet before the Fortress smashed into the ground at Wilbarston, some 16 miles from its base. There were no survivors. A court of Inquiry found the most likely cause of the accident to be premature engagement of the auto-pilot, before stabilising procedures had been effected, causing the pilot to become disorientated in cloud.

So far the few operations had been carried

out without hindrance from the enemy but catching one of the vaunted Fortresses became something of a challenge for the Luftwaffe. The time required to reach the bomber's operating altitude did not leave much loiter time with the short endurance of Me 109s. A successful interception depended on an early precise and accurate vector from the fighter controller and on August 2, 1941 that was forthcoming.

Plt Off Frank Sturmey's crew was one of two despatched for an attack on Kiel. It was their first operation and in *F-Freddie* they were to have followed the experienced Flt Lt Mathieson and crew in *C-Charlie*. But the Fortress they tracked after take-off began to take a course different from that briefed and the Sturmey crew discovered they had mistakenly joined up with a Fortress on a training flight. After landing back at Polebrook, *F-Freddie* was refuelled and set off again at 1715 hours to attack Emden. Finding thickening cloud over the Frisian Islands, Sturmey

Below: Fg Off F. W. Sturmey (third from the left) and crew. Flt Sgt Fred Goldsmith, who won the DFM for his conduct on August 16th, is extreme right. Only the captain of the original combat crew survived the World War 2.

Bottom: The cockpit of AN519. Sqn Ldr Alex Mathieson is in the first pilot's seat with his hands on the B-17's renowned throttle levers. Mathieson and crew were lost without trace on the disastrous second raid to Oslo.

elected to bomb Borkum, visible through a gap in the undercast. At 2020 hours on the return trip, while some twenty miles north of Texel and at 22 000 feet, two Me 109s were seen climbing to attack. The fighters made seven individual attacks turning in from 250 to 750 yards and scoring several hits on *F-Freddie* although none of the damage caused was serious. The Fortress gunners returned fire and after three bursts had been seen to hit the engine of one Me 109 the enemy aircraft broke off the engagement. *F-Freddie* returned to base without further trouble.

This action, recorded as an inconclusive skirmish by the British participants, was of some historical significance. Three Me 109Fs of 3/JG52 had taken off from Wangerooge to intercept at 1925 hours. In the attack Feldwebel Wihelm Summerer's Me 109 was apparently hit in the engine, forcing him to bale out over the sea and he was never seen again. Both the other German aircraft were also hit by defensive fire, one severely as it was later forced to belly-land at Alphen near the Meuse in Holland. The third aircraft sustained only slight damage and made a normal landing at Katwijk airfield near the Dutch coast. The Fortress's first air battle gave substance to the name.

Plt Off Sturmey's crew were also involved in a drama played out over the English Channel on August 16, following another attempt to bomb the German battle-cruisers holed-up in Brest. Three minutes after bombing, at 1109 hrs, two enemy fighters were sighted about 1 000 feet below to the right of Fortress *D-Dog* and shortly afterwards five more appeared from the same general direction. Flt Sgt Fred Goldsmith, the fire controller, identified the first two as He 113s (erroneously as the type never served operationally with the Luftwaffe) and the rest as Me 109s, all with yellow noses and rudders. It was Goldsmith's duty to observe the enemy manoeuvres as they prepared to attack and alert the gunners and pilots. *D-Dog* was at 32 000 feet and as Sturmey had been unable to coax the bomber any higher during the flight he now relied on making evasive turns. The first attack, from astern, hit the aircraft and cannon shell shrapnel wounded Goldsmith in the left hand and leg. Sgt H. Needle, the wireless operator/gunner, could not get the twin upper guns to fire, probably because of freezing. In a series of attacks several cannon shells were put into the rear fuselage, one mortally wounding under gunner Sgt M. J. Leahy in the head and neck, Sgt S. Ambrose the beam gunner was killed and Sgt H. Needle was hit in the stomach. In this desperate situation Sturmey put *D-Dog* into a dive, losing 2 000 feet a minute, but the Messerschmitts followed. Although wounded, Goldsmith continued to give Sturmey warning so the pilot could take evasive action every

Below: Wreckage of WP:D, AN525, at Bygland, Norway, photographs from the album of Lt Alfred Jakobi who shot down this first of thousands of Fortresses to fall in World War 2. Much of the wreckage – shown here are an engine and the left side of the fuselage waist – was transported to Germany for detailed examination. The graves of the crew in the local cemetery are still regularly tended by the villagers.

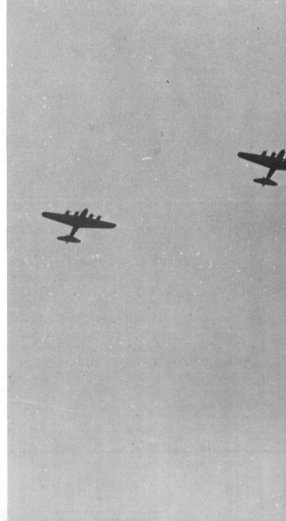

time a 109 came within range. Black smoke was streaming back from the damaged No 4 engine when, providentially, a patch of light cloud appeared ahead. The fighters did not follow through and when Sturmey levelled *D-Dog* out some 2 500 feet above the sea there was no sight of her tormentors. The Fortress had suffered 26 attacks in 23 minutes at the hands of the experienced pilots of JG 2.

It was believed that Needle and Leahy were still alive and Goldsmith attempted to go to the rear to give them first aid across the catwalk over the open bomb-bay which was festooned with a mass of broken wires and cables and from which the guide ropes had been shot away. He had to be restrained, almost by force, from making the attempt. The bomb aimer, Plt Off A. J. Mulligan then tried to cross, once with a parachute, but the obstacles made the task almost impossible. By this time the pilots had brought the badly damaged aircraft within sight of the small airfield at Roborough near Plymouth. Sturmey, and Plt Off T. Franks the second pilot, managed to get it down despite having little rudder control, an inoperative aileron, no tail trim and the tail wheel stuck halfway down. The brakes had also been wrecked and *D-Dog* careered across the small grass field running into a hedge and a concrete tank trap where it burst into flames. The survivors were soon out of the bomber and some re-entered the fuselage to rescue their comrades. Leahy, still alive, died later in hospital; the other two gunners were dead. While the last flight of *D-Dog* said much for the robust nature of the Fortress it also emphasised the deficiencies in armour protection for the crew. As a result of this experience some experimental installations were put in hand, notably blanking off the fuselage aft of the waist guns with a sheet of armour plate.

During August 1941 the number of American personnel at Polebrook increased to a score as General Arnold, the USAAF commander, anxious to see the RAF experiment have every chance of success, sent over more technical experts. Nevertheless, despite intensive crew training and attempts to eliminate technical troubles, it was never possible to despatch more than four Fortresses on a single operation and bombing results were always poor.

It transpired that the first American subject to drop bombs on Germany from a Flying Fortress was a civilian! Sperry's technical expert on the RAF's bomb aimers bomb sight criticised them and rose to the taunt that couldn't do better. He was allowed to don RAF flying clothing and act as a bomb aimer on *N-Nan* in a raid on Bremen's shipyards carried out on September 2. Some cloud obscured the target but Mr Vose was satisfied that the bombing run and lining up of the aiming point had been accurate. However, photos showed strikes three miles wide of the

Below left: A rare sight; five Fortress Is in formation over Polebrook. A display for the film 'Flying Fortress'.

Below: A warrant officer takes details from disembarked crewmen after one of the last Fortress sorties by 90 Sqdn. The twin .50s in the upper gun position are visible on 'B-Baker', AN518. The US Sergeant was one of the technical advisers at Polebrook whose presence was a guarded secret at the time.

Top: AN530, in which Frank Sturmey's crew fought the first engagement with enemy fighters on August 2nd.

Above: Dusk falls: 'J-Johnny', AN532, at Shallufa, Egypt. No 90 Sqdn Detachment had great difficulty in maintaining the aircraft due to an inadequate supply of parts.

target. After this it was concluded that the stress imposed on mental and physical faculties at great height was the root cause of bad bombing.

Early in September a detachment of Fortresses was sent to Kinloss in Scotland for the purpose of carrying out raids on the pocket battleship *Admiral Scheer* reposing in a ship-building and repair yard at Oslo. The first operation was carried out as planned, but the bombs missed their target. A second raid was flown on September 8, 1941 but this time Me 109Ts of 13/JG77 at Stavanger-Sola were alerted when the approaching force was detected on the German radar sited on the Norwegian coast. Four Fortresses had been despatched from Kinloss but *N-Nan*, piloted by Sqn Ldr Alex Mathieson was delayed ten minutes after the others. To obtain better bombing results the attack was to be carried out from 26 000 feet after which altitude was to be increased to evade possible interception. Flg Off David Romans in the new *D-Dog*, flying ahead of Plt Off Sturmey in *J-Johnny* and Flt Sgt 'Mick' Wood in *O-Orange*, was intercepted at 1127 hours when nearing the Norwegian coast by two Me 109s. During the first exchanges of fire, Lt Alfred Jakobi took hits in the right wing of his Me 109T but pressed his attack and scored several hits on *D-Dog*. With port engines on fire the bomber turned sharply to port, went into a dive, and apparently broke up before crashing at

Bygland, a mountainous area some 75 kilometres north of Kristiansand. All seven crew members were killed. The first Fortress had fallen in battle.

Crews of the following Fortresses witnessing the interception realised that it would not be expedient to complete the mission; *J-Johnny* returned safely to Kinloss without further incident but *O-Orange* did not escape so easily. Sgt Wood was flying about four miles behind and some 3 000 feet above the unfortunate *D-Dog*. He immediately applied full power, jettisoned bombs, and climbed to 35 000 feet as he turned for home. At this altitude there was less risk from interception but voices on the intercom became very indistinct due to insufficient vibration of the vocal chords in the rarified air. A beam gunner, mistaking an order, exchanged his main oxygen supply for a portable emergency bottle and collapsed on the floor after a few minutes. Another gunner going to his assistance also collapsed having failed to connect his oxygen line correctly to a portable bottle. It was some time before the pilot, failing to get any response over the intercom from the gunners, realised something was miss and sent the radio operator to see. On the report that both were unconscious, and fearing for their lives, Wood dived *O-Orange* towards denser atmosphere. During this dive a tell-tale vapour trail was emitted and spotted by Unteroffizier. Woite, another Me 109 pilot who, closing

from astern to 50 yards, fired a long burst before peeling off. From *O-Orange* smoke streamed back from a blasted glycol tank. The two unconscious gunners were hit by cannon shell fragments, Sgt Tait being wounded in the legs and Sgt Wilkin was killed. The aileron controls would not operate, one engine was damaged and later a second failed, and there were many shell and bullet holes all over the aircraft. In this battered state Wood was able to bring *O-Orange* back to Kinloss where complete hydraulic failure necessitated a crash-landing. No trace was ever found of Sqn Ldr Mathieson's *N-Nan*, although a sea search was carried out next day. The assumption is that some accident caused loss of control.

For RAF Bomber Command this operation was final proof of the vulnerability of the Fortress to fighter attack and an affirmation of the inadequacy of its armament. Operations were still conducted on a limited scale from Polebrook but only relatively safe diversion attacks, the last three of these being carried out by the most experienced crew, Plt Off Sturmey's, with the finale in the new *B-Baker* on September 25. Although the Squadron remained on operational status, no more Fortress I raids were made from Britain. Twenty-four operations had been flown amounting to 48 individual sorties of which 26 were abortive in that the bombers had not attacked their objectives. Most of the in-

effectual attacks were due to cloud obscuring the target, while only five per cent were attributed to mechanical troubles. The RAF's Director of Bombing Operations was now in no doubt that this experiment had failed when, on the same day as Plt Off Sturmey was making the final sortie, he outlined the reasons why the Fortress I was not suited to operations in North-West Europe in a letter to the AOC-in-C, Bomber Command:

1 The Fortress cannot rely on evasion of enemy aircraft below 32 000 feet.
2 Once intercepted the Fortress has little chance against modern fighters.
3 Despite reputed accuracy of the Sperry sight, precise bombing with the Fortress above 32 000 feet is extremely difficult, due to physical and mental strain imposed in using equipment at that great height.
4 Dependence on suitable weather to carry out attack limits the frequency of operations.
5 Condensation trails can cause a raid to be abandoned. Gives away position of the B-17.
6 The average bomb load is uneconomical in relation to the manning and maintenance effort.

During September 1941 interest was shown by the RAF Middle East Command in having

Top: AN537, one of the four Fortress Is inherited by 220 Sqdn and used primarily as trainers during the Squadron's conversion to the Fortress II for marine reconnaissance.

Above: AN520 spent most of its life with Coastal Command and still wore the white sea-patrol camouflage, when, in the spring of 1944, it arrived at Sculthorpe to serve as a trainer for RAF Bomber Command's 214 Squadron, then using later model Fortresses for radio-countermeasures operations.

the Fortresses transferred to that theatre where conditions might prove more amenable and reduce the danger of enemy interception. This request was met after improvised dust filters were installed on the engines; five aircraft and crews set off. However, *A-Able*, after showing a marked reluctance to start at Polebrook, suffered a blown cylinder head on No 4 engine and got no further than Portreath in Cornwall. On October 28th Sqn Ldr McLaren in *C-Charlie*, Plt Off Stokes in *B-Baker*, Flg Off Sturmey in *K-King* and Flg Off Stevenson in *J-Johnny*, departed England for Malta. *C-Charlie* and *J-Johnny* had flown in more missions than any of the other No 90 Sqn bombers with nine each to their credit, the former having flown the very first operation in July.

The Fortresses remaining at Polebrook were joined by the last two replacement aircraft from the Burtonwood depot early in November, for although operations had been halted, training and experimental flights continued. Not only were endeavours made to resolve the remaining difficulties with the aircraft and equipment (the oil throwing and freezing of guns had by this date been largely eliminated) but even higher altitudes were sought. On one occasion a lightly loaded Fortress was flown to 40 000 feet but usually the tests were made to 36 000 feet. Here the lack of atmospheric pressure brought additional discomforts for crews as it caused bladder incontinence. To avoid clothing being wetted and consequently freezing, a rubber tube was rigged up to run down inside the leg of the flying suit and then out of the flying boot onto the cockpit floor. This led to a disconcerting experience for Flt Sgt Ron Hartwell piloting at 35 000 feet when he found he could not move his leg. His immediate thought was of paralysis, then he discovered that escaping urine had frozen his boot to the cabin floor!

The very high altitude experimentation continued into 1942 under constant observation from RAF medical officers and technical experts. A great deal of valuable information was gained on the effects of stratospheric flight on both man and machine. But plans were already afoot to turn over the remaining Fortresses to RAF Coastal Command, where it was felt their endurance would allow them to play a useful part in anti-submarine patrols. Before this happened on January 9, Fortress *M-Mother* crashed with the loss of all five crew members while on a routine training flight over Cambridge. At about 13 000 feet speed apparently fell away and the aircraft stalled. *M-Mother* was seen to come out of cloud in a left-hand spin and, although the crew had donned parachutes, it appears that the order to jump was never given which

suggests that the pilot hoped to make a recovery. The five remaining Fortresses at Polebrook were sent to No 220 Squadron at Nutts Corner, Northern Ireland, in mid-February, their formal transfer being on the 12th, after which 90 Squadron ceased to function as a Fortress unit.

Meanwhile, the detachment sent to the Middle East had not fared well. Operations had begun from Shallufa in early November but it was found that the hot atmosphere slowed the rate of climb and reduced the ceiling to around 28 000 feet. Engine temperatures rose to near danger levels and petrol consumption became excessive, difficulties later attributed to lack of instruction in the technique of operating radial engines in hot climates. During the first operation to targets in the Tobruk area, the veteran *C-Charlie* ran out of fuel, forcing Fly Off Swanson to land behind enemy lines. The crew, failing to get the aircraft to burn, machine gunned the bomb sight and other components before making a successful bid to reach British troops.

Some weeks later *K-King* was being flown locally by Flg Off Sturmey when an engine caught fire – through a propeller over-speeding – and the crew were ordered to bale out, one man being killed when he hit the tail. The remaining *B-Baker* and *J-Johnny* were chiefly employed in sea reconnaissance flights at around 20 000 feet, searching for the Italian fleet. On two occasions when enemy fighters endeavoured to intercept, the Fortresses managed to evade. Lack of spares and blowing sand compounded the maintenance problems and brought long periods of unserviceability. The detachment was made over to No 220 Squadron in February 1942, with the intention of sending it to join the other Fortresses in Northern Ireland. An order to this effect was issued for April 9 but it appears to have been countermanded as the two bombers were directed to India. Due to lack of spares the two Fortresses did little flying after their arrival and in December both were handed over to the USAAF who were operating a small number of B-17Es in India. Unfortunately, *J-Johnny* suffered an engine fire during a test flight and crashed. *B-Baker* was completely overhauled to become a VIP transport in the theatre. The Americans too, had found this early model Fortress unfitted for combat after experience during the initial stages of the war with Japan. As for the RAF crews, the planned two-month detachment from England had grown to a frustrating nine months leaving them 'tired and dejected'.

General Arnold was later to write that the RAF never gave the Fortress a chance and that the B-17C had been badly handled by Bomber Command. In this he was influenced by reports from his observers and his knowledge of the RAF's preconceived notions that any attempt to employ the Fortress in daylight was almost certainly doomed. The advised technique of the USAAF differed from that actually undertaken, in that they would have operated from 20 000 feet and flown the aircraft in close formation to obtain a better defence through the co-ordinated fire of several guns. While this would undoubtedly have given better results in delivering bombs on targets, the inadequate armament and armour of early Fortresses gave little reason for supposing such a formation would have been effective.

No 90 Squadron may not have inflicted much hurt on the enemy but they did provide for themselves and their Allies some knowledge of high altitude operations, as well as highlighting weaknesses in the B-17 and its equipment. From these early endeavours the Fortress emerged with a tarnished image for the British, derision from the Germans – and there were also many in America who doubted its prowess. But the USAAF was by then committed to large numbers of B-17s for daylight precision bombardment – a weapon in which they retained their faith, to pursue a policy undeterred by the experience of others.

The 20 RAF Fortress I (B-17C)

British Serial	90 Sqn Code	90 Sqn Service From	Subsequent To	Service and Remarks
AN518	WP.B	9/8/41	3/2/42	220 Sqn Det as MB.B. To India 1/7/42 to USAAF 1/12/42
AN519	WP.H	3/6/41*	15/10/41	A&AEE Farnborough. 206 Sqn
AN520	?	1/11/41	12/2/42	220 Sqn. 20/6/42 CCDU. 214 Sqn 2/44. Scrapped 1/9/44
AN521	WP.K	25/5/41*	8/1/42	Crashed near Shallufa, Egypt
AN522	WP.J*	4/6/41	22/6/41	Crashed Catterick Bridge, Yorks.
AN523	WP.D	25/5/41	16/8/41	Crash-landed Roborough, Devon
AN524	—	None		Damaged at Burtonwood on delivery
AN525	WP.D	?/8/41	8/9/41	Shot down, Bygland, Norway
AN526	WP.G	3/6/41		Became instructional airframe 4429M
AN527	WP.A	25/5/41	12/2/42	220 Sqn
AN528	WP.B	4/6/41*	3/7/41	Burnt out, Polebrook
AN529	WP.C	11/5/41*	8/11/41	Destroyed behind enemy lines, Libya
AN530	WP.F	10/7/41*	12/2/42	220 Sqn. NR:F CCDU 20/6/42. Scrapped 206 Sqn 11/9/43
AN531	?	1/11/41	12/2/42	220 Sqn. 206 Sqn. VX.V
AN532	WP.J	22/7/41	1/2/42	220 Sqn. Det 1/2/42. India 1/7/42. To USAAF 1/12/42
AN533	WP.N	?/8/41	8/9/41	Missing, fate unknown
AN534	WP.E*	7/5/41*	28/7/41	Crashed Wilbarston, Northants
AN535	WP.O	?/8/41	8/9/41	Crash-landed Kinloss
AN536	WP.M	29/7/41	9/1/42	Crashed Shepreth, Cambs
AN537	WP.L*	23/7/41	12/2/42	220 Sqn NR.L

The ten aircraft originally prepared for 90 Sqn at Burtonwood were WP.A AN527, WP.B AN528, WP.C AN529, WP.D AN523, WP.E* AN534, WP.F AN530, WP.G. AN526, WP.H AN519, WP.J* AN522 and WP.K AN521.

*Conflicting information but most sources point to the detail as given.

The B-17C was in production August-November 1941 and aircraft for Britain were drawn from a pool established at McChord Field, Washington. The US Army serials prefaced 40- were: 2043, 2044, 2051, 2052, 2053, 2055, 2056, 2057, 2060, 2061, 2064, 2065, 2066, 2068, 2069, 2071, 2073, 2075, 2076 & 2079. Entries in pilots flight logs show that the allocation of British serials did not follow in consecutive order as is generally supposed. For example AN518 was 40-2066 and AN537 was 40-2055.

A Grand Churchillian Gesture

Tom Danby

'F-Freddie', the Fortress in which Tom Danby and comrades flew the abortive Berlin operation. Prominent in this view are the turbo-supercharger turbines on the underside of the engine nacelles, the partly exposed wheels in their retracted positions, and the 'bathtub' gun emplacement in which the gunner took a prone position.

'In what has been up to now a very private file of souvenirs, are a few newspaper headlines "Slim Supermen of the Stratosphere',' etc. I was one of the slim types who, when the occasion presented itself, alternated flights in the stratosphere with active operations at squadron hostelries in Norwich and Peterborough in the summer of 1941.

'The headlines in the press allude to the first major daylight Bomber Command raid on Brest, when B-17Cs, the original Flying Fortresses of the Royal Air Force co-operated with British-built bombers to try to sink the ghost ships of the German Navy – the *Scharnhorst* and *Gneisenau*. Then the public knew about our existence. The exciting time of preparation, of preliminary raids has never, to my knowledge, been made public – and to my mind again – has been forgotten by all except the aircrew who participated in the trials, the hopes and heart tremblings of the early days of the Fortress Squadron.

'His Majesty, and the Royal Air Force, were given a present of 20 B-17Cs from the USA. In the beginning, aircrew were selected from truly operational types. After a strange medical we became two-legged guinea pigs. The USAAF had never flown the B-17s as high as we wanted to go. Oxygen and intercom presented great hurdles. Nowadays the stratosphere is flown through and round about with gay abandon. Then – well I remember not one but several really experienced operational types who'd flown in daunting war raids in "Wimpey" ICs and never deigned to leave last letters – who before a height trial in Fortresses, carefully put their effects in order, left last letters, and then went out to fly high over England. They hadn't bothered about such things before – anyhow it never seemed a wise thing to do. On the very early height tests – to 30 000-

35 000 feet doctors used to fly with us – to carry out experiments. On most occasions we flew with all internal doors open, wearing differing types of oxygen masks, to see which one of us passed out first. At that height you might recover if someone helps you quickly. The intercom, which was super-perfect on the ground used to go unserviceable at height – at times very embarrassing. In spite of all the setbacks there was the finest of feelings in the Squadron – everyone was happy and eager. Very different from the "couldn't care less' attitude which unhappily came over many servicemen before the end.

'We had hosts of semi-heavenly bodies descend on us from even a greater height than that to which we were accustomed. Their Majesties the King and Queen, Mr Winston Churchill and others visited or met the Fortress crews. Rumour had it that there was a private line from the PM to the Squadron Commander. I still believe there was. There was a sense of urgency I've never experienced before or since and the result was the first operation of the Flying Fortresses.

'Most people know now the briefing and pre-operational procedure of the RAF. One delightful Sunday three Fortresses set off to drop the first bombs in daylight from the stratosphere on to German soil. I was a gunner in the Squadron Commander's kite. We climbed, flew to Wilhelmshaven. It was bright outside, but surprisingly dark inside the bomber. We reached Wilhelmshaven. Below we saw the harbour and the white marks of ships there. We dropped our bombs. The Squadron Commander circled until the other aircraft had unloaded and then set off home. We couldn't talk to each other. The intercom was unserviceable. I noticed two climbing black specks in the sky and hoped our captain was aware of them. He was.

Flt Sgt F. A. 'Mick' Woods and crew.

Our aircraft tilted its nose into the rare air and climbed easily but after a few thousand feet the German fighters came level with us. They flew around our bow and I expected the turn in toward for an attack. I was on the beam guns. The slipstream and the cold were forgotten. I followed one Jerry as it flew flatly around out of range to our quarter – I began to squeeze the trigger. The bead sight was on the tailplane as I waited for him to make his attack proper. Slightly we turned. As the fighter tightened so he literally fell out of the sky – and I would like to know what happened to him!

'We felt grand when we got back. Just that one trip had paid for all the trials, the voluntary imprisonment in camp, the cold that was so intense that one's eyelashes tended to stick over one's eyes because heating for gunners wasn't at that time mastered.

'The celebration party was forgotten. Men, who liked a pint of beer, morosely sipped lime juice and lemonade – for now a greater thing was in store. For days the briefing went on. Secrecy was everywhere. The locals of Peterborough went without our custom. A tremulous yet smug air pervaded the camp. This was going to be something. And then, on July 23 we took off on a daylight raid for Berlin. A grand Churchillian gesture, and we were – and those of us left must still be – proud of our participation. We climbed. The 2nd pilot niggled about oxygen supply. We had to do with less. Even if we did come back from Berlin, we would never be able to fly back at our safe height of about 32 000 feet – we would end up by wave hopping. The gunners spoke of their fishing lines! Over the North Sea. It was cold. Over Denmark came the curse of those early flying days – condensation trails streamed in white revolving tell-tale clouds behind us. Far below, we could see ominous black specks. Across Denmark – turning towards Berlin. And then – stretched high and wide before us, the great grandmother of all weather fronts – a wall of white impenetrable cloud. Back we were forced. Bitterness, frustration palled the aircraft.

'My co-mate and brother in exile at the back was shivering. He was a Pig Islander. A grand type. We came lower and let our oxygen masks dangle from our helmets. Mop-head's face was frostbitten. He looked grey. I got permission to open the emergency rum. Poor old Mop-head. His heating had been unserviceable and he'd never spoken about it. He swigged the rum and vituperative invective streamed. I had a mouthful of rum and burnt the lining of my mouth. It seemed to have little effect on Mop-head at the time – and he kept sipping from the bottle. The Wireless Operator had a mouthful – and in the warmth of his cabin tapped out strange signals. Forty miles from the English coast we saw small ships. If we had got to Berlin and had got back we would have landed about there. The wind had shifted and the pre-flight plans seemed to have gone wrong.

'It seemed all the crowned heads of the RAF were at base to meet us. We stood back until our Squadron Commander had climbed down the ladder. Mick, a "parfair knight", an Australian took charge of events in the belly of the Fortress and, as usual, Mop-head became his concern. Mop-head stood at the top of the steps. Two of us caught him as he fell and put him in the blood wagon. VIPs looked – asked questions. Our captain muttered, "Oxygen trouble, no doubt." We all took showers. Two hours later our crew stood in the Wing Commander's office, propping up Mop-head. "Have you any suggestions or complaints, Sergeant?" He replied, "Sir, the heating in my suit was cold, Sir".'

The three gunners on the Berlin raid, Dennis Clifford, Tom Danby and Tom Imrie.

Right: Before the United States officially entered the war USAAF aircraft were flying anti-submarine patrols over the western Atlantic. These two B-17Cs of the 41st Reconnaissance Squadron operated from Newfoundland in the autumn of 1941.

Below right: The first of the big tailed Fortresses, B-17E 41-2393. The remotely controlled ventral turret is extended and the blister for the periscope sight can be seen further back under the fuselage.

Below: A power operated turret was an urgent requirement to improve the Fortress's defence. The Sperry model used on the B-17E was first experimentally installed on a Wright Field B-17C, seen here during a visit to Rockcliffe, Ontario, Canada on November 22nd 1941.

The Big Ass Bird

Three days before the first Fortress fell in battle during the RAF's disastrous second mission to Oslo, a completely new model of the Boeing bomber first took to the air. This was the B-17E incorporating so much re-design that, apart from the wing, it bore little resemblance to the Model 299 prototype of six years previous. So rapid were the advances in aerodynamics and the field of military aviation under the stimulus of the war in Europe, that many aircraft types ordered by the world's air forces were approaching obsolescence by the time they entered service. The sleek four-engine all-metal Flying Fortress monoplane was unquestionably the most advanced bom-

ber of 1935, but by 1940 it was outclassed in many respects by the new medium and heavy bombers of Britain, Germany and, more crucially, that of another US firm, Consolidated, whose four-engined B-24 had greater range, heavier bomb load and better defensive armament.

While the Army Air Corps was sensitive to any outside criticism of the small force of B-17s it had obtained prior to the outbreak of war in Europe, its technicians were by no means blind to the deficiencies of their prized heavy bomber. Long before the RAF encountered the lateral instability of the Fortress I at high altitude, Boeing engineers were

working on the problem, although admittedly it was not so evident at the reduced altitude the Army Air Corps planned to operate. Ironically, the principal deficiency of the early Flying Fortresses was inadequate defensive armament; they belied their name.

The enemy opposition RAF bombers had met in their daylight bombing raids in the opening months of the war had left US air observers in no doubt that armament had to be improved. The main deficiency of their B-17 was in rearward defence, the quarter from which fighter attacks were mostly directed. A tail turret was imperative, but its incorporation into the tapering rear of the B-17 fuselage was impractical, if not impossible.

To retrieve the B-17 from the verge of obsolescence, Boeing designed a new rear end for the aircraft. The fuselage was lengthened by some six feet and deepened towards the rear to incorporate a tail gun position. Even so, there was insufficient room to install one of the new power turrets in which gunner and weapons revolved together. Boeing were forced to devise an emplacement where two .50 machine guns, projecting from the open tunnel-end of the fuselage, were traversed manually and aimed with a remote sight from the gunner's glazed cabin. The field of fire, restricted to a 30 degree cone, was considered acceptable in conjunction with cover afforded by other new defensive positions. These were a Sperry two-gun power turret sited in the upper fuselage, just aft of the pilot's cabin, giving a field of fire from the horizontal plane to an all round 75 degree elevation. Not depressing the field of fire below the horizontal allowed a very low profile turret, thus keeping down drag. Under defence was also catered for by a power turret. Located just aft of the wing root this semi-retractable turret was operated by a gunner sitting in the fuselage above with a periscopic sighting device.

In addition to the new defensive positions, both the hand-held guns firing through the fuselage waist or beam openings were retained and also one in the radio operator's cabin. The waist windows were enlarged and made square to give better fields of fire. The nose armament of a single rifle calibre machine gun remained unchanged, whereas all other weapons were of the larger .5 calibre with greater range and hitting power. With this improved armament of ten guns the Flying Fortress really lived up to its name; it was then the most heavily armed bomber in the world. But the effectiveness of this armament still had to be proved. Even with the prototype the Army Air Force found the lower ventral turret impractical. Searching with the periscopic apparatus proved unsatisfactory and this turret was to be superseded on production

aircraft by the Sperry 'ball turret' which got its name from the compact spherical shape. Barely four feet in interior diameter, a gunner of small physique was needed to be comfortable in the doubled-up position between the two guns and the ammunition. The whole turret was suspended on a tripod structure permitting full traverse and depression below the horizontal. It was an ingenious design and proved highly effective.

Apart from the new empennage of the B-17E, both vertical and horizontal surfaces were enlarged and the fin swept forward to form a spine along the fuselage top to a point level with the trailing edge of the wing. This overcame the lateral instability of previous models at high altitude. With this new tail the Flying Fortress was 'as steady as a rock' at 25 000 feet and provided the stable platform essential for precision bombing. This comparatively gigantic empennage was an inviting subject for airmen's wit and the B-17E and succeeding models were tagged 'The Big Ass Bird', a crude appellation often camouflaged in a painted adornment as 'The Big-gass-bird'.

In effect, the B-17E was a new aircraft. Only the wing and centre-section of the Model 229 prototype remained basically unchanged. The bomb-bay, incorporated in the centre-section, could not be enlarged. This limitation on both total weight and size of bombs was not at this time of major concern to the USAAF, who believed the advantages their technique had in accurate delivery overrode considerations of bomb size. So, when the up-dated Flying Fortress appeared in the autumn of 1941, its internal bomb load was no more than the new B-26 Marauder medium bomber, and only a third of that of the new British heavies – Stirling, Halifax and Lancaster. The capability to lift heavier tonnages was there, the capacity was not.

Even while the first B-17Es were coming from the production lines at Boeing's Seattle factory, their design engineers were preparing to introduce further improvements. These chiefly concerned internal equipment and components, culminating in the B-17F which replaced the B-17E on the Seattle lines in May 1942, and that summer was also being produced by Douglas at Tulsa and Lockheed-Vega at Burbank, California. Outwardly the F model could be recognised from the E by the new moulded nosepiece devoid of framing, but the major difference was new model Cyclone engines driving larger diameter propellers with wider blades. Among the improvements, which affected the turbo-superchargers in particular, were some resulting from the RAF's experiences.

The B-17F became the standard combat model and, weighing half as much again as the Model 299 of 1935, its performance was for all practical purposes little different from the other heavy bombers. The major advantage over British contemporaries, and for that matter over the B-24 Liberator, was its combat ceiling. The Fortress could go to war with ease at 25 000 feet while, for example, the RAF's Stirling was hard put to maintain 15 000 feet. An altitude of 25 000 feet however, no longer rendered the Fortress immune from enemy fighter interception and heavy anti-aircraft fire as had been hoped during its development. To survive in daylight operations the B-17 would, indeed, have to be a Flying Fortress.

At the time of its introduction the B-17E had the heaviest defensive armament of any bomber and rearward cover was particularly good. Five defence points are visible in this view.

A Fighting Plane for all Purposes

By 1941 most American military leaders believed it was only a matter of time before the United States became actively involved in the war raging in Europe. To this end plans were already being made for the employment of heavy bombers in a strategic bombing campaign while the expansion and training of this force was primarily in daylight precision attack from high altitudes. The B-17 was the principal instrument in these preparations but the first USAAF Flying Fortresses to go to war did so in a defensive and tactical role.

This initiation was painful as the battle ledger shows.

When, in December 1941, the Japanese attacked Pearl Harbor and swept down through the islands of the south-west Pacific, the USAAF had 150 Flying Fortresses, a third deployed in these areas. The Hawaii defence force included 12 B-17C/Ds among a mixed collection of 131 military aircraft, while 176 warplanes in the US protectorate of the Philippine Islands, included 29 B-17Ds and 6 B-17Cs deployed in four squadrons, one

assigned to the 7th Bombardment Group and three to the 19th Bombardment Group – but all under the control of the latter. The 7th was in the course of moving to the Phillipines and another of its squadrons plus a fourth for the 19th were actually in the process of air movement via Hawaii when the Japanese attack was made.

In the strike against Pearl Harbor four B-17Ds and an itinerant B-17C, unfortunately arriving during the raid, were destroyed. In the Philippines fourteen of the 19th Group's B-17s were wrecked on their Luzon base and in brave, but largely fruitless, attempts to strike back at the Japanese invasion fleet and forces during the following two weeks another seven were lost. By the end of the month the bases in the Philippines were no longer tenable and the remnants of the Group were withdrawn nearly 2 000 miles south to Darwin in Northern Australia – only to be despatched 1 500 miles north-west to Java for further action. Of the surviving B-17s reaching Australia only ten were fit for further operations, but with Japanese landings in

Borneo and other points south only the B-17s had the range to reach these widely scattered places and all were needed.

Reinforcements came in the form of B-17Es direct from the production line flown by hastily trained crews. Despatched from America in flights of three to six along an eastern route through the Caribbean, Africa, India and so down to Java, the first aircraft reached their destination in the second week of January 1942. The spearhead was composed chiefly of the remaining units of the 7th Bomb Group followed by crews assigned to the 43rd Bomb Group. Such was the shortage of B-17s that LB-30s – early versions of the B-24 Liberator – repossessed from a consignment awaiting delivery to Britain, were used to equip one of the 7th's squadrons.

Of 53 B-17Es setting out from the US for Australia and Java between December and early March, only 44 reached their destination. Five crashed en route, one was delayed for repairs while another turned back with mechanical trouble; two that found their route barred when Java fell, remained in

Two B-17Es of the 19th Bomb Group being serviced at Port Moresby on August 19th 1942, while a Douglas DC-5 transport takes off from the runway behind them.

An invasion of the
Hawaiian Islands was
expected after the attack on
Pearl Harbour and the small
force of B-17s available there
flew oceanic patrols
whenever weather
permitted. There was a
shortage of servicing
equipment and ordnance.
Here four men are
manhandling bombs to be
winched into the bay of a
B-17D. The assorted bombs
range from 100 to 500 lb HE.

India subsequently to form another bombing force. Two months of combat from Java reduced the total of 49 B-17s that reached its airfields to 19 – two B-17Ds and 17 B-17Es. Only four of the 12 LB-30s survived. Of 30 B-17s lost only six had fallen in air fighting while 19 were destroyed by enemy air attack on their airfields and another five had to be abandoned and destroyed during the evacuation. Leaving aside the debacle at Hawaii, from the opening of hostilities with Japan, 52 B-17s had been lost out of the 80 available in the combat areas. Indeed, the picture was even more unfavourable for another six B-17s were written off in accidents in Australia.

In three months the Japanese offensive had secured vast areas of South-East Asia and the western Pacific, with some 270 thousand square miles under Japanese domination. This had been achieved at remarkably little cost in ships and aircraft in contrast to the crippling punishment sustained by the Allied sea and air forces which had been found unprepared, ill-equipped and tactically outclassed.

The operations of the B-17 units during these first three months of the Pacific war were notable for heroics rather than military achievement, for few of the bombs they dropped destroyed or damaged enemy targets. At the time the record did not look so dis-

appointing for crews were often convinced that their bombs had found the target. The history of air warfare is marked with such over-optimistic reports from combatants, resulting from the speed of actions where a fleeting glimpse by an excited individual brought wrong or distorted impressions. For the men in the B-17s, from two to four miles above, accurate observation was barely possible. Japanese records later showed that of three warships and eight transports claimed during this period only two could have been sunk by B-17s – and this in some 350 sorties of which a third had not reached the target area. Hitting a fast manoeuvring ship from high altitude proved virtually impossible and the most successful strikes had been made at much lower altitudes, where the B-17s then ran the risk of being brought down by anti-aircraft fire. The bombers were further handicapped by the extreme range at which they had to operate and on many missions it was necessary to carry an auxiliary bomb-bay tank of 365 US gallon capacity. With this installed the bomb load was often halved and to targets 700-1 000 miles from base, 2 500 pounds of bombs was a very small payload. Moreover, the bomb bay tank, devised only for long-range ferrying, was non-self-sealing and thereby a fire hazard in battle. It could be jettisoned, but this was only done in an emergency as no replacements were on hand.

If the B-17 had achieved little in its bombing expeditions, failure could be largely attributed to the hostile environment. Apart from missions being at extreme range they were often flown in poor weather when cloud and storms predominated and targets were hidden from view at high altitude. These flights put a considerable strain on aircrew who at times even had maintenance tasks to perform on their aircraft after a return to base. Shortage of parts, tools and specialised equipment hindered servicing and standards inevitably fell. On top of all this, frequent and well co-ordinated attacks by enemy aircraft on bases gave little respite to the weary personnel.

With the new B-17Es came crews less well trained who were thrust into the battle. Often new bombers required extensive maintenance after the 12 000 mile ferry flight from America and some aircraft were simply used to supply parts to keep others in the air. Rarely did the number of B-17s despatched on a mission run to double figures; often only three or four aircraft composed a strike force. That losses were not higher can be attributed to weaknesses of the Japanese, their lack of radar or organised warning system to facilitate interceptions. And when there were clashes, the ruggedness of the Flying Fortresses was a significant factor in their survival in combat.

At this time the principal Japanese fighters – with one exception – were only armed with two rifle-calibre machine guns each. A considerable expenditure of rounds was required to bring down such a robust giant as the B-17, particularly the B-17E which had some armour protection. On the other hand the Japanese fighters were comparatively fragile machines designed primarily for dog-fighting and were without armour plate for the pilot or self-sealing fuel tanks to lessen the risk of fuel fires and explosions, factors which made them extremely vulnerable to the bombers' defensive fire. The B-17C and D models with their hand-held armament did not present such a threat as the B-17E with its power turrets and this newer model quickly earned a reputation as a formidable opponent amongst Japanese fighter pilots.

The only operational Japanese fighter with a substantial armament was the Navy Type O, popularly known to Allied pilots as the Zero*. Two 20-mm cannon supplemented the stan-

dard rifle calibre machine guns giving the fighter firepower similar to the German Me 109E/Fs that had intercepted the RAF's Fortresses. The Zero also had a much better all-round performance than the other Japanese fighters and its Allied counterparts of that period in the Pacific area. Land and carrier based Navy units with a total 140 of these fighters dominated the air fighting during the opening months of the Pacific war, the Zero's vastly superior manoeuvrability and acceleration making it an act of suicide for any of the motley collection of largely obsolescent British, Dutch and US fighters to engage it in a dog fight. However, like the other Japanese interceptors, the Zero did not have self-sealing tanks or armour protection and was susceptible to fire.

The Zero became the B-17's antagonist for it alone possessed armament heavy enough to deal adequately with these large machines. Nevertheless, in the classic mode of interception of a bomber, from the rear, Japanese pilots soon found that even with 20-mm cannon the big bombers could absorb a large number of hits without going down. This was primarily due to the fusing of the Japanese 20-mm shells which exploded on impact so that damage was often superficial. The Japanese also discovered that whereas the B-17C and D models were ill-defended in the rear and the gunners without protection quickly silenced, the armoured tail position and upper power turret of the B-17E made an attack approach to that quarter particularly hazardous. The early B-17Es were not adequately protected from attack from below because of the difficulty in siting the remotely controlled under turret which, in the opinion of most crews, had little more than scare value.

As the most sophisticated warplane encountered – larger than anything in their own flying services – the B-17 became an object of considerable fascination to Japanese flyers, so much so that three of the dozen or so discarded wrecks in Java and the Philippines were laboriously rebuilt and flight evaluated. But the immediate value of the broken and burned examples on captured airfields was the intelligence they yielded on defensive armament. The B-17E's deficiencies in forward firepower were plain to see: the rifle calibre machine gun in the nose had to be man-handled from various sockets to meet attacks from different quarters; the upper turret could not fire below the horizontal, and while the ineffectiveness of the under turret may or may not have been fully evident at this time, the impracticability of its tricky manipulation to deal with fast-closing fighter assaults against forward areas was certainly apparent.

Provided with their analysis of B-17 de-

*The Type O designation came from the Japanese year of design. The aircraft was further identified as the Mitsubishi A6M. During the opening months of war with Japan the majority of their fighters encountered were radial-engined and all were invariably identified as Zeros such was the poor standard of aircraft recognition.

fence potential, Japanese fighter tacticians experimented with attacks on the Boeings from ahead and slightly below with encouraging results and by the summer of 1942 a three-quarter frontal pass had become virtually the standard method of fighter attack. The Americans were quick to counter this move by field-improvised mountings for twin 5-inch guns firing through an aperture made high in the nosepiece. Often another of these weapons was placed in the nose ventilating door and in some instances a fourth gun in a fixed position was fired by the pilot. The additional nose weapons tended to hamper the bombardier and had a limited field of fire, although the fusillade of lead unleashed was undoubtedly formidable if not accurately aimed. Even so frontal attacks continued to be the chief Japanese tactic for it could stop engines or kill the occupants of the nose section. Luckily for the B-17 crews the high rate of closure in frontal attacks – something in the region of 500mph – made an extremely difficult target for the Zero pilot, particularly if the bomber took evasive action. The enemy fighter pilot would open fire as soon as he was in range, getting away fifteen 20-mm shells on average, before diving away beneath the bomber, rolling his fighter to provide a difficult target for the gunners.

Japanese fighter pilots were generally tenacious and usually continued attacks until fuel or ammunition were low, but they were nonetheless respectful of the B-17's armament. A Zero could normally make no more than five or six firing passes at a B-17 on one sortie because of depleting ammunition and oxygen. Two Zero pilots with B-17 combat experience during 1942, Lt Cdr Kofukuda and Lt Kono, wrote a detailed report on air fighting revealing concern over the difficulties of shooting down the big bombers. They were respectfully aware and critical of the Zero's deficiencies in armoured protection and the lack of self-sealing tanks – 'the majority of fighters are destroyed by fire'; they also complained of limited oxygen and internal fuel supply. They summed up the difficulties – 'Since shooting down B-17s which have executed a raid requires a pursuit of considerable length and exposure to their many guns, we should in the future provide the Zero type planes with armour and heavier weapons.'

The improvised nose armament of the Fortress was far from satisfactory and the need for a power turret in this position was an early request to the manufacturers. Among other weaknesses in B-17E armament was irregular belted ammunition feed to guns and faults in the electrically operated turret equipment. The door hinges of the new ball turret were originally too weak and doors had broken away during missions; the gunner held by his safety straps was secure but the position was

Co-pilot's view from a B-17E. The aircraft ahead, 41-2656, served with the 19th Bomb Group and other SWPA units for many months. The red 'meat ball' in the US insignia was deleted early in 1942 to avoid confusion with the Japanese marking.

not really tenable in such circumstances, or 'really hairy' to quote one gunner who experienced this failure three miles above New Guinea. Telescopic sights on some hand-held guns were found to restrict vision and be prone to misting, so these were replaced by ring and post sights.

By the end of March the initial Japanese thrusts had largely foundered through supply problems, giving the Allies time to re-group their forces. Signs were that the enemy would take New Guinea and then assault Australia. The remnants of the Allied forces that escaped from Java were reformed and rested, the tired men of the two B-17 groups among them. The 7th Group was moved to India leaving most crews and aircraft to bolster the 19th. A new group, the 43rd had been ordered to move from the USA to Australia in February and the ground complement had arrived the following month. Aircraft and crews, however, were used to fill the gaps in the ranks of the 7th and 19th Groups and it was several months before the 43rd was ready to go to war.

In May the Japanese moved an invasion fleet against the Port Moresby area of New Guinea, the last Allied stronghold at the western end of the island. They were met and turned back by US Navy carrier aircraft; this success removed the immediate threat of invasion of Australia. Japanese expansion now shifted three-thousand miles north-east to the western-most island of the Hawaiian group, Midway. US intelligence, having broken the Japanese wireless code, were forewarned of an impending invasion; naval and air forces were on hand to meet and check the Japanese fleet. The 5th and 11th Bomb Groups on Hawaii had been quickly bolstered with new B-17Es to meet this threat but detachments operated from Midway with little success and again it was the Navy dive and torpedo bombers that won the day.

Back in Australia the 19th Bomb Group returned to operations having 45 B-17Es, many with the new, effective, manned ball turret to protect their undersides. Most operations were long range reconnaissance or bombing missions to ports and airfields used by the Japanese in New Guinea plus the occasional thousand-mile marathon to the major enemy base at Rabaul in New Britain, staging through Port Moresby. By August 1942 enough crews and Fortresses were on hand – including a number of the latest B-17F models – to allow two squadrons of the 43rd Group to operate from their Northern Australian bases; the other two squadrons did not enter combat until later in the year. At that time the 19th Group was completely withdrawn from operations and long serving personnel were returned to the United States. The recently arrived crews were transferred to the 43rd, as were many of the aircraft. The 5th Air Force, the USAAF establishment in Australia and New Guinea, then had some 80 B-17s to keep this lone Fortress group operational.

The Allied theatre commander was making plans to take the offensive in the summer of 1942 and started in August by invading Guadalcanal in the Solomon Islands, some 600 miles east of New Guinea, that marked the southern-most limit of Japanese conquest. To back up this campaign the B-17E squadrons of the 5th and 11th Groups were gradually transferred from Hawaii to the New Hebrides and New Caledonia island chains south of the Solomons and a thousand miles east of Australia. A new command, the 13th Air Force, was created for the Solomons campaign and B-17 units were eventually assigned to it.

The first elements of the 11th Group arrived in New Caledonia in July 1942 but it was some time before facilities permitted all their 35 B-17Es to be accommodated. Many of these bombers were from a batch originally built for the British, distinguished by azure blue lower surfaces, the colour deemed suitable by the RAF for high altitude daylight operation. The 11th's main base was nearly a thousand miles from Guadalcanal and missions were staged through the airstrip at Efate, an island in the centre of the New Hebrides group, still over

Below: Hit by strafing Japanese fighters, a B-17E burns on Anchi airfield in Java.

Bottom: Such was Japanese fascination for the Fortress that they rebuilt one of the B-17D wrecks left by the 19th Bomb Group at Clark, and two B-17Es found in Java. To accomplish this components were taken from several aircraft. The venture was successful and the three Fortresses were subsequently flown to Japan for evaluation, but by this time the USAAF had decided to withdraw the B-17 from operations in the Pacific and Asian areas. The B-17D was 40-3095, and remained in the natural metal finish it had at the time of the first attack on Clark Field.

The few B-17Es reaching India were used to re-establish the 7th Bomb Group. Although this group had officially existed in Java none of the personnel assembled there knew it! In India maintenance proved very difficult, as there were no spares, and the high day temperatures brought problems with engine over-heating.

seven hundred miles from the objective. A new airfield was being constructed on Espiritu Santo, one of the northernmost islands of the Hebrides to give the B-17s an advanced base only 600 miles from Guadalcanal, placing less strain on fuel reserves on the long tedious flights over the ocean. The four squadrons of the group were often separated at different bases and at times squadrons were split from forward echelons moved nearer the combat area. Bases were exceedingly primitive, being simply cleared patches of mosquito-ridden jungle where the terrain was considered sufficiently level to put down a mile-long runway. Perforated metal planking formed the basis of the runways but even so these airfields were alternately choking dust bowls or mud traps as the intermittent blazing sun and torrential rain of the tropical weather decreed.

The climatic obstacles of dust and damp severely handicapped maintenance crews, making it exceedingly difficult to keep aircraft serviceable. Rarely was a squadron able to launch more than half-a-dozen bombers in the early days and the whole group effort was frequently no larger. The tropical weather was also a constant worry with massive storms making flying itself hazardous. On some missions, after have been airborne for several hours, a formation might encounter a weather front stretching away to the horizon on either side of the flight path and twenty thousand

feet or more into the heavens. The mission leader would have to decide whether to climb over, or seek a way round, rather than abandon the mission; but with critical fuel supplies there was little time if the mission was to be accomplished. Entering such a front was risking structural damage, for a 25-ton Fortress could be tossed about like a leaf in the turbulence. If the cloud was broken then the bombers might attempt to pass through. These weather fronts were considered by many crews a greater hazard than the enemy and, in fact, in seven months of operations the 11th Group had only six B-17s fall to the enemy while double that number were lost as the result of weather conditions.

On one occasion a flight of three B-17Es were on the return leg of a mission when they encountered a seemingly limitless front. For four hours they endeavoured to find a way round but eventually, lost and running out of fuel, all were forced to ditch in the sea. Fortunately all crews were rescued but one spent seven days in a damaged life raft during which time one man died.

Used tactically to bomb enemy ground installations, airfield and shipping in direct support of the Solomon Islands campaign, the attack altitudes of the Fortresses varied for the type of target attacked. Missions were often of ten hours duration, and the long flights to and from the target area were made below oxygen level to assist in crew comfort. While some attacks on land objectives were made from 18 000 to 20 000 feet, for the most part bombing was performed from medium altitudes and for shipping as low as 6 000 feet. Apart from a better opportunity for accuracy it was found that 5 000 to 6 000 feet was the optimum altitude for minimising the effectiveness of anti-aircraft fire, being too high for small arms and low enough to cause sighting difficulties for the heavier ship-mounted guns.

Approved formation for bombing ships at sea was a vee of five aircraft stepped down from the leadplane and releasing on its signal to obtain a pattern drop effect. Sometimes a sixth aircraft would be placed in between the two trailing bombers of the vee. Pattern bombing gave a much better chance of obtaining hits in shipping strikes for it was far more difficult for a vessel to evade all bombs by abrupt changes in course.

Confidence in the Fortress was always high amongst men of the squadrons operating in the South-West Pacific. It was considered a 'rugged ship', highly durable in which aircrew felt they had a chance and were quite able to give any formation of Zeros a tough time. In fact, gunners claimed the destruction of one out of every four Japanese fighters reported attacking. A Japanese assessment of the B-17

referred to it as 'a fighting plane used for all purposes' rather than a heavy bomber. This attribute was not without foundation, for apart from general bombing, patrol, reconnaissance and even transport, there were several instances when the Fortress had been used as a gunship, low-level strafer and even pursuit plane. Lt Tom Trent, pilot of an 11th Group B-17E on a shipping reconnaissance to Kapingamarangi Island near the Caroline Islands, spotted a vessel standing offshore which his crew identified as a Japanese radio ship. The Fortress carried no bombs so Trent dived the aircraft down to about 50 feet above the sea and proceeded to make low level runs round the ship for 25 minutes while his gunners hammered it with machine gun fire, after which the vessel was well ablaze.

Fortresses also 'intercepted' and destroyed a number of enemy patrol bombers. One such incident involved a Kawanishi H6K 'Mavis' which a lone Fortress on oceanic patrol encountered. Captain Walter Lucas took his aircraft in to attack coming up below the four-engined flying boat so that the top turret and waist guns could bring fire to bear. Then, pulling up abreast of the enemy, a twenty minute running battle took place, until the Mavis had an engine catch fire and was forced to land in the sea where it was enveloped in flames.

With the capture of the airfield on Gaudalcanal – known as Henderson Field – B-17s frequently used it as a staging base for raids on other Japanese strongholds in the Solomons, chiefly Bougainville the largest island in the group some 400 miles to the north. For several months Henderson Field was a target for Japanese bombers which damaged some 11th Group B-17s in one raid.

The first of the 5th Group's squadrons arrived in September 1942 and by January 1943 all eight squadrons of the two groups were on operations in the SWPA. Air Force commanders wanted more B-17s, but by the summer of 1942 the decision had been made to send the Fortress to Europe and eventually to replace those facing the Japanese with the Liberator. The latter had an extra 200 miles radius of action, a significant factor in bomber operations where such vast distances lay between bases and targets. The numerical peak of B-17s ranged against the Japanese was reached in September 1942 when the 19th, 43rd, 5th and 11th Groups had 125 Thereafter few new aircraft arrived and with the withdrawal of the 19th in October and the 11th in the following February, numbers declined rapidly. The 11th returned to Hawaii to convert to B-24s, its Fortresses being handed to the 5th Group. Within four months the 5th was also converting to the Liberator and the 43rd Group too, both flying their last B-17 sorties in September 1943. A few Fortresses were retained in the Pacific as command transports.

There were never more than 20 B-17Es in India with the 10th Air Force and the main squadron operating these, the 9th, was sent to Palestine in the autumn of 1942. The remainder became maids of all work, frequently troop transports, conveying two dozen men and their equipment.

A Formation of One

Durward W. Fesmire

There were few survivors from the B-17 crews who faced the Japanese in the Philippines at the time of Pearl Harbour but one became a legend in his own time. 'A frank, good-natured hunk of man', Durward Fesmire took part in no less than 92 missions in Fortresses in the South-West Pacific, and if that were not enough war for any man he then went on to fly two tours with the 8th Air Force from England, to make a grand total of 133 combat missions in B-17s during World War 2. The Korean conflict found him back in bombers again, this time Douglas B-26 Invaders, in which 66 operations were completed. No wonder his old CO, General Harold Bowman once said of him, 'He was the only guy I ever knew personally who actually had no fear.' Perhaps 'Fes' would disagree but he could not dispute the facts of risking his life 199 times, which signifies a toughness far beyond the pyschological stamina of most warriors. This coolness and dedication enabled Durward Fesmire to achieve the best bombing record of any AAF bombardier in the early days of war with Japan. All the more remarkable in that he had no formal training as a bombardier. These are his memories of those days in 1941-1942 when there were very few Fortresses at war.

Durward Fesmire back from mission 93.

'I enlisted in the Army as a private in 1930 and was eventually assigned to bombardment at Hickam Field, Hawaii. When expansion hit the US military services in 1939 there just weren't enough flying officers to go around, particularly bombadiers and navigators, duties which had been largely handled by surplus pilots. Now every pilot was wanted, so they decided to train some enlisted ground men as a stop-gap. At the time I was working as an armourer, in charge of bomb scoring for my squadron and maintenance of bomb sights, which made me a natural to be picked for bombardier training. Three enlisted men were teamed up for each crew and we learnt the trade from the fliers on the base. Then I was taken out of bombardment and sent back to Training Command in the States, but finally managed to work a posting to the 19th Bomb Group which was preparing to go to the Philippines with B-17s. All of a sudden the bombsight had become very secret and now they wouldn't let me go near one! They preferred an inexperienced 2nd Lt to a Sergeant with the know-how. So I was left behind at March and had to start agitating until I got a transfer to join the Group. I rode a boat to the Philippines and on arrival was attached to the 93rd Squadron at Del Monte in Mindanao, 300 miles south-east of the 19th's main base at Clark in Luzon. They viewed things differently out there and I was immediately assigned to 1st Lt James T. Connally's* crew as bombardier. In addition to my bombing duties I was also put in charge of the 93rd armament section. At that time they wouldn't allow us to carry any more than 25 rounds per gun on the B-17's point fifties because they were not handled by qualified gunners. This didn't make sense to me and after a lot of argument we did manage to have an armourer as the waist gunner, so with the bombardier there were now two qualified gunners on each crew. My ship was a B-17C and we liked it because it was faster than the D model which predominated in the squadron.

'We got in a few training missions before the war began for us. I heard the news on the radio when I woke that morning but a lot of fellows wouldn't believe it until later in the morning one or our ships went up to Clark Field and pretty soon we got word that it was coming back with battle damage and injured aboard. Next day we started our operations. Our targets were mostly those of opportunity because things were very confused and we often didn't know where the Jap invasion forces were. We were lucky in surviving, only about 10 per cent of our group got out of the Philippines. For some missions we were reduced to flying a formation of one!

*This is the same James Connally who, earlier in the year was with the RAF's 90 Sqdn in England. Later in the war he commanded the B-29 equipped 504th BG and was killed during a raid on Japan in February 1945.

On December 14 we set out from Del Monte to bomb the invasion fleet off the Philippines with six aircraft which was a very big formation. Connally was the lead but when we were taxiing out a tyre blew and we didn't get to go. The rest did and two of the five were so badly shot up they never made it back to the field. Meanwhile we had a real good day. There was a wrecked B-17 at the end of the runway that was being cannibalised so we went down and were able to get a wheel off to bring back for our own B-17C. To fit it was a different matter because we had no tools or jacks. There was an air base unit that had only arrived at Del Monte from the States a few days before and I went to see if I could scrounge some tools from them. They had plenty but I couldn't talk the officer in charge into parting with anything as all were still packed in protective material. Then I recalled that the night before an old buddy of mine, a line chief, had said he knew this maintenance officer and that he didn't take official action against enlisted men who stepped out of line, preferring to 'go up behind the barn' with them to settle differences. So, knowing this, I suggested to this officer we go out behind the tent; if he won he could court-martial me; if I won I'd get the jacks. But he wouldn't hear of it so I still didn't obtain the jacks. In the end we changed the wheel with an automobile jack by cranking it up under the wing an inch or two at a time. We were none too happy knowing the proper jacks were on the field and we couldn't get them. Apparently with the first news of the Jap landings preparations were in hand to move out of Del Monte. There we were trying to get our ship into flying condition and needing spares and help while some people were more interested in getting out. We tried to get mechanics but they told us they had no men that could help us. There was one high ranking officer going around picking up equipment ready for the move. He had a truck back up to our parking area where we lived under the B-17 and while we were busy he had some men load, among other things, our personal gear. I caught up with him just as he was having it unloaded and told him to take it back. He threatened to have me court martialled; probably would have done if Connally hadn't come along and spoken up for me.

A few days later we took our B-17 down to Batchelor Field, near Darwin, Australia, because the Japs had started air raids on Del Monte. This made us safe from attack but meant we had a 1 500 mile trip to reach the Philippines when we flew a mission to hit Jap ships at Davao a day or so later. After this mission we put down at Del Monte to refuel and re-arm. At the end of December we moved to Singosari, a Dutch military field in Java, and staged through Borneo or Celebes on missions. This brought us nearer our targets but still cut our bomb loads to under two tons as an extra fuel tank had to be carried in one half of the bombbay. If it was an extra long trip they would sometimes put another gas tank in the nose with me; made me think! Although they were the type that collapsed, they weren't *supposed* to be dangerous!

'On one of the first missions out of Java we were to bomb an airfield at Jolo and go on into Mindanao afterwards and pick up some of our people. When we got to Jolo it was socked in, we couldn't see a thing, so we headed on towards the Philippines without dropping our bombs. I took the head of the bombsight and laid it down because it was in my way. I was sitting there reading a book when the weather began to clear. Looking down I saw one of the biggest boats I'd ever seen, a tanker of around 15 000 tons, with an escort of destroyers. Cecil Combs, the group CO – he had been our Squadron CO when war started – was in the right seat next to Connally that day. I called upstairs and told them what I could see. They said okay, take the big one. I said the bombsight wanted warming up so would they give me a long turn – I didn't tell them it was off and completely out of the way. I've never hooked up a bombsight faster than I did that day! We had six aircraft in two three-ship formations and each had seven 100 kg bombs and a gas tank in the bay and we were at 7 500 feet. Of the 21 bombs dropped by the first flight, one went into the water one side of the tanker and two the other side and 18 hit it. Where the 21 bombs from the other three ships went no one ever knew because one of our gunners called out, "You've hit him; he's blown up." It must have been loaded with high test gas because it really did blow all to hell. That was one of the few missions I flew with Connally that was perfect.

'We had some of the best mechanics you could want; they were all regular Air Corps old timers and they knew how to make an airplane fly. We didn't have much mechanical trouble on our B-17C although we did have a bomb door that would shut but not open. One day when we were after shipping near Mindanao the navigator went back to crank open the door by hand and stayed there under the misapprehension that he had to crank it up again. Just as soon as I dropped the bombs I hit the closed switch. The handle was still on the crank and this flew round and almost knocked the navigator out of the bay. Boy was he sore!

'Flying out of Java we used Dutch bombs which were 100 and 300 kilogram weights. They fitted our bomb bay shackles and we didn't have much trouble using them. I'm not likely to forget them either. On one mission we staged through Balikpapan in Borneo, going in there for more gas and bombs. We had no help on the ground and we had to load 300 kg bombs ourselves, rolling them under the airplane and cranking them up by hand. Then this British newsreel photographer arrived on the scene and he got Connally to have us roll the bombs all the way up to the front of the aircraft and then back under the nose to the bay just so he could get some good footage. It meant we had to roll them three times as far; it was hotter than the hinges of hell and we were tired, dirty, hungry and above all thirsty. Right then I hated the British and cussed that guy. We went out on the mission and came back into Balikpapan again. First person we see on getting out of the plane is this movie man. He had a keg of beer, iced down and ready to serve! Boy, never was beer so welcome or so good. I loved the British from then on!

'New crews with the B-17E model began to reach Java while we were there. One day our old B-17C had an engine shot up and we needed a new one. A B-17E came in, straight from a 14 000 mile flight from the factory, over-ran, skidded and wrecked the landing gear. The field was sod and it rained a lot and there was often a slick on the surface. So we had a brand new B-17E to provide us with a new engine. Next day our B-17C was test-hopped over Singosari by another crew. The Japs jumped them right over the field and shot them down.

'The crews loved the old C and D models although we knew the B-17E was much better and safer to fly in combat. It was better at altitude, too. On the morning the Japs moved into Bali we were sent after their ships. The cloud base was 4 000 feet and we had to come in under it. Our target was a destroyer and all I could see through the bomb sight were flashes from his guns as he fired broadsides at us. He didn't get us. We went back that afternoon and it was clear. Remembering all the stuff that had come up in the morning the pilot called down and said give me an indicated altitude that will give us a true 35 000 feet. That was the highest I ever flew in any plane during the war and we got hits on a couple of ships.

'Connally was made Group Operations Officer and didn't fly as much so I began to go with anyone and everyone who wanted a bombardier, finally joining with Lt Elliott Vandevanter and staying with them until the remnants of the Group were evacuated to Australia. We hadn't been paid since the war started so it looked good when I got to Melbourne with the promise of two weeks rest while we were waiting to be reprocessed. However, when I walked into camp next morning I found myself picked for one of two crews that were wanted up at Townsville for a B-17 squadron that had just come in from Hawaii after flying ocean patrols and was supposed to be combat weary! Stayed with them a couple of months but only got to fly one mission. This was to Rabaul and the target was a big cruiser tied up in the harbour. There were four B-17s on the bomb run and we were flying on the left wing of the lead plane. I set my bomb sight for range and while the indices were still quite a way apart I suddenly saw the other three ships drop their loads. I didn't drop with them preferring to trust my own sighting. Their bombs hit way down near the harbour entrance and mine exploded near the bow of the cruiser but not near enough to do any harm, if I'd been sighting for deflection I might have hit him. When we got home somebody came out and said 'Congratulations, you sank a cruiser.' I said, 'We didn't sink a thing, we just killed a few fish.' I had to report to Major Carmichael who wanted to know why I hadn't dropped with the others. He started to give me a bad time. He kept insisting we sank a cruiser. Finally I said 'All right, they sank a goddam cruiser' and walked away. He didn't take any further action against me but I wasn't happy in this outfit. A few days later Connally flew into the field. He was now a Lt Colonel in command of the 19th; in fact, he had gone from 1st Lt to Lt Col in three months. When I heard he was there I went up to his plane and waited. When he came I asked him to get me out of this lousy outfit, only I used stronger words. He agreed to take me to Cloncurry, giving me just fifteen minutes to collect my things but I made it.

'At Cloncurry I flew with quite a few made-up crews. Connally as CO had no crew of his own and my other old pilot, Elliott Vandevanter had been sent home to form a new B-17 group and would take it to Europe. Connally later went back to the States too, and was killed near the end of the war while leading a B-29 group over Japan. My old squadron, the 93rd, was being got together again with crews evacuated from Java and some fresh from the States. It was sent to Longreach in May and I went with them. The commander was Major Felix Hardison who had brought a new B-17E into Java during February and done well. Two of his original gunners had gone sick and the replacements were two old timers, John Geckeler and Bill Bostwick, whom I had served with before the war. Hardison's bombardier was killed in a Jap air raid after the evacuation from Java to Australia and as there was no replacement Geckeler and Bostwick recommended I get the job.

'My trial period took in four missions in

four days. On the first we bombed a ship off Timor. Our navigator passed out through lack of oxygen, collapsing on his table during the bomb run, so after we'd dropped I had to go back and take care of him. He made it all right. We had a General with us that day, he was looking out of the bomb bay and he said we hit the ship. Next day we went back to the same area and hit an airfield. The Japs had a neat line of aircraft and we marched our bombs up the lot. Then we went to Rabaul on a high altitude day raid, staging through Port Moresby and landing back there afterwards to load up again. This time we went back to Rabaul at night and low down. After bombing Hardison came down to the deck so that Johnny Geckeler could shoot up anti-aircraft emplacements firing at higher aircraft. Back over Port Moresby we ran into bad weather and they radioed that we couldn't land because they were socked in all the way to 25 000 feet, and to go on to Horn Island. When we finally saw land we were so short of gas that Hardison had her running on only two engines and throttled back and losing altitude. We had missed Horn Island for the land turned out to be the tip of the York Peninsula. The Old Man saw a clear spot in the trees and said he was going to set her down. He said, "I'm going to try and save the airplane", named *Susy-Q* after his wife, "and you guys can get out now or ride on in with me." We all stayed. It was hard to see how he got her down in one piece with no damage for when we got out we found the clearing was less than a thousand feet long and full of large melon holes. I had my picture taken in one that was in between the main wheels and it came up to my chest – and I'm six feet one!

'Our radio man finally got an SOS out and after four days Australian Beauforts dropped us food and equipment. Later trucks brought us gas and the melon holes were filled for an attempt at flying the *Susy-Q* out. Guns and anything that could come out to save weight were taken off and Hardison had only a skeleton crew. He held her on the brakes and gave her full power until the tail pulled up and then let her roll. About a third of the way down he gave her one-third flaps and when they reached the end of the strip and pulled her off she was only doing 80, but they made it.

'From then on I had a regular job. Felix thought I was the best bombardier in the world; I wasn't, but that was all right as I flew with him for the rest of the time I was out there. He was the best B-17 pilot for me and a master at flying the PDI (Pilot Direction Indicator) on the bomb run, which is why I hit so many targets with him. *Suzy-Q* was a lucky ship and no one was ever killed or wounded in her, although that goes for all the

ships I flew while in the SWPA. We didn't ever get into any real trouble with fighters. The best defence was to try and fly at 30 000 feet as the Zero got real sloppy on the controls at that height and couldn't stay with you. They usually attacked singly and in the early days attacks were all from the tail. When we got the E model they started coming in at the front. From my point of view the biggest weakness on the early B-17s was the old .30 calibre gun in the nose. There were a lot of ports and you had to keep pulling the gun out and pushing it into a new port to follow attacks – and it needed a great deal of effort to do this at altitude. We took the early under-turrets out because they were useless. The Japs probably found out about this because they tried a new tactic when we attacked Lae airfield on July 4, 1942. Coming in under us out of gun range, they'd pull up sharply in a sharp climb and just sit there hanging on their props and spraying us.

'We got more planes in the summer of 1942 but the largest formation I was ever in was only 13. Because the Jap defences were getting good most of the missions to Rabaul were then at night. On my last mission with the 19th we had about 20 B-17s but we went in individually. One plane carried flares and we went in first with the others stacked up behind at different levels to lessen the risk of collisions.

'A new group started to take over our work in August and the 19th Bomb Group was gradually withdrawn and most of the old timers sent back to the States. They flew *Suzy-Q* home too for a flag-waving tour. She was a great ship, but then what B-17 wasn't?'

Fesmire's 'office' for many of his missions.

Big League

On the first day of July, 1942, a Fortress wearing the white star insignia of the United States touched down at Prestwick, Scotland, vanguard of a host totalling more than eight thousand that would be involved in the aerial onslaught against the European Axis. Three-quarters were destined to be destroyed as a result of these hostilities.

The decision to standardise on the B-24 Liberator in the war with Japan, while concentrating all B-17s in Europe was basically a matter of range. For the Fortress's 500 mile radius of action, the UK was a suitable base for a campaign of strategic bombing on German war industry, in which the Americans were eager to join with the British. While the RAF carried out heavy bomber operations almost exclusively in darkness, the USAAF persisted in its determination to operate by day although their battle-experienced partner cautioned against it.

The first Fortresses to reach Britain were three dozen B-17E models, equipping the four squadrons of the 97th Bomb Group, which were, coincidentally, allotted the base from which the RAF B-17Cs had gone to war – Polebrook. All other Fortress groups arriving during 1942 had the new B-17F model. The intention was to provide a combined B-17 and B-24 establishment for the 8th Air Force, the UK operating agency, and though two groups of Liberators did arrive in the autumn of 1942, it was found technically impracticable to operate the two types of bomber in the same strike force. Handicapped by acute shortages in crews and aircraft the B-24 units were often employed in supporting roles or detached to the Mediterranean war zone. For a year, until the late autumn of 1943, the US strategic bombing offensive in Europe was pursued chiefly by the Fortresses of the 8th Air Force, a period that proved to be the most crucial for the whole campaign.

The 97th Bomb Group began operations on August 17, 1942 when 12 aircraft raided Rouen. The debut of the USAAF Fortress in the European Theatre of War came at a most opportune time, the Luftwaffe fighter units defending the west being hard pressed by superior numbers of British fighters and the serious situation on the Russian front precluded reinforcements. In this situation the Luftwaffe fighter commanders in France and the Low Countries chose to conserve their forces, only committing them to battle when there appeared to be an advantage. Thus many of the early B-17 raids, heavily escorted to targets within Spitfire range, were hardly challenged. The bombing was mostly inaccurate but improved during the winter months, bringing sharper reaction as the Germans appreciated the potential of a heavy attack by the four B-17 groups then in action. The 8th Air Force B-17s were not without some of the problems encountered by the RAF in the damp air of North-West Europe but their usual combat altitude, being from three to ten thousand feet below that at which the RAF chose to operate, did not impose such severe strain on men and aircraft. The secret of the American success, albeit erstwhile, was numbers; tight formations of a dozen or so bombers providing gun cover for each other. In fact, a substantiation of the technique that they had long practised and preached.

The two oldest B-17 groups in the 8th Air Force were taken to support the Allies North African venture in November, 1942 and another two groups originally destined for England were redirected early in 1943 to bolster the bombing force in that theatre. The four B-17 groups remaining in the UK operated for six months before further groups joined the fray, providing the 8th Air Force with the strength to embark on a combined bomber offensive with the RAF – 'round the clock'. In the meantime, the basic operational procedure for the B-17 strikes was evolved and remained little changed throughout the rest of the hostilities. The Fortresses would take off, usually around dawn, and spend some two hours climbing to combat altitude while assembling formations. It was necessary to be at this height to minimise the effects of anti-aircraft artillery fire when penetrating the enemy coast. A three-plane vee flight was the basic element of a formation with two to four of these making a squadron, while three squadrons usually composed a

USAAF Fortresses return from their first combat operation over Europe. Among the waiting 'top brass' on the Grafton Underwood control tower is Gen Carl Spaatz first commander of the 8th Air Force in the UK.

group box formation of between 18 to 27 aircraft, although later in the war 36 became the standard number.

Squadron or group formations dropped bombs on the sighting and release of the lead bomber flown by a specially trained crew. Set up correctly, the Norden sight could produce a very accurate drop from 25 000 feet and the bomb loads from a group formation, all detonating within a quarter square mile area, often produced great destruction at a target. While the B-17s maximum long-range bomb load of 4 000 pounds was small in comparison with those carried by RAF heavies on their night raids, it transpired that this was not so important as the inability to take any bomb larger than a 2 000 pounder in its bay. Far more telling destruction could have been obtained by 4 000 pound bombs on the industrial installations that were frequent targets.

The few B-17Es in Europe were withdrawn from combat units after eight missions and used for training. For a year the B-17F, the first really battle-worthy Fortress, was the model used for operations in both the UK and North Africa. The most notable change during the production of 2 300 F models was the near doubling of fuel capacity by installing nine additional fuel cells in the wing, outboard of the engines, and adding another 250 miles to the B-17's practical radius of action. Known as Tokyo tanks – theoretically they permitted the B-17 to make a one-way trip from the US to Tokyo – they were fitted in most of the B-17Fs equipping the new groups reaching England in the spring of 1943.

During the summer of 1943 the 8th Air Force strength was increased to sixteen B-17 groups and missions with between two and three hundred bombers were flown to targets deep in Germany. Luftwaffe fighter strength was rapidly increased and vast air battles became an almost regular feature of every mission as the Fortresses were assailed by the defenders. For intensity, scope, and duration these air battles probably have no equal; there were occasions when individual formations were under almost constant attack for three or four hours. Amongst American participants this offensive was known as 'the Big League of sky fighting', and it certainly was with an average 35 per cent chance of surviving the 25 missions each man was required to fly to complete a combat tour.

Although the claims of enemy fighters destroyed by gunners proved highly exaggerated, the Fortresses were going out unescorted and fighting their way through to targets often four hundred miles inside hostile territory without once being turned back, heavy as the losses might be. At first the

Luftwaffe, confident that such raids by large slow bombers could be quickly countered, tried conventional tail attacks but finding the defensive fire ferocious turned, like the Japanese, to assault the poorly defended frontal areas of the bomber. This manner of interception was soon recognised as requiring considerable skill and best undertaken by experienced pilots. With a growing realisation that the bomber boxes were not to be easily deflected, let alone destroyed, heavier ordnance was brought into use. By the late summer and autumn of 1943, the Germans had evolved new tactics using twin-engine fighters armed with large calibre cannon and rockets. These were fired out of effective range of the Fortresses' guns to disperse the formations so that the single-seat fighters could then deal with individual bombers.

A Fortress did not die easily as German pilots involved will testify. The bomber could absorb an extraordinary number of cannon and bullet strikes without going down. The Luftwaffe deduced that on average twenty 20mm hits were needed to destroy a B-17. While a single hit on some vital part could bring disaster, there were examples of Fortresses returning to base with evidence of far more than a score of cannon shell strikes. The most vulnerable parts were the Tokyo tanks, for while affording much needed extra range, they were a fire hazard. Fumes tended to gather in the outer wing sections where an incendiary strike could cause an explosion that might rip off the whole wing. Only in the final days of the war was a successful venting system introduced to reduce this danger.

The B-17G, which began to reach the groups in September 1943, featured a remotely controlled Bendix turret under the nose, commonly known as the chin turret. In combat trials this turret had proved far superior to other forms of frontal defence installed in Fortresses. The G model also introduced a number of internal changes and many others were made during the course of production. The B-17G remained in production until the end of hostilities and was the major Fortress model, 8 680 being delivered by the three manufacturing plants.

The dominance of the German fighters had, by the autumn of 1943, made obvious the pressing need for long-range escort fighters if bomber losses were not to become prohibitive. Bolstering the range of existing American fighters by the use of pressurised drop tanks and introducing the P-51 Mustang, to which no part of Germany was out of reach, brought a changed situation. The value of the escort fighters was endorsed by incidents that involved their absence. This was when the German controller was able to vector his interceptors to places along in the bomber

stream where escorting fighters had failed to materialise. Individual formations of B-17s were decimated when the Luftwaffe introduced tactics of mass assault with heavily armed and armoured FW190s and Me 109s.

The four B-17 groups in North Africa with the 12th Air Force became part of the newly formed 15th Air Force in November 1943 and moved to the Foggia area of Italy. The 15th was primarily created to carry out a campaign of strategic bombing in southern Germany and the Balkans, areas which could not easily be reached by the 8th Air Force. All but two of the new groups sent from the United States to complete the complement of this new air force were B-24 equipped. Only a solitary B-17 wing of six groups operated from Italy and in the early months suffered as grievously, if not more so, than the Fortresses flying from England.

From the spring of 1944, with the growth of American fighter support, the heavy bombers frequently went about their work unmolested by enemy interceptors. Having lost the mastery of the air, Germany increased and improved its anti-aircraft artillery defences, with higher velocity guns, gun-laying radar and better battery control techniques, making 'flak' the foremost bomber killer in the last year of hostilities. At vital installations, such as synthetic oil plants and refineries, several hundred guns were deployed and over such targets as the Merseburg complex as many as 50 B-17s were crippled or fell in a single mission. Altitude was still a factor in minimising the effect of flak and because the

B-17 had a five thousand feet advantage over the B-24, Fortress groups were frequently allocated the most heavily defended targets.

As the war progressed the standard of bombing achieved by USAAF heavy bombers gradually improved. Many spectacular results were achieved but equally there were instances when the target was missed completely, through human or mechanical failings or weather difficulties. The B-17 proved a very stable bombing platform for high altitude sighting although some of the best results were obtained from lower levels – around 20 000 feet. While the internal bomb load was limited for practical purposes to 6 000 pounds the Fortress could lift as much as 20 000 pounds by making use of under-wing racks. In the last two months of the war a special unit in England made a number of strikes on E-Boat pens with the concrete-busting rocket-boosted bombs which weighed 7 000 pounds each and were carried one on each wing rack.

In May and June 1945 over 2 000 Fortresses from England and Italy were redeployed to the United States. For the vast majority of their flying days were numbered and most were flown to Kingman, Arizona, to be parked in the arid desert plain where eventually they were reduced to scrap. From the battles over Europe some 4 500 B-17s were lost and another 2 000 written off through damage received or in accidents. Fortresses averaged $238 070 apiece to build, and to train and equip a ground and air crew took another $100 000, at a time when the average factory worker's wage was 40 dollars a week.

The ultimate model of the Fortress, the B-17G, devoid of camouflage paint. All Fortresses left the factory in 'silver' finish from January 1944 onwards.

Ten Little Fortresses

Ten Little Fortresses

Ten little Fortresses, all was going fine
'til one got bombed and then there were nine

Nine little Fortresses homing rather late
One ran out of gas and then there were eight

Eight little Fortresses caught in Satan's heaven
One met Messerschmitts, then there were seven

Seven little Fortresses lost without a fix
One hit a hill top and then there were six

Six little Fortresses, one went in a dive
Winding up in the brine, then there were five

Five little Fortresses, with one late for war
A prop wouldn't feather, then there were four

Four little Fortresses high above the sea
One got its tail knocked off, then there were
*   three*

Three little Fortresses, looked like winning
*   through*
One became a flying bomb, then there were two

Two little Fortresses, their combat days done
One wasn't safe to fly and then there was one

One little Fortress survived for quite a run
The French let it fade away, so there were none.

The fortunes of a specific band of flyers
engaged in hostilities are inevitably those of
diminishing numbers. Naturally, the rate of
attrition varied; in some cases a new unit
committed to battle might be decimated in a
few days, while another, in a less hostile
theatre of war, could endure for many months
without suffering loss. The crews and B-17s
of bomber squadrons arriving in England
during the spring and summer of 1943 did not
remain upon the scene long. Most fell in
trying to sustain the VIII Bomber Command
offensive in unescorted deep penetrations of
Hitler's Reich. There follows the story of one
squadron, typical of any of the four dozen
B-17F squadrons committed to battle during
that period. The story of the ten Fortresses is
not unlike the nursery tale on which the
opening poem is a parody.

The 562nd Bombardment Squadron (H)
was officially activated on Christmas Eve 1942
at Gower Field, Idaho, as a component unit of
the 388th Bombardment Group (H). While a
squadron was the basic flying unit in the Army
Air Force, operations were normally conducted on a group basis, particularly in the
case of heavy bombardment. Each bomb
group (bombardment was commonly shortened to bomb in Air Force jargon) had a
complement of four squadrons, which normally remained with the group throughout its
existence. Those completing the complement
of the 388th were the 560th, 561st and
563rd.

At first only a small number of men were
assigned, the main raising of the Group
taking place at Wendover Field, Utah, during
February-April 1943. Here aircrews and
ground personnel, fresh from training establishments, were added to the nucleus of flying
personnel. Well-worn B-17D and Es were
assigned to training crews for bombing and
formation practice, although squadrons had

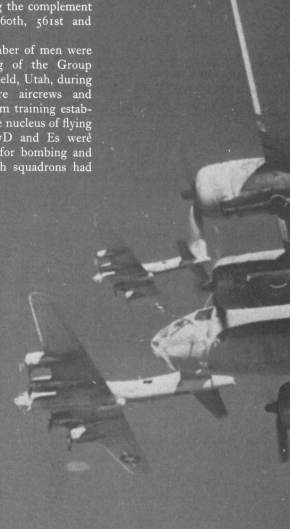

Top: The hole made by a .50 calibre bullet in the co-pilot's window on 'Charlene'.

Above: The Squadron Staff Ship after her crash-landing on a wheat stubble near Stanton, Suffolk. The tail emplacement has wrenched off and the ball suspension frame has broken the spine of the fuselage making repairs impracticable.

only six apiece by the end of April. Rumour, always rife at military establishments in those days, held that the Group would take these bombers to war; a story happily proved unfounded when the 388th moved to Sioux City Army Air Base in Iowa during the first two days of May. Here brand new B-17Fs were forthcoming, mostly Boeing made, but a few from both Douglas and Vega factories were included. The unit establishment of a squadron was 10 aircraft, one being assigned to each of the nine combat crews, the tenth being the 'Staff Ship' crewed by the squadron commander and senior personnel, although they did not constitute a combat crew and this aircraft was really a reserve. Two B-17s assigned to Group Headquarters were also in effect reserves. A total of 42 B-17Fs were readied for overseas movement in early June but one aircraft, 42-30228, of the 562nd Squadron never started the trip. Lt Ivan Willson's crew nearly didn't make it either, as co-pilot Charles Seymour relatés:

'We were on an air-to-air gunnery mission at Casper, Wyoming, where we were required to fire at a tow-target pulled by another '17. The procedure was to fly parallel with the target plane, off to the side and above, then peel off, come down, letting the forward guns of the aircraft fire, making a tight turn around the back of the sleeve and as we went away the idea was that the waist gunner, and eventually

the tail gunner, could get a shot at the target. We did this once or twice but on our next go, while in a steep bank we had a high speed stall, a snap and a spin from which we didn't recover until some 10 000 feet later. When Ivan recovered from the spin, the tail gunner called: "Gee, that was fun. Let's do it again", although I don't think the rest of the crew were that enthused about the manoeuvre. Anyway we flew straight and level for a while, got the aircraft trimmed up, and returned to base without any further incident. Other members of our Group, who had been up there flying near us and had seen the B-17 spin into the clouds below, thought that they had seen the last of us. We found that the rear fuselage had been twisted so that the tail was some twenty degrees out of true. Also the wing tips had been bent up about four feet giving added dihedral. The Boeing reps took a look and decided the aircraft was no longer airworthy. The intent was to run some static and dynamic tests on it to see how close we had come to the failure point of the aircraft. We were given another B-17 for combat. The obvious choice for a name was *Second Chance*.'

Aircraft nicknames were a permissible adornment on the bombers' noses in most units destined for combat theatres. The official serial number of an aircraft was a tedious identity, whereas individual names

were popular as an easy and more personal reference among group personnel. Every one of the original B-17Fs of the 562nd Bomb Squadron was eventually labelled. Apart from *Second Chance* there was *Homesick Angel*, *Quarterback*, *Charlene*, *Lil' One*, *Wailuiku Maui*, *Plain Mister Yank*, *Wolf Pack*, *Little Lass* and *Sondra Kay*. They set out across the Atlantic from Gander to Prestwick direct during the Group's overseas movement. One aircraft of the 563rd Squadron disappeared en route but between June 23 and July 12, 1943, 41 B-17Fs reached the 388th Group's wartime location in England, their base for over two years. This was Knettishall, situated between the village of that name and Coney Weston in north-west Suffolk, about 35 miles from the east coast. The location was among well-wooded farmlands bordering an extensive heath and conifer forest area known as the Brecklands. Knettishall was still under construction although the flying field, apart from a few hardstandings, was complete. Only one hangar was available and several of the hutted living sites were unfinished so that initially the ground crews were given tented accommodation. Despite the lack of facilities life in this rural setting was not unpleasant during the warm summer days.

Preparations for combat were hastened, notably indoctrination of the crews in theatre procedures. The Fortresses were modified to the 8th Air Force standard, which involved among other things radio changes and the installation of a .5 machine gun in the transparent nosepiece.

The 388th's introductory mission was a shallow penetration to bomb a target at Amsterdam on July 17. Thereafter, despite its inexperience, the Group was committed to the 8th Air Force's major offensive during a week of fine weather late in the month. This was against targets five or six hundred miles from base with many hours in hostile airspace. Known as 'Blitz Week', this series of missions introduced the 388th to the harsh realities of combat. In six days the Group lost more than a quarter of its strength; good morale faded as young men faced the prospect of oblivion. A Norwegian target was the opening gambit on the 24th and from this, the Group's second mission, all returned safely. The following day brought the first flight into Germany where enemy fighter opposition was experienced, but attacks were not pressed against the 388th. One bomber from 563rd Squadron was seen to drop out of formation for unknown reasons and did not return, presumably having been picked off by fighters. It was the first loss for the Group.

When, for the third day running, the 388th went to war seeking a rubber factory at Hanover, it attracted considerable attention from the enemy. Under almost constant attack

Bob Pfeiffer and the crew of 'Lil' One'. Pfeiffer's wife was expecting their first child which was referred to as the 'Lil' One', hence the name for his bomber. Barbara was the navigator's wife or girl-friend.

by fighters and anti-aircraft artillery while in enemy airspace, five of the Group's Fortresses failed to return and another ten of the 21 despatched suffered battle damage. One of the first to fall was a 562nd Squadron aircraft. Shortly after crossing the German coast, an enemy fighter flying about a thousand feet above the formation dropped a time-fused bomb which apparently exploded against the wing root of *Plain Mister Yank*, flown by Lt Denton's crew. A bomb-bay tank immediately took fire and the bomb-load was salvoed as the blazing bomber gradually slipped behind the other aircraft. The bale-out order was given but only navigator Bill Davis had time to escape before an explosion sent the bomber spinning out of control. The remainder were held immobile by centrifugal force as *Plain Mister Yank* spiralled down. A further explosion blasted bombardier Arthur Basham out of the nose, radioman Frank Glose through the radio room hatch, and gunner Ivan Walter from the right-hand waist position, these with Bill Davis were the only survivors. Arthur Basham, who was knocked unconscious, reported, 'I came to at about 10 000 feet after falling through the air for some 13 000 feet. My hip was injured when I was blasted out of the plane so I had to slide my 'chute straps down to my knees as I floated to earth. Bill Davis saw this from two miles away and thought it looked like two guys

in my 'chute (I'm 6ft 6ins). We were all together within an hour at the "Flughafen" at Vechta'.

During the demise of *Plain Mister Yank* another 562nd B-17, Lt Bliss's *Charlene*, was in trouble. No 4 engine began to lose power, presumably damaged by shrapnel, and the propeller had to be feathered. Bliss moved to the centre of the formation, for more protection from fighter attacks that were developing. Flak was encountered again in the target area and *Charlene* picked up a few holes in the tail and wings while some other bombers were badly damaged. The remnants of the 388th then joined on to the rear of the 100th Group for the journey home, but fighter attacks did not cease until the bombers were well out from the German coast. Lt Charles Zettick, bombardier takes up the story of *Charlene*:–

'We were about 15 miles out to sea when a 20-mm shell from an FW190 came through the front windshield on the co-pilot's side and exploded inside the pilots' compartment, and the pilot was hit in the left arm by flying pieces of steel. The co-pilot, Lt Duncan, took over the controls. The fighters had thinned out by this time but there were still too many around for comfort. We were now flying on the underside of our formation and on the right wing of the lead ship. Two FW190s singled out our ship, probably because they saw one engine

First replacement B-17F in the 562nd was 'Mister Yank II', 42-5954, seen here with the Bensel crew prior to the Regensburg mission in August 1943. Its unlucky predecessor, 'Plain Mister Yank', got its nickname through pilot Paul Bensel's habit of alluding to himself as 'just a plain Yankee'. 'Homesick Angel' is the B-17 in the background.

feathered, and made repeated attacks on the nose from 2 o'clock. One of the bastards had a yellow nose and the other one looked like checker board, with black and white squares painted on his cowling. After about six passes they disappeared and were lost to my sight for good. We continued with the formation for a while after the fighters left us until we decided it was necessary to lighten the ship in order to save gas. Then we left the formation and started throwing things overboard, guns, ammunition, tool kits, extra radio equipment, etc. We were letting down all the time so we'd be able to take off our oxygen masks and before long we had dropped to 2 000 feet. At this point No 3 engine started acting up; the rpm got out of control so we had to cut the engine and feather the prop. This left us with two good engines on one side, a wing on the other and a prayer in the cockpit. However, the prayer wasn't necessary for we still had two very capable men there. They not only held a straight course for the rest of the trip but gained 2 000 feet altitude before reaching the English coast.

'We were running very low on gas so we all kept an eye open for the first air base we could find. We soon spotted one but found it was still under construction. We flew on and soon saw another one to our right (Saltby, Lincs). Lt Bliss took over the controls and made a beautiful wheel landing. He had to

lock the brakes to keep the ship from going off the end of the runway and when we'd nearly reached it the right tyre blew out. We skidded to a stop just short of the end.'

When ordnance experts examined *Charlene* they discovered that it was not an enemy 20-mm shell that had penetrated the windscreen and wounded Charles Bliss, but a .5 bullet, obviously fired by some careless gunner in another B-17 ahead. She did have plenty of genuine 20-mm damage elsewhere, and flak holes plus damage caused by an empty ammunition can falling from another B-17.

An acute shortage of replacement parts made the maintenance critical during these early days, often grounding aircraft for long periods so that some crews had to fly missions in aircraft assigned to other crews. This was the case for Lt Henry Rodgers' crew whose own B-17, *Wailuiku Maui* suffered a failure in No 2 engine during one of the early training missions over England. Because a replacement engine was not available *Wailuiku Maui* was grounded for the best part of a month during which time numerous parts were 'borrowed' from it to keep other Fortresses flying, earning the aircraft an additional nickname at Knettishall field – *Tech Supply*. The position got so bad that Crew Chief Walter Corsa began to think he would never get his charge into the air again, and as a deterrent let it be known that he had permission to stand

The crew of 'Sondra Kay'. Back row l to r Frank Broach (B), Albert Runin (CP), Henry Cox (P) and Willis Eddy (N). Front row: Herman Ball (TT), George Martin (BT), Joshua Lewis (TG), Otto Kloza (WG), Paul Gomis (RO) and Francis Curry (WG). All except Eddy, who had been transferred to Bliss's crew, were killed in a crash 36 days after this picture was taken. The bomber was named for the baby daughter of Joshua Lewis.

'Charlene' had only two missions to her credit when this photograph of Charles Bliss and crew was taken at Knettishall on August 30th, 1943. Crew are l to r: standing: John Harlan (N), wounded September 6th, 1943; Charles Bliss (P), Vernon Duncan (CP) and Bernard Quenneville (B), ex-Pfeiffer crew. Kneeling: Robert Brailey (BT), Albert Brown (TT), Herman Mays (WG), Lawrence Ruddell (WG), Edmund Wilbert (TG) and Henry Rotell (RO). The aircraft was named after Bliss's baby daughter.

guard on *Wailuiku Maui* with a machine gun. The bomber did not fly its first mission until August 12 but three days later the No 1 propeller ran awry on take-off and Rodgers was forced to abandon the mission and return to base.

On August 17 the 388th Bomb Group took part in the first 8th Air Force shuttle mission, striking at the fighter factory at Regensburg and then flying on to land at bases in North Africa. Lt Rodgers' crew went in the Staff Ship *Homesick Angel*. Over the Mediterranean the navigator, pilots and engineer conferred and agreed it would be necessary to leave formation and fly a more direct route to their destination to conserve fuel. In consequence *Homesick Angel* was the first 8th Air Force B-17 into Bone where a reception committee of high ranking officers were rather deflated to find the aircraft piloted by Second Lieutenants and not the mission leader Brigadier-General Curtis Le May who was expected to be the first arrival.

The 388th returned to the UK with the rest of the B-17 'shuttle' force on August 24, bombing an airfield at Bordeaux en route. The flight again entailed over 11 hours in the air and many of the B-17s were low on fuel when landfall was made over southern England. Lt. Rodgers and *Homesick Angel* reached home base but while in the landing pattern all four engines suddenly stopped, starved of fuel, although the gauges showed a substantial reserve in the tanks. Rodgers was able to make

a successful belly landing on a wheat stubble near Stanton. The crew were uninjured and sat in the bomber eating water melons brought from Africa until help arrived. *Homesick Angel* was, however, beyond economical repair.

The next few missions were less eventful for the 562nd although on the last day of August *Charlene* again suffered damage from 'friendly fire'. After a cloud-foiled operation over Belgium a .5 hole was found in the tailplane, presumably the result of a gunner's negligence while test firing over the Channel.

What should have been a major mission to Stuttgart on September 6 turned into disaster for the 8th Air Force and especially for the 388th. Weather deteriorated and the bomber stream was scattered by heavy cloud. Near Strasburg the 388th, flying the vulnerable low group position in the wing formation, came under concentrated attack from fighters. The Group's low squadron, made up of 563rd aircraft, was completely destroyed in the battle that followed. All told the 388th lost 11 of the 21 B-17s that crossed the enemy coast but only one, the first to go, was a 562nd aircraft. Edward Wick's *Wolf Pack* lost an engine before the IP, lagged behind the formation and was pounced on by fighters just before the target. It was seen in flames and four of the crew, pilot, co-pilot, engineer and right waist gunner, parachuted into captivity. Wick's crew had previously had some near misses. On an early mission the fin of another

'Tech Supply' alias 'Wailuiku Maui', and crew. Back row l to r: Jerome Flohr (N), Henry Rodgers (P), Pat Lewis (CP) and Seldon Smith (B). Front row: William Sawyer (TG), Kelly Hill (WG), Ed Pawlicki (BT), Jack Ford (WG), Joe Hallam (RO) and Eddie Franklin (TT). The dog is 'Peggy'.

B-17 had damaged the tailplane of *Wolf Pack*. On another occasion flak hit a propeller which could not be feathered and windmilled until it 'melted' off.

Stuttgart proved to be the 388th's most costly mission of the war. Shortly after this disaster the Group historian wrote: 'Airmen were impressed with the idea that their chances of surviving a tour of operations were next to nothing and gave opportunity for the thought to enter their minds, as well as to the minds of ground personnel, that Germany might yet win the war because in attacking the enemy our strength was being drained'. Indeed, in the unfortunate 563rd Squadron only one complete original crew and one original Fortress survived after Stuttgart. An outcome of this mauling was the installation of extra armour plate in what were considered exposed positions on the B-17s. As a standard fitting three pieces were added in the nose section, a piece under each pilot's seat and one piece for the floor of the waist gun positions. Some 30 tons were secured from the RAF for these modifications – primarily against flak splinters – and did much to raise aircrew morale.

In an endeavour to hoax the enemy into believing an invasion of the Channel coast was imminent, many of the missions undertaken during the remainder of September were to attack airfields and other installations in France. These penetrations, usually shallow, were less fraught with danger but an exception was La Pallice, a submarine base on the French Atlantic seaboard, a secondary target which was attacked on the 16th. A long flight skirting the French coast involved over nine hours in the air and brought the Fortresses back over England in darkness. An extensive weather front barred the way on return and groups made their own way – over, through or under. The 388th became widely dispersed in the cloud and some aircraft became lost. Seeking landing fields in the murk, some crews were apparently unaware of the high ground in south-west England. Shortly after 2200 hours, Lt Cox and his crew were killed when *Sondra Kay* struck Rhiw Gwraidd hill, a few miles south-east of Rhayader in Wales. Two other 388th B-17s came to grief that night including the last of the 563rd originals. *Sondra Kay* was on its 13th mission.

The superstitious may have reflected that the next original of the 562nd to fall was also on its 13th mission. During the bomb run over Munster on October 10th, Paul Williams' *Little Lass* was seen to nose down and dive out of formation during a lull in fighter activity and was never seen again. Most of the crew were on their 18th mission, and co-pilot Israel Rogg was on his 21st. *Little Lass* was the only 388th loss on a bad day when a total of 29 B-17s of the 3rd Division failed to return. Her demise had been quite spectacular and Paul Williams relates: 'I had trouble with No 3 engine about 50 miles from the target and had to carry excess power on the other three. Frankly I do not know what happened to cause No 3 to start acting up but it could have been hit by a stray bullet or a flak fragment. Unfortunately No 2 engine would not develop full power, probably due to the oil lines to the superchargers being frozen up. On the IP run No 3 started to run away and I controlled it with the feathering button. Flak was moderate and a few fighters were about. Immediately after bombs away No 3 surged again and this time would not feather. I did not feel I could now maintain formation and gave the abort signal and dived out of formation heading for the deck – straggling behind the formation would have meant certain elimination. On the way down six or so Me 110s picked us up and started attacking. No 3 engine was finally feathered again but during evasive manoeuvres the two men in the nose, evidently believing the aircraft was out of control, baled out. The engineer, thinking the signal to jump had been given, also left. I quite understand, given the situation, how this could happen. In any event we reached ground level and both Israel Rogg and myself believed we were the only occupants left in *Little Lass*.

'We were still travelling at high speed from the dive and I pulled the aircraft up sharply to get enough altitude so we could get out ourselves, for with no gunners it was only a matter of time before the fighters got us. It was then we heard guns firing and realised the rear crew was still there. I headed due west and stayed close to the ground hedge-hopping. The Me 110s pressed their attacks but evidently had very inexperienced pilots as we were only hit by small calibre fire. The 20-mm shells were arcing overhead and exploding forward of us. The fighters then overshot us, two of them actually appearing alongside, not 60 feet from our wings. The waist gunners claim to have hit these. All the time I was taking extreme evasive action and probably ran No 2 engine into a pole or obstruction although it could have been due to the hits we were taking from fighter fire. Anyway it ceased to function and feathered without trouble. We were now on two engines and down to about 120mph. Luckily the fighters were suddenly gone – perhaps out of fuel or ammunition.

'We continued westwards and were suddenly over the sea. I thought: "We've made it." My optimism was premature for the temperature of the two good engines began to pass the safe limits. We started dumping equipment overboard but it didn't help. Knowing the engines were unlikely to last much longer I warned the crew to prepare for ditching. We gradually lost speed and I decided to ditch while we were still above stalling speed. The contact was smooth except for the final thrust into the water but no one was hurt. I immediately opened the cockpit window and tried to get out. I was terrified to find I couldn't and then realised that in my panic I had not removed my chest 'chute. Once free of this the exit was easy and despite the delay I was amazed to find I was still the second man out. We got into our rafts without trouble. The sea was relatively calm but it began to get choppy as time passed. It became very cold and when, some ten and a

Rear fuselage of 'Little Lass' served as an unusual location for girly art. Life size, it was based on an Esquire Magazine pin-up. Standing in the crew pose are: l to r: Paul Williams (P), Israel Rogg (CP) and Edwin Garver (N). Crouching: Ralph Cornwall (WG), Alfred Gardin (RO), Ray Harwood (TT), Roland Conners (TG), Maynard Rollins (WG) and Harold Moore (BT).

half hours after ditching, a German mine-sweeper picked us up we were glad to see anyone.'

Better weather during the first two weeks of October enabled the 8th Air Force to carry out precision attacks deep in Germany. The opposition was the stiffest so far encountered and many groups suffered heavily; in contrast the 388th fared comparatively well. Yet after three months of combat there was little left of the old order in the 562nd. Major Gilbert Goodman had taken command, four of the crews and six of the aircraft had been lost. There had been changes in all the remaining crews, some due to promotion of officers to lead crews; illness, personality clashes, wounds and injuries. In mid-November Bliss's crew was broken up, he and engineer Sgt Albert Brown being re-assigned to 482nd Bomb Group for Pathfinder work. Co-pilot Duncan took over the crew and other men were assigned to fill the vacated positions.

Personnel were rarely interchanged between squadrons to fill a crew gap for a combat mission, but if maintenance problems were particularly acute in one squadron aircraft from another were utilised by its crews. One such occasion arose on November 13 when Lt Robert Simons of the 560th had a tyre burst while moving out for take-off. As no spare aircraft was available in his own squadron, he was ordered to take 562nd's *Lil' One* which had been readied for the mission but held. This delayed Simons ten minutes. Three-quarters of an hour later, still attempting to locate the 388th formation over east Suffolk at 16 000 feet, manifold pressure on No 4 engine dropped and rpm decreased by 150 followed by a runaway propeller which neither Simons nor his co-pilot could feather: 'I should have known that any aircraft with its serial number ending in 13 would not bring us much luck on the 13th day of the month. The engine literally started to tear itself and the rest of the aircraft apart and caused great difficulty to normal flight. Parts of the cowling and engine were striking the wing. I was in the process of returning to base when the ball turret gunner informed me that we were on fire. I immediately ordered everyone to bale out and attempted to steer the aircraft toward the coast. I baled out and delayed opening the 'chute until approximately 1 000 feet above the ground. I landed rather hard and was in the process of gathering up my 'chute and was still in somewhat of a daze when I heard the thrashing about of a rather angry bull. He evidently did not look kindly upon my intrusion and seemed to be in the process of doing something about it. All this time I was trying to get out of my 'chute and find my way out of the pasture. Finally, I decided I could not get through in time or

before the bull decided to do something drastic, so I pulled out my Service .45 automatic and fired four shots near the bull which made him stop and think. I then fired five more which put him in the middle of the pasture still wondering what to do about me. I was in the process of putting in another clip of ammunition when I noticed a commotion on the other side of the hedgerow. I looked over and staring through an opening in the hedgerow was an English boy of about 7 or 8. His eyes were as big as saucers, having heard the shots from the other side. When he gazed upon my condition he could only say one thing: "Are you a German?" I told him I was not and needed some help. He immediately got on his bicycle and rode off down the road.'

A police officer from Beccles arrived in a car soon afterwards and helped Simons, who suffered spinal injuries in his landing that were to keep him in hospital for nearly a year. *Lil' One* flew on for some 15 minutes after the crew had left, heading west towards her base and finally crashed not far away in open country three miles north of East Wretham.

In November the flow of new bombers from the factories was such that, despite the heavy operational losses the 8th Air Force had incurred, it was possible to begin raising the unit establishment of each squadron from ten to 14 aircraft. This in turn led to each station being able to despatch larger numbers on each raid. For the 388th, November 26 was significant in that it was the first occasion that the Group was able to put up two separate formations on a single mission (45 all told). It was also a day marked with particular tragedy as the two bombers lost were victims of accidents in which the enemy played no part. While one 388th formation was over the target at Bremen a B-17 was struck by bombs released by 96th Group aircraft flying above. The other loss was another 562nd original. At 1228 hours, as the formation was withdrawing a strange B-17G was seen to join the formation, get into turbulence, nearly collide with the lead bomber of the second element in the high squadron, slide off to the left onto *Second Chance* in No 3 position of the 2nd element of the lead squadron, completely severing its tail before finally peeling off to the right, apparently under control. *Second Chance*, flown by 2nd Lt D. H. McCown's replacement crew, turned over twice, went into a spin and was seen to hit the ground. There were no survivors. Men of the 388th who witnessed this incident were inclined to believe that the interloper was being operated by the Luftwaffe for deliberate ramming tactics. In truth the Fortress was *Fancy Nancy* of the 401st Bomb Group, taking part in that organisation's first operation. *Fancy Nancy*, which struck *Second Chance* with its port wing root

Below: NOSES: September 19th, 1943. 'Second Chance' was Ivan Willson's second B-17F. Co-pilot Charles Seymour did the paintwork which included two red dice with matched sides showing lucky seven. Black bars on bomb symbols indicate group lead, a position from which 'Second Chance' had been relieved due to obsolescent equipment – after only a month!

Right: Wailuiku is a town in Maui, an island of the Hawaiian group. Every member of Henry Rodger's crew suggested a name for their bomber, settling the issue with slips in a hat, bombardier Seldon Smith being the lucky drawer. 'Wailuiku Maui' (pronounced Wy-loo-coo Mow-ee) was the home address of a fellow student in flying school. Seldon Smith liked the way it rolled off the tongue and thought it would be a nice gesture to his friend.

Below right: Tail gunner M/Sgt Roland Conners suggested the nickname for the Williams' crew Fortress. This was Vega built and like other B-17Fs from this source in the original 388th complement had the old-type cheek gun windows.

and left fuselage side, was able to reach England and land although it never flew again. A gunner in the ball turret, thrown from the machine at the time of impact, was the only casualty in the crew, who incidentally, maintained that it was the 388th's plane that was out of control and had hit their aircraft.

Another 562nd original was nearly given up for lost on that day. Lt Watts flying *Quarterback* experienced engine difficulties and was forced to abandon the mission at 1205 hrs over the North-West German coast when the turbo on No 3 engine failed and No 2 was running roughly. The bomber, then at 25 000 feet, jettisoned bombs and headed back over the North Sea. It soon transpired the crew were lost, finally making landfall in southern Scotland. *Quarterback* did not land until 1615 hours, long after all the other Knettishall aircraft on the raid had returned.

On operations December 5, a 388th gunner achieved what many had believed unlikely, the completion of a tour of 25 missions. Thereafter several other men reached this goal making them due for return to the USA. Henry Rodgers' crew became the first in the 562nd to finish, returning safely from a raid on Bremen on December 20. Of the original crew the co-pilot had transferred to Cox's ill-fated team and been killed. Navigator Jerome Flohr didn't arrive at dispersal one morning; in the dark he had been knocked down and killed by a truck while leaving the parachute store. *Wailuiku Maui*, the bomber in which most of their missions had been

flown now passed to other hands but on December 24 a new crew crash-landed it at Knettishall after its 20th mission. A new left-inner main wing panel had to be installed and the aircraft was out of commission for weeks and was later relegated to training at another UK base. Robert Pfeiffer, one time pilot of *Lil' One*, had been assigned to Group operations as an instructor after his 15th mission although he subsequently became a Command Pilot and flew several more missions later in the war. His crew completed their tour at the end of 1943 with the exception of the tail gunner, James P. Riley, who was lost on November 29, in a ditching with another crew. Paul Bensel's crew, whose assigned bomber *Plain Mister Yank* had been the first loss to the squadron, completed their tour in March and returned to the States. The co-pilot, however, had been given his own crew after a few missions.

Members of Ivan Willson's crew (*Second Chance*) all survived although the crew was broken up after a few missions when the pilots were taken to form a lead team in which Charles Zettick (late of the Bliss crew in *Charlene*) was bombardier and John Flor (ex-*Little Lass* and Williams' crew) was navigator. Willson's original navigator went to *Little Lass* and became a POW when it was lost. Zettick eventually became Group Bombardier.

As for the three remaining original aircraft, *Charlene* and *Wailuiku Maui* were retired to non-combat duties, the former

Top: Old 'Quarterback' rolls out with 15 missions to her credit. Denton's crew were recognised as the squadron's most proficient in bombing and navigation during training and they were often used to 'call the signals' for the rest of the team as the quarterback does in American football.

Above: Denuded of camouflage paint, 'Bir Hackeim' (ex-'Charlene) taxiing at Dijon, France in 1953. The tail call-number and letter were retained, repainted above the cross of Lorraine. Additional windows have been added in the former radio-room and waist, while the tail gun apperture had been faired over.

Above right: Grand old lady. Wearing the flags of 20 countries visited during her career, Charles Bliss's old bomber sits on a hardstand at Dijon awaiting propellers. The forward insignia commemorates the round-the-world flight, noting places visited.

serving on radar calibration duties, flying up and down the English coast. Only *Quarterback* continued on operations with the squadron into the spring of 1944, ironically the bomber assigned to the first 562nd crew lost in combat. Yet the record of 388th original aircraft was better than that of any other of the seven 3rd Division groups that had started with B-17F models, for by April 1944 the Group was still operating seven – a total greater than the combined total of the other groups.

Quarterback soldiered on until declared 'War Weary'. New crews did not like flying the older aircraft, believing them to be more prone to malfunction, and gradually the B-17Fs were withdrawn. For *Quarterback* the finale was spectacular. In July 1944 the 388th was given responsibility for support of a hush-hush, highly secret project codenamed 'Aphrodite' carried out from nearby Fersfield. It involved stripping armour, armament and other equipment from war weary B-17s, filling them with 20 000 lb of a volatile explosive called Torpex, and installing special radio-receiving apparatus which was linked to the controls. The bombers were flown off Fersfield manually by a crew of two who baled out once the operational altitude had been reached and control of the aircraft passed to a radio transmitting 'mother ship' that followed. The object was to direct these explosive laden aircraft across the North Sea and then dive them into a suitable target – such as submarine pens or V-weapon sites. They were literally flying bombs. Radio control equipment was primitive and little success was achieved in this venture. *Quarterback*

became one of the early missiles of the experiment being launched to its destruction on August 6. The planned journey was never completed as the control apparatus went awry and the aircraft plunged out of control into the North Sea.

Of the Group's aircraft, the last of the B-17Fs of the 388th that had reached Knettishall in early July 1943 to remain in combat was *Blind Date*, a 560th Squadron machine, which finally suffered an engine fire and crashed at Walpole after setting off on its 67th mission. This was on October 7, 1944, coincidentally the same day that Colonel David, who had led the Group to England, relinquished command and returned to America. Of the 41 original Fortresses, 23 were listed 'Missing In Action' with the 388th and nine had crashed in England; the 562nd's contribution to these totals was five and three respectively. By the end of hostilities the Group had received over 270 B-17s losing 178 operationally and 34 in accidents or through damage. Some 450 crews served the 388th, 135 being 'Missing In Action'. Only a handful of the original flying personnel remained to the end mostly in staff positions; but the original ground echelon were still at Knettishall in May 1945. Crew Chiefs administered in some cases to as many as eight different B-17s through successive losses of their charges.

Two veteran Fortresses of the 562nd survived the war in Europe. But *Wailuiku Maui*, after training duties, was deemed too worn to make a trans-Atlantic flight home and was scrapped in June 1945. *Charlene* however, did not meet this fate. Having been converted for local transport flights by Air Service Command, in 1945 she was given as a personal gift from General Eisenhower to the Free French General M. P. Koening, hero of Bir-Hakeim, the Libyan village where French troops were beseiged by Rommel's forces in June 1942. In his honour *Charlene* underwent a change of name and became *Bir-Hackeim*. Koening was the C-in-C of French Forces in Germany from 1945 to 1949 and used *Bir-Hackeim* extensively. As a flag-showing gesture, a round-the-world trip was made in the autumn of 1945. Starting on September 6, *Bir-Hackeim* left Paris and returned on October 2 having spent 137 hours in the air, visiting 12 countries including the USA. Lt Melvin Lynch was the pilot. For most of its service with the French Air Force, *Bir-Hackeim* was based with unit ELA 54 at Baden-Oos, a small airfield three miles north-west of Baden-Baden. Once it had its tail shot up when straying from an air corridor to Berlin: a hot incident in the Cold War. In 1955 it was struck off charge and sold with a full cargo of spares to the Institute Geographique National at Creil, an organisation already using converted B-17s for high-altitude photography. The sum involved was a token one franc! Here the aircraft languished in a hangar and although the intention was to overhaul and put it in flying condition again, *Bir-Hackeim* became a source of parts to keep the other B-17s flying. At Creil this famous old aircraft gradually faded away, sustaining younger brethren. How long parts of it remained at Creil is not known but certainly until the mid-1960s. The career of 42-30177 alias *Darklock F-Freddie* alias *Charlene* alias *Bir-Hackeim* was unique among all the thousands of Fortresses.

This then is the story of the men and machines with which the 562nd Bomb Squadron entered battle. In itself it is a tale of death and destruction yet one that was very quickly vindicated in the continually revitalised status of a squadron at war. Crews and aircraft would come and go but the enemy could never destroy a squadron; only a written order from an administrator could do that!

Crews and B-17s with which 562nd Bomb Squadron started Combat Operations

B-17 Serial	Letter Borne	Nickname	Fate & Date	No of Missions	Crew Captain	Crew Fate
42-3289	A	*Wolf Pack*	MIA 6/9/43	7	Edward A. Wick	MIA 6/9/43: N, B, LW, BT, RO, TG & TT. KIA; rest POW (P, CP, & RW)
42-3295	B	*Wailuiku Maui*	SAL 45	22	Henry J. Rodgers	CT 20/12/43
42-5898	D	*Little Lass*	MIA 10/10/43	13	Paul E. Williams	MIA 10/10/43 All POW
42-5906	E	*Sondra Kay*	C 16/9/43	13	Henry O. Cox Jr	All KAS 16/9/43 Cilgu, Wales
42-30177	F	*Charlene*	Survived War	15	Charles C. Bliss	Crew broken up 11/43
42-30212	G	*Quarterback Aphrodite*	MIA 6/8/44	15+	John R. Denton	MIA 26/7/43 N, B & RO, POW, rest KIA
42-30213	H	*Lil' One*	C 13/11/43	20	Robert L. Pfeiffer	CT
42-30225	J	*Plain Mister Yank*	MIA 26/7/43	2	Paul P. Bensel	CT March 1944
42-30317	K	*Second Chance*	MIA 26/11/43	19	Ivan M. Willson	CT CB
42-30230	L	*Homesick Angel*	C 24/8/43	6	Staff aircraft	

See page 72 for details of abbreviations.

Left: Two camouflaged B-17Gs, resplendent in recently applied red identification markings of the 1st Combat Bomb Wing, fly low over the East Anglian countryside, summer 1944. The bomber with the original type tail gun emplacements was later lost; 42-31570, VP:W, 'Lucky Me!' being shot down in September 1944 . More fortunate was the aircraft with the Cheyenne turret, 42-32025, VP:P, 'Dream Baby,' which survived the war with more than 1 000 combat hours. Both served with 533rd Bomb Squadron, 381st Bomb Group.

Departure

Members of the crew who flew in the forward section preferred – if they were not too heavily laden – to enter via the nose hatch. Opinions differed as to the best style of entry. At the 390th BG this flyer preferred the cupid's leap – with assistance. At least this way if you missed and fell out you landed on your feet.

Top left: S/Sgt William Mulgrew of 303rd BG used the swing-one-leg-up technique which involved a good deal of twisting and squirming to enter via the nose hatch.

Centre left: Taxiing out required a weaving pattern in order to see ahead and avoid running off the hard into winter mud. Behind these 463rd BG Fortresses on the Celone taxiway can be seen the cloud-shrouded foothills of the Apennines which claimed several bombers.

Bottom left: The leading elements of the 305th BG bunched on the end of a Chelveston runway awaiting the 'start' signal flare from the control tower. In order to achieve the 30 second interval between each bomber commencing its take-off, the whole force was closely marshalled and in the correct order for gaining their allotted place in the formation.

Above: 'Royal Flush', 91st BG, lifts off. Although the prescribed maximum gross weight of a B-17F or G was 32 tons, the loads of fuel and bombs carried by 8th AF Fortresses often took the gross weight to 36 tons. In such circumstances every bit of a standard 4 400 ft runway was usually needed to get safely airborne.

Below: A collision appears imminent. The illusion is created by the distance and height of each aircraft from the photographer. This fighter type, close staggered, take-off was a stunt and not the normal way B-17s were flown off Glatton runways by the 457th BG.

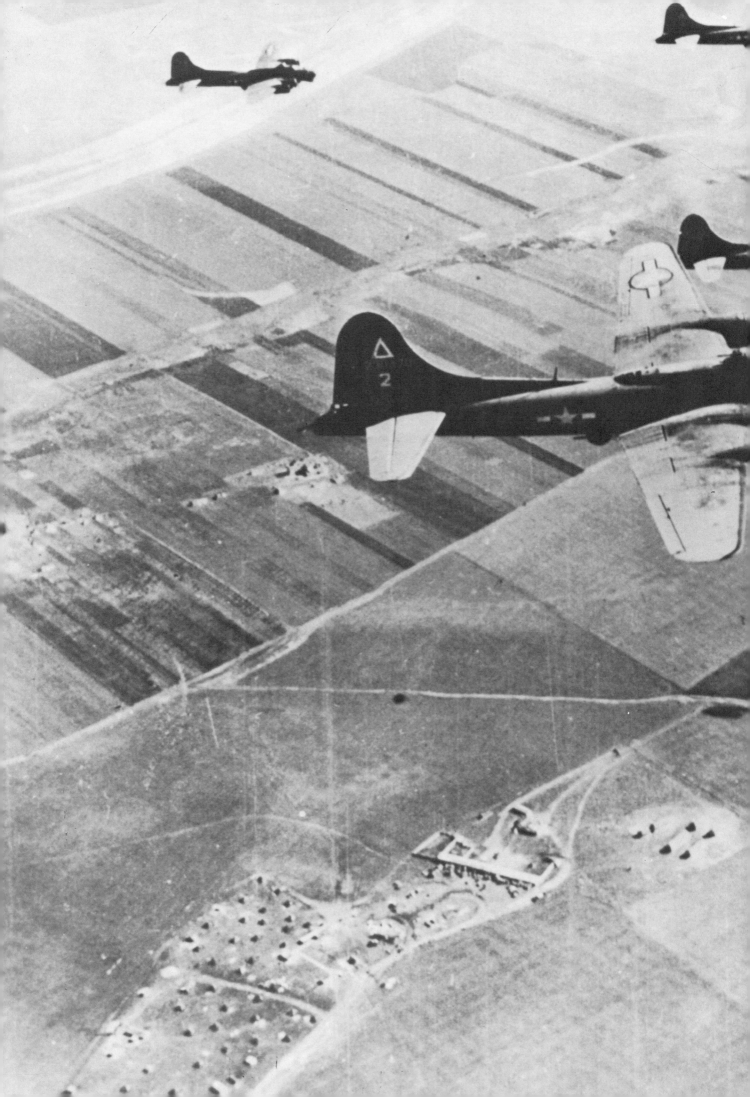

Formations

In a good combat formation the wing aircraft in a flight fly just half a B-17's wing span behind the flight leader and half a wing span from his wing tip. Difficult to maintain and not always as good as in this 97th Bomb Group formation over Italy.

Above: Three bombers made the basic vee flight. In this instance the two camouflaged aircraft are Pathfinders with H2X radomes in place of ball turrets.

Right: Two flights make a squadron, the trailing flight being stepped down below the first.

Below: Three squadrons make a group, the left squadron flying low and the right high to the lead and both trailing it.

Below right: A Combat Wing was made up of three groups staggered in similar fashion to squadrons within a group formation.

Bottom right: Later in the war an extra B-17 flew in the 'slot' position at the rear of each flight and an extra flight in each squadron made a standard group formation of 36. This 457th BG formation is flying 4-plane flights.

Far right: Heavy cloud often caused a formation to spread losing much of its defensive potential.

Far bottom right: Contrails also tended to spread a formation, particularly the trail elements. These 381st BG Fortresses are having to fly through the trails of a preceding group.

Problems and Solutions

By any contemporary standard the Boeing Fortress was a soundly designed aircraft and practically viceless. Crews had an unshakeable faith in its reliability. However, there is a limit to inherent stability and to meet the contingencies of war the gap between operational limit and actual abuse was narrow and often obscure. Of major significance in determining the limitations was the environment in which the aircraft operated. As related, there was a considerable difference in performance in warmer climates where moisture was quickly dissipated and that in the persistent damp of north-west Europe – the Fortresses' principal theatre of war. It should be appreciated that all military aircraft operating to sub-stratospheric heights in that theatre were affected to a degree by these atmospheric conditions, some disastrously so. The problems that arose were not at first recognised, and understandably, for when all systems of an aircraft functioned perfectly at 30 000 feet over the Utah Salt Flats, it was to be expected that this situation would obtain elsewhere in the world. But the high humidity of the air and extreme cold, particularly in winter, brought forth a rash of technical problems on B-17s operating in Europe, some of which had only partially been solved by the end of hostilities.

Initially the B-17's Wright R-1820 Cyclone engines were a persistent source of trouble, primarily because they were pushed beyond design limitations in alien atmospheric conditions. The engine, designed in the 1920s, had proved a good reliable power unit in other military aircraft during the following decade. A nine-cyclinder, single-row radial, it had a good power/weight ratio and was easy to maintain. In the early Fortresses it proved reliable, but then it was rarely operated over 15 000 feet. With the turbo-supercharger installations on the B-17B and subsequent models, the engine was subjected to greater strains as ceilings rose above the 30 000 feet mark into the stratosphere. Even so, the engine appeared well able to meet requirements. The first signs of trouble came when the RAF's ventures into the stratosphere brought abnormal discharge of sump oil from engine breathers. The cause was moisture laden air diluting the oil which then became sluggish in the 50 degree below zero temperatures and was drawn out of the sump in damaging quantities. The problem was aggravated by Wright's practice of inverting

Left: A navigator moved quickly when an inboard propeller started to windmill. This 385th BG B-17F managed to land before the propeller on No 2 finally parted company and cut into the fuselage.

Below: When 'The Lost Angel', B-17G 42-38183, returned from a mission with undercarriage trouble, the ball turret was jettisoned to avoid the yoke breaking the fuselage in the belly landing which was successfully made. With bent propellers and skin damage to the undersurface of the fuselage the bomber was raised and repaired.

Top: A feathered propeller on a 452nd BG B-17G which failed to return from the mission of May 8th, 1944.

Above: A crew member of the 390th BG's 'Spot Remover' took this photograph of the bomber's ball turret being jettisoned over the sea. Later the B-17F was able to make a successful belly landing at its base. It took an average of 20 minutes to unbolt and detach the turret.

one ring on each piston to ensure adequate lubrication and prolong cylinder life. Engineers found an immediate remedy through baffles placed inside the breathers and also in recommending more frequent changing of the oil. When the 8th Air Force brought its B-17s to Europe and flew winter missions where temperatures were as low as minus 60 degrees F, engine oil changes had to take place even more frequently to prevent the build-up of sludge. But this did not prevent a greatly reduced engine life. In the USA engine replacement was advised after 500 hours flying time, but there were cases of engines running to 900 hours before being changed. In combat areas the engine change time was 350 hours, but again individual engines endured for double that period.

The four 12th Air Force B-17 groups in North Africa found sand storms a constant menace to engine life, and fine grit also proved a problem in the South-West Pacific. The 43rd Bomb Group engineering section made 42 engine changes on its B-17Es and Fs during the first three months of operations from New Guinea and of these some 30 were due to excessive oil consumption.

Nevertheless, radial engines were remarkably hardy and would often continue to function with substantial damage. What a radial could not withstand was a runaway propeller which was an all too frequent occurrence in the first three years that the Fortress was at war. The Wright 1820 swung a Hamilton Standard three-blade propeller of 11 feet 6 or 7 inch diameter and weighing 500lbs. A governor mechanism in the hub automatically adjusted the pitch of the blades to meet the variance in air density through changes in altitude, and so maintain a constant engine speed. The intricate hydraulic mechanism in the hub gave some problems, mostly associated with the damp and cold of the European winter. In cases of complete failure when the pitch went haywire and the propeller over-speeded, the pilot had to press the button on his instrument panel to feather the blades in alignment with the flight path of the aircraft, and bring the propeller to a standstill. Far too often the propeller failed to feather and would continue to windmill, turning the engine at such high speed that extreme vibration would set in. The usual outcome was that the propeller 'melted' its shaft and flew off. Sometimes it seized up and caused the whole engine to break from its mounting usually leading to the loss of the aircraft. Technical experts concentrated upon finding a solution to the feathering troubles by modifying the hub mechanism, apparently overlooking that in the stress of protracted operations at high altitude, other factors played a part. The extent of this problem was only realised after an analysis of incidents, in which a particularly revealing piece of evidence came from repatriated aircrew prisoners showing that in many instances their bombers had been lost directly, or indirectly, due to the inability to feather a propeller. The oil for the feathering mechanism was drawn from a standpipe in the engine sump and this pipe was found to be too short. What happened in many cases when the pilot 'hit the button' was that the sump oil had already fallen below the point where it could be drawn into the feathering mechanism. A modified standpipe was the immediate remedy while a separate oil reservoir in later engines all but eliminated the problem.

Efficient functioning of the turbo-super-charger was essential in maintaining high altitude performance. The turbo-super-charger was driven by engine exhaust gases blowing a turbine bucket wheel to compress rarified air at high altitude and provide the engine carburettors with the necessary volume of air for efficient combustion. The turbo had to be regulated to maintain the correct and constant boost required, for overspeeding brought disintegration and loss of power. Regulators were installed to control turbo speeds and in the first instance these were hydraulically operated. With the extreme cold at high altitude both 8th and 15th Air Forces found that the oil in the hydraulic lines to the regulators became sluggish or froze solid. A way to prevent this was for the pilot to exercise constantly the turbo controls, a tedious operation. At the end of 1943 a new electronic regulator was introduced and fitted to all but the first few hundred B-17Gs. This was a vast improvement and by the late summer of 1944 both air forces were retiring most surviving B-17Fs and early G models fitted with the hydraulic type.

Another problem with engine accessories that developed in the winter of 1943-44 concerned engine oil coolers. For some time a proportionately high number of these copper core units had been replaced because of leaks but once again operations undertaken in extremely low temperatures increased the failure rate to alarming proportions. On one 8th Air Force station over 200 oil coolers failed in a four-month period, a problem compounded by the fact that repaired units were found to be doubly prone to fracture. Frequently engines seized because of oil loss. A combination of the hydrostatic pressure, vibration, torsional stress and minus 60 degrees F was more than the component could stand. Special reinforcement had to be made on repaired units until strengthened

coolers became available from production.

Paradoxically, while extreme cold was a hazard to the smooth functioning of the engines there was also a problem of overheating. The B-17 was flown with a gross loading of up to 72 000 lbs, some 6 500 lbs more than the recognised maximum. This left little reserve of power although bombers were consistently and safely flown off at such gross weights. However, in climbing from low altitudes, engine temperatures hovered near the danger mark and in several instances engines overheated, failed, and sorties had to be abandoned. The root cause was conflicting instructions to pilots under training. In the US, where a more cautious view of aircraft loading and engine operation was taken, pilots were taught to arrest engine temperatures in a way that had a different effect under combat conditions. Engine cowlings had gills which could be gradually opened to increase the flow of air around the engine. On seeing the temperature needle approach the red danger mark, the freshman pilot would open the cowl flaps fully. The aircraft would then lose speed, so the pilot would apply more power which in turn would raise temperatures still further. What was happening was that the flaps of the gills, extending out from the cowling, acted as miniature air brakes. Keeping the flaps

Below: The nose section was not damaged in a good B-17F belly landing but with a B-17G the chin turret usually stove in the underside. Both aircraft in these pictures – 'Ole Puss', 42-30872, 96th BG and 'Hey Mabel', 42-31169, 447th BG, have the Norden bombsight uncovered. Extra ammunition has been stacked in the plexiglass nose of 'Ole Puss'.

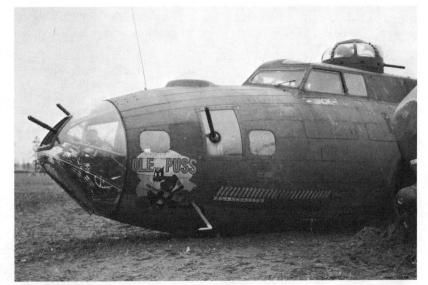

practically closed and allowing the temperatures to ride the red line on the gauges – they were found to be far too conservatively placed, anyway – caused no harm, but new pilots had to be re-educated in this matter. Later, shortened gills helped to reduce drag in the fully open position.

There were numerous B-17 modifications and changes to improve performance in combat and particularly to enhance the chances of survival. In combat theatres a constant programme of experimentation was under way, notably with the Air Technical Section at Bovingdon in England. One of the most trying combat problems was that arising from the introduction of the so-called Tokyo Tanks half-way through B-17F production. The extra tankage was needed by the 8th Air Force to extend operations further into Germany. The 4th Bomb Wing had first priority for B-17Fs arriving in the UK with the long-range wing, and it soon became evident, from an analysis of losses that this Wing was losing a larger number of bombers through wing explosions than the 1st Wing operating short-range B-17Fs. The Tokyo Tanks were self-sealing like the main wing tanks, but whereas the latter could absorb enemy fire, the former invariably exploded. This was attributed to an accumulation of fumes in the tanks after the fuel had been consumed – as it usually was by the time enemy fire was encountered. The pumping of inert gases into the tanks as they were emptied

was experimentally tried by the 8th Air Force but, though partially successful, tankage had to be reduced to accommodate the gas cylinders and range was lost as a consequence. In any event, it transpired that the most frequent cause of these outer wing explosions was petroleum fumes leaking from the tanks and accumulating in the wing tips. The 15th Air Force was the first to highlight this and successfully devised extra air venting in the wing tips to carry the fumes away. A substantial reduction in wing explosions resulted.

An investigation of a spate of top turret fires during the last winter of the war found that the majority of aircraft involved were veteran B-17Gs with first examples of the later model turret. The cause of the fires was traced to electrical wiring and the oxygen line running up the centre post of the turret. These were not as well secured as in the previous model turret and, after considerable use, the pivoting of the turret frayed the electrical wiring and fractured the oxygen line, with a resulting ignition of the oxygen and often severe burns for the gunner. Until a redesign of the turret post could be made to overcome this trouble, it was decided that filling the space around wiring and oxygen line with some non-combustible material would prevent fire if a fracture occurred. Finding a suitable material to pour into the turret post was the problem, eventually resolving itself to one material – cement. The knowledge of this

A veteran B-17G of 398th BG (42-102593) on its 102nd mission. One of a few B-17Gs that had their chin turrets removed late in hostilities, it benefited from the extra speed.

would probably have left the B-17's designers aghast, beset as they were with the perpetual problem of restricting the aircraft's weights. But the trouble was solved and it is a fact that many older Fortresses flew cement-laden to combat.

The operational problem of icing affected many of the aircraft's components, notably the bomb shackles, bomb-bay doors and the guns. All were overcome by special oils and procedures to eliminate moisture contamination on the ground so that freezing at altitude was forestalled. The cold could also affect oxygen equipment but several changes eventually produced a very reliable system. Cabin heating and electrical clothing also had to be improved. One of the more personal crew problems, but nonetheless crucial in the matter of crew comfort, was overcome in an ingenious way at one 8th Air Force station as the commander, then Colonel Harold Bowman, relates:

'Those who designed the B-17 were aware that on long missions some modern conveniences must be provided. So at each station small funnels were attached to outlet tubes. What the designers, sitting in their comfortable offices, failed to realise was that at 50 degrees below zero it wasn't long before the ball-turret gunner's plastic bubble was covered with human frost and the relief tubes were frozen solid. So, of course, we had to shut them off. But we were unable to shut off people. We tried everything. Personally, I hung a one-quart canteen on the control wheel, but what with heavy flying clothing, flak vests, parachutes, lap straps and temperatures, there were some problems in meeting the little container. Some of the boys took off their "tin hats" for the purpose. Of course that also relieved them of the protection but it had one advantage, at the end of a mission it was easy to knock the ice off on the ground and be ready for the next mission. But we had far too many crew members in hospital with frostbite. The problem caused much concern. So the two problems finally met.

'I woke up one night with the solution: prophylactic rubber condoms. Over-zealous planners had supplied us with enough rubber safes to last thru' World War Ten. I jumped out of bed and phoned the Group bambardier, Major Julius Pickoff, and said: "Pick, you are hereby appointed Group Pee Officer. Before today's mission I want 2 000 rubbers distributed!". He said: "Oh boss; at 0200 hrs you call me out of my much needed sleep just for a funny?" I finally persuaded him I was serious and he then 'phoned the Group supply officer, who answered in a very sleepy voice out of the sack. Pick demanded: "The Old Man wants 2 000 safes and he wants them right now." The irate supply officer said "That old Son of a Bitch!" and hung up. Pick had to go over and pull him out of bed to get the job done. The system may not have been equal to Savoy Hotel facilities – but it worked.'

The open cockpit of 'Gremlin Gus II' (42-30565) showing the cut down decking in foreground.

A view of the same aircraft taxiing shows control antenna on nose. The white paintwork was to make it easily seen. This photograph was taken surreptitiously from an airfield building.

Forts and the Luftwaffe

Top: An Me 109 curves in
for a beam attack.

Above: An FW 190 making a
beam approach faces the
massed fire of some 50 B-17
guns.

Below: An assault on the
95th BG going to Bremen,
October 8th, 1943. A Ju 88
flies parallel to the B-17s,
out of range, tracking the
formation.

Left: Sun glints on an FW 190 as B-17s take evasive action.

Below left: Another FW 190 pulls away after a frontal attack on the same B-17 flight.

Below: The famous 'split-S' manoeuvre. An FW 190 having delivered a frontal attack, rolls over to curve away down.

Right: Frame from the gun camera film of an FW 190 showing cannon shells bursting along the fuselage of a 3rd Division Fortress.

Below right: Fortress Killer. Major Heinz Bar was one of the most successful Luftwaffe fighter aces operating on the western front having over 30 B-17s to his credit in a total of 220 victories. Here he is inspecting 'Miss Quachita', a 91st BG B-17F shot down February 22nd, 1944.

Bottom: Air launched rockets bursting behind a B-17 of 381st BG.

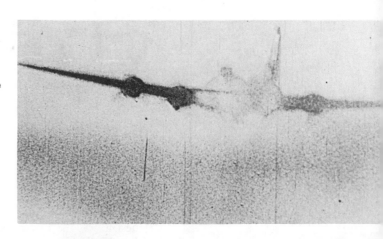

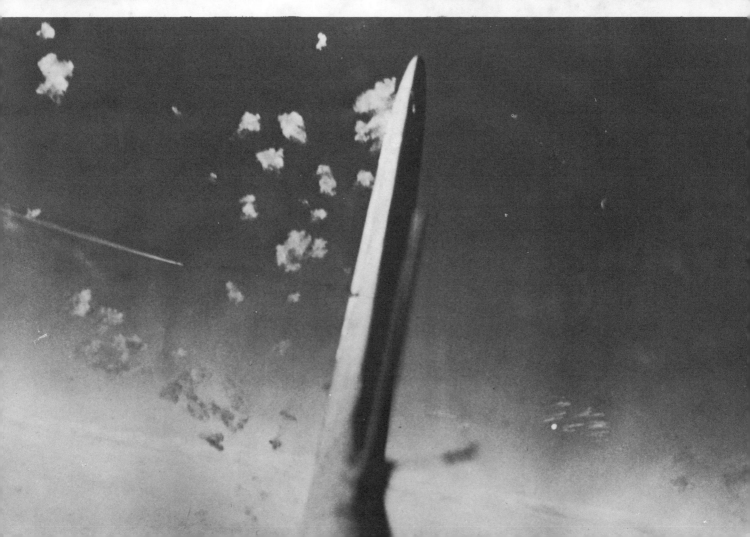

Fort v Lib

The Consolidated B-24 Liberator, although a later design, was the B-17's contemporary in the heavy bomber squadrons of the US Army Air Force. Inevitably the virtues and vices of the two aircraft were endlessly discussed but nowhere more avidly than among those who flew or serviced them. Basically the two bombers had similar specifications and per-formances, both being designed and developed for the same purpose. On the other hand each had distinctive handling qualities and operational characteristics. For the men who entrusted their lives to one or the other there was no debate: if you flew a Fort then the Lib was the inferior aircraft, and vice versa. Reason did not enter into it, as a few

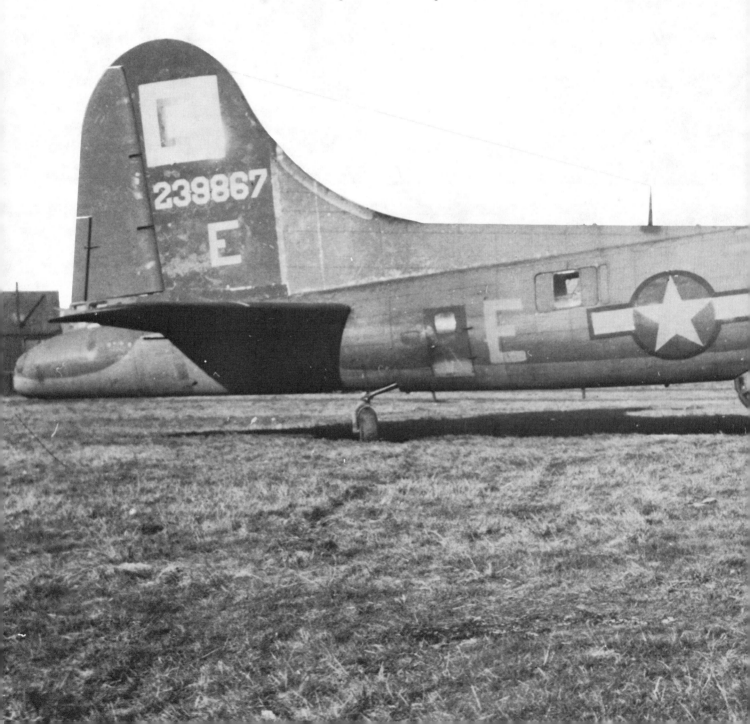

B-24H 'Foxy Phoebe' (left) and B-17G 'Hang The Expense III' (below) posed in profile illustrate the vastly different configurations of the two types built for the same mission.

English landlords and Italian bistro proprietors discovered when this championship developed forcefully on their premises.

Verbal antagonism was common. To the Fortress men the B-17 was the 'Queen of the Sky' and the B-24 'that Banana Boat'. To the Liberator adherants the Fort was 'that heavy bombardment training plane' while their own charge was 'a real man's ship'. Most of the derogatory remarks were levelled against the B-24; there was the unkind story about it having been designed as a flying boat but leaked so badly they decided to put wheels on it: and the other oldie, 'the B-24 was the packing case they sent the B-17 over in'. A more truthful jibe, originating with a very distinguished B-17 group commander: 'Who needs escort when there are B-24s around' – referring to the lower altitude at which B-24s were forced to operate making them inviting targets for both flak and fighters.

The boisterousness of youth expressed this one-upmanship in subtler if more dangerous ways. Performing some aerial manoeuvre for which a B-17 or B-24 was not designed in the presence of operators of the other type was a not infrequent occurrence, although liable to get the rogue pilot grounded if witnessed by authority. On one occasion the crews of a B-17 formation ploughing across an overcast at 150mph during a training mission were amazed to see an old B-24 suddenly go sailing past at what must have been twice their speed. Two backsides were framed in the waist window in vulgar gesture. The Liberator pilot apparently attained this turn of speed in a dive from higher altitude. Buzzing or shooting-up (very low flying) airfields was another highly dangerous and 'grounded-if-you're-caught-activity' indulged in by banner waving B-17 and B-24 pilots. In such circumstances it was easy for someone to take the number and make a report. But pilots still took the risk to cock-a-snook and sometimes got away with it as in the following incident recorded April 20, 1944 in the Flying Control Log of the B-24 base at Hethel.

'I have seen a lot of buzz jobs in my time but today I saw a buzz job that took the cake. A B-17 was approaching the field from the north-east. The Airfield Flying Controller had his head out of the porthole of the caravan but not for long. The Fort came down so low over the caravan that he had to pull his head in for fear of getting hit by the belly turret. After he passed the caravan he went still lower, heading south-east. He was not more than six feet from the ground when he passed the tower and they all thought he was going to make a belly landing. Everyone was holding their breath. He finally swerved up to the right at the end of the field. He passed on, not knowing all the suspense he caused, and we still don't know

who he was, where he came from, or why he did it.' On the last point one can be sure that most personnel on the B-24 field did not share the seeming naivety of the record keeper.

Probably the ultimate in B-17 one-upmanship was a prank performed by a pilot assigned to the hush-hush *Aphrodite* unit at Fersfield in England. (*Aphrodite* was the code name for experimental operations using war-weary B-17s filled with high-explosive and guided by radio control to a target and dived onto it.) One veteran B-17F *Gremlin Gus II* was selected for a special project which involved installing British torpedoes for an attack against the battleship *Tirpitz* in a Norwegian fjord. To instal these items it was necessary to cut away the upper decking of the B-17 fuselage up to the cockpit windshield, but before the work was completed the *Tirpitz* was hit by RAF bombers and the plan dropped. Instead, *Gremlin Gus II* was used as a hack ship, the decking was repaired but the cockpit left open. This unique machine caused considerable interest wherever it appeared and being some three tons lighter than an empty combat Fortress, due to its gutted state, *Gremlin Gus II* had a considerable turn of speed. A Liberator could normally out-pace a Fortress so that every B-24 pilot knew he was unlikely to be overtaken by the Boeing. The operators of *Gremlin Gus II* delighted in exploiting this situation. A story is told about Major Hayes of the *Aphrodite* unit who would stalk a B-24 formation, amble alongside and then smartly advance all throttles to full power, whereupon *Gremlin Gus II* would speed by. As the head of the formation was passed, Hayes would stand up in the open cockpit and salute!

On a more serious level the virtues and vices of both bombers are probably most truthfully obtained from those pilots who had extensive combat in both types. The 3rd Division of the 8th Air Force was originally composed partly of B-17 and B-24 units. The operational difficulties presented in using the two types in the same bomber stream caused the Division to convert the B-24 groups to B-17s in the late summer of 1944, in contrast to the Pacific where the previous year all B-17s had been replaced by B-24s. In both theatres there was a marked fondness among aircrews for the Fortress which, when all their reasons were taken into consideration, came down to the simple fact that they believed their chances of survival were higher in that type. Nevertheless there was mutual respect among B-17 and B-24 crews, despite the provacative rivalry displayed. Some of the notable differences between the B-17 and the B-24 are noted in the following comments from pilots of the 490th Bomb Group, one of the 3rd Division groups that used them both.

William Whitlow, who flew 500 hours in Liberators and about 400 in Fortresses, had no doubt which he and the majority preferred in his Group. 'The main thing the B-17 had over the B-24 was that it could get up to 27 000 feet and more on a mission with no trouble and take you away from a lot of the flak. Once you got past 20 000 feet in a Lib' the controls started to get mushy. That Davis wing just wasn't made for taking heavy loads much higher and if you went to 24 000 feet, formation flying became really tricky. On the other hand the Fort' could be flown in formation with little trouble, 5 000 feet higher than the Liberator – and that's a lot of altitude when people on the ground are shooting at you. Over 20 000 feet the B-24 needed a lot of work by the pilots. The B-17 didn't drain your physical strength like the B-24 did. The B-17 was strictly an aileron control type aircraft whereas with the B-24 you had to use rudder.

'I never met anyone in our group who regretted the change to B-17s. The conversion was fairly easy and the only real difficulty was landing. Each pilot had one and a half to two hours flight instruction before going solo. The B-24 was easier to land as it had a tricycle gear and you'd bring her in and plonk her down with little trouble. The B-17 had conventional gear and the technique was quite different; she tended to float along over the runway and you had to develop a more delicate touch. It could be tricky in a strong crosswind. On the runway a B-24 definitely had better directional stability but needed a longer run on take-off if similarly loaded to a '17. We had a few accidents after conversion which were probably due to insufficient training. We did have a few B-17s slam into one another because the pilot wasn't up to par or forgot he was in a Fort and instinctively acted as if he were still in a B-24 using rudder instead of ailerons. We had a collision happen right in front of us over the field one day and both B-17s went down. A horrible thing to watch as men fell out with no parachutes.'

Bill Whitlow's co-pilot, James Mynatt, had a reservation: 'When flying light and below oxygen altitudes I preferred flying the B-24. The cockpit was more comfortable and had a better layout and was much quieter than a B-17's. You had a better view of the ground too. But for combat give me the Fortress. It was much easier to fly in formation at high altitude. As far as I am aware the rest of the crew also felt the B-17 was better in combat. The bombardier and navigator definitely had much better visibility out of the nose. The interior of the B-17 seemed cleaner. Perhaps it was because it had mostly electric systems whereas the B-24 had hydraulics which were always a plumber's nightmare.'

John Stewart went from B-17s to B-24s and then back again: 'In one of the typically ridiculous situations the Army was famous for, I trained to fly B-17s, got my crew, and to my consternation found on arrival at my new group that they were using B-24s. The B-24 was undoubtedly a trickier plane to fly with the heavy loads we carried and you really had to work at the controls to keep formation. The B-17 was easy; you could fly feet off the rudder pedals and up on the dash' if you wanted! I liked the arrangement of the throttle levers; you could get much smoother control over all engines in one movement; it was particularly good if you had to fly on just two. The Wright Cyclones were good reliable engines but much noisier than the Pratt and Whitneys on the B-24. They sounded particularly rough when they started. Most pilots flew with the earphones off the right ear so they could hear what the co-pilot said without going through intercom. Likewise co-pilots flew with the left ear uncovered. This is the reason why a good many old B-17 pilots are hard of hearing in their right ear and ex-co-pilots a bit deaf in the left. I certainly can't hear too well in my right. The Pratt and Whitney was a much quieter, tighter running and cleaner engine. One of my first thoughts on flying the B-24 was why they didn't fit the Twin Wasp in the B-17.'

For John Jurkens the Fortress was the preferred aircraft to be in if you were in trouble: 'They were both fine aircraft but any pilot who is honest will admit that the B-17 was easier to fly on a combat mission. There was a feeling of more positive control at high altitude. Hitting prop wash while in a formation was something you tried to avoid in any ship but in a B-24 it could be disastrous; you'd drop right out. Recovery was far easier in a B-17. I always felt less concerned about losing an engine in a B-17 than I did in a B-24. If it happened on a Fort she would swing because of the high dorsal fin and you had to put both feet on one rudder pedal to get her back on an even keel to get your trim in. Once she was trimmed you were in good shape and you could hold your place in formation even if you began to lag. With a B-24 you lost speed fast and you usually had to dip your nose to make up airspeed and get power on again. Both bombers were pretty tough and would take a lot of punishment but the Davis wing on the Liberator was more sensitive to damage. The B-24 cruised around five miles an hour faster than the B-17 on a mission but apart from the altitude advantage of the B-17 the real difference was in control rather than performance. If you want to romanticise the difference for a pilot; you had a sense of flying the B-17 and driving the B-24.'

The Saga of 'Mary Alice'

Many airmen had a feeling for their aircraft. Mere structures of metal that they were, the aircraft was the very fabric in which a crew were brought together in the air – and brought back to their base. It was their shelter from the elements and at times was nursed or coaxed as occasion demanded. Some had distinctive characteristics of their own – their virtues were exploited and their vices countered. Small wonder that some aircraft were personified, not merely by a name and motif, but to a degree that only those who flew them, or knew them, would really understand. Here is the story of one outstanding personality; her name was *Mary Alice*.

B-17G serial number 42-31983 left the production line at the end of 1943, one of the last batch of olive drab and grey painted Fortresses to come from Boeing's Seattle plant. Accepted by the USAAF on January 10, 1944, '983' went to Grand Island Nebraska, where it was assigned to the recently trained combat crew of Lt Dan C. Knight. The pilot deciding on a more personal label for his charge, had his mother's Christian names, Mary Alice, painted by the ball turret gunner Sgt William 'Mack' Mackowiach. The crew flew *Mary Alice* across the Atlantic as part of the 457th Group for the 8th Air Force but ended up as a replacement with the 615th Bomb Squadron of the 401st Bomb Group at Deenethorpe, England. Here *Mary Alice*

assumed an additional identity, formerly that of a Fortress that had fallen in action the day they arrived. This letter 'G' and the 'IY' identification code of the 615th, were painted in yellow on both sides of the fuselage; the G was also applied below the original serial number on her fin and above this a blue 'S' in a white triangle denoted the 401st Group.

Mary Alice and her crew first went to war on February 22, 1944, bombing Oschersleben. The initiation was not without incident, for top-turret gunner Bill Sartor caught his arm in the turret mechanism which put him out of the crew for a month. The second mission was to Berlin on the first major American attack. Here enemy fighters appeared and gave *Mary Alice* a hard time. Additionally a flak burst blasted away the top of the radio room, severely wounding the operator, Charlie Atcher, in the head and chest. By the time the bomber reached England she had two engines out of action on one wing and had to make an emergency landing at Horsham St Faith. Unable to taxi, she had to be towed off the runway.

On another trip to Berlin, later in the month, the bomber had to be flown all the way back with the bomb-bay doors stuck open. On a long haul to Sorau in eastern Germany on April 11, waist-gunner Charlie Wilson was wounded in the ear by flak. A mission to Dessau on May 28 brought up the Luftwaffe

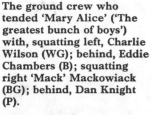

The ground crew who tended 'Mary Alice' ('The greatest bunch of boys') with, squatting left, Charlie Wilson (WG); behind, Eddie Chambers (B); squatting right 'Mack' Mackowiack (BG); behind, Dan Knight (P).

for a determined assault on the 401st Group, and it shot down seven B-17s and badly damaged several others. *Mary Alice* came back with perforations and a live 20-mm shell which had come to rest just behind tail gunner Charles Paceley. On June 25, Knight and crew finished their tour in spectacular form having flown most of their 30 missions in *Mary Alice*. The bomber was now turned over to other crews.

When the 401st, a group with a low loss rate, had met trouble, *Mary Alice*, was nearly always there in the thick of it. With a new crew she exhibited no inclination to lead a more docile existence. 2nd Lt Harry Haskett took her on his fifth mission, to Munich, on July 13. Positioned in the rear of the Group formation *Mary Alice* was the recipient of a hit-and-run attack by fighters. Cannon shells exploded in the vicinity of the No 2 engine putting this out of action and holing a fuel tank and the bomb bay. Other shells hit the tail, blasting a tremendous gap in the left tailplane, wrecking the tail gun position and mortally wounding the gunner. Haskett nursed *Mary Alice* for three hours and with little fuel remaining, made the RAF airfield at Beccles near the English coast. After that episode *Mary Alice* acquired a new tail turret and tailplane.

The Luftwaffe attacked *Mary Alice* again during a raid on Weimer, August 24. This time cannon fire perforated the left elevator and right flap with a great many holes, severed control cables and exploded splinters into the fin, fuel tanks, radio room and No 4 engine. Again the veteran bomber made it back to an emergency base. The repair crews were now making no attempt to apply matching camouflage paint to the pieces that covered the battle scars. The contrasting olive drab and natural metal of the repairs gave *Mary Alice* the look of a complicated cross-word puzzle block. By the law of averages the bomber had now seen more than her share of action and her patient ground crew had lost count of the total number of wounds she sustained. But her finest hour was yet to come.

On November 2 Lt George Cracraft and his crew came to Deenethorpe as replacements and found to their dismay they had been assigned not only the oldest B-17 on the base, but the most scarred. The ground crew proudly pointed out that until her 66th mission, November 21, when an oil line broke, she had never had to turn back for mechanical failure and that she had also survived some of the most punishing missions the Group had undertaken. On their second mission Cracraft's crew found *Mary Alice* was as true as her record.

On November 30, 1944 the crew were amongst the B-17 force participating in the

Below left: Dan Knight examining the damage to his old charge in a hangar at Beccles. Decoration of A-2 flight jacket was work of 'Mack'.

Below: Tail emplacement shattered by a 20 mm cannon shell which killed the gunner. Note face decoration on gun shield.

View through the large hole in the right stabiliser made by cannon shells on July 13th, 1944.

Hoag was awarded the DSC, second highest US decoration for valour, and the only one among more than a thousand decorations awarded men of the 401st Group during the war.

It is said that when *Mary Alice* returned to Deenethorpe, veterans long since satiated with the fortunes of war took time off to view this legend.

On February 16, 1945 Deenethorpe tower received the familiar message that *G-George* was in trouble coming back from a mission. George Cracraft this time had an even more difficult job, for two engines were disabled on the one side and the pull from the remaining engines caused a crabbing course. But the old lady didn't let him down and he made the RAF airfield at Lissett for a safe landing.

It was March 12 before *Mary Alice* came home to Deenethorpe to be transferred to the 613rd Squadron as the 615th had from the first of that month become the Group's 'lead' squadron with only PFF radar-equipped aircraft assigned. In her new unit with a new ground crew she led a calmer life, although going out on more missions. On the date of the Group's last operation she was on standby.

Flown back across the Atlantic early in June 1945, *Mary Alice* lingered at the storage depot at South Plains until November when she joined the thousands of other bombers in the arid desert 'boneyard' at Kingman, Arizona, where eventually the breakers did what Hitler's flak and fighters failed to do.

Perhaps of all the events involving *Mary Alice* the most incredible is that of her last mission with her original crew on June 25, 1944. The story is recounted by Dan Knight:

'The target at Montbartier, south of Bordeaux near the Spanish border, was an underground fuel storage dump, and target information had been furnished by the French underground. As we were told at briefing, there was no way we could be positive that the information was correct, but we were going on this mission on the assumption that it was. There would be no visible target, only some co-ordinates by a railroad track. It was all underground and from the air looked like all the other woods – all trees and wilderness. Colonel Seawell (Group Leader) said that since we were going to come back to England over the sea where there was no fear of flak, he was going to bring us back 'on the deck'.

'The Colonel was flying the lead and I was number two, flying as Deputy Group leader on what was to be a long haul of an estimated 9 hours 50 minutes from take-off. The trip to the target was pretty routine although we got some light accurate flak crossing the coast. We went over the target at 22 000 feet. As I mentioned it was a patch of woods by a railroad track, and as bombs were away I know we all had the same feeling;

most disastrous of missions to the German synthetic oil plants, when the bombers were devastated by the flak defences. *Mary Alice* was ploughing through an intense flak barrage over Bojlen when three shell bursts bracketed her just after the bombs had been released. No 2 engine was crippled and No 3 sustained damage which meant feathering the propeller. The co-pilot's controls were inoperative and the forward oxygen system ceased to function. Shell fragments had riddled the tail, wings and fuselage in many places. An exploding oxygen bottle knocked the top-turret gunner off his stand, injuring his leg, while a piece of shrapnel hit a waist gunner in the right hand, severing two fingers. Shrapnel blasted through the underside of the nose, smashed the navigator's table and sent long jagged splinters of wood into navigator Carl Hoag's face, blinding him in one eye and injuring the other. Despite the pain from his wounds Hoag remained at his post making mental calculations and devising a flight back to friendly territory. For almost five hours Cracraft and co-pilot Martin Karant nursed *Mary Alice* home on two engines, for much of the 500 mile journey alone over hostile territory at 10 000 feet. Late in the afternoon they reached England and located Boxted airfield, making a successful landing on the third attempt. For his part in this mission

was this a target or just a bunch of trees. We made a turn as soon as we dropped and watched to see what would happen. We didn't have to wait long for the answer. Those woods erupted into a big ball of fire and a towering pillar of smoke that was visible all the way to the coast, rising almost to our altitude.

'We crossed the coast near Bordeaux and Colonel Seawell, true to his word, descended until we were probably no more than 100 feet off the water. It did feel good to get the oxygen mask off, and being over water, not have the worry of flak.

'The weather was bad, one of those murky days when everyone looked like they were in haze. We were flying our usual tight formation that the 401st was famous for, with wings overlapping. My left wing tip was almost in Colonel Seawell's right waist window when we ran into a dense patch of fog coming up from the water. When I say dense, Colonel Seawell's plane disappeared completely from view at the tip of my wing. From that moment on everything happened much faster than the time it takes to tell. I kicked rudder to the right and dropped the nose. Right then we came out of the fog and I saw the water coming up. I hauled back on the wheel, the plane mushed down and the ball turret hit a wave. I bounced up, glanced above me and

there was Colonel Seawell's plane coming down. I shoved forward but not in time to avoid hitting him. My vertical stabiliser hit the side of his fuselage, knocking a hole in him and bending over about three-quarters of my tail.

'All my rudder control was gone and to keep going in a straight line I had to fly in a bank. I asked Bill Huegin my co-pilot to take over and went to the top turret to take a look at the damage. The tail was fluttering and looked as though it might break off completely any minute. With the drag the tail was causing I couldn't keep up with the rest of the group, so we had to limp back on our own.

'All the balloons were up in the Channel when we finally got there and we dodged all around them trying to find the closest field in England. The weather was terrible but we finally spotted Weston Zoyland where I put down. We called Deenethorpe to report that we had made it and they sent a plane for us.

'One person I'll never forget was "Mack" who didn't have to be in the ball turret on that mission because he had completed his tour the day before, but he had always said from the start of our tour that he was going to be along on my last one and he was. For a moment we thought it was a last mission for all of us!'

William 'Mack' Mackowiack, the tail gunner who had a dip in the channel, watches a mechanic make adjustments to the vessel in which he was riding at the time.

A cloud of acrid smoke
billows up into the rain
swept English sky from
B-17G 42-31513, which
caught fire on a training
flight. Abandoned by Lt
Kuehl and crew on the
Bassingbourn runway the
bomber became a mass of
flames before fire tenders
could reach it. Once the fuel
and oil tanks were alight a
B-17 was quickly gutted by
fire.

Death

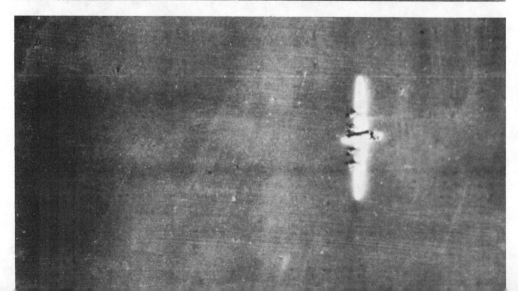

This page: 'Lady Liberty', a
B-17F of 305th BG, setting
out for a mission to occupied
Europe on August 19th, 1943.
Over Flushing the aircraft
took a direct hit in the
fuselage severing the tail
and scattering fragments
far and wide. A camerman
caught these pictures of the
bomber's final plunge.

Right: 'Wee Willie', B-17G
42-31333:LG:W, of 323rd BS,
91st BG was a fortunate ship
until April 10th 1945 by
which time another 123 bomb
symbols had been added to
its nose tally since the first
picture was taken 17 months
before. A direct flak hit in
the fuel tanks blasted apart
the left wing – the tip can be
seen at the left of the
second photo, above the
flames sweeping back from
the burning fuel. This
picture and the following
two were recorded by a
target strike camera in a
B-17 above, operating at 3
second intervals. The two
main pieces of 'Wee Willie'
had not fallen far before the
tanks in the other wing blew,
completely distintegrating
the wreckage. The rear
fuselage can be seen, the
tail having broken off.
Miraculously some of the
crew survived.

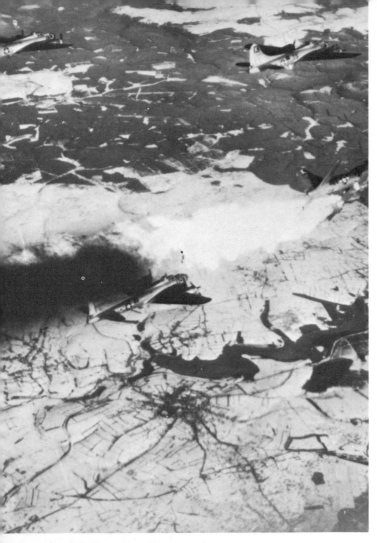

Left: Concentrating on the leading elements of the largest bomber operation of World War 2, December 24th, 1944, German fighters hit this 447th BG deputy lead in the Tokyo tanks. The Fortress, 44-8355, is a pathfinder and has the H2X radome lowered. Another pathfinder flies the lead of the flight.

Above: A victim of the infamous Merseberg flak, a B-17G with most of its tail blasted away plunges inverted towards the ground; November 2nd, 1944.

Below: With number three engine in flames, the pilots dive B-17G, 42-37958, 'Old Faithful', in an effort to extinguish the fire during the mission to Toulouse, June 25th, 1944. Lt Peter Mikonis was able to bring this badly flak-damaged 91st BG bomber back to England only to crash with the loss of all on board.

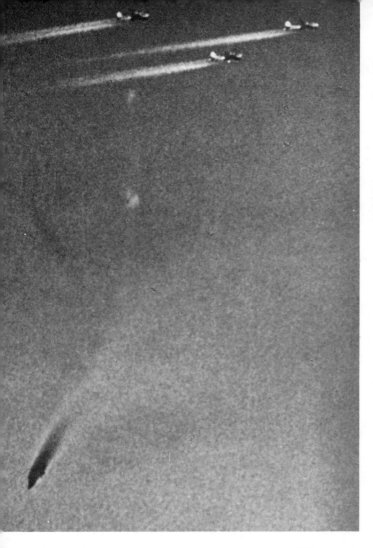

Left: Destruction could come quickly in the cold thin air at 25 500 feet. One moment this Fortress was flying in formation; the next a falling flaming mass.

Above: The oil fields around Ploesti were defended by the largest concentration of flak in south east Europe. A direct hit has ignited the left main fuel tanks of this 15th Air Force B-17.

Below: A Fortress was large enough to cause a great deal of damage if it fell in the wrong place. This 96th B-17F was abandoned by its crew over the south coast of England but instead of plunging into the sea the stricken bomber ploughed down a street at Dymchurch: February 6th, 1944.

Queen of the Skies

Above: 'Mon Tete Rouge II', 452nd BG, on her way to Chateaudun, France, March 28th, 1944 at 17 900 ft. Oil and exhaust stain the bright aluminium.

Left: Unusual close-up plan view of 398th BG's 43-88708 reveals considerable detail. Fuel filler caps can be seen on wing.

Top right: Pilot's view of 463rd BG Fortresses flying tight on the grey painted Pathfinder during a 15th Air Force mission to Regensburg, February 7th, 1945.

Centre right: On their way home from the first Italy-Russia shuttle mission 97th BG Fortresses cross the Alps. Camouflage was abandoned on new USAAF heavy bombers at the end of 1943 although it was February and March 1944 before the 'silver' bare metal finish aircraft began to appear in combat.

Bottom right: Dead astern view clearly shows the armament that could be brought to bear on a fighter making an approach to that quarter.

Air Crew

Affection for the Fortress, the theme running throughout the following nine personal accounts, tends to belie the fact that operating in this exalted bomber was, the enemy apart, far from pleasant. The crew were subjected to the incessant noise from the engines and conversation was achieved only by shouting; at most stations there was also constant vibration. The sub-zero temperatures at high altitude necessitated wearing a great mass of uncomfortable clothing besides the discomfort of wearing an oxygen mask which, after a few hours, felt more like a muzzle than a life-sustaining aid. When not on oxygen crews endured the odour of oil and petrol-tainted air. All far removed from the accepted luxury of air travel a few years later.

Pilot

James W. Johnson

Above: Lt James W. Johnson.

Below: Pilot's sliding window on a Fortress. It was possible to escape through this in flight – if your parachute went first – but many who did were killed by striking the tail fin. Glass was laminated and toughened but not bullet proof.

Skipper, Captain, Boss, Old Man, were names commonly used by the other members of a B-17 crew for their pilot, endearing epithets engendered through his satus as the bomber's commander. While the pilot might show exceptional skill in handling his bomber, he also had to have the essential qualities of leadership if the crew were to develop that mutual confidence which could be so vital in an emergency. The average age of a B-17 pilot was 21 and his responsibilities were made easier by the implicit belief that the bomber he took to war was dependable both as a flying and a fighting machine. This is made clear by James Johnson's observations on his own experiences in the left-hand seat of the Fortress.

'The Fortress inspired a tremendous confidence. It was the only propeller driven aircraft I have flown that was completely viceless; there were no undesirable flight characteristics. The directional stability was excellent and, properly trimmed, the B-17 could be taken-off, landed and banked without change of trim. Both ailerons and elevators were particularly responsive for such a large multi-engined airplane, so there was normally no effort at the wheel even at quite high altitudes. The B-17G was a totally predictable aircraft. Most warplanes were given to

some scary situation and you could, of course, get into trouble with any of them. But in normal circumstances, you had to be a really sloppy pilot to get into trouble with a B-17. I never had one in a spin and understand it was difficult to get into one accidentally because of the inherent stability. Stalling characteristics were good; she would fall off straight ahead in a stall, power off or on.

'To see how students would react, instructors often deliberately produced emergency-type situations. A favourite was to cut an engine during take-off. This was done to me just after we left the runway and before I could catch the drop of the wing, the landing gear on that side struck a farm windmill, but we kept in the air! Undoubtedly, the hairiest situation of all occurred while flying the radio beam at Lockbourne, Ohio. For this, clip-on blinds were 'fitted over the cockpit windows to simulate instrument conditions. I was flying the south leg when a corner of the blind in front of me came unclipped and fell down. Coming towards us on a collision course was another B-17! I immediately pushed the wheel forward to take the aircraft down. The instructor, who had been turned in his seat talking to another trainee pilot thought I'd lost control and tried to compensate by reversing the controls. Since then, I have often reflected on the good fortune of that blind working loose at that moment.

'Training complete, I sailed with my crew for England on a troop ship late in 1944, going to a replacement depot at Stone where we were given an assignment to the 100th Bomb Group. At the time, it meant nothing particular to us but we were soon enlightened that this was the hard luck outfit of the 8th Air Force that had become known as the "Bloody Hundredth" due to the heavy losses it had taken. However, when we joined the Group,

we, like the rest, tended to take a sort of pride in this reputation; during leave, we always let it be known we were part of a real fighting outfit. Pride and patriotism played an important part in our young careers. To go through flying school was a big accomplishment for somebody under 20; to captain a crew and an aircraft like the B-17 even bigger.

'Of course, we were young and with the exuberance of youth, we never really considered our situation. I often think back to some of the things we did then as almost a matter of routine. We weren't smart enough to realise the risks in what we were required to do. For instance, on missions we would take off every 30 seconds and often disappear straight into the overcast. Bombers from all the other airfields in East Anglia were doing the same thing, and somebody was bound to get lost or off course in the clouds. I've known times when we would suddenly flip through turbulence which was obvious prop wash, and realize someone else had been there only seconds before.

'The reputation of the B-17 as a rugged fighting machine was well-known in the Air Force, and I was reassured of this on many occasions by what I saw and heard. Once when our group had been attacked by fighters, an Me 109 collided with a B-17 taking off most of the rudder and left stabiliser as well as slashing several holes in the fuselage. It was almost unbelievable that the B-17 could keep flying, but it did and managed to make a safe landing at base. Another time, I saw a B-17 hit by flak lose about four or five feet of wing back from the tip, and that aircraft got home too. Although it was late in the war when I started combat flying, the 100th was still seeing plenty of action with the Luftwaffe. During my last raid on Berlin near the war's end, we took the brunt of an attack by Me 262 jets. Usually when there were enemy fighters approaching, somebody on the crew saw them in the distance and called them out several times before they actually made their pass. This time almost as soon as they were called they hit us and were away before we really knew what was going on. The Fortress above us was crippled and went down and so did one in our flight. He had a large hole ringed with fire in his wing, and as I watched, the hole gradually enlarged. He then fell away from my view, and I was unable to see what finally happened. I don't think we ever considered just how vulnerable the B-17 had become with the appearance of the German jets. We were fortunate in that not once during our missions did we ever get more than superficial battle damage to our B-17.

'My crew got along well, and I never had to overtly exert control. In the cockpit, I shared

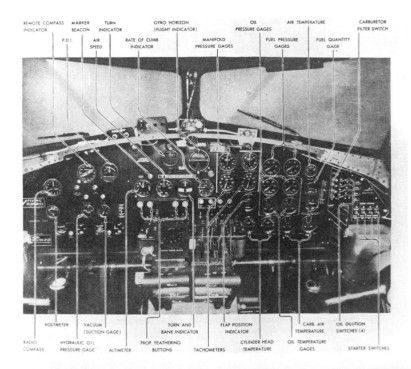

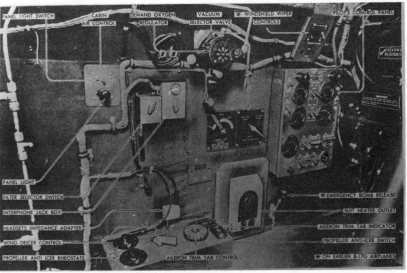

duties with my co-pilot and we generally flew turns of 15 minutes at a time in formation. I can recall that we used to line up the tip of the VHF antenna on the leader's fuselage above the radio room with the star of the national insignia on his far wing. By relating these two points to one another, it gave you the right distance and position to fly. Formation flying was also helped by those magnificent gate-like throttle levers which made it so easy to make power changes. You could move all together or any combination, or manipulate each lever separately; and all with one hand.

'After 25 missions, you cannot be without some sentiments for the aircraft that has been strapped to your back-side, sometimes for 10 hours at a stretch. I must be but one of many former B-17 pilots who still experience nostalgia in terms of the reliability of the aircraft and the affection we all had for it.'

Top: Instruments of B-17G.

Above: Cockpit controls: pilot's left side.

Co-Pilot

Jim Fletcher

The Fortress, like other American medium and heavy bombers, was designed to carry two pilots, a specified requirement of multi-engined US Army aircraft for many years. Other air forces considered this an extravagance in skilled manpower, but the policy was thoroughly vindicated in combat. The rigours of close formation flying for long periods would have placed undue physical and mental strain on a single pilot and for that reason alone the co-pilot or 'guy in the right-hand seat' was essential. There were also many occasions when one pilot became a battle casualty and the presence of the second saved both crew and aircraft. Jim Fletcher learned the hard way that in emergencies both pilots' hands were often needed to keep a B-17 under control.

'My original pilot and crew were lost on their opening mission which happened to be the Eighth's first successful raid on Berlin. I was in hospital at Bedford with sinusitis at the time, so when I returned to Bassingbourn I became a fill-in co-pilot with other crews. My early missions were flown with Lt Howard Weber's crew in a Fort' called *Destiny's Child*. When I joined them they were an

Lt James Fletcher wearing parachute harness and Mae West.

experienced bunch, well on their way to completing a combat tour. After a trip to Rheims, and an introduction to flak, we went to Brunswick. Approaching the target area bandits were being reported but I'd never seen a fighter before from the perspective of a cockpit and the specks out ahead looked something like the distant flak I'd seen the previous day. It wasn't until those specks began to grow rapidly in size and suddenly started blinking at us that I realised what was happening. Almost simultaneously the sky around us was lit up like the Fourth of July as 20-millimetres exploded all around our '17. My initial reaction was to duck my head down below the instrument panel and keep it there! This was a new experience and I can tell you I was concerned! I was brought out of it by Weber shouting "Help me" and thumping my side with his hand. We were one wing low, peeling out of formation to the right and Weber couldn't hold her alone. With both of us on the controls we managed to right *Destiny's Child* and keep her in the bomber stream. One cannon shell had hit the leading edge of the right wing and exploded in between the tanks, puffing out the skin of the wing so you could hardly see the aileron. This distortion of the airfoil had thrown us out of formation. Fortunately the Focke-Wulfs didn't come back; it had been a single head-on pass by about fifty and they had knocked down several of our ships, including Lt Anderson, our element lead. Andy was my room-mate – a grand guy; this was his 25th mission and would have marked the completion of his tour.

'With No 3 engine out and a damaged wing we couldn't regain the formation and had to come home on our own. Upon reaching the North Sea the navigator got us a Gee fix and we headed for Bassingbourn alone letting down through 12 000 feet of solid rain cloud. Sitting there watching the wing skin flapping made it seem like an eternity but we came out of the cloud, lined perfectly with the runway. The navigator had done a tremendous job. Trips like this taught you how dependent crew members were upon each other. Later that day the ground crew found a 20-mm cannon shell in a fuel cell on *Destiny's Child* which would have been fatal had it exploded.

'I flew with several crews before joining Lt Bob Langford's about halfway through my tour. A co-pilot had a natural hankering to get a crew of his own, and I was no exception. However, when the opportunity to check out came I had already flown several missions with Bob and felt at home with him and the crew. This relationship became more important than acquiring a crew of my own. It was a team effort and everyone knew his job on this plane, *The Peacemaker*. The relationship between Langford and myself was one of mutual confidence and this was important in the cockpit. Personality clashes between pilot and co-pilot could seriously impair the essential teamwork during the stress of combat; squadron commanders were quick to make personnel shifts when such differences became evident.

'When you fly with a fellow a lot your tasks in the cockpit become automatic and this is how it became with Langford. When we arrived at the plane we would chuck our gear up into the nose hatch, swing ourselves up and check out the cockpit switches. We would then come out and give the plane a ground inspection after which we would wait for the signal from the tower for engine time, when we would take our seats and begin the pre-start check. I had a one sheet checklist which I would call out for Langford. Most of the engine controls were situated on a pedestal between the two pilots' positions and were readily accessible from either side, although the control switches nearer the co-pilot were usually his concern. There were items on the co-pilot's right which were normally always operated by him – the bank of intercooler shutter levers for adjusting the temperature of supercharger air, a hand pump for the hydraulic system in case of power failure and the engine primer. On completion of the checks we would hit all the necessary switches and I would prime and start each engine, Nos 1 to 4, as the starting controls were all on the co-pilot's side of the instrument panel. The co-pilot was the engineering officer of the crew and his special duty was to monitor and adjust the power systems. Once the engines were running we would warm them up at 1 000 rpm, checking the prop feathering three or four times and then run up each engine to maximum to test magnetos and turbos.

'As other B-17s moved past your dispersal you watched for the tail number you knew you must follow to make the correct place for take-off. When this was seen I would release the parking brake and out we would roll on to the taxiway. The tail wheel lock control, not unlike a car hand brake lever, was situated on the cockpit floor at the foot of the control pedestal on the right side for co-pilot operation. Working this lever was always a chore for it had to be unlocked and locked often while taxiing, particularly on curving perimeter taxiways. Strong crosswinds acting on the large tail fin of the '17 added to the problem. For taxiing the two inboard engines were set to idle at about 800 rpm and the outers provided the power for manoeuvering. When our turn came to take off the pilot would line her up and I would lock the tailwheel. At this critical point I had to keep my eyes on the instruments, particularly the

Jim Fletcher (right) and other crew members examine damage to 'The Peacemaker'.

boost, revs, pressure and temperature gauges as the pilot advanced the throttles. The co-pilot followed through with the throttle controls taking them over from the pilot as soon as maximum power was reached, by which time the plane would be pulling 2 500 rpm and going straight, keyed in for the far end of the runway. We normally used every bit of runway with a full bomb load, putting the tail up a little and getting as much speed as we could before pulling her off at between 110 and 115mph.

Once off the pilot would call and signal for gear up and this was the co-pilot's job, while touching the brake pedals gently to stop the wheels spinning. As soon as the cylinderhead temperatures reached 200 degrees I had to open the cowl flaps to prevent a further rise, and once we were climbing out I would have to bring the engine revs back a couple of hundred as the pilot reduced power slightly. Climb speed would be around 140mph straight out from the runway for a minute when we would begin a lefthand turn to assume a course towards our assembly area and buncher beacon, usually south of the field over north London. Assembly altitude depended on weather but was generally quite high, just below oxygen level. Often you'd see the sun begin to come up or you'd fly into the early morning light. It could be tricky because everyone was supposed to be going the same way but you could be sure some guy would get lost, start searching for his formation and wind up going the wrong way. If it was pretty dark it was hard to spot these jokers, so you really had to keep looking around all the time. By the time the group had made the Division

107

stream we would be up at 20 000 feet. If the target was in northern Germany we nearly always passed over Cromer on the way out.

'When we got moving the co-pilot normally flew the plane just as much as the pilot where there was mutual confidence. If we were flying a left wing I would fly more than the pilot; when we were lead the pilot would do most – but just by fine adjustments to the turbo-knob. If we were on a right hand wing then the pilot would fly most because he was on the side nearest the wing plane. Formation flying was tiring; sitting there with your eyes glued to another aircraft for up to 9 to 10 hours. Even when enemy fighters and flak were around you couldn't look away; you just had to keep zeroed in on that wing. The pilot who wasn't flying watched the air and the instruments and monitored the intercom. The ease with which a formation could be flown had a lot to do with the leader. If you had a man out front who flew erratically and your position was way at the back you were forever jockeying the throttles to keep in your slot. It also depended on the altitude you were at. Sometimes we'd go to 28 000 feet and up there it was awful sluggish and you'd be working twice as hard. If the lead made a turn and you were on the inside you'd be

throttling back to hold from over-running and come near to stalling. If the leader was smart he kept the speed up and gave people at the back plenty of latitude to move.

'The cockpit heating in the B-17 was good and I can't ever remember being cold. Hot air was ducted into the cockpit from a special glycol heater in No 2 engine nacelle. It was so efficient that I never had the need to wear an electrically heated outfit, preferring nothing more than the light-weight gaberdine flying suit over my uniform and an A-2 flight jacket.

'Wearing armour was a matter of taste for the day. As the pilots' seats were armoured we were provided with flak vests for chest protection, but I rarely used mine in the prescribed way. I usually sat on mine with part of it projecting out under my legs – flak fragments tended to be blasted upwards! When you were on the bomb run over places like Berlin, Hamburg, Munich you knew damn well you were going to go through eight to ten minutes of real heavy flak and there was nothing you could do but sweat it out. I always tightened my seat belt when I saw it coming; I don't know why, I guess it just made me feel safer. In the heat of battle when things were looking bad you might pull

Not the regular co-pilot of 94th BG's 'Raider' but comedian Bob Hope posing for photographers. Visiting celebrities were often invited to 'take a seat' in a B-17.

108

your 'chute out from under the seat and hook it on in case the plane exploded – the pilots usually had chest packs.

'The Leipzig mission was the roughest of my 32 and I guess we came very near to getting it that day. We were under attack for 16 minutes by 50-plus fighters although in the cockpit we couldn't see much as they were coming in from the rear. Our Group was flying a poor formation that day, and the Luftwaffe were quick to take advantage of this opportunity. They hit us hard from the rear. I only saw one fighter and then because he over-shot, coming right by the nose. They almost wiped our squadron out that day and only four of us got back. I watched one Fort' in the lead squadron disintegrate in front of my eyes, he didn't blow, the metal just peeled away. Our plane, *The Peacemaker*, had been hit all over, No 3 engine was knocked out, so was the oxygen, and all communication equipment except the transmitter – although at the time we didn't know it was working. We lost altitude down to around 17 000 feet before the fighter attacks ceased and some of our own fighters picked us up.

'When we were under attack the tension was high and you acted automatically with no time to be scared. Far worse was seeing some-one else getting hit. One of the most unnerv-ing things I ever witnessed was a group of B-24s being annihilated by German fighters. They were way out ahead of us and we could see bombers being picked off and every so often one would get hit and explode. Seeing it like that had far more impact; you had time to think what might soon be happening to you.

'On the home leg of a mission people tended to get tired and tetchy and the forma-tion would loosen up a little. In the landing pattern the co-pilot lowered and checked the gear and put down half flaps when the speed dropped below 145mph, and full down on the final approach. We'd come in around 120 and roll the full length of the runway with little use of brakes. The co-pilot would cut out the inboard engines for taxiing back to dispersal and it was his job to check out the engine switches and locks before leaving the aircraft.

'Since those World War II days I have flown some 15 military aircraft including several jets, but none of these have surpassed the "Flying Fort" as a pilot's aircraft. It seemed to meet every requirement and anyone who flew a combat tour in the Fort' would swear by it. It was majestic in appearance and will remain the Queen of the Skies to those of us who knew her.'

Cockpit controls: co-pilot's right side.

PANEL LIGHT OXYGEN REGULATOR INTERPHONE JACKBOX HEADSETS IMPEDANCE ADAPTER RADIO FILTER PANEL LIGHT

RUDDER PEDAL ADJUSTMENT INTERCOOLER CONTROLS ·SUIT HEATER OUTLET· ENGINE PRIMER HYDRAULIC HAND PUMP

Bombardier

John C. Minahan

The object of any bombing mission was to deliver the bombs accurately on the target to achieve its destruction. To this end both bombardier and ordnance had to be positioned precisely for an accurate sighting and release. To navigate to that point, through cloud and clear, evading or countering the enemy's defences, was an achievement in itself; yet all was to no avail if at the very crux of the mission the bombardier failed to be precise in his aim. The USAAF eventually came to entrust the sighting for a whole formation to one highly skilled bombardier in the leading aircraft. Lead bombardiers were selected with care and schooled for perfection, and with the advent of radar aids the art became even more complex. However, the basic principles of high altitude precision bombing remained unchanged from the early

days, when John Minahan became one of the first formally trained bombardiers in the Force.

'I was put into the Air Corps Technical School at Lowry Field, Denver, Colorado, in January 1941 and graduated in April of the same year. There had been two previous classes of bombardiers but they were trained as instructors and had not been required to qualify. As a result we felt we were the very first class of bombardiers the US Army Air Corps ever had. Fifty-one of us started but 23 were eliminated. The 28 who passed were divided between the only three B-17 groups then in existence, the 2nd at Langley, the 19th at March and the 7th – which I joined – at the old Airdrome Lease just outside Salt Lake City, Utah.

'I was assigned to the 11th Bomb Squadron and my introduction to the B-17, a C or D model, was simply a walk through with a team of men, the pilot, navigator and a gunnery sergeant, explaining the layout. The Norden sight and bomb racks were familiar because they were essentially the same as those we had trained on in the Douglas B-18 at Denver.

'Some of my first flights were in connection with a problem encountered by the RAF with their B-17Cs during very high altitude flights. Apparently the guns and bomb doors froze and jammed and we were requested to conduct some tests. I flew on three of these tests during which time we would go to maximum altitude over the bombing range at Wendover Salt Flats in Utah. The highest we ever got was 36 000 feet. On each mission we dropped bombs and fired guns and in each case the guns operated and so did the bomb-bay doors without malfunction of any kind*. By way of citing the virtue of the Norden bombsight, we dropped a string of eight bombs from 36 000 feet with a deflection error of less than 100 feet, and the mean point of impact for the string was about 250 feet short of the target.

'We were using oxygen masks for the first time on these missions, an early type with a balloon fabricated onto the bottom. After a while moisture would condense inside the balloon and had to be drained out through a bung hole in the bottom. This was fine on normal operations but at these extreme altitudes the balloon tended to freeze up. On the first mission we got to 32 000 feet when the waist gunner passed out because the mask had frozen. The pilot immediately dived the aircraft, at such a steep angle that when he attempted to pull out at 14 000 feet it took him another 10 000 feet before we were going straight and level again!

*As explained in Chapter 2 the difference in experience was caused by the high humidity in Europe.

Lt John Minahan being decorated by General George Kenney, 5th Air Force commander.

'Prior to the oxygen masks we simply had oxygen bottles fastened in the rack close to us with a rubber tube coming from it. Flights had not often been above 15 000 feet and seldom higher than 20 000 feet and we had drawn oxygen through the rubber tubes. As the tubes were not very palatable we fitted a pipe stem – usually purchased at Woolworths – into the end. I remember some friendly bickering as to which was best a straight pipe stem or a curved one; personally I liked the curved one better.

'Later in 1941 I went to Geiger Field, Washington, where a new bomb group was being formed, and on return was assigned to the 88th Reconnaissance Squadron of the 7th Group. The 7th was scheduled to move to PLUM, which I later discovered was the code name for Mindanao in the Philippines, and the 88th was the first squadron to go. We had been equipped with some of the first of the new B-17E models with tail guns. The squadron flight echelon began its overseas movement from Hamilton Field, California, where we took off for the leg to Hawaii at 2300 hours on December 6. Our plane developed engine trouble and we returned to Hamilton, the others going on to Hawaii and arriving just as the Japanese made their assault on Pearl Harbour and our air bases. My crew never rejoined the 88th as our B-17E was taken as a replacement. We subsequently crossed the Pacific in an LB-30 to begin operations in January from Java, where the 7th Bomb Group was eventually established. After the withdrawal to Australia, surviving personnel were merged with those from the 19th Group and I flew most of my 47 missions with the 28th Bomb Squadron operating B-17Es out of Mareeba.

'In my opinion the B-17 was the finest combat airplane the Air Force has ever had. It had one major disadvantage of course, in that it carried quite a small bomb load. Our normal loading was eight 500lb bombs while operating from Australia; although there were bigger bombs in the theatre they were rarely used by my group. In Java we were using Dutch 300kg bombs – 660lb – on the same shackles as for 500-pounders and the airplane could carry eight of these without any trouble. The B-17 was capable of carrying much more weight than we ever put into it: the problem was the configuration of the bay. If we used 250 or 300lb bombs we could carry 14 and if they were 100-pounders then 20. There was some rearrangement of bomb stations for the smaller bombs in later B-17s permitting a few more to be carried.

'On a mission the bombardier's real job began at the IP (Initial Point). This was the point at which the bombing run on the target was commenced, preferably some prominent

Three .50 guns installed in togglier B-17E of 7th Air Force, New Caledonia. (41-2463, 11th BG).

landmark which could be easily recognised but in the South-West Pacific it was often just a set of co-ordinates over the sea. The technique was to make a turn into the IP so that the enemy would not know exactly where we were heading until we actually commenced the bomb run; that was the theory though in most cases he knew very well what we were after.

'Few, if any, bombers equalled the B-17 in the visibility afforded the bombardier. Sitting on the low, fixed armour-backed seat, right behind the bombsight at the lip of the nose, you could see a long, long way; the view was marvellous. On the left side of the nose was a control panel fastened below the observation windows. It had a number of switches for predetermined selection of the order and interval of bomb release, together with an air speed indicator and altimeter to provide information necessary for setting up the sight. Just prior to reaching the IP the bombardier would set the intervalometer on this panel for the number and spacing of bombs to be dropped, selecting to drop a "stick" (in train) or only one or two bombs from the load carried. Next the Pilot Directional Indicator (PDI) was turned on, plus the bombsight switches to activate the whole system.

'Fixed to the floor, below the control panel and level with the base of the bombsight, was a quadrant with two levers. The lever nearest the control panel was moved to engage the system for the selective drop previously set up, or right forward to allow the bombs to be salvoed – instantaneous release of all. The other lever on the quadrant opened the bomb-bay doors, which was the next move; a red

111

'Top: Normal B-17E nose armament of 'Baby Doll', 41-9026, 97th BG; one .30 with three firing locations in plexiglass nose and two .50s in side windows.

Above: Early B-17F nose with sockets in plexiglass for .30 Browning and apertures in flat side windows for .50 cheek guns.

IP and see that it was strictly maintained during the run. With the PDI it was essential that the pilot flew a smooth course because any skidding or slipping could upset the precision of the instrument and cause a bombing error. However good the bombardier was in setting up his sight, if the pilotage was sloppy there was little chance of an accurate drop.

The Norden was a marvellous piece of mechanism for its day. An intricate system of gyroscopes and computers, it simplified the bombardier's job considerably by taking into account factors of altitude, airspeed, ground speed, ballistics, trail and drift, and automatically fixed the correct spot on the bomb run where bombs must be released to strike home. If the bombs failed to hit it was a variation in course, or of the data fed in, that was at fault – not the Norden. Altitude and airspeed were, of course, dependent on the pilot's performance in following the PDI, but the other requirements were either fed in by the bombardier or computed by the sight itself.

'The optical part of the Norden was a small telescope. If the bomber was on a correct course the bombardier would first locate the target by looking over the instrument and through the plexiglass nosepiece. Once the target was seen he would try to line it up in the telescope, not always easy early in the run and often requiring several head-up glances to find the target again. There were two cross hairs on the telescope, one to show drift left or right of target, the other to establish the "rate" of closure, both hairs being centred on the target. Located on the right side of the telescope were two indices, one displayed the bombing angle established by the bombardier, the other, the "rate" index; this would move toward the former, synchronised to the forward speed of the aircraft. When these two indices met the bombs would release automatically.

'However, in the early days I, like most bombardiers, did not trust the intervalometer and preferred to release my bombs by hand using the toggle switch attached to the forward end of the control panel. By practice with a stop watch a rhythm could be established that would effect the required spacing. To get a Mean Point of Impact on a target the first bomb had to be dropped short. Hence I would start to toggle the bombs slightly before the indices met.

'The Army Air Force concept was formation bombing but in the early days of the war with Japan there was rarely anything approaching a reasonable sized formation. If three B-17s went out we would fly the standard vee flight in bombing. The bombardier in the lead aircraft would sight for both range

light showed when the doors were fully down but another member of the crew carried out a visual check as doors could stick through freezing.

'Everything was now ready for the bombardier to go to work with the sight. The Norden was composed of two units, the base unit was called the stabiliser and was a box-shaped affair fixed to the floor directly aft of the lip of the nose. The top unit was the actual sight, largely cylindrical in shape and with an optical eye-piece and the necessary adjustment controls. A basic principle of the bombing technique was that the bombardier controlled the airplane on the bomb run, either through the auto-pilot or the PDI. With the former the bombardier actually had direct lateral control of the aircraft; linkage between the bombsight and the auto-pilot causing adjustment of the sight to operate the auto-pilot. However, on early B-17s this system left much to be desired and as far as I am aware only the PDI method was used in the SWPA. With the PDI the changes desired in the flight pattern were transmitted by adjustments of the bombsight to a visual display on the cockpit instrument panel for the pilot to follow. Whichever system was used the pilot had to trim the aircraft for a precise altitude and airspeed at the

Single .50 nose gun
installation standardised for
B-17F ('Short Stuff', 42-30332,
FC:N, 390th BG) in 1943.

(forward travel of bombs) and deflection (distance bombs will drift due to crosswind) while the two wing aircraft would sight for range only, relying on the leadplane for lateral positioning.

'The first occasion to my knowledge that B-17s used the drop-on-leader technique for a large formation was at Vunakanal airstrip near Rabaul on August 7, 1942. Each formation dropped on the release of bombs from the lead B-17. Despite being under heavy attack beforehand the strike was quite effective. My own airplane had an engine knocked out on the bomb run so as we were lagging behind I had to make my own sighting. The drop-on-leader technique became standard in Europe. By using the most skilled bombardiers in the lead this certainly produced a better strike pattern on a target. The bombardier also made greater use of the auto-pilot system over there.

'At the start of the war in the Pacific we were bombing from altitudes of between 25 000 and 30 000 feet. We found that our bombing accuracy from these heights generally wasn't too good and particularly when we were under fighter attack. So when there was a specific objective of great importance we were required to go in much lower to ensure drops were more effective. In the summer of 1942 we reached the point between bombing accuracy and battle losses where it was deemed much better to go in at night, and indeed we got much better results. Most of the night missions were run against the Jap's major supply base in the SWPA, Rabaul in New Britain, which had a most distinctive horse-shoe shaped harbour. There is always a contrast between land and water even on the darkest night and it was not difficult to locate the target area – which was usually a part of the harbour. In these missions we flew at under 10 000 feet, bombing individually, and a decent crew could put a bomb within 50 to 60 feet of the aiming point. Each crew had their own philosophy about Jap gunfire and could choose its own altitude providing there was no conflict. Our crew believed the lowest the safest and usually went in at 4 000 feet; their small arms couldn't reach us and the heavy stuff couldn't get that low. These night raids caused a lot of trouble for the Japs; we would frequently fire a fuel dump or explosives store.

'The bombardier was also responsible for the armament on the B-17 although in practice each gunner was an expert on his weapon and pretty self-sufficient. Originally the bombardier had a .30 rifle calibre gun in the plexiglass nose of the B-17E but when the Japs turned to frontal attacks an improvised mount was rigged up at air depots in Australia to take a pair of point-fifties in this position. The guns were mounted high and to the right of the bombsight, firing through an aperture cut in the top of the nosepiece. When not in use, a rubber cord kept them stowed out of the way of the bombardier's head. As soon as the bombs had been dropped and the bay closed, the Norden was quickly and easily removed from its base and put on the floor behind the bombardier's position: then the two fifty calibres could be brought into play. They had limited travel and you could not fire far below the horizontal. As a result Jap fighters came to make climbing attacks from twelve o'clock low and only the ball turret could reach them before they rolled away down. I would often see them coming in but couldn't bring the guns to bear. I hate to say it but the fighters looked pretty in a horrible sort of way, glistening in the sunlight.

'In the early days the Japs found it very difficult to down at B-17. They would come down to 150 yards behind the tail in the blind spot and just sit there and empty their guns. Their principal weapon was the .303 rifle calibre gun and this used a copper jacketed bullet with a .25 needle-nosed armour piercing slug in the centre. When the bullet penetrated the skin of the airplane the copper

peeled off and the only thing that came in was this little armour-piercing core. We had a lot of people wounded by these but as the bullet did not fragment they left a very clean wound. I've known a man able to walk away from his plane with one of these bullet holes clean through the calf of his leg. These small slugs didn't penetrate the B-17's armour plate. You could sometimes scoop up a handful of them from the bottom of the fuselage where they had hit the armoured bulkhead behind the cockpit. The Japs had a 20-mm cannon on the Zero but it took them some time to get the fusing right. At first it was instantaneous so the shell exploded on contact and rarely penetrated; blowing a hole in the skin but not getting to the vitals of the bomber.

'You can understand how in the early days we came to think of the B-17 as a really great combat aircraft. My introduction to its toughness was at Batchelor Field near Darwin on my way to Java. There was an old B-17C or D named *Old Miss No 2* on the field, which had come down from the Philippines. It was riddled with holes and the crew had circled each with chalk. There were hundreds and hundreds yet the plane had kept flying.

'I've always felt that a Tech' Sergeant named Louis Silva played a big part in teaching the Japs to change their tactics. Silva was known to everyone as "Soup" and to me he is

Twin .50 nose guns in 8th Air Force toggler B-17F. ('Martha II', 42-29761, VP:W, 381st BG). Note chute to deflect spent cases from plexiglass and non-standard togglier – visiting British Armoured Corps soldier.

one of the great unsung heroes of the war. When the first B-17E came into Java "Soup" was the senior ordnance man in the outfit and he would not permit anyone else to fly the tail guns in that airplane, flying every mission himself. He loaded the guns without tracers so the Japs wouldn't see where the fire was coming from. On his first mission he sat there in the tail behind those twin 'fifties, waited for the first fighter to come down on the rear in the usual way, let it come in to 150 yards and then opened up with a short burst and down it went. He got five that day. Next mission he went out and did the same thing getting six. He flew every mission adding more Japs to his score. The Japs soon figured out where it was coming from and began to change their tactics. There was another story about "Soup" shooting down three fighters while showing a private how to handle a gun. "Soup" was later killed in an accident near Townsville. Some experiments were being run on the use of flares for night bombing and "Soup" was in a B-17 that exploded when the flares ignited somehow. In all "Soup" shot down some 18 or 20 Japs and these were confirmed. In each case members of his or other crews came back raving about "Soup's" kills. His achievements were common knowledge at our base. It is almost unbelievable, here was one of the great gunner aces of the war yet he never received any official recognition. Due to the disorganisation in Java there were no written records to acknowledge his many victories.

'On nearly every one of my daytime missions in B-17s we encountered fighters. I guess like most I came out of my tour with a kind of fatalistic attitude about being killed. There were a couple of incidents that helped engender this attitude. Once at the start of a bomb run I had sat back from the sight to scan for a target. At that moment a 20-mm shell came through the plexiglass and exploded against the bombsight which distintegrated. I was completely untouched by the fragmentation. On the other occasion the reverse happened. We were on our way home from a night mission when I noticed a hole in the fuselage side on my left. Looking round I saw that there was another hole high up on the right side of the nose. The line between the two holes passed somewhere through the upper part of my body! Obviously I had been leaning over my sight on the bomb run when a shell – happily a dud – had gone clean through the nose a few inches over my back. And neither the navigator nor myself were aware it happened. This sort of thing made you believe that there is a God in heaven and nothing was going to happen until it was supposed to.'

Below: Hoisting 500lb HEs from bomb trailer prior to loading 'Whaletail II', 42-5845, GD:A, 381st BG.

Right: Bombing instruments and controls on left side of B-17G nose interior.

Below right: Controls and equipment on the right side of bombardier's position.

CHIN TURRET CONTROLLER (STOWED POSITION)   PORTABLE OXYGEN RECHARGER   INTERPHONE JACKBOX   OXYGEN REGULATOR

DEFROSTER AIR DUCT   GLIDE BOMBING ATTACHMENT STATIC PRESSURE SELECTOR VALVE   OXYGEN PANEL   CAMERA RECEPTACLES AND SWITCH

BOMB RELEASE LIGHT   ALTIMETER   ULTRA-VIOLET LIGHT CONTROL   BOMB INDICATOR LIGHTS SWITCH

AIR SPEED INDICATOR   BOMB DOOR WARNING LAMP   BOMB FORMATION LIGHT & SWITCH   BOMB ARMING SWITCH & LIGHT   BOMB RELEASE SWITCH

ULTRA-VIOLET SPOT LIGHT   BOMB RACK SELECTOR SWITCHES   PILOT CALL SWITCH & LIGHT   INTERNAL BOMB CONTROL LEVER   BOMB DOOR CONTROL HANDLE

INTERVALOMETER CONTROL PANEL   BOMB INDICATOR   EXTERNAL BOMB CONTROL LEVER   EMERGENCY REWIND WHEEL

117

Navigator

Frank D. Furiga

Determining the position of an aircraft in relation to the earth is a simple description of air navigation. Far from simple in practice, navigation is a highly exacting art demanding a quick mind and a penchant for mathematical calculations. A navigator had to give constant attention to his task in order to know the exact position of his aircraft at all times, even when guided by a formation, for situations could change rapidly and a crew could not risk not knowing where they were over enemy territory. Navigation was the key to reaching the target and returning to base; the pilots flew the aircraft but the navigator supplied the course they must fly. Navigation could be by pilotage (visual reference to the ground), dead reckoning (keeping account of heading and speed and assessing departure from the last known position), radio and celestial (astronomical) means, or any combination of these four. Dead reckoning, making use of pilotage and radio aids, was the usual practice in US heavy bomber formations.

Frank Furiga describes dead reckoning and

Lt Frank Furiga.

other normal duties of a B-17 navigator in the course of his 25th and most crucial operational mission, the attack on oil plants at Zeitz in the Leipzig area on November 30, 1944, the day the Eighth Air Force suffered its heaviest losses at the hands of the German flak defences.

'The truck stopped and I climbed off onto the revetment. Our ship stood clothed in the early morning mist, bomb doors open, while the ground crew huddled around the put-put charging motors. The whole air base throbbed with the phut-phut of these small engines; it was a sign that the take-off was near. *Fightin' Hebe* was painted in bold black letters across the nose of the plane and I reflected that the original pilot might have been a Jew. Lt Gene Goodrick, the pilot, walked over to me and said that I had done a good job navigating for another pilot the day before and requested I do the same for him. He also asked for a copy of the course headings, times and changes before walking away to make his own pre-flight check of the plane. I struggled to get up into the nose hatch and got assistance from one of the ground crew. It was quiet in the nose and as I looked around I noticed the gunners had already installed my side (or cheek) guns.

'The nose compartment was roomy and I could just stand in it without stooping. The navigator's table was fixed at the rear of the compartment against the left side and I sat at this on a tiny swivel seat facing two small windows beyond which the propeller of No 2 engine was poised. Immediately above these windows two vital instruments of my trade were suspended from the fuselage formers. Nearest the rear bulkhead was the gyro magnetic compass and to its right the radio compass, both with dials facing me at an angle that made it easy to observe the fluctuations of the pointers. The gyro compass was a complex instrument in which the Earth's magnetic field was used to monitor a directional gyroscope. One of the navigator's jobs was to align the master gyro before take off. The radio compass was linked to a rotating loop aerial housed in a plastic fairing suspended from the underside of the fuselage just forward of the bomb bay, and to a fixed whip 'sense' aerial further forward under the nose. The signal received from a radio beacon was presented visually on the compass face as a relative bearing, or as an aural 'rule' signal through the headphones. The controls for the radio compass were on the bulkhead just above my table but they could be remotely operated by the pilot from switches in the cockpit ceiling. On the opposite side of the fuselage behind my seat the drift meter was located in a bracket below the rearmost window. This was used to determine the angle between the heading of the aircraft and its track over the ground, the amount of drift being essential in the calculation of the wind velocity element of dead reckoning. Another important radio/radar aid was the Gee Box unit which had a small circular television-like screen and was located at the right end of my table.

'I was tacking down my plots on the navigator's table when I noticed someone was trying to squeeze by me. I looked up into the face of Lt Jim Cresto, one of our Group and Squadron lead bombardiers and I asked him what he was doing in our plane. He stated that he had volunteered for a "togglier" mission as he was getting sick and tired of waiting for a lead mission. "Togglier" was the term used for the man who released the bombs on the drop of the lead plane and he had no need for a bomb sight and there was none in our plane now. Jim was now busying himself by lugging the flak suits up into the nose compartment. Soon the rest of the crew scrambled aboard the plane as it was nearly time for engine start. A brilliant green flare arched up over the control tower into the morning sky. Out pilot called "Mesh 1, Start 1" and the co-pilot laboured with the priming pump, slowly awakening each one of the giant engines until their throbbing shook every bone in my body. From my seat in the nose compartment I could hear the brakes squeal as we moved out of our revetment into the perimeter track for the take-off; there was a whole line of B-17s waddling along the taxiway now just like a gaggle of geese going to a pond.

'We were amongst the first to take off as we were flying in a lead squadron and I tensed up as I saw the end of the runway coming and felt the last light touch of the tyres as we were airborne. Then we were started in the pattern climb out of the aerodrome and I breathed a sigh of relief – there was always the fear that an engine might fail and the nose was not the place to be in a crash landing. The sky was showing some more light now as the first fingers of dawn began to poke above the horizon, however, inside the plane we were still in a partial darkness. Turning on the radio compass I tuned in the frequency of our base radio range beacon and watched the needle swing around to our compass direction from the field. For the time being the pilot would circle the field using this radio beacon as a homing point as we climbed higher and higher into the cold blue sky to make our assembly.

'With assembly completed we were off from point A on the flight plan, Clacton-on-Sea. There was some cirrus stratus cloud layers above us and to the east traces of stratus

Navigator peering into the Gee box. Flexible eye shade was necessary to see the 'blips' clearly in daylight.

cumulus appeared. I plugged in my electric cords and turned up the rheostat in order to get the heated suit to function. The bombardier, Jim Cresto, was now sitting crosswise in the nose, his sole duty for a while to make an oxygen check at every one thousand feet. The crewmen would check in over the intercome beginning with the tail position and ending with me. If one of the crew did not acknowledge the call the man nearest was despatched to investigate; life was short at high altitude without oxygen.

'I tuned in the Gee box and began to plot our course. Gee was a radar instrument that worked on one master beam and two slave beams. By reading some numbers off on a superimposed grid scale on a cathode ray tube, then plotting these numbers on a special chart, the exact location of the crossing beams was found and that was our position at that precise moment. This was a splendid system developed by the British. I handed the pilot a copy of the mission course headings, times and airspeeds and received a cheerful thanks. We were now at 16 000 feet and the crew were chattering over the interphone. I was asked by one how long we would be in the air today; I estimated about nine hours and thirty minutes. "Roger, thank you. Oh my achin' back!" he said.

'As we joined the Division and began the long journey to our objective only the radio operator, pilots and myself were working.

Every four minutes I checked our position and entered it in the log on my navigator's table. Because of a swift tail wind we were now passing over the Channel very rapidly. Glancing at the altimeter I saw we were at 20 000 feet as Ostend hove into sight on the sandy coast. Ball-turret called and asked what was the name of the town below, so I knew that he was down in his fish-bowl watching the vast panorama of moving scenery below. Short puffs of contrails were whipping by us now from the planes ahead. As Liege, astride the Meuse river, passed below I gave the pilot an "On course, On time" call over the intercom. Some of the crew began to put on their flak suits and as we crossed the German border I notified the pilot and he called for a test fire of the guns. The whole ship quivered as the men fired and as all the other ships in the group would be doing likewise at around the same time, I often wondered what the Germans thought whenever they heard that racket. I was musing now that on the plane I was flying today I only knew a few of the crewmen – the pilot, co-pilot and, of course,

the bombardier. I did not know any of the sergeants as I had never flown with them before and if something were to happen then I might never know who had been along.

'Around 1315 hours I informed the pilot that we were coming to the IP so that he was prepared for the big turn the formation would make. The altimeter was now fluttering at 25 000 feet as we crossed the IP and began our bomb run which would take six minutes to the target. The ship groaned and bucked as the bomb bay doors went down. Chaff dispensed from the leading planes filled the air to confuse the enemy's flak radar. The temperature outside was near 50 below zero yet I was sweating. I tightened up my nerves and pulled the flak helmet down tighter on my head; we knew we were going into one of the most heavily flak defended targets in Germany. I watched the radio-compass closely now and wished that I'd stayed in bed that day! I readjusted my flak suit again; heaven knows I did that about a thousand times. I ran my finger along the chute rings to be sure I'd be hooked to the harness. Jim Cresto had his eyes

Navigator's station.

RADIO COMPASS CONTROL BOX ULTRA-VIOLET SPOT LIGHT ULTRA-VIOLET SPOT LIGHT CONTROL SWITCH GYRO COMPASS INDICATOR
INTERPHONE JACKBOX GYRO FLUX GATE COMPASS AMPLIFIER GYRO COMPASS CAGING SWITCH

OXYGEN REGULATOR MICROPHONE SWITCH OXYGEN PANEL RADIO COMPASS
HEADSETS IMPEDANCE ADAPTER TABLE LAMP SWITCH PORTABLE OXYGEN BOTTLE RECHARGER

glued on the lead plane so that he could release his bombs at the precise time as the lead bombardier.

'Suddenly the intercom came to life "Pilot to bombardier, pilot to bombardier, over." "Bombardier, Roger." "Pilot to bombardier, we are not going to drop our bombs but will go to the last resort target." "Bombardier to pilot; Bombardier to pilot; bomb bay doors going up". What was wrong? I peered over the bombardier's back; the target area was covered by a dense pall of smoke; a smoke screen was that the reason we were turning? We hadn't seen a bit of flak yet. Surely they were tracking us below with their guns. I looked at the compass and was horrified to see that we were going back onto the same heading again. "Pilot to bombardier, pilot to navigator, we are going to make a PFF run on the same target." Our Group leader had obviously decided this important target warranted another try. A quick peek at my wrist watch, it was 1343 hours and there were two minutes to bombs away; a long time to be playing games over the target. We were really asking for it now and sure looked as if we were going to have some trouble.

'The ship vibrated as the bomb bay doors went down again. The bombardier sat there with the same transfixed stare on his face watching the lead plane. Suddenly there was a violent explosion and we seemed to wallow all over the sky. The oxygen tanks behind me in the passageway from the pilot's deck burst into bright flame and light blue smoke started filling the nose compartment. Casting a quick glance at the sky I saw huge clouds of flak at our level and a B-17 ahead going down leaving a plume of grey smoke. The oxygen tanks were burning fiercely, fed by the released oxygen in a sort of chain reaction. Flak was still slamming around the plane. I stood up in time to see the engineer come down and kick out the forward escape hatch. The bombardier turned round, surprised to see the engineer and co-pilot bale out. In his determination to fulfil his duty he hadn't noticed the conflagration behind us. We dropped our flak suits simultaneously and Jim motioned for me to bale out. I looked at the flak-studded sky and shook my head. Too much flak. Without deliberation or hesitation he shoved me aside and plunged head-first out of the hatch. Kneeling on the floor I could see bombs bursting on the landscape below. I tried the intercom but there was no response, it must have been destroyed. I then figured that the ship was mortally wounded and that Gene Goodrick was holding her on an even keel until we all got out. Evidently something terrible had happened to make the co-pilot and engineer hit the silk. I took a couple more swigs of oxygen, tossed the hose aside and picked up my officer's hat and GI shoes off the drift meter. I wasn't going to wait around until the ship blew up. Oddly enough I wasn't frightened at the thought of jumping. Resting the rip-cord in my right hand and with a prayer on my lips I now leaned out into the slipstream head first; my helmet was fiercely torn loose and I tumbled out into space.

'The slipstream was very powerful and made me gasp for my breath. I began to tumble, turning and dropping slowly, glimpsing the earth and sky revolving. When I decided I had dropped below flak level I started tugging on the rip cord, on the third attempt it came loose yet nothing went by my face. Then I felt an intense pain in my groin and pressure on my arms and looked up at the most beautiful sight an aviator in distress can behold; the enormous white canopy of a parachute. Looking down I saw I had dropped the rip cord but incredible as it may seem I still had the cap and shoes in my left hand. Some silvery chaff was still drifting about but I could not see a single plane, the great armada of bombers had departed home while I was on my way to a broken foot and prison camp.

'It was many months later that I learned all that had befallen *Fightin' Hebe* and the rest of the crew on that mission. The second run on the target had been made because smoke palls from enemy smoke pots obscured the aiming point. The flak shell had exploded under the pilots' compartment almost bouncing the pilots out of their seats and igniting their oxygen supply. With flames and smoke creeping up the sides of the compartment the engineer and co-pilot were convinced that it was only a matter of seconds before the plane exploded. The fire subsided and Goodrick salvoed the bombs to stick with the aircraft. The intercom to the rear of the plane was still working and he managed to call up the ball turret gunner, Lee Pierce, who came to his aid; just in time as Goodrick had then been without oxygen for four minutes. The flak had put electrical and hydraulic systems out of action; the bomb bay doors wouldn't close and the undercarriage kept lowering and re-tracting itself until it was manually cranked into a fixed position. Tagging behind the formation, night was falling when *Fightin' Hebe* reached Grafton Underwood. Another B-17 acted as a "seeing dog" guide to mark the runway line as with no flaps or brakes Goodrick brought the Fortress in to touch down at over 125mph and in the darkness. Though they over-ran the runway to end up in a field, none of the six remaining crew members were hurt. Ironically, in abandoning the plane we appear to have saved it, for the fierce draught through the open nose hatch is credited with blowing out the fire!'

Flight Engineer

George W. Parks

No other crew member of a Fortress had such a wide knowledge of the mechanism and functions of the bomber and its equipment as the engineer. He was capable of servicing the aircraft if it landed away from the home base and if need be he could turn his hand to most jobs normally handled by the ground crew. Apart from the ability to maintain airframe and engines, the engineer was an armourer with a detailed knowledge of the aircraft's guns and the operation of the bomb racks. He also understood the oxygen equipment and could tune radio transmitters and receivers if necessary. In an emergency he was a key man, being trained in procedures to adopt in particular situations. However, the engineer's 'regular job' was manning the B-17's upper turret on combat missions,

M/Sgt George W. Parks

explaining why he was frequently referred to as 'Top Turret' rather than by his correct calling. Because of their technical expertise with power units and flight controls many engineers could, in an emergency, take over from one of the pilots and help fly the aircraft; although they were not trained to do so. Many engineers had previous experience as crew chiefs on heavy bombers, and one such was M/Sgt George Parks who volunteered for a flight posting. He flew 37 missions over Europe in 1944, some rough, some smooth. This is his account of his roughest:

'Pushing my parachute up through the nose hatch I pulled myself up after it, crawled through the passage under the cockpit and up onto the flight deck. The worst part of any mission was the time on the ground beforehand, getting ready and waiting. I was always scared – and any flyer who says he wasn't is a liar – so I was glad to get in the airplane; it wasn't so bad then, you were committed and there was work to do.

'My parachute stowed against the left hand side of the rear bulkhead where I could get it quickly in an emergency, I started my pre-flight check on the turret. Climbing onto the circular stand around the turret pivot post I looked the guns over and when the self-contained hydraulic unit that provided the power had warmed up, clutched in, put the switches to "On" and swung the turret. The operation was controlled by two cycle-like hand grips. The left had the gun trigger and a press-in safety lever: the moment you took your hand off the grip the lever came out and cut all power. The right handle worked the range finder of the optical sight through a twisting motion. Pulling the handles up elevated the guns and pushing them down brought the guns back again. Pressure to left or right on the handles rotated the turret in that direction.

'Having found everything okay I parked the turret with the guns pointing aft, which would keep grit that might be thrown up during take-off out of the barrels. There weren't enough serviceable airplanes in our own squadron that day and we had been allocated one in the 323rd across the field. I was pleased it had the new high dome turret and not the squat type of the B-17F and early G models which was around six inches lower. Being 6 feet 3 inches tall and 180 pounds I could not stand completely upright in the old type without my helmet hitting the top, so I normally stood on one leg resting my other foot on a stirrup. The sling type seat was useless as far as I was concerned for I was too big a man to get into it and be comfortable. Neither could I wear the bulky sheepskin jacket as there wasn't enough room in the turret. So I had to rig myself up in my own choice of clothing, usually an electric suit, an A-2 flying jacket, a black silk scarf round my neck – actually one of my wife's old nightdresses – black silk gloves under RAF felt gloves, and RAF flying boots. We preferred the RAF boots because they were longer in the leg and stayed on your feet if you had to bale out. The American issue could and would leave your feet, and who wants frost-bitten toes! My helmet was also an RAF type because they were more comfortable. Under it I wore a green baseball cap with long peak to shade my eyes so I could lay my head back and look up into the sun.

'I spread a couple of flak vests around the deck of my turret. There was no room to wear one in there and as flak fragments were blasted upwards this seemed the most useful place to have them so they protected the family jewels! Had to keep my eye on the flak vests for sometimes another member of the crew would steal one as he passed to pad around his own station.

'At engine start and run-up I stood behind the pilots' seats checking the fuel and engine gauges, everything was fine. I remained there while we taxied out and during the take-off called off the airspeed readings for the pilot so he could concentrate on keeping the airplane headed down the runway. Once airborne I climbed up to give the engines and gas filler caps on the wing a visual scan, coming back to the flight deck to keep a check on the fuel gauges and gas consumption as we climbed for assembly. Some engines were fuel hogs; we reckoned those Studebaker made were particularly so and it paid to watch how the gas was going.

'The date was Sunday April 19 and the target an assembly plant for Focke-Wulfs at Eschwege just outside Kassel in central Germany. As we winged high over the spring greenness of England the sky was clear and visibility unlimited, the best weather we had seen for some time. Leaving the coast far below it was time to climb into my turret to charge and test fire the guns. Swinging the turret round and aiming out where my fire would be safely away from other B-17s I let go a quick burst. There were around 750 rounds in the ammo' boxes only you could never afford to waste one at this stage of a mission. The view from the top turret was probably the best in the whole airplane. Looking back towards the tail I could see the radio operator's gun swinging freely but I could not see any other members of the crew. Our B-17 was lead of our element of three in the high squadron and, as our group was flying the high group position, I could see the lead group way ahead and down to our left, and the low group further down to the left and

Surveying the damage to the tail of 42-37938, OR:E. l to r: Lt Thomas H. Gunn, T/Sgt George Parks and S/Sgt Robert D. Smith, tail gunner. George Parks is wearing the longer RAF flying boots.

parallel with us – perhaps 50 to 60 bombers. The sun blazed down and there was not a cloud in sight. Just a mass of B-17s in a blue void. Our pilot Tom Gunn called "What a beautiful Sunday and we have to go to war".

'Rotating the turret slowly I scanned the sky. There was not even the ugly black puffs of smoke that meant flak at our level. As the guns panned over the nose I noticed the antenna sticking up and made a mental note to remember it. On previous missions I had twice shot this off while following a fighter. The turret mechanism incorporated a special cut-out that stopped the guns firing when they were aimed at the propeller arc or the tail but there was no cut-out for the antenna.

'After an hour in the turret the noise and the sun beaming through the plexiglass began to make me drowsy; it had happened before and was a job to shake off. Even with the dark glasses I was wearing the sun hurt my eyes if I looked too long in that direction, only it was from there that Jerry was most likely to come if he put in an appearance. The sun still blazed down on the plexiglass; I put out my hand to touch it, it was as cold as hell.

Early Sperry upper turret
was particularly cramped
with little headroom.
(306th BG, B-17F: Sgt Joe
Collette.)

'After over three and a half hours in the air
we were approaching the target. If they were
going to hit this was the most likely time; that
knowledge subdued the drowsiness. Over the
intercom there was some talk between the
pilot and bombardier from which I understood the formation was going to make a 360
degree turn right for another run on the
target. Owing to our position way out on the
right, we were racked in tight to hold with the
formation as it turned and the pilots were
using all their skill not to over-run.

'No one shouted a warning, no one saw
them coming in time; they must have been
up there in the sun waiting their chance. The
first thing I knew was that the pleasant Sunday afternoon was shattered by smoke and
flame. A wave of fighters flashed by us through
the formation, Lt Gunn hauling back on the
wheel to get above their line of fire. As I spun
my turret I saw one of our wingmen explode
in flame. Another Me 109 was boring in
head-on at the squadron. Frantically working
my range finder to frame the accelerating
target, I gave a number of quick bursts. The
guns rattled and the turret shook. The
Messerschmit smoked and crumpled away
past. "I've got one!" I yelloed on the intercom. Suddenly I realised smoke was filling
the turret and looking down I saw a fire in the
bomb-bay. Spinning the turret round I slid

out, grabbed a CO_2 extinguisher from the wall
and sprayed it into the flames. Thankfully the
fire went out. Turning I saw that the flight
deck was filled with smoke and that the
co-pilot had been hit in the legs, a cannon
shell having burst somewhere below the
instrument panel. Trying to move forward to
help proved difficult, the airplane was now in
a flat left hand spin and the G forces were
building up. I saw Lt Gunn trying to attach
his chest pack 'chute. The acrid smoke was
now so dense that it was almost impossible to
see through the windscreen. Lt Gunn forced
his side window open. Then I realised the
instruments were shattered and he had no way
of telling our flight attitude unless he could
see the horizon. How we came out of that
spin I don't know and neither did Gunn but
we did and he managed to bring her straight
and level.

'I got the co-pilot out of his seat and back
through the bomb-bay into the radio room.
He wasn't badly hit. I then went back into the
cockpit and got into the co-pilot's seat to help
the pilot in any way possible, calling one of
the waist gunners up to take over the upper
turret. Lt Gunn wasn't a big man and he was
having a hell of a time keeping the airplane
flying with the wheel hard over to the right.
He motioned for me to take over and instinctively I started to bring the wheel back.

Immediately the airplane fell off to the left again. I kicked the rudder bars but there was no response, they were quite free and we had obviously no rudder control. We managed to haul the airplane back and maintain level flight at reduced speed by the use of full right aileron.

'We were now alone and down at 15 000 feet. Seeing a marker flare over the target we managed to edge the bomber in that direction and give the bombardier a chance to jettison the bomb load in the right area. Now to get home. We all knew what happened to stragglers and I guess we all prayed secretly that the 109s wouldn't return. Everything had happened so fast I wasn't aware of how much damage we had until now. Not only were most of our flight instruments gone and the rudder controls severed by a shell that had blown a large hole in the fin, but we had a hit on the main left wing gas tank, a turbo out, engine damage, elevators shot up and some aileron damage. Full right aileron being necessary to keep her level, Lt Gunn could only control direction by using the engines. Other shells had exploded in the nose, cockpit and bomb-bay and besides the co-pilot, the navigator had wounds.

'Presently somebody at the rear called the word we had all been dreading "fighters". With the damage we had there was no question of evasive action; we had to sit there and wait for them to hit us. There was no fire from our guns so the fighters were obviously out of range, looking us over before the kill. I looked up out of the right window and saw them. What sweet relief: I recognised P-51s. They edged in towards us and after a while the leader broke radio silence: "Big Friend, will stay with you until you go down." They had no doubts we were doomed. Happily they were wrong and we kept going thanks to the skill of our pilot.

'Seven hours and five minutes after we left the place we caught sight of dear old Bassingbourn. Lt Gunn brought her in smoothly and on touch-down we found the right brake was locked, causing our landing roll to veer slightly off the runway onto the grass. I tumbled out with the rest, the tension over, now tired and edgy. Fire trucks and meat wagons came to meet us but our wounded could get out of the airplane under their own power. Tom Gunn went down and ran his fingers through the grass in pleasure; we all knew how he felt and right then he was the best pilot in the Air Force as far as we were concerned. A big crowd gathered around to view the damage. The Boeing rep came up and asked Lt Gunn what he thought of the B-17. It wasn't the right time to ask and the answer he got wasn't what he was looking for!'

Later turret had higher dome and more side glazing. Reflector sight is visible just in front of gunner T/Sgt John M. Graham's face. Grips attached above his head are the gun charging handles. (384th BG).

Radio Operator

Martin Goodman

Probably the most unglamorous post in a Fortress crew was that of radio operator. Tucked away in the middle of the bomber, isolated from his comrades and with restricted outlook, the radio man usually had to sit at his receiver and 'sweat out' the battle that raged outside. Yet he was a key member of the team, handling the vital communications equipment which frequently proved a life saver for the crew. Marty Goodman sweated out 30 flak-filled missions in the radio room with the 401st Bomb Group during the latter half of 1944.

'My duties as a radio operator on a B-17 were manifold. After the main briefing on the morning of a mission, we radio operators went to the radio shack on the base for our separate briefing. There we were given the code of the day which was changed for each mission. This was simple in form, merely one letter of the alphabet standing for another; as an example, the letter D in the code would stand for F. We were given the code written on paper similar to tissue and we were instructed to destroy it should anything go wrong and we came down in enemy territory. This paper was supposedly edible if there wasn't time to dispose of it by some other manner.

'We were also given the check points of the mission. These were certain co-ordinates along the route, points over which the lead radio operator would transmit a coded message to 8th Air Force headquarters. The main purpose of this was to enable fighter cover to rendezvous with us, and as soon as headquarters received the check point message the fighter planes were informed of our position.

'The first thing a radioman did on taking his position in the plane was to tune his equipment and make sure the frequencies were correct. The signal was strong at the base and over England, but the further away a mission took us the weaker it became and the more static the man had to contend with. All morse code· transmissions from our base or Division HQ were sent slowly with dots and dashes given distinctly so messages could be easily understood. The radioman worked in the same manner so even though the signal might be weak, and contain static, the code could be understood. At 50 degrees below zero you couldn't remove your glove as your finger would stick to the key. This made transmitting code all the more difficult.

'Each mission had a primary and secondary target and if the lead pilot felt that adverse weather or operational problems made the primary a bad risk, he could elect to hit the secondary. It was the duty of the radioman to inform headquarters immediately as to which target was bombed and if the results were good or not good as the case may have been. Right after the bomb run the lead radio operator sent these details in coded message. The information contained in this message often started the wheels turning on planning the next days mission.

'All along the route of this mission, the radioman had his headset on his ears listening for any messages that might come from headquarters, such as a decision to scrub the mission and order all planes to return. This was not an easy job as there was a great deal of static and to listen to static for hours on end was in itself difficult.

'Another of our functions was to receive a radio position fix. At times the navigator lost his position for one reason or another, or perhaps he wanted to check and see that his calculations were correct. He would get on the intercom and request the radio operator to get a radio fix. Spread over England were installations with highly sensitive radio compasses. The radio operator would contact certain of these installations and ask for a fix. He would then hold his morse key down to give a solid signal for approximately one minute. This signal was read at widely spaced stations which were inter-connected and a line projection of these readings were made on a map. Where lines intersected would be the position of the plane. This position was then radioed back and within minutes the navigator was informed. The same procedure was used should a B-17 be forced to land on water. If the plane was within friendly limits the radio operator would send a distress message and then hold his key down. The plane's position would immediately be given to the air/sea rescue service and help would be on its way.

'The radio compartment was situated between two fuselage bulkheads, one at the rear of the bomb bay and the other just forward of the ball turret, adjacent to the trailing edge of the wing. A plywood door in each sealed the compartment although I always kept them open during a mission. The radioman sat facing forward on a swivel seat located on the left side of the compartment with a work table in front of him. The liaison radio receiver and transmitting key were located on this table, while the liaison radio transmitter was fixed to the bulkhead directly behind the operator's seat. These sets were used for long-range communication in morse and to avoid confusion with vocal broadcasts this form was known as wireless telegraphy or W/T. Normal receiving was via an aerial attached to the plane's skin but a trailing aerial reel was available for difficult and distant reception. On the right-hand side of the rear bulkhead were five W/T transmitter tuning units.

'Also on the right side of the radio room, attached to the forward bulkhead, were two transmitters and three receivers for the Command radio. Known as the R/T (radio telephony) its purpose was short-range vocal communication with nearby aircraft or ground stations for navigational or traffic control reasons. The pilots used the Command radio and the controls were located in the cockpit ceiling.

'Receivers and other equipment for the Indentification Friend or Foe (IFF) unit, a radio device that as the name implies, differentiated between enemy or friendly planes approaching from the rear, were situated on the right side of the aft bulkhead. A crash button in the cockpit could explode a small charge in the secret IFF receiver if there was any likelihood of the aircraft crashing in enemy territory.

'The radio operator was also trained as a gunner to operate a flexible point fifty machine gun in the top of the compartment. On early B-17s the hatch was removed so the gun could be manoeuvred but this let in the cold and made the radioman's job very uncomfortable. Later B-17s had the gun in a special swivel socket so that the top hatch did not have to be removed. However, the field of fire was very limited and as there was rarely time to spot enemy fighters approaching due to restricted view from this position, the value as a defence point was in doubt. Eventually the gun was removed – and this was the case on all of my missions. About the same time only one waist gunner was assigned to fly with each crew and if enemy fighters attacked, and the radio man could be spared from his post, he would man one of the waist guns.

'In the floor of the radio room there were trap doors covering a well containing a large K-24 or F-24 (British version) camera. This was fixed vertically with the lens pointing through the bottom of the fuselage. On the bomb run the radioman activated a switch that started the camera automatically taking pictures at ten-second intervals. The resulting strike photos were put up on the bulletin boards at the base so that all could view the results of each mission. It proved a very good morale booster as one could see that all the effort was getting results. The camera could be used for individual shots and a viewfinder was incorporated for the radioman to use in such an event.

Sgt Martin Goodman.

'The radioman was also trained as the first-aid man of the crew. In the radio room we carried a large bag filled with a first-aid kit and other extra items such as an oxygen mask, heated suit essentials, and so on. This bag helped to save the life of our ball turret gunner on one mission. His oxygen mask became inoperative and if it wasn't for the extra mask in the bag he would have died. Other emergency equipment and tools were located in the radio room which was considered the safest place in the plane during a ditching or crash landing. In the event of such an emergency all crew members other than the pilots would come to the radio room and brace themselves, backs towards the forward bulkhead.

'To the left of me as I sat on my swivel seat was a window from which I could see the left wing with its two engines and also a panorama of the sky on that side. As the engines drowned out any noise I was only

Above: Gunner handling .50 gun installation fitted to B-17E, F and G models until late in 1944. Note raised slipstream deflector shield forward of gun pit and the aerial which was sometimes shot off. This view also shows the forward facing glazed area in the early upper turret.

Above right: View through rear radio room doorway showing gunner in firing position. (Sgt Frank Kimotek, 'Hells Angels', 303rd BG).

Right: Installing the strike camera in the well beneath the radio room. Camera could be fitted either internally or externally. ('Short Stuff', 390th BG).

aware that we were going through flak by seeing the black puffs in the sky; I never heard them. The intercom also kept me informed of the situation and all the members of our crew knew it was important to let the others know what was going on; we respected each other and had complete faith in every man to do his job. As I never closed the radio room doors I could see the waist gunner to the rear and also through the bomb bay into the cockpit. Right after the bombs were released I checked to see none were hung up due to a faulty release mechanism, if they were then they had to be pried loose by hand. Thank the Lord I never had to do this in combat; I did on a practice mission over the Isle of Man. Practice bombs were light and often did not trip the release mechanism, so I had to go out on the catwalk over the open bomb bay and force the release manually. All I can say of that experience is, now I know how a tight-rope walker in the circus feels.

'The Politz mission (October 7) was my

roughest. The sky was black with flak over the target. Suddenly a big hole appeared in the left wing outside my window and my radio went dead. If one believes in fate or God or luck that hole was positive proof of something. It was the size of a manhole cover. There were two types of flak shell; one burst on contact and the other was fused to explode at a specific altitude. The shell that made the hole was set for altitude and we happened to be flying below. If it had been three feet to the right it would have gone through the radio room and I wouldn't be writing this; if it had been three feet to the left it would have hit our gas tanks and our plane would have blown up. When we landed at base we all stood under the left wing looking up at the gaping hole. None of us said a word. We were amazed that we were alive.

'Despite such incidents combat did not produce the most traumatic experience of my tour. I was a member of a replacement crew and when we arrived at our base in England

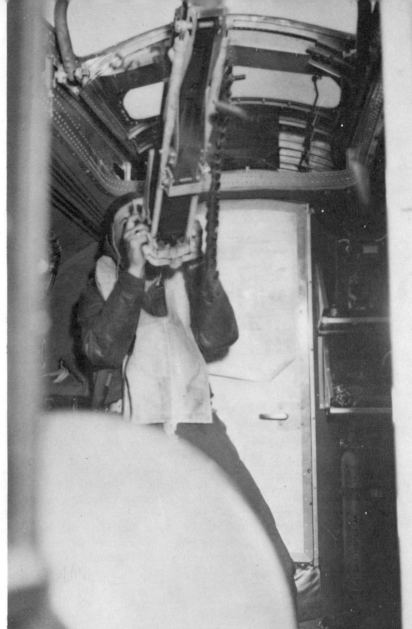

I was assigned to a hut with five other enlisted men from another crew. They were a
great bunch of guys. I think of them often.
There came a day when this crew were
scheduled for a mission that our crew was not
to fly. On that day I sat alone in the hut
sweating out the return of the mission. The
B-17 with the crew that I lived with made it
back to base with two engines shot out on the
right wing. When the pilot attempted a turn,
he lowered the right wing a little too far and
the plane spun into the ground killing the
entire crew. The next morning a corporal
from the orderly room came into the hut. He
had five black barracks bags and went from
one bed to another putting the personal
belongings of each man into the bags. Of all
the experiences I had in the service, that day
in the hut watching the corporal fill the black
barrack bags, is the most haunting. Another
group of men moved into the hut but I
never got too close with them as I couldn't
take losing another group of friends.'

Waist Gunner

William Hess

The waist windows of the Fortress provided excellent defence stations but the intricacies of flexible gunnery were such that great skill or good luck were required to obtain strikes on an enemy fighter hurtling past. Nevertheless, the waist guns were an important feature of the defence scheme for the American bombers, filling the lateral fields of approach around a formation with fusillades from the massed firepower. Waist gunners incurred a greater number of casualties than men at any other Fortress crew station. Allowing that for the most part there were two waist gunners in each crew, this unenviable record stemmed from their being the least well protected from shrapnel and bullets by the structure of the aircraft and armour protection. Also, standing at their guns, their bodies filled a larger area than was the case for the rest of the crew who were hunched in seats. Bill Hess was one of the luckier men who vouches for the exposed nature of the waist position.

'In July 1944 I joined the 340th Squadron of the 97th Bomb Group in Italy. As I was only there in the summer, living in tents wasn't that unpleasant. We did have to keep mosquito nets over our cots, though. Malaria isn't generally considered a problem in Europe but it certainly was with us down around Foggia. The base was Amendola and the area was not unlike the western part of Texas, sparse scrub vegetation and blowing sand. The runways were steel matt and boy was it rough on the planes. Every time we landed you thought the bottom was going to fall right out.

'My crew received a very brief orientation, only lasting about three days, before we flew our first combat mission. They did not have a whole lot of crews at the time; the 15th Air Force was always short of crews, aircraft and equipment. I should have been the ball turret gunner on our crew but I swopped places with the armourer gunner and after checking out in his duties started flying the left waist position. It was my job before and after each mission to look after my own gun, one of the chin turret guns and one of the cheek guns in the nose manned by the navigator. These guns had to be cleaned down and put in shape after each mission. On early B-17s waist window covers were on slide rails and had to be opened before a mission so that the guns could be swung out from their stowed positions inside the fuselage. With the open waists, gunners had to stand in an icy slipstream when at their weapons, although there was a deflector in the side of the fuselage that could be pushed out and lessened the force of this blast. Improvements were introduced in later B-17Gs. New gun mounts fixed to the inner sill of each window and incorporated in a permanently fixed plexiglass cover meant that gunners didn't have to freeze to death. Fortunately all the planes I flew in were this later type or had been modified to take the new mounts. At the same time as the new gun mounts were introduced the waist window on the right side of the fuselage was positioned further forward to stop gunners getting in each other's way. In the older B-17s with the side-by-side waist windows you had difficulty moving around without bumping the other gunner. The old types also had the intercom cords and oxygen lines hanging down overhead and it didn't take long to get in a tangle. A guy could easily lose an oxygen connection if his attention was distracted by combat and when that happened it wouldn't be long before you passed out.

'The oxygen equipment was difficult to get used to and the mask was awfully tight on your face, but it was reliable which is more than I can say for the heated suits. I know, because I burned out three in three days once. The best sort that I found were the Baby Blue Sleeper type (The F-1 model one-piece used in the early days of combat in Europe). They didn't make you look very pretty but they were darned warm and very efficient.

Below: Sgt William Hess.

Right: Waist gunners assuming firing positions in original rear fuselage design where windows were directly opposite and gunners could, in the heat of battle, get caught in each other's equipment. ('Hell's Angels', 303rd BG).

The later overall type with a little bolero were rather shoddily made and I know I had a lot of trouble with them burning out. When that happened you had to get out of that suit in a heck of a hurry and put on another before you became chilled to the bone. Normally I just wore my khakis or sun tans – as we called them in Italy – with the electric suit on top of that, and wool gaberdine coveralls to finish off. It was a very lightweight outfit and very comfortable when your heated suit worked properly.

'The fifty-calibre machine gun was a heck of a fine weapon. It was a weighty bit – about 65 pounds but not that difficult to carry. I never had any real problems with one and freezing up was not a trouble as they were fitted with efficient heaters. Firing it hand-held meant it was hard to steady. You had to lean back off the spade grips as you lined up on the ring and post sight. Of course, deflection shooting was not easy to master. When a fighter attacked it always seemed un-natural to aim between him and the tail of your own plane. But if you were going to hit him this is what you had to do because the forward speed of your plane was always added to the speed of your bullets no matter what direction you aimed. This meant that bullets would always strike forward of your point of aim. I only ever fired a few bursts in action myself for we were never under heavy attack. The only fighters encountered on my missions were usually fly-throughs by one or two aircraft which would come down, make a fast pass, do a split-S and go on down and out of our formation. By the time we got over to Italy they had decided that tracer rounds were causing more confusion than they were doing good so all that we carried was ball ammunition, armour piercing and incend-iary. The usual supply on hand was 300 rounds for each waist gun but we had extra ammuni-tion boxed near the radio room and it was one of my duties to keep the tail and ball gunner supplied if they ran short. During a mission a waist gunner did little else but wait and watch; at least you could move around whereas the ball and tail gunners were in pretty cramped conditions for hours.

'Our outfit had seen some heavy fighter attacks earlier in the year but by the time I joined them flak had become our primary opposition – and believe me they had some flak guns up there in Germany and Austria. Our intelligence officer didn't mince his words when briefing us on the strength of the batteries round Vienna; he used to say: "Well, if you guys have been up there you know what to expect. If you haven't then you ain't seen nothin' yet!" We flew a mission up there one day and were right in the middle of this flak over Vienna when all of a sudden Nos 1 and 2 engines quit. We immediately fell

External view of early waist position with gun mount inside fuselage. Forward deflector could be opened to lessen slipstream. (92nd BG).

off on the right wing, lost about five thousand feet, skidded out of one flak area into another before the skipper could trim her up on one side. What had happened was the new co-pilot flying with us that day had not kept a tight check on the fuel gauges and the usual job of transferring fuel before we reached the IP had been missed. The engineer had to go back in the bomb bay and hammer on the transfer valves until he could get the fuel through so we could get the two engines going again. We had to come back by ourselves that day and were fortunate in being able to contact the P-38 escort. Four of them played around us all the way home; it was real good to see them out there.

'The only protection the waist gunners of a B-17 had was their flak suits and helmets. Our B-17s had armour plate, curved to the fuselage contour, fitted below the waist window but it proved to be of little protection as I discovered on my last mission, September 13 1944. We were flying the deputy lead in our formation to the synthetic oil refinery at Blechhammer, near the German-Polish frontier. Apparently we were the last group over the target and those flak boys up there had got our altitude right and started tracking us and hitting real darned hard. Our plane took quite a number of hits on the left wing and we lost Nos 1 and 2 engines. A shell went into No 2 oil tank and the entire wing was covered with oil.

The auto-pilot was shot out, the bomb bay doors shot open, and we lost a complete set of controls in the tail section. My side of the waist was all blown in with holes everywhere and my plexiglass window was gone; in fact we were just about like a sieve. There was even two holes through the armour plate you could poke two or three fingers through. My flak suit and helmet saved my life. The helmet had a dent in it you could lay your hand in and the front of the flak suit was just shredded and the metal parts were falling on the floor. Everything happened so fast that afterwards my memories were rather vague. I can recall a hissing which was an oxygen line shot out over my head; and I do have a very vivid memory of looking out and seeing the sky full of debris with chutes going down in the flak. I plainly recall seeing the wing of one of our B-17s drifting down like a leaf with the props still turning.

'We were at 28 500 feet when hit and were losing a thousand feet a minute when the skipper signalled us to abandon the plane. Our squadron lost four out of the seven in the formation that day and ours was the only one that didn't blow up. Our crew all got out successfully. We were carrying an extra man that day, a special radio operator whose job was monitoring the German fighter frequencies, and he was the only one to evade capture.'

Later form of enclosed waist position with gun mount on sill. Looking from tail.

Ball Gunner

Ben H. Phelper

Sgt Ben Phelper.

Ask any man who went to war in a Fortress which was the worst crew position on the aircraft and the chances are he will immediately reply, 'The ball turret'. Indeed, this tight little glazed sphere buttoned to the underside of the fuselage needed a stout-hearted occupant, immune from claustrophobia and bolstered against the thought of being without a parachute if the aircraft was suddenly stricken. So cramped was the gunner's position that an early British assessment of the turret considered it quite untenable for long flights – there were many American airmen who would have agreed. If one had no qualms about the angle at which the world below was viewed, the ball provided an extraordinary vantage point. Ironically, far from being the most dangerous place in a B-17 as the majority thought, statistical evidence later proved it to be the safest – at least so far as battle wounds were concerned. This is explained by the huddled posture of the gunner, back against the armour plated door. Towards the end of the war in Europe, when fighter attacks became rare, there was a plan to remove all ball turrets from B-17s to save weight – substantial at 1 200 lbs plus the gunner – and add speed through reduced drag, but this was never instituted. However, in the summer of 1943 the ball turret was still a key defence point of the Fortress, and young men like Ben Phelper knew that they were likely to engage the enemy on nearly every mission.

'We had been alerted at 6.30 the night before; we had breakfast at 1.00 am and briefing at 2.00. I noticed my name was not on the blackboard with the rest of my crew. I asked my bombardier why. He said that I was grounded but if I wanted to go he would see what he could do. Certainly I wanted to go to Africa on the first shuttle raid!

'I did not know why I was grounded until Lt Zavisho told me I could go and that he had to get permission from the hospital. Then I remembered: on August 12 I had frozen my feet and passed out from lack of oxygen and been kept in hospital until the doctor was sure I would be all right. Hastening to the dressing room, I struggled with my flying equipment along with the rest, pushing, shoving and jostling in that mad scramble for equipment.

'Jumping a truck I was taken back to my hut for my oxygen mask that I had left drying after washing it the day before. I shook hands with Rude as I left; he was ill and grounded so had stayed in bed. I felt a bit more for him that the rest of the crew because it was he who had pulled me from the turret and saved my life on the 12th.

'Back to the hardstand we sped through the night. Swiftly I put my guns in the ball turret, this I did from the ground, removing a small cover each side of the turret entrance door so that I could slide the guns into their rigid mounts. Having secured the guns and given the turret a pre-flight check, I tugged on my flying clothes. Lying down I put my head on a parachute and fell asleep.

'About 5 o'clock Lt Roti, the co-pilot, startled me awake by kicking my foot. I gave the ball a last minute check and the pilot, Lt Reichardt warmed up the engines. Roti gave out the escape kits and some gum.

'All over the field the ships were warming up and the first taxied out to the runway. Bidding the ground crew goodbye and shaking hands all around we climbed aboard *Sack Time* and she moved slowly out into the ramp. As we reached the taxi strip the ground crew gave us the good luck sign.

'Plane after plane took off until it was our turn. Reichardt eased into position, jabbed the brake and revved up each engine separately. The ship next to us slid out and down the runway throwing bits of dirt, paper and grass swirling back. I climbed up on the rim of the radio hatch as we began to move.

'At first we gained speed slowly, but suddenly all four throttles were opened fully and with a breath-taking surge we sped down the strip. With the radio gun muzzle swinging in my face, wind tearing at my clothes, I thrilled and gazed about me. As we passed a jeep I saw Captain Benner (Squadron CO) standing on the far side and I waved, he waved and I motioned for him to come and he made as if to leap over the hood of the car and chase after us. After one or two long bounds we rose into the air and I slipped down into the radio room. The ship arose very slowly because we had an unusually heavy load. This trip was a long one and gas was in the regular tanks and "Tokyo Tanks" out at the end of the wings. No one cared for them; those tanks, if ever hit, would blow off the wing tips and sometimes blow up the ship itself. We gained a little altitude and at the same time began making formations.

'It was now time to load the ammunition boxes in the turret. With the guns stowed in a rearward facing horizontal position – which they always had to be for take-off and landing so that the barrels did not strike the ground –

the two covers were exposed inside the plane's fuselage. Removing the covers I fed belted ammunition into each box until each was full with about 250 rounds. Replacing the covers I prepared to enter the turret. The whole unit was suspended on a gimbal with the central tube of the structure attached to the ceiling of the fuselage. For elevation the ball hinged on the frame each side of the guns while the yoke of the gimbal pivoted giving the turret movement in azimuth. To enter, the turret had to be moved in elevation so that the guns were pointing straight down bringing the door inside the fuselage. I took the hand crank from its holding clip, fitted it to the manual shaft, shifted the elevation clutches from power to hand operation, loosened the brake with one hand while cranking the turret until the door could be swung down. Reaching inside I clutched in power operation again, removed the crank handle and returned it to its clip.

'I changed my shoes and put on my heavy flying boots. After putting my GI shoes in a parachute bag I hooked my oxygen mask on and descended into the turret, hooked in my throat mike and earphones, checked the escape door fastening and fastened my safety belt. Turning on my main power switch I swung the turret down. Everything was okay. In the turret I was hunched with my back against the armoured door and my legs bent and spread so my feet were on rests each side of the 13 inch diameter armoured glass panel, which provided my chief outlook on the world. My face was about 30 inches from this panel and suspended in between was the optical display of the computing gunsight. A pedal under my left foot adjusted the red reticles on this glass and when a target was framed therein the range was correct. In sighting I was looking directly between my feet. Two post handles projected rearwards above the sight and flexing these worked valves in the self-contained electric-hydraulic system, giving movement to the turret. In the end of each handle was a firing button for both guns and to move the turret and fire my arms were arched and my hands above my head. The whole hunched position was quite comfortable; the real trouble was that one couldn't stretch. The two Point Fifties were only a few inches away from my head and the ammunition boxes above them.

'I fixed the oxygen tube so it would not cut off my breath. Checking my rheostat on the sight, I hooked the heat cord up and settled myself more comfortably. The ground had been covered by grey fog, but viewed from up above it shone fleecy white in the morning sun with an occasional church steeple or tree poking through. Above us another layer of clouds had to be flown through and as we came

out on top Lt Reichardt kept the ball just below the top cloud for a few minutes. I could not see so I swung round to the rear. Swirling clouds made a valley formed by the slipstream.

'We had taken off about 6.15 after an hour "delay time", formed and headed for enemy territory. We turned on oxygen, checked through and when the lead ship began test-firing its guns we had reached the middle of the Channel. I heard the navigator, Lt Sullivan, say "We will reach the enemy coast at 9.15." My turret and guns were working perfectly.

'The first black puffs of flak came as we neared the Belgian coast. No one was hit although one burst raised our ship up a little and metal clanged on metal. The ship flew on with a ragged hole here and there that I could see from the ball. Back of us I could see groups of B-17s all over the sky, but never did see our fighter escort. Way down below us a B-26 outfit slipped quickly away and for a few moments nothing happened.

Below: One of Ben Phelper's sketches illustrating his last mission. This was done in Stalag XVII B and hidden from the guards.

Bottom: The 385th BG en route to Regensburg, August 17th, 1943.

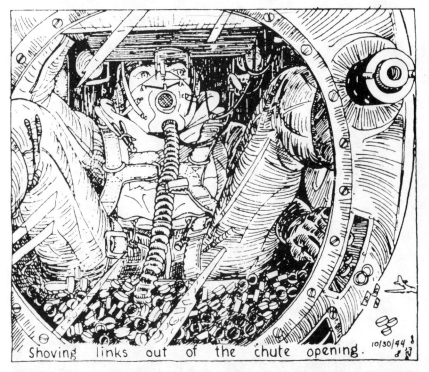

Shoving links out of the chute opening. 10/30/44

'Suddenly the interphone began to shout: "Fighters at six o'clock . . . high," "Fighters at eleven o'clock . . . level," "Two at one o'clock". It sounded as if everybody had gone crazy. I could hear them firing through the intercom. Then, zip-zip-zip . . . fighters . . . past me and diving downward and I opened fire but they were too far away.

'One of the ships behind me began belching smoke and flames. Immediately figures began hurtling from the escape hatches; leaping, tumbling and turning until suddenly they were jerked to a stop, then swung lazily back and forth suspended from snow white parachutes. I counted one, two; looked back and saw the ship turn lazily over on its side as a wing and one engine pulled off. Both wing and ship twisted out of my sight. The interphone crackled, "Fighters . . . level!" At top speed I turned my turret around just as a Focke Wulf flashed by the end of our left wing followed by six more. "Chung, chung, chung, chung, chung", my guns roared and my turret bucked. The sight bounced about – on the target, off, on, off, on again, as I fired and followed them around and down out of range.

All of them were smoking, but one had a lick of flame at his engine cowling so someone had hit him. I didn't have a chance to watch him for the interphone was humming and fighters were coming in from every direction. Fighters came in, their noses and wings blinking their little red eyes at me. Tracers flicked red trails out to meet them and my guns filled the turret with haze. The spent links from the ammunition belts scrambled and churned around the lower part of my glass. I could smell burnt powder and vaguely realized my oxygen line was leaking. My guns were red hot and the turret filled with links when the last fighter dove out of range and disappeared.

'I was wet with sweat as I swung my turret scanning the sky and giving the ship the once over. "Whew!" What a relief! No new holes; everything okay! As I gyrated slowly back and forth, from nose to left wing tip, downward, back to nose and repeat, I was shoving links out through the link chute opening. I watched another group behind us go through a black wall of flak. Two ships which had been just below me were gone.

'We droned on and ran the gauntlet of flak again a few moments later. From above a B-17 dove into my vision, fire streaming from every part of it. Nose down, pointed toward the earth and like a bursting sky rocket she exploded. Millions of pieces, fire streaming after each, swept down. I called the navigator, "Did you see that?" He answered gruffly "Yeh!" Not a chute had come out of her; it happened in the space of four or five seconds.

'More fighters came and went, more flak gauntlets were run. We were beyond the escorts' range and deep into Germany when our last battle occurred. Everyone on the ship had begun calling fighters and I had spotted eleven coming up on my left and as they reached a point about ten-thirty level the lead plane banked into us. Followed by the rest he dove at my group. I concentrated my reticles on that first fighter and pressed hard on my range finder at my left foot until the reticles were as close together as possible. As his wing tips widened into my firing range I pressed down on the fire button with my thumbs, but nothing happened. Fear shot through my brain as I glanced at the main firing switch, but it was on. Then I realised that I was aiming at those fighters through the propeller circle where firing was automatically stayed. I kept my triggers pressed and when the muzzels depressed below the circle, the guns blazed. Out and through the first one my tracers ripped and he disappeared. The second came on apparently unhit, but the one behind burst into flames and whipped underneath me followed by the rest. "Swish", I turned to fire after them and then our ship turned up her

Below: Few changes were made to the design of the Sperry ball turret on Fortresses. An idea of its compact nature can be gauged from the RAF and US airmen under this 97th BG B-17E.

Bottom: The entrance door of the turret could be lowered externally for maintenance work. Guns were installed and removed through the detachable panels located one each side of the door. T/Sgt Robert Myllykoski in turret talking to S/Sgt John H. Jessup. (B-17F 42-29900, RD:J, 306th BG).

belly. I found myself staring up at our group and they were slipping quickly away from us. Two German planes on fire were twisting between us and the formation.

'I whirled around madly. Terror hit me. Smoke was pouring away from No 2 engine. I dimly remember a huge hole in the wing. An object hurtled by me and I swung around in time to see a parachute open. I thought to myself: "Poor devil" and then noticed a fighter diving in and I fired a burst at him, another and then the ship levelled off. I saw another object pass and this time I saw it came from the escape hatch in the nose and it dawned on me the crew was baling out. "My God, they are leaving with me trapped in the ball" I thought. "What if the electric system got shot out? ? ? What if we dove straight down and I couldn't get out before she hit the ground?" This was the thing I had dreaded, made horrible nights of my sleep. In my frenzy I turned the turret into correct exit position, turned the guns down, flipped off all the switches and tried to open the clasp on my safety belt, but in my excitement I pressed my back against it and for a moment I fumbled unable to release it. Forced to my senses I relaxed. Instantly it slipped free and with no more trouble turned the escape door handles above and behind my head and pushed the door open. Without undoing my oxygen, earphones, or heater cord I stood up and this yanked them loose. I put one foot out of the turret and Mike Khoury, the radioman, must have seen my door open and made a dash for the waist. I hopped out, grabbed my chute, sat down, twisted it upside down but turned it back on seeing my mistake and snapped it on. Now that I was out of that "death trap" and had a chute on I was much relieved. As I stood up I could see most of them were okay, none seemed wounded. Cohan stood in the middle of the waist talking on the interphone, Curry was working on his gun and trying to fire. Khoury yanked the emergency release on the waist door and it fell out and swept away to the rear as Kelaher, the tail gunner, came crawling past the tail wheel.

'I glanced out of the right waist window, saw a fighter diving from four o'clock – high and grabbed at the gun waving the muzzle upward, but our ship went into a dive. I was thrown onto the ceiling and pinned by centrifugal force unable to move. I thought it was just about over, but she levelled up and I grabbed the gun. The ship was making wide circles to the left with that wing slanted down a little.

'A fighter was coming in level and behind the end of our right stabilizer. I fired through it chewing off the tip as he dove down under the ship. I poked Curry and pointed down on his side, but his gun would only fire one

shot after charging. An Me 109 dove from high up three o'clock and I triggered at him a couple of times. The gun ran away and I let go. As he passed level and on down I pushed the gun handle up and let the muzzle follow him even though I was shooting at random. The weight of the cartridges stopped it.

'How many planes I fired at I'll never know, but a Ju 88 swooped down beside us. It jockeyed and bounced; about 100 yards out from the nose of my gun. I noticed then that it didn't have a sight post at the end. I think it was gone before I grabbed the gun, but I'm not sure. As he floated into position beside us I opened up. My tracers shot through, over and under him, but he still sat there. Curry grabbed me by the arm, but I yanked away and kept on firing. He pulled me away forcibly and pointed towards the cockpit but I didn't comprehend. Turning back to the window the Ju 88 had disappeared. Cohan and Curry said he went down flaming fiercely.

'No more ships were in view and sensing something screwy I clambered around the ball and into the radio room to the bomb bay. Looking through I could not see any legs. Neither the co-pilot's or the pilot's! Then I realised – no one was flying the ship! Wow! Back I scrambled; yelling, pushing and trying to tell them to get out. Finally when I shrugged my shoulders, pointed towards the cockpit and pointed downward they understood. Khoury didn't hesitate – out he went but the others held back. I decided to go before the ship exploded. Smoke was beginning to whisk through the waist and flames were sweeping past the left waist window. Snatching my mask from my face with my left hand by the oxygen hose and making sure I had my right hand on the ripcord ring I pushed out of the door. The slipstream shoved me against the side of the door and I was yanked out. My last contact with our plane was when my boots thudded against the frame of the door. I believe it stopped me from somersaulting. As I dropped away I recall seeing the tail wheel down but it still didn't make me realise that our ship, technically speaking, had surrendered long before.

'There I hung, swinging back and forth. From roaring chaos to a beautiful world of sunshine, peace and quiet, broken only by the faraway sound of engines. Looking over my shoulder I saw my ship coming in a huge circle; smoke and flames streaming from both wings now. She turned her nose down and dove for mother earth. As I watched a huge blast came up to me and then a column of red smoke lacked with black; boiling like a volcano, changing into a pillar of black, rolling gently upward. That was the end of poor old *Sack Time*.

The Sperry computing sight used in both upper and ball turrets of the B-17F. When jettisoning the ball turret prior to a belly landing, air crew were advised to save the sight because of its cost. (306th BG).

Tail Gunner

Gerald Dial

The tail 'stinger' of the Fortress was the most important defence point on the bomber as the natural area of closure for an intercepting fighter was from the rear. Tail gunners inflicted the most telling fire on the assailants and in consequence the elimination of the tail gunner and his weapons became the first aim of the fighter pilot attacking from astern. During the great air battles over Europe during 1943 rarely did a B-17 return from a mission without the tail guns having been engaged, whereas in the final winter of the war the efficiency of Allied fighter escort made enemy interception rare and the majority of gunners never once fired their weapons at the enemy. Yet there was always the possibility that the Luftwaffe might appear with deadly account and later gunners could afford to be no less alert than earlier comrades. This is the account of one such 19-year-old's vigil in 35 long missions, usually tedious and often fearful, out of not-so-sunny Italy.

'I left the United States on September 9, 1944, with a replacement crew in a brand new B-17G bound for a combat theatre. We took off from Grenier Field, New Hampshire on the first leg to Gander, Newfoundland. Once airborne Pat O'Neil (pilot) opened sealed orders we received before departing Grenier and told us over the intercom that we were headed for Italy. We flew via the Azores, Marrakesh to Tunis, and then to Gioa, a replacement depot in Italy. There the plane was stripped of all extras including bomb-bay gas tanks, ammunition loaded on and a complete pre-flight and checkout performed. Here we were given our operational assignment which was with the 99th Bomb Group based at Tortorella, a few miles south of Foggia on the eastern side of Italy.

'We finally made our war base at ten o'clock in the morning of October 2 and spent our first day setting up six man tents in the rain, the frequent rain we were to get used to. These tents were to be our only shelter and we lived in them all through the winter months. We did our best to make them comfortable and keep out the wet and cold. Heating was from an improvised stove run on 100 octane gas. The stove was made from a 50-gallon oil barrel and the gas was piped to it underground from a storage tank outside the tent. We used discarded hydraulic lines from B-17s to pipe in the fuel. It really worked quite well though we did have some tent fires! There were a few prefab buildings around the field for headquarters and supply but officers and enlisted men alike all lived in tents. Conditions on the base were bad and it was always wet, cold and muddy. However we kept so busy we did not have time to think about this too much. The food was very poor; I went from 180lbs down to 134 while there. We found we could trade cigarettes with the Italian kids for fresh eggs and potatoes, etc, two packs being worth eight eggs or eight potatoes so a guy like me could fry some fresh food for a change.

'The field was one of several on the flat plain around Foggia. It had a corrugated steel plank main runway with a dirt strip running parallel with it on which emergency or crash landings had to be made to avoid blocking the main runway. Each revetment for parking aircraft was also corrugated steel plank. We found that the 99th shared the field with two RAF bomber squadrons which operated at night so it was quite a busy base for 24 hours a day.

'Our crew was processed on joining the 99th but we all remained together with O'Neil. "Oh-three-six", the plane we had brought in

Sgt Gerald W. Dial.

was, however, turned over to our squadron (the 348th) for the whole outfit to use. Crews were not assigned a particular plane, flying whichever were serviceable when a mission came up, although we did get to fly "036" several times during our stay. All the enlisted men on our crew had gone overseas as corporals and were now made up to sergeants. It was an air force rule at the time that we could not enter combat until at least a staff sergeant: something to do with if we were shot down and captured we would then receive better treatment.

'O'Neil's crew flew their first mission ten days after joining the 99th. The target was a troop concentration near Bologna which was bombed from 20 000 feet. We thought there was quite a bit of flak although this was really a fairly mild run in comparison to what we were to find next day over Blechhammer up on the German-Polish border, where a terrific barrage put several holes in our plane. One of the roughest and coldest we were to fly as we went over the target at 30 000 feet – the highest attack altitude of my tour – and it was 42 degrees below zero. The oil plants at Blechhammer and Vienna were the most strongly defended and we were hit by flak fragments on every occasion we visited them. If the plane was damaged on a mission over Germany or Austria there was always the worry about the 10 000 feet barrier of the

Alps. The group lost four in the Alps during November 20 mission to Blechhammer. We dropped out load of sixteen 250lb RDX high explosive from 29 000 feet. At that height the flak was very heavy but it was worse for the following B-24s who couldn't reach as high as we were. I saw two go down over the target area.

'We went back to Blechhammer again on December 2 attacking from 26 000 feet and at this lower altitude were in the midst of very heavy and accurate flak, losing a few ships from our formation. Two of the engines on our own plane were knocked out so that we had to jettison some ammunition, plus flak jackets and armour plate on the way back to get up over the Alps. I flew a further two missions to Blechhammer but on December 23 word was posted from S-2 (Intelligence) that Blechhammer had been knocked out. This gave a good feeling and something for the crews to celebrate. After each mission we were issued two ounces of bourbon to take the chill out of our bones and ease the tension a little bit. Some of it was saved up and after deals like this there was a celebration in adjoining tents.

'There was still plenty of flak at other targets. The closest shave of our tour came on February 21 when we attacked marshalling yards at Stuttgart. Shortly after we dropped our load from 27 000 feet the B-17 took a

Below left: Bomb bay of Pathfinder B-17G 44-6413, looking up at forward end shattered by direct flak hit. Doors have been blown off.

Below: Tail gunner's view as B-17Gs of the 99th BG leave Foggia in morning haze.

Bottom: Crew quarters, Italian style. Tortorella.

Below: Original tail gun emplacement featured two .5os in a tunnel type opening. The ring and bead sight was placed externally outside the gunner's window and linked directly to movement of the guns by bell crank devices. The backlash in the joints was such that it was difficult to harmonise guns and sight accurately. (S/Sgt Antoni Bednarchuk with his British pet. (303rd BG).

Bottom: The later type tail turret was more compact and had a better angle of fire. Known as the Cheyenne turret it was introduced experimentally on a number of B-17Gs passing through the modification centre at that Wyoming location prior to being introduced on all production lines. (Sgt Frank Domitz, 483rd BG).

Below right: The nose was the usual place for pin-ups but in the 15th Air Force many appeared on tails and were tolerated. (Bob Gibbs, 463rd BG).

direct hit in the bomb bay. No one was hurt and O'Neil managed to get the wreck home and land safely on our dirt runway. Damage to the plane was so extensive that it never flew again.

'There was often quite a while between missions and this was mainly due to weather. Either it was too bad so that we couldn't get over the Alps or the targets would be socked in. On one occasion we had flown clear to the Alps when we hit a front and had to turn back. This took in about six hours flight time – wasted time. We lost many B-17s while I was there and probably more through accident or bad weather than to German flak or fighters. These losses were kept from us as much as possible, if you didn't see one go you didn't know until a crew failed to show up for briefing.

'My final mission was on April 24 to Dahlburg, Austria and in contrast to most of the others it was an easy one. I had flown 35 missions as a gunner but without firing my guns in action or even seeing an enemy fighter. O'Neil's crew was lucky for the worst we suffered was a little frostbite. Even so, each mission was a long and tiring experience. H-Hour – the time they called us in the morning – was usually between 3.30 and 4 o'clock. We would dress and after chow would go down to operations for gunners' briefing. They would tell us take-off time, the altitude

we would be flying, flak and fighters to expect in the area of our route. From here we would go down to the line to pick up our equipment where we had our own bin holding a bag with our oxygen mask, parachute, Mae West and other survival equipment, binoculars and a .45 pistol. Our machine guns were also kept in the bin. From here we would be conveyed to the plane where the guns would be installed and the turret inspected with the ground crew. Then it was waiting around for the flare from the tower signalling the mission was go or scrubbed.

'On take-off all the gunners in the rear of the ship would assemble in the radio room. There were two reasons, it was the safest place if there was a crash, and it also moved the weight nearer the fulcrum of the plane making control easier for the pilot during take-off and climb. Once in the air we would go back in the waist and start dressing for altitude. To prevent frostbite we wore silk socks and gloves. Over our GI longhandles (wool combinations) we wore our heated electrical suit and on top of that a sheepskin flight jacket and trousers. Fleece-lined helmet and flying boots completed the kit and finally the parachute harness and Mae West were strapped on. Combat positions would then be assumed and I would go back and climb round the tail wheel, taking my parachute with me. In the turret I would plug in my

heated suit, oxygen and intercom. The gunner took a kneeling position: there was a seat to sit on but your knees rested on padded supports and your legs were doubled back under your buttocks. The seat was about a foot higher than your leg rests. It did get rather uncomfortable after long periods although I would partially stretch my legs in front of me by manoeuvring around, but a bigger man couldn't accomplish it.

'The two guns which were manipulated by hand were mounted on a tripod arrangement. The back plate of the point fifties had a spade grip and you could control and fire the guns with both or either hand. Most of the B-17s I flew in had late type turrets with a little more room and much more plexiglass so your range of vision was improved. The main advantage was that it gave you a few degrees more coverage with your guns both horizontally and vertically. The old type had a ring and bead sight outside the turret moved through linkage to the guns: in the new turret we got an electric sight (N-8) which was a great improvement. Box shaped, about five inches square, it illuminated a red circle with a central dot when switched on. Using this type it was both easier and quicker to line up on a target. The ammunition ratio was five armour piercing to one tracer, in the belts of 250 rounds for each gun and stored in boxes on each side of me.

'By 8 000 feet I had checked my equipment and reported to the bombardier that everything was AOK – he was the gunnery officer on the crew. The group would by this time have assembled over the Adriatic and I could test fire the guns with a short burst into the sea before the formation began its climb to clear the Alps. From here on it was observe formations, if there was no undercast report any unusual ground or water traffic that could be seen, as well as watching for any unidentified aircraft. Early in February 1945 O'Neil's crew became a leadcrew and we often flew the "Mickey Ships", which were distinguished from other B-17s by being painted grey. I then had the extra job of reporting to the flight deck the positions of our wing planes and if we were keeping a good tight formation. I was the only man who could see each and every plane in the group and it didn't take long to discover who were the good pilots and who were just so-so.

'Flying in the tail was not bad although there was quite a lot of up and down movement when the pilot worked the rudder and elevator controls. In some cases it could be very extreme and throw you off balance, so you learned to clamp your legs back around the seat and ride it out. You got so that you moved with the plane as if you were part of it. Can't say it was lonely as we talked on the intercom and checked visual sightings and so forth as I was in contact with the crew all the time. The rear of the plane was the coldest part and my only real problem in 35 missions was when my heated suit went out on the Christmas Day mission in 1944. Going to the target wasn't so bad as the sun was shining into my position, but coming home I was in the shade and began to get mighty cold indeed. It was on this mission that we picked up the ETO radio beaming Bing Crosby singing White Christmas and O'Neil plugged it into the intercom. I was a very blue GI in another sense for a few minutes.

'There was a fine view from the tail position, especially when conditions were good and you could see the beauty of the Alps. The most spectacular sight I had during my tour was during the big drive in the Po Valley in April 1945. Visibility was good and when I looked down it seemed that everything was on fire on the ground. Through my binoculars I could actually see tanks and trucks moving through the smoke and flame. A more unnerving sight when nearing a target was to look down and see flashes of the flak guns as they fired at us.

'In none of the planes I flew was there armour plate in the tail, as the weight made the ship hard to control. Instead I had a flak vest and helmet. The vest covered the chest area and the back down to my waist, the helmet was similar to the pot worn by ground troops. However, both were so heavy and uncomfortable that you generally only put them on from the IP to the target. Also, the thinking among gunners was how they were going to get out of flak vests and get a parachute on in an emergency. I always made a point of keeping my 'chute just behind my right foot so it was easy to reach. When a plane went out of control there was very little time to get to the escape hatch, a small door under the right stabiliser. This had an emergency release; jerk the lever upwards and out came the hinge pins, then you could kick the door loose with no problem. I only made use of that door on the ground as it was easier to remove the tail guns through it than clamber over the tail wheel well.

'There was always relief after leaving the target area and also after we had re-crossed the Alps and come down to 10 000 feet where we could go off oxygen. After landing and reporting to Intelligence we would clean and oil our guns – quite a job as they were hard to clean – and then return them to the store. After that back to the squadron for bourbon and chow. It was often a 14 hour day. My respect and admiration for the B-17 grew with each hour in the air. It could take a terrific beating and still fly. I still feel it was the greatest plane of its time.'

She sure was Rugged

B-17G, 42-31779, of the 379th
BG after a collision with
another Fortress. (May 24th
1944).

Below: Right stabiliser completely severed, rudder jammed, B-17G, 42-39789 of the 379th BG made a normal landing at base.

Right: B-17G 42-31855, of the 97th BG damaged by cannon fire over Styer, Austria.

Bottom: Flak burst under bomb bay over Berlin, March 6th, 1944: three men killed. (M/Sgt J W. French).

Above: A cannon shell hole large enough for Crew Chief T/Sgt A. T. Dykes to poke through. (Berlin, March 6th, 1944).

Centre left: A direct flak hit nearly severed the fuselage of B-17G 42-38078 (2nd BG) but it held together until the bomber landed.

Bottom left: Cannon fire from an Me 262 did this wing damage. (390th BG, March 3rd, 1945).

Keeping 'em Flying

George Cuda

'There was no such thing as regular hours for a B-17 ground crew; you worked until your plane was fit to fly and often you could only eat and catch a little sleep while it was out on a mission. You knew that a lot of guys' lives might depend on how well you did your job; if the plane never came back you didn't want to feel it might be because of something you hadn't done. I'd say the mechanics in my outfit were a dedicated bunch; they knew the dangers the flyers faced and saw to it that the B-17s were in good shape.

'The engineering section of a bomber squadron had two officers and around a hundred enlisted men. The officers had a hut on the technical site from which they and the specialist engineers worked. Out on the squadron dispersal the line chief was in charge and he had three flight chiefs, 12 crew chiefs and 48 mechanics. A crew chief with his four mechanics looked after one B-17 when my group, the 398th, was first formed, but later, after we moved to England, they raised the number of aircraft in a squadron from 12 to 18 so six more crew chiefs were needed and the number of mechanics on each B-17 was cut to two or three. The rest of the engineering personnel were electrical, instrument, sheet metal and propeller specialists and they worked as required on all the B-17s of the squadron.

'I was flight chief for C Flight of the 600th Bomb Squadron and, like the line chief and most crew chiefs, a Master Sergeant, which was as high as an enlisted man could get in squadron engineering. My job was to oversee work on B-17s of my flight and deal with any technical problems the crew chiefs had. Actually I did a lot of work on the planes, standing in for my mechanics. The one thing they hated having to do was kitchen duty down at the Mess Hall and sometimes, if I wasn't busy, I'd stand in for them during the day. I was back around 6 o'clock to work on any problems they were having on the line.

'Our hardstands were around two miles from the Mess Hall and I had to go even further to my billet, which wasted a lot of time. Finally, I built myself a shack out of old wood bomb boxes, just off the dispersal among some trees, so that I could live and sleep near my work. Eventually two other guys who had had enough of tracking back and forth to the camp moved in with me. We collected our own store of food from the mess and cooked it in our shack.

'The boys put in a lot of hours and to keep them happy I used to take a couple of jerry cans and go off across the fields to the nearest pub and bring back nine gallons of beer. Major Weibel, the CO, knew about this and didn't mind as he never had much cause to complain about our work.

'The weather could be rough out there on dispersal and you were pretty exposed. I think fog was the worst but we did get a lot of snow and ice during the winter of '44-'45. If you were working on the plane the weather didn't really trouble you; the clothing was good and warm and we could rig a canopy over a stand if it was raining. We also had portable generators and good lights for working at night. Once we had a German plane strafe the field and shoot out our lights, damaging the plane my mechanics were working on. No one knew there was a raid on because although Operations would telephone a raid warning to the clerk's hut on dispersal; if we had an engine running and no-one in the hut, the 'phone wasn't heard. We tried to get a Tannoy fixed after that.

'When the planes returned from a mission a crew chief would get the pilot to make out the Form 1A on any troubles or damage to his plane. If there was a major defect to rectify then the crew chief would put a red cross in the status column on this form. If the plane was flyable but not perfect then a red diagonal would be marked; a red dash meant that an inspection had not been carried out yet. Then the crew chief and his men would set to work. If they were lucky there were only normal maintenance checks to carry out and they could be through in a few hours. If the plane had any mechanical trouble or battle damage they might have to work all night to get the plane in shape for the next mission. Most nights some crew was out on the line.

'The engines and their accessories had to be in peak condition and the turbos, magnetos

M/Sgt George Cuda.

and plugs were carefully checked. Tyres were another item that had to be closely inspected after every landing to see there were no cracks or bad burns. With heavy battle damage it wasn't always possible to get the plane ready for the next mission. Holes in the skin could be fairly easily patched by the sheet metal men but if we had damaged flaps or control surfaces these usually had to be replaced.

'When a mission was planned Group Operations would call us and say how many planes they wanted us to put up. This was usually around the early hours of the morning and from then on we had to be pre-flighting the aircraft to warm up engines. Ordnance people would truck in bombs and ammunition and load up while we worked on the plane. The gas wagons would come round to top up the tanks to the required number of gallons. On long trips the full 2 800 was put in and that kept the fuel boys busy around the base filling every B-17 going on the mission.

'When the flyers arrived at the plane the ground crew had to be there. The crew chief would get the pilot to see the Form 1A and sign it if all was okay. He would walk round on the pilot's pre-flight check of the plane pointing out any problems they had. Some crew chiefs were a bit protective and would caution pilots who they thought were heavy-handed. Even after the planes had gone it was necessary to hang around in case any aborted and came back. We'd try and fix

it if it was something simple so they could take off again and catch up with the formation. I'd say very few aborts were due to sloppy work by the mechanics. The Group was very hot on the reason for aborts and required full details. I suppose there were a very few pilots who knowing the target was a tough flak spot would use the slightest pretext to abort. We had a few cases of co-pilots over-priming the engines when they started them so they caught fire. As they had been cautioned about this often it looked deliberate to us.

'We would get a good many Tech Orders giving modifications that were required. There had been a lot of trouble with engines burning up in flight because pilots couldn't feather the props. The tech people found out this was due to lack of oil reaching the mechanism, so a standpipe modification had to be installed and this made a hell of a lot of work. We also had to remove all the rubber de-icing boots along the leading edges of wings and tail. It was found that if these were damaged in combat they would flap about, break away and probably wrap around part of another plane in the formation.

'We did engine changes on the line with the help of a crane and I'd say we changed 150 in our squadron during a year of combat. Engine life varied quite a bit and we'd run regular compression tests on them, although once a Wright started to push an excessive amount of oil out of the breathers it was generally a

sign of wear. The heavy overloads that the engines had to meet took many hours off engine life. One of the worst jobs was removing the fuel tanks if they were damaged. They were collapsible but to get them out we had to get the smallest guy around up inside the wing to wriggle along to disconnect them. The tanks were of a jelly rubber material and the job was always a real struggle. One of the other squadrons had a B-17 backfire and blow the wingtip out while taxiing. They found that when a fuel tank had been replaced it hadn't been secured properly and had leaked fuel into the wing. The sub-depot on the technical site near the hangars did most of the heavy work like changing wing panels. They also did the engine rebuilds and instrument work we couldn't handle out on the field.

'In my opinion the best mechanics were those who picked the job up as they went along. A lot of those who passed through maintenance school never showed the same ability. They automatically got three stripes and extra pay but when it came to knowing the job they were always having to be helped out.

'Some flight and crew chiefs could pretty well fly a B-17. We had to taxi them to and from the hangar and, when a new engine was installed and had to undergo the hour and a half slow time flight before the plane was allowed to fly missions, the pilot would often take a chief along and let him fly it.

'Some B-17s would give little mechanical trouble while others always seemed to have things go wrong; you just couldn't account for it. Crew chiefs became very attached to their B-17s and there was quite a lot of competition as to who would knock up the most missions without an abort for mechanical reasons. Some wouldn't take any leave because they didn't trust others looking after their plane. The boys took it pretty hard if they lost a B-17 they had nursed for a good number of missions. When you almost lived night and day with your plane it was more than just a machine to you. I remember one of my crew chiefs, Joe Goeller, had a Fort that went 54 missions before being lost after a raid on Merseburg. He nearly cried when that '17 crashed. The next plane he had was also lost. Bob Phelps, on the other hand, had the same Fort all through the war. This was *Was It Well* and she put on 112 missions, more than any other B-17 in the 600th, but was also the only one in my flight to have aborted. Of the eight B-17s that were in C Flight, two were lost in combat, two in landing accidents and the rest survived. The whole squadron used 40 different B-17s during our stay in England, 15 were Missing in Action, eight crashed and five were left on the Continent because of heavy damage.

Nuthampstead, England, home of 398th BG. George Cuda's flight was sited on the loop hardstands at the inner side of the outer perimeter track, nearest the small wood. Living quarters were in the maze of roads visible in the far righthand corner.

Left: Knowledge of metal fatigue was rather limited in WW 2 but towards the end machines such as this fluoroscope were in use at air depots to X-ray components.

Above: Refueling 'Boomerang' (B-17E, 41-9148, 92nd BG). A fully laden Fortress had a healthy thirst to quench; over 400 gallons an hour climbing to altitude and 200 cruising to the target.

Centre right: PULLING HER APART. In 1942 and 1943 a shortage of parts led to the 'cannibalisation' of any B-17 that crash landed. Here B-17F 42-3085, QE:N, 94th BG, is gradually dismembered.

Bottom right: 'Hangar Queen' with very little left but the centre section (Nuthampstead 398th BG).

Prang

Tom Wrigley

Wreck of Z9:A – the broken radio room shows in this view. Forward of port wing is one of the dinghies.

The law of gravity being what it is, the several tons of metal and other materials that constitute an aeroplane can return to earth with violent contact when things go wrong. If one had to be in a crash, the Fortress was a good aircraft to be in as it held together better than most. After a controlled crash-landing both men and bomber would often fly again and even in many uncontrolled reunions with the earth men survived the wreck. There were, sadly, situations where the chances of coming out alive were remote. This is a story of such a situation,

'The morning was bright, crisp and not at all unpleasant, I thought, for flying the first operational sortie of my Royal Air Force service. I had been posted to Wick, near the north-east tip of Scotland a few weeks before, having recently completed my advanced training as a pilot. My new posting was No 519 Squadron, a meteorological unit recently equipped with Fortresses. Having never flown anything larger than the twin-engined Oxford and Anson trainers it was a big step for me, particularly as this first operational flight was also to serve as my first training flight in a Fortress. I only had one opportunity to familiarise myself with the cockpit layout and receive a few tips from experienced hands before this occasion. Admittedly, at this stage in the war – the date was January 31, 1945 – there was little danger of

Tom Wrigley joined the RAF in 1940, serving in fighter operations units before being accepted for training as a pilot in 1944.

encountering enemy aircraft, although we were armed and carried gunners just in case of the remote possibility that we should encounter a long-range raider from Norway.

'In any case, I could not have been in better company that morning for the Fortress was being flown by the "Gen Crew", made up of men recognised as the most experienced and proficient in the Squadron. Flt Lt "Bluey" Humphries, an Australian, was captain of the aircraft and Flg Off George Pullen, a Yorkshireman, his No 2. As the third "dickey" on this trip, I positioned myself just behind them where I was in a good position to study control procedures.

'We took off at 0900 hours and set course over the bleak but beautiful scene below, the wild hills and moors of Caithness lapped by the icy North Sea. Our ten hour flight would take us beyond the Orkneys and Shetlands to the Arctic Circle and back, ranging through heights from sea level to 25 000 feet. The code name for this operation was "Recipe II", the second of two such flights north that the Squadron aimed to undertake every twenty-four hours. The Squadron also had to undertake daily met' flights in a southerly direction as far as the north Norfolk coast and these were known as "Rhombus I" and "II".

'The Weatherman – a Flight Sergeant – in the nose of our Fortress *A-Able* began taking readings from special apparatus attached just outside the right starboard nose window. At varying heights he reported data to the Wireless Op' who transmitted it to base where the work was done on preparing up-to-the-

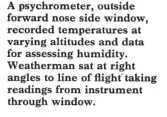

A psychrometer, outside forward nose side window, recorded temperatures at varying altitudes and data for assessing humidity. Weatherman sat at right angles to line of flight taking readings from instrument through window.

The two port engines of Z9:A have broken away.

minute weather forecasts for use in planning combat operations. These two men were busy all the time but for the three gunners the trip must have been one of prolonged monotony. After a while I was allowed to take over the controls from one or other of the pilots while they had a break. To my comfort I found the Fortress was a very gentle old lady to fly and no problem for the novice. I was quite enjoying the trip. As the morning wore on we began to meet the odd snow flurry until we climbed well above the oxygen-on level. The temperatures outside were extreme and the weather was generally deteriorating.

'Some 700 miles out we reached the outward limit of our sortie and turned on the home leg in a gradual descent, the weatherman continuing to give regular readings from his instruments. Soon after that I became aware that the pilots were having trouble with the superchargers and eventually two ceased to function, resulting in a loss of power. In my position behind the pilots' seats I had no intercom and therefore could not hear the conversation between the rest of the crew. I realised the pilots were a little concerned with the situation as I was no longer invited to take a turn at the controls. To add to their problems ice kept forming on the leading edges of the wings and tailplane, now and then breaking away in lumps.

'As it started to get dark and we were still some three hours away from base the snow became almost continuous, streaming back over our cockpit. We were now flying com-pletely blind, relying on instruments and our Gee Box. Watching the altimeter it appeared that we were losing height faster than the pilots would have liked. They were quite calm but something about their intent manner made me feel a trifle apprehensive in spite of the confidence I had in them.

'At last my watch showed that we must be approaching home ground and this was confirmed when the weatherman and navigator came up out of the nose and pushed by me on their way back to join other crew members in the wireless room. The pilots had obviously advised them we were approaching the airfield when it was usual for everyone except the pilots to gather in the wireless room, warmest and supposedly safest part of the aircraft.

'The darkness of the cockpit was relieved only by the green glow from the instrument panel and the white mass of snow sweeping incessantly onto the windscreen. I guessed the conversation "Bluey" and George appeared to be having was with Flying Control at Wick; perhaps we were going to be diverted to another airfield. Not being connected to the intercom gave me a rather lonely feeling. I leant back against the turret supports and looked out at the windscreen wipers straining against the oncoming blizzard. We must be somewhere out over the sea preparing our landing approach.

'CROINCH! The Fortress shuddered: there were brilliant flashes outside the window: I was pitched forward. During the silent

On the right hand side of this photograph the markings 'Help 4 Alive' can be seen marked in the snow. (There were actually 5 alive then). The word 'Fags' can also be seen, apparently a request to the search aircraft that located the survivors.

hiatus that followed the thought flashed through my mind that we had bumped into another aircraft in the snow clouds and were falling from the sky. It was only momentary for again CROINCH, my world spun round. With no securing straps, for a second or two I must have bounced around like a ball between the back of the pilots' seats and the turret structure. The rending torrent of noise ceased abruptly and I heard the skipper shouting for "everybody out". As I pulled myself up he and George Pullen were forcing open their side windows. A quick call to see if I was all right and they squeezed through dropping silently out of sight. I followed Pullen and fell, landing in slush and bog up to my thighs. It was pitch black, cold and the falling snow whipped into my face. An icy hell in retrospect but at the time the discomfort was as nothing compared to the fact that I was somehow alive. Recovering from the initial shock and waiting a few minutes until satisfied there was no sign of fire, Flg Off Pullen climbed back into the cockpit and brought out a flare pistol. He shot several signal flares in the hope that they might attract anyone in the vicinity. As the flares arched up into the darkness they illuminated the scene and we could see that the rear portion

of the Fortress lay some yards away on its side. The first impact had broken the fuselage in two just behind the wing and through the wireless room where the six other members of our crew had been. All was still and as our eyes became accustomed to the gloom we started looking for survivors, a difficult task as each step might immerse one in snow and slush up to the waist. Eventually we found two of the others, both badly injured. We got parachute silk and carefully wrapped around our injured men, putting them in dinghies that had automatically ejected and inflated in the crash. We pulled these under the shelter of the wreckage and did what else we could to make the men comfortable. A further exhaustive search failed to locate the others but from the way the radio room had disintegrated we felt they must be dead.

'We decided to spend the night in the broken rear section of the aircraft in case something in the wing section was smouldering and the fuel tanks might suddenly catch fire. I don't think any of us got much sleep. It was a wild night and the gale constantly rattled the torn metal of the fuselage. Perhaps we pilots had time to reflect on our miraculous escape and say our own little private prayers of thanks; we had crashed blind and unsus-

pecting into hilly ground. The other two were held by their seat belts and apart from the shock of the incident were unharmed. I was badly knocked about and had a painful foot yet amazingly there appeared to be no broken bones.

'When morning came a desolate scene was revealed; snow as far as the eye could see with no sign of habitation. Our injured men were still alive but Flt Lt Humphries went on a search and reported back that he had found the four other crew members all dead. We imagined we must be somewhere in the hills near our base but it would have been imprudent in the conditions to set off walking. The skipper also retrieved the Gibson Girl portable wireless (so called because of its shape) from the wreckage; we flew the kite aerial and took turns to crank the handle to send out the automatic distress signal. From the dinghy kit we took a dye marker pack and spread this around making patches of fluorescent green on the snow. It was also used to mark out a message "HELP 4 ALIVE" in the event of a search aircraft coming. We were not to be disappointed, our signal had been picked up by a Spitfire searching along the coast. Some time later the sound of engines reached us and a Warwick flew directly overhead to drop a canvas bag of supplies; hot cocoa, oranges and so on. To our dismay the parachute failed to open and the bag plunged into the deep snow. We managed to retrieve it but the flasks were smashed. Shortly afterwards distant figures could be seen approaching and these turned out to be a crofter, Mr Sutherland, with his son and his dog. They had heard our Fortress pass low over their cottage the previous night and then the crash. The hot tea and whiskey they brought were very welcome, even more so was the relief in knowing that somebody knew where we were. Around 1 o'clock the mountain rescue team reached the wreck. It was a relief to see among the rescuers the familiar face of "Doc" Gossip, our station MO who, after a quick word with us went off to tend the injured. Then they put the injured on sledges – sadly they later died in hospital – and took us all down to the crofters' cottage. By this time I was stiff and sore from my bruises, and suffering delayed shock, so I got a sledge ride too. We had crashed near Loch Rangag, about 12 miles south-west of Wick, and somehow hit a 700 feet high hill in a slightly nose up attitude.

'A few weeks later I made my second Fortress sortie. I am, however, never likely to forget the circumstances of my first.'

Do 200

On December 12, 1942, 21 B-17Fs of the 303rd Bomb Group took off from Molesworth, England for a mission to the Rouen Sotteville marshalling yards in north-west France. The Group was still very much a freshman unit and this, its sixth operation, proved to be a painful experience. Separated from other formations, it was set upon by an estimated 30 fighters and attacked all the way from Beauvais to the target. During this battle one bomber was shot down in flames and shortly thereafter aircraft 41-24585, better known as *Wulf Hound*, was seen to drop out of formation, steadily lose height and disappear into clouds. Returning crews reported that

this Fortress was fatally stricken. In fact, beneath the clouds the pilots of *Wulf Hound* were able to make a wheels down landing on a French field, presenting the Germans with their first intact example of the redoubtable bomber that had been making frequent penetrations of continental air space during the past four months. The prize was of particular value in that it allowed the Luftwaffe to develop tactics against *Wulf Hound*'s kin, apart from revealing full details of performance and equipment.

With the American stars replaced by German crosses, 41-24585 went to the Luftwaffe flight test station at Rechlin and was later

Right: 'Wulf Hound', the first flyable B-17 captured by the Germans.

Right: The second B-17F obtained by the Luftwaffe photographed at Orly late in 1943.

Below: 'Phyllis Marie', after her landing near Brandenburg, being inspected by Luftwaffe officers.

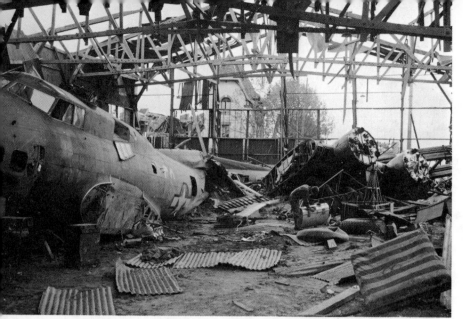

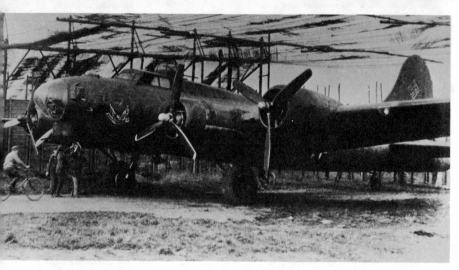

Top: The remains of a
390th BG B-17G, one of three
being cannibalised for parts
by the Luftwaffe in hangars
at Orly and found by Allied
ground forces.

Above: KG 200's B-17G at
Hildesheim. The aircraft is
known to have flown several
supply dropping sorties to
beleaguered German Forces
on the French coast during
the winter of 1944-45. It is
believed to have been
destroyed during the transit
flight of April 6th 1945.

demonstrated to most fighter Gruppen in the Reich and in France. After further trials with a fighter tactics unit, the aircraft was ferried from Rechlin to Berlin-Rangsdorf on September 10, 1943. Here it joined I/KG200, the most secret of all Luftwaffe combat organisations, which was engaged primarily in ferrying and supplying agents in enemy territories.

The nature of I/KG200's commitment was so tightly guarded that many of the ground personnel were unaware of the nature of the operations they sustained. A varied number of types were employed by I/KG200, including large transports such as the FW200 and Ju290. To facilitate clandestine missions, the Gruppe had a small collection of aircraft captured from Germany's enemies to which the B-17 was a useful addition. In keeping with its new role the Fortress received a cover name, Do 200, a non-existent type designation.

The Fortress proved very popular with pilots having to undertake special missions over Allied territory as it was able to pass as just another ubiquitous B-17. Efforts were made to obtain other airworthy Fortresses from the many brought down, but even machines that belly-landed were generally

beyond repair as on impact the ball turret support frame broke through the tail spine seriously distorting the fuselage. However, another intact example was acquired in 1943 and a further chance came during the second major American air raid on Berlin, March 8, 1944. One of three bombers lost by the Framlingham based 390th Bomb Group was 42-30713 *Phyllis Marie*, which was seen to go down under control with several crewmen bailing out. Some minutes later *Phyllis Marie* made a wheels down landing in a large field where one undercarriage leg ran into a drainage ditch. The Luftwaffe were delighted for, apart from a bent propeller on No 2 engine, they had another little-damaged B-17F. This aircraft soon appeared in the ranks of I/KG200 with German insignia. But strangely, in spite of the hundreds of B-17 wrecks in German hands a replacement propeller was not obtained and a German make of slightly smaller diameter was fitted.

Soon afterwards the Luftwaffe acquired an early B-17G in flyable condition and by early May 1944 I/KG200 had three Fortresses on strength. Although the headquarters of the organisation was variously at Berlin-Rangsdorf, Finow and Berlin-Finsterwalde during 1944, operations were carried out by detachments operating at forward airfields on all fronts. B-17s used for sorties over the Balkans flew from Weiner-Neustadt, and an airfield near Bordeaux was used for an agent-dropping flight to Ireland. The most successful of I/KG200 operations with Fortresses took place in the spring of 1944 when one, rigged out with extra fuel tanks, flew from Marseilles to the Algerian desert where a chain of secret landing grounds and fuel dumps were established. In October 1944 a B-17 flew from Athens-Kalamaki to drop agents in Transjordan.

In the face of Allied airpower, I/KG200's activities in the West became expectionally difficult. However, the Gruppe is only known to have lost one B-17 during operations, this – believed to have been engaged in supply dropping missions to German forces beleaguered at Brest – was shot down at night near Frankfurt by a Mosquito. At the turn of the year the weight of Allied bombing was producing such havoc to industry and communications in the Reich, that the captured B-17s were to be utilized in a plan to disrupt the US bomber bases.

Since early 1943 US bomber aircrew had often reported strange B-17s during combat missions and it was accepted that the Luftwaffe was using captured examples to pace US formations and direct fighter attacks. There is, however, no evidence to substantiate this and Luftwaffe fighter commanders have pointed out that such a practice would have been far too dangerous with the risk of German-crewed B-17s being shot down by their own side. Indeed, most of the strange B-17s reported during that time were aircraft that had become detached from their own formations and were seeking protection of another. Now, in January 1945, a plan was put into action whereby the captured B-17s of I/KG200 would try to join 8th Air Force formations returning from missions, fly with them to their base and then attempt to shoot down B-17s in the landing pattern.

One of the pilots for this ambitious operation was Unteroffizier Schubert, who was introduced to the B-17 at Burg airfield near Magdeburg early in January. After cockpit familiarisation and a short briefing, he undertook a 5 hour training flight to gain experience, taking the aircraft up to 20 000 feet. He found it surprisingly easy to fly compared to the He177 and FW200, which demanded constant attention at the controls and likened its stability to driving a bus. Schubert took part in two of these daylight intruder missions which apparently had to be abandoned after the US formations became suspicious. Flying with false American insignia the crew were understandably apprehensive about being captured fearing that, in these circumstances, they would be executed.

It is possible that it was one of these occasions that Lt James W. Johnson, an 8th Force B-17 pilot, witnessed returning from a mission. 'Our squadron had reached the vicinity of the German coast when we noticed a lone B-17 off to one side, some distance away. As we progressed it began to edge in towards us and at first we assumed it was a straggler from another group. Something didn't look right, it seemed to have an odd colour. Our squadron leader tried to call up the stranger over the radio; we could hear him call but he got no response. Our leader then became very suspicious and came on the radio to tell us to have our gunners bear onto this stranger. So every gunner in our outfit who could, lined up on him. The pilot, whoever he was, must have understood the message because almost immediately he started to pull away from us and kept going. From his behaviour we believed this Fort was enemy-operated.'

By the spring of 1945 I/KG200 had its aircraft at Hildesheim, secreted away from Allied attack under camouflage structures. Advancing Allied armies soon threatened this base and I/KG200 prepared to move. The three B-17s and a lone B-24 they held were to take-off at first light on April 6 and fly at low level to a destination in Bavaria. The crews felt the trip would be extremely hazardous; while flying at low level gave a better chance of eluding Allied fighters, there was a grave risk

of being shot down by small arms fire from German troops believing the bombers to be enemy-operated. With the breakdown of communications it was impossible to ensure all ground units along the route could be warned in time. These fears were well founded, because one B-17 was shot down killing the crew; another hit a fog shrouded hill in the Thureinger Wald, and the B-24 had to make a forced landing due to flak damage. Only one B-17 survived and landed at Altenburg south of Leipzig.

This Fortress was still reposing there when, just over two weeks later, the US 1st Army captured Altenburg. The GIs were surprised to see the familiar shape amongst the many German aircraft on the landing ground. They were curious about the nickname *Phyllis Marie*, the accompanying 35 mission symbols and six swastikas recording her American service that her more recent operators had allowed to remain on the nose. Inside they found wooden bracing to take a portable floor in the bomb-bay and bloodstains in the fuselage waist, but no other clues to the extraordinary service this old lady had given for her erstwhile enemies.

In KG 200 service the B-17G had mottled night camouflage. Motif is of Luftwaffe origin.

Odd Forts

Left: YB-40 was the designation given B-17Fs modified as escort gun ships with additional armament. Apart from twin .50s in the waist positions and an extra power turret over the radio room, the YB-40 was fitted with the first Bendix 'chin' turret. An operational trial with the 8th Air Force in summer 1943 proved these aircraft to be of little value in defending formations. (42-5741, UX:H, 92nd BG).

Left/below: The mass of autographs on these two Fortresses signifies something special. Boeing workers adorned the Seattle plant's five thousandth B-17. Later 'Five Grand' served with the 96th BG in England and survived combat to return to the USA. 'Hell's Angels' was the first British-based Fortress to complete 25 missions and after 48 was sent home carrying the inscriptions applied by men of the 303rd BG.

Top right: Glide bombs, basically 2 000lb bombs with wings and empennage, were an attempt to hit targets without penetrating their flak defences. Success was dependent on calm conditions, rarely encountered over north-west Europe and after use against Cologne rail yards in May 1944 the scheme was abandoned. A B-17 carried one glide bomb on each external wing rack. (303rd BG).

Centre right: The 8th Air Force's Night Leaflet Squadron operated black painted B-17s for dispensing propaganda material over enemy and occupied territory during darkness. Although converting to B-24s in the autumn of 1944, a few B-17s were retained. 'Tondalayo' was the last and came to grief in a British 'ack-ack' barrage during a flying bomb attack. The Squadron CO, Major Aber was among the crew that perished.

Below: A cargo far removed from the normal. Food packages going into 'Bomb Bay of Blues' for the April 7th, 1945 supply mission to aid starving Dutch civilians. (43-38285, H, 493rd BG).

Above: The Fortress
returned to the Pacific war
in 1945 in the role of life
saver. The 6th Emergency
Rescue Squadron used B-17Gs
with radar search units
under the nose and
parachute lifeboats attached
under the bomb bays. (Luzon
June 1945).

Centre left: General George
Kenney had such a liking for
the B-17 that he retained one
as a personal transport after
Fortresses were withdrawn
from combat in the Pacific.
His last was B-17G, 44-83477,
seen here at Yotan airstrip,
Okinawa, near the end of
hostilities. The crew take
shade beneath the wing. Note
embossed plate carrying
Kenney's four star rank!
There were also curtains at
the waist windows.

Bottom left: Known as 'The
Spotted Cow' this war-
weary B-17F (42-3441) served
the 384th BG as formation
'assembly ship', tow-target
plane and general hack.
Colour scheme was white
with blue polka dots.

Photo Credits

J. Archer: 62 (T), 84 (T), 84 (C), 185 (B), 186
Australian Official: 34
R. Besecker: 8, 30 (lower inset)
Boeing: 11 (inset)
British Official: Title page, 12, 13, 14 (B), 15, 111 (B), 170 (T)
P. Chryst: 167 (C)
Via S. Clay: 10, 26, 32, 77 (T)
Columbia: 6, 190
Via T. Cushing: 23 (B), 181
Via G. Collins: 76 (B)
G. Cuda: 161
G. Dial: 97 (CR), 148, 149
Via T. Danby: 16, 19 (T), 28, 29
F. Domitz: 150 (BL)
S. Evans: 118, 184 (T)
J. Fletcher: 116, 117
R. Gibbs: 109 (TR)
Via W. Girbig: 20 (L), 91 (CR), 179 (lower inset)
J. Harlick: 108 (B), 109 (TL), 154 (lower inset)
W. Hess: 140
E. Huntzinger: 80 (TL)
Imperial War Museum: 17, 18
K. Kössler: 180 (BL), 181
D. Knight: 100, 101, 102, 103

V. Maslen: 48, 97 (TR)
J. Minahan: 120, 121
M. Osborn/V. Jenkins: 110 (B), 164 (T), 165, 167
B. Phelper: 144
Public Archives of Canada: 30, 30 (inset), 168 (inset)
J. Rabbetts: 171 (top)
B. Robertson: 170 (BR), 171 (C), 171 (BL)
Royal Netherlands Air Force: 39 (TR)
Via K. Rust: 125 (BL)
R. Sturges: 87 (B)
USAF: 46, 76 (C), 81 (B), 88, 89, 90, 91 (T), 91 (CL), 91 (B), 98, 110 (T), 111 (T), 111 (C), 121, 154, 156, 158 (TL), 158 (B), 159 (B), 164 (BL), 166, 182, 184 (T), 184 (B), 185 (T), 185 (C)
USAAF: 21 (BR), 36, 38, 42, 45 (B), 53, 56, 58, 59, 74, 76 (T), 78, 96, 97 (B), 122, 123, 124, 125 (TL), 141, 142, 143, 145 (B), 146 (T), 146 (B), 147, 148, 152 (T), 153 (B), 154 (inset), 158 (B), 159 (T), 159 (C), 167 (T), 178, 180 (T), 184 (C), 188 (C), 188 (B)
Via T. Wrigley: 172, 174, 176, 177
11th BG Association: 43 (inset), 44

BOOK TWO

B-29 SUPERFORTRESS
AT WAR

This book is dedicated to the kids who were
there, and to the grown-ups who remember

The bombs are 500lb incendiary clusters; the bombers are the B-29s of the 98th Bomb Wing, over the target in North Korea. / *USAF 78774 A.C.*

CONTENTS

Acknowledgements

A-44 from the 871st Bomb Squadron, 497th Bomb Group is parked in the early afternoon sun and is the centre of some attention from the men around her. A thermos jug, canteen, and probably some food stand in the sun near the left nose wheel. Nonchalant pilot and aircraft commander, hands on hips, socks rolled down and shorts rolled up, stand and wait at the nose of the aircraft. / *Dr Lyman C. Perkins*

The response to my original request for assistance in telling the story of the Superfortress at war was overwhelming. Some of those who answered told their experiences by letter, by telephone, on tape, or — later — in interviews. Others loaned reference material: books, unit histories, clippings, copies of *Brief* magazine. Still others loaned their priceless collections of photographs, original negatives taken during the wars, collections of colour slides. A few did all of these.

Those who helped with this work, who made it possible, then and now, are listed below:

T. H. Brewer; Jack J. Catton; James B. Cliver; Gerald Coke; Ferd J. Curtis; Eugene L. Davis; William F. Dawson; H. W. Douglas; R. A. Ebert; Fleming Fraker, Jr; Paul Friend; James J. Garrity; Robert F. Goldsworthy; George S. Gray; Haywood S. Hansell, Jr; Charles B. Hawks; Ingram T. Hermanson; Don C. Hetrick; Robert B. Hill; H. D. Hollinger; Elmer Huhta; Mrs Thomas Isley; Mike Janosko; Richard M. Keenan; Philip J. Klass; W. B. Leake; Olinto F. Lodovici; John F. Loosbrock; Prescott Martin; David W. Menard; A. F. Migliaccio; Donald L. Miller; Francis B. Morgan; Charles R. McClintick; Glenn E. McClure; Bernard J. Mulloy; Kenneth E. Neff; W. A. Pearce; Alberto R. Pearson; Dr Lyman C. Perkins; Denny D. Pidhayny; Vern Piotter; J. R. Pritchard, Jr; Del Shaffer; Murray Singer; Frederick M. Smith; Ben H. Tucker; E. L. Tyler; Roger Warren; Eric Weber; Gordon S. Williams; Fred Wolfe; Ron E. Witt; John Zimmerman.

Those who were there are further identified in the text. For their enthusiastic cooperation, I am deeply grateful.

The experiences related here, the quotations, the loaned materials are theirs; but the context, views and opinions are mine, and I'm responsible for them.

David A. Anderton

Ridgewood, NJ, USA
September 1977

Notes on the photographs

Good photographic coverage of the B-29 in action was limited by a number of factors. The island bases were really isolated; everything had to be brought in from distant supply bases, and such luxuries as camera film were rare. Fine coral dust, sand and fungus attacked cameras and film. High temperatures plagued processing. Photo labs, like all other supporting units, had heavy work loads as routine, with little time available for private and unofficial work.

The bright sunlight overpowered many of the cameras and films of the day. It produced very high contrast between the highlights on a B-29 fuselage and the shadow under the aircraft. In the amateur films, paper and processing of the day, this resulted often in chalky white highlights and black blobs of shadows, devoid of any detail.

Photography in the air was another difficult matter. The pressurised B-29 had no open hatch or window for photography. All air-to-air pictures had to be taken through a layer of glass or plastic, with their inherent distortion, internal reflections, and other deterrents to good, clear pictures.

In spite of all that, the photographs in this book require no apologies, just explanations.

During the preparation of this work, at least 500 photographs were either printed from original negatives, or copied from loaned prints, then processed and printed. Several collections of negatives were loaned by their owners, and one of them demonstrated clearly the hazards of wartime photography on the islands. Several negatives had tiny grains of coral or fine sand embedded in the emulsion.

Copies of black-and-white photos were made with a Hasselblad 500C using the normal 80mm Zeiss lens and an extension ring, or a +1 diopter close-up lens, or both. Kodak Plus-X Pan Professional film was used, processed in Kodak Microdol-X in a 1:3 dilution.

All black-and-white photos, whether copied or printed from original negatives, were printed using a Beseler 23C enlarger on Ilfospeed paper of proper contrast grade, and processed in Ilfospeed chemicals.

Several collections of colour transparencies were loaned for this book. They were copied with a Canon F-1 and Canon FL bellows on Kodachrome II Professional (KPA135) film, using an Aimes-Hershey light box. Colour processing was done by Kodak.

Special thanks are due to Dr Lyman C. Perkins, who loaned his entire collection of hundreds of documentary negatives taken on Saipan during World War 2; to then Sgt William A. Dawson, B-29 gunner in the Korean war, for the loan of his negative collection; to Vern Piotter, a navigator in both wars, for loaning his colour transparencies; to Ingram T. Hermanson, for loaning a set of colour transparencies taken on Saipan by himself and Kenneth E. Neff; and to Eric Weber, then an engineering maintenance officer in the Second Air Force, for sending his collection of outstanding, professional-quality colour slides of the B-29s and their elegant noses.

There's always something to do on the damned engines; they're older now, and they've got a lot of time on them. So two of the 343rd Bomb Squadron's mechanics scramble over the cowling, wrenches in hand, and work on the engine in the Yokota winter sunlight.

Introduction

The people who finally put the Boeing B-29 Superfortresses over targets in the Japanese home islands were pilots and file clerks, bombardiers and engineers, Rosie the Riveter and Rosey O'Donnell, and hundreds of thousands of Chinese farmers and Mao Tse-Tung.

The Chinese built the airfields in their country, the Indians in theirs. The US Naval Construction Brigades (Seabees) levelled and surfaced the Marianas runways.

The Army and the Marine Corps took the Mariana islands — Guam, Saipan and Tinian — where the B-29s were to be based. The Navy got them there, and softened the Japanese defences with shelling by warships and strikes by carrier-based aircraft.

And when the B-29 operations started, a closer liaison between the Army Air Forces and the Navy also began. The B-29s reported shipping locations and other maritime observations directly to the Navy on a secure communications channel. They flew reconnaissance missions from Guam with naval observers on board.

When the B-29 force shifted a portion of its effort to mine-laying in Japanese waters, naval mine fuse specialists assigned to B-29 units worked side-by-side with the air and ground crews.

Air-sea rescue was a joint operation that used both Army Air Forces and Navy aircraft for search and location, and Navy submarines and surface ships for pickup of crews from life rafts or sinking aircraft.

When the *Enola Gay* made her historic flight to Hiroshima, a naval officer was the first nuclear weapons specialist who went along to assemble and arm 'Little Boy', the first atomic bomb.

It was, in every sense, a joint operation all the way. True, there were high-level political moves to attempt to seize control of the B-29s, or their missions, or both. There were inter- and intra-service squabbles, jealousies, rivalries, and enmities that had to be factored in.

But at the working — and dying — level, the B-29 airmen understood that they were no more responsible for winning the war than soldiers or sailors or marines or even civilian production-line workers.

This is, properly, a book about the Boeing B-29 Superfortress in combat. For that reason, it must exclude with regret the story of the B-29 in many of its non-combat roles. There are no pictures of the B-29s that carried research aircraft aloft to their drop altitudes, no stories of weather reconnaissance flights out of northern bases during the Cold War, and nothing about the existing B-29s in museums or on flight status.

Further, this book is of finite size, and there is no way in the world that it could be, or pretend to be, the definitive history of the B-29 in combat. It took almost 400 pages in the official history of the United States Army Air Forces in World War 2 just to summarise the B-29 story in that war. This book had to be selective; the selection was the author's.

The Boeing B-29 saw combat during the closing days of World War 2, first from India and China, and later from the islands of the Mariana group. It had a brief rebaptism of fire during the Korean conflict, when Strategic Air Command and Far East Air Forces B-29s were assigned to bombing missions.

Its combat life was short, but its accomplishments were many and great. This book attempts to create the mood of those days, and to tell the story of the men and machines in the words of those who were there.

Superfortress

She was born in Seattle, grew up in Wichita, and died in the skies over Japan. She was the Boeing B-29 Superfortress, loved and hated, Queen of the Skies and an aborting bitch.

She was graceful, with a long, sleek body that caught the sun in dazzling highlights. Her wings were wide, with a gentle taper and a slimness that hinted at effortless flight. Her power lay inside four huge engine nacelles, crowding forward from the uncluttered wing, bulging with steel and aluminium and magnesium that had been alloyed and shaped into cylinders, gears, rods, cases, and twin superchargers.

She was clean, aerodynamically smooth, with countersunk rivet heads lying flush with the aluminium alloy skin surfaces. Drop the landing gear, and her drag doubled.

She spawned superlatives: highest, fastest, biggest bomb load. Slowest-turning, biggest metal propellers. Largest cowl flaps. Heaviest and longest aluminium extrusion.

And the ultimate superlative: She dropped the first — and then the second — atomic bomb.

She was the pivotal airplane in the long and difficult transition from a subservient strategic air force to an independent United States Air Force.

Let's look at her from the start.

The Beginnings

The United States Army Air Corps, as it was then, often organised boards of officers to study the needs of the growing air arm. Early

in June 1939, one such board began its deliberations with the goal of guiding future development of aircraft for the Air Corps. The board's report, issued at the end of the month, recommended among other things that several long-range medium and heavy bombers be developed during the next five years.

Late in 1939, Maj Gen H. H. Arnold sought and received the authority to let some study contracts for a very long range heavy bomber, and he gave instruction to Capt Donald L. Putt, then working in the Materiel Division at Wright Field, Ohio, to write the statement of military characteristics for the airplane.

On 29 January 1940, the Air Corps mailed its Request for Data R-40B to a number of aircraft companies. Four were to respond: Boeing, Consolidated, Douglas and Lockheed.

It took a while for the mail to get to Seattle, Washington, and the desk of Philip G. Johnson, then the president of the Boeing Aircraft Company. On 5 February Johnson read the letter and its enclosures: R-40B and Spec XC-218. They called for a proposal for the design of a bomber with a range of 5,333 miles, with more speed and bomb load than the Boeing B-17, then just entering service. And the letter asked for the designs to be submitted within 30 days.

Boeing beat the deadline with a week to spare and sent details of its proposed Model 341, a bomber that could carry 2,000lb of bombs and could fly faster than 400mph.

The exercise was not a completely new one for the company. They had been asked in March 1938 to submit ideas for pressurising the cabin of the B-17, and had begun work on two parallel studies. Design teams worked the Boeing XB-15 design into the Model 316 and altered the B-17 into the Model 322. The Boeing teams drew on that experience and forged ahead with their concepts of a heavy bomber. In January 1939, before the Air Corps had produced its own requirements,

Progenitor of the long line, the first experimental Superfortress stands in the September haze at Boeing's Seattle plant. She is officially XB-29-BO, serial number 41-002, and her lovely lines are swathed in olive drab and dark grey camouflage paint. She had three-bladed propellers, streamlined gunners' sighting blisters, and a fixed tail bumper. Her Sperry gun turrets were retractable. / *Gordon S. Williams*

Boeing had designed Model 333. It had tandem engines, tandem bomb bays, two pressurised crew compartments connected by a tunnel, and tail guns.

The design was refined further into Model 334-A, with a higher wing loading and other features that qualify that design, seen with the benefit of hindsight, as the first real ancestor of the B-29. By August, Boeing had the Model 341, with wing loadings as high as 64lb per sq ft, a 12-man crew, and the calculated ability to carry 2,000lb of bombs for 5,333 miles. Boeing was serious enough about the design to begin work on a full-sized mockup at company expense in December 1939.

By April 1940 the realities of modern war were sinking in. Early air combat in Europe at the beginning of World War 2 showed the many weaknesses of contemporary aircraft, with their conventional fuel tanks, little or no armour, small calibre machine guns. The Air Corps re-thought its needs and updated its request for proposals in a letter to the bidders: Include leakproof tanks, armour, heavier-calibre machine guns and cannon, and multiple gun turrets.

Out of this came the Boeing Model 345, powered by the new Wright R-3350 twin-row radial engines, and defended by four retractable turrets mounting twin machine guns and a tail turret with twin machine guns and a cannon. It was a pressurised airplane, capable of hauling one ton of bombs over 5,333 miles. Its maximum bomb load was to be 16,000lb. It had a 12-man crew. Its landing gear was tricycle, with double wheels all around. The wingspan was 141 feet 2 inches; length, 93 feet; design gross weight, 97,700lb. The formula was fixed, and on 11 May 1940, Boeing submitted the design for Model 345 to the Air Corps.

Later that month, Boeing and Lockheed were selected as winners of the competition, with the Model 345 considered to have the edge. The Air Corps gave it the XB-29 designation, and named Capt Putt as project officer. Lockheed's entry became the XB-30. In June, both companies received contract awards for mockups and wind-tunnel tests, and the Air Materiel Command was directed to begin negotiations for price and delivery dates of a pair of prototype aircraft, with an option to buy 200 production bombers.

On 24 August, the Air Corps decided on Boeing and signed a contract with the firm for the development and construction of two prototypes and a mockup at a cost of $3,615,095. By the time the contract had its official approvals on 6 September, Lockheed had made a policy decision to get out of bomber design, and Consolidated had been selected to develop the XB-32 as a parallel project. The remaining member of the original four bidders, Douglas, had been working its basic DC-4 transport configuration through a series of designs that might have become an XB-31, but the project never got beyond paper studies.

Late in the year, the Boeing mockup was inspected, and in November the company got an order for a third prototype and a fourth

Top right . . . Soaring past Mount Rainier in the pose that is still a Boeing photographic trademark. The third XB-29 (serial number 41-18335) had the hemispherical gunners' blisters that were standardised in production aircraft. The positions for the .50-cal machine gun turrets can be seen on the upper fuselage. Her fabric-covered ailerons, elevators and rudder were painted olive drab and grey camouflage. She carried anti-icing boots on the leading edges of the stabilisers, dorsal fin and vertical tail. / *Boeing X-45*

Bottom right: Weight lifting off the wheels, the third experimental Superfortress rolls down the runway at Boeing's Seattle plant. / *Gordon S. Williams*

Below: Under a leaden sky, the short-lived second XB-29 (41-003) is readied for flight. / *Gordon S. Williams*

airframe for static tests. The B-29 was on its way. Less than four years later — a remarkably short time for the design, development and deployment of a new weapon and its crews — the first B-29 mission was flown against the enemy.

Building and Flying

All the times seem short, anyway. True, aircraft design was simpler in the 1940s. But the Boeing B-29 was as much of an advance over its contemporaries as a Mach 3 fighter is today. The first engineering drawings were sent down to the shop floor on 4 May 1941. The work statement called for the first airplane to be completed in August 1942: 15 months to go.

Then began the almost endless number of small and large changes, policy decisions, Air Corps — and after 20 June 1941, Army Air Forces — modifications. The first was the conditional contract of 17 May. Under its terms, Boeing was asked to build 250 B-29s and 335 additional B-17s, conditional upon the expansion of its facilities at Wichita to meet production goals of 65 B-17s per month by 1 July 1941, and 25 B-29s per month by 1 February 1943. Boeing broke ground at Wichita 25 June 1941, for the expansion around the nucleus of the plant of the Stearman Aircraft Company, which had become a wholly-owned subsidiary of Boeing in 1939. The programme was proceeding at an accelerated pace when all hell broke loose at a remote Navy base called

Pearl Harbor, and the United States was at war.

In the days that followed, the Air Forces moved fast on all their programmes. On 31 January 1942, the Air Staff ordered 500 B-29s and $53 million worth of spare parts for the planes. The final production programme for the B-29s came from a meeting of military and industrial representatives in February. Boeing-Wichita would have the responsibility for production and assembly of the B-29s. Bell Aircraft Company would build B-29s at a plant yet to be erected at Marietta, Georgia (now the Lockheed-Georgia factory). North American Aviation, then a division of General Motors, was to build the bombers at its Kansas City plant. General Motors' Fisher Body Division would produce B-29s at a Cleveland, Ohio, plant then unbuilt.

In April, the Wright Aeronautical Corporation was ordered to triple the quantity of the original order for the big, new R-3350 engines for the B-29s. And in August, after the Battle of Midway and the planning changes it forced, the Army and the Navy shuffled their plants and projects at two locations: Boeing at Renton, Washington, and North American Aviation, at Kansas City. The Navy took over the Kansas City plant; the Army got Renton. The Boeing Sea Ranger, a prototype Navy flying boat, was cancelled to free the Renton factory. North American built B-25 bombers at Kansas City and some of them went to the Navy to meet their urgent need for medium bombers. Fisher Body was pulled out of B-29 production plans to concentrate on the P-75 fighter, and the Glenn L. Martin Company got the job of building B-29s at its huge Omaha, Nebraska, plant.

In early September, Boeing workmen hauled the first XB-29 out of the assembly shed with tractors, and the flight crew ran up the engines and made the first taxi tests. A few days later, the XB-29 taxied fast and hopped — maybe 15 feet into the air — three times, touching down on the long runway at the Seattle plant.

Then, on 21 September 1942, the flight test crew headed by Eddie (Edmund T.) Allen climbed aboard, fired up the engines, taxied out and flew. They came back one hour and 15 minutes later, with generally good impressions and a few gripes.

The second XB-29 made its first flight 30 December 1942. Less than two months later, it was a heap of burning wreckage that killed Allen and the flight test crew. A fire had begun in the number one engine — the first of many that were to plague the programme — and had burned through the wing structure.

Bomb bay doors yawning wide, a Renton-built Boeing B-29A-5-BN (serial 42-93844) poses in the cloudless skies over Washington. Superfortresses had two bomb bays, one forward and one aft of the wing carrythrough structure, and could lift a variety of bomb loads to a maximum of about 20,000lbs. Early production B-29s had electrically driven bomb-bay doors that took many seconds to open and close. Later models had pneumatic actuators that snapped the doors open and closed in a fraction of a second. / *Boeing*

The third prototype XB-29 made its first flight 16 June 1943, and during July, Boeing made its first delivery to the USAAF, which accepted seven of the YB-29 service test series from Wichita.

Only three experimental prototypes were built at Boeing's Seattle plant. All production aircraft came from four sources: Boeing's new facilities at Renton, Washington, and Wichita; Bell's Marietta plant; and the Martin plant at Omaha.

Boeing-Wichita delivered the first 175 B-29s by 1 March 1944. This was the initial batch of aircraft to equip the 58th Bombardment Wing (Very Heavy), the first unit to receive and operate B-29s. But these aircraft were not combat-ready right off the line; they had to be modified extensively. The 1,000th B-29 was delivered in February 1945, and by the following month, production schedules had stabilised at 100 B-29s per month at the Wichita plant alone. In July 1945, Wichita workers were turning out an average of more than four B-29s each working day.

The contracts for the big bomber called for a total of 6,289 Superfortresses to be produced, with deliveries to continue well into 1947. The total actually produced and accepted by the AAF was 3,960 B-29s.

Production was not all of the B-29 story. The modification programme accounted for an enormous number of workers and time. During the latter half of the war, the B-29 modification programme took over a major share of the country's total modification capacity. At the AAF modification centre in Birmingham, Alabama, almost 9,000 employees were assigned to work on the Superfortresses.

Describing the B-29

On the ground, the Superfortress spanned 141 feet 3 inches, and stretched 99 feet from nose to tail turret. Its tall tail towered 27 feet 9 inches into the air, or — as Boeing publicists were fond of saying — as high as a three-story house. It was designed to operate at a gross weight of about 120,000lb, and at a maximum overload of about 135,000lb. But B-29s were operated at weights as high as 142,000lb, and probably heavier at times.

There were three basic B-29 models, differing only in detail. The standard B-29, built at Wichita, Marietta and Omaha, had a continuous wing centre section to which the outer panels attached. The B-29A models, produced at Renton only, featured a five-piece wing, with a separate centre section, outboard and inboard panels. The fuel capacity of the B-29 was 9,363 gallons; on the B-29A it was 9,150 gallons (or 213 gallons of wing joints, as one engineer observed).

The B-29B was a special model for night precision attacks using radar bombing techniques. It had only a tail turret for defence, all other armament having been removed. It carried the AN/APQ-7 Eagle radar, updated Loran equipment for more precise navigation, and the AN/APG-15B

Top right: Before there were transistors, there were vacuum tubes, and the black boxes in the radio operator's position in the B-29 housed dozens of tubes. The primary radio receiver is mounted at the back of the table (centre) with the antenna switching unit above it. The transmitter is mounted at the right, as are the oxygen system controls, the interphone controls, the trailing antenna reel drive and controls, and a rat's nest of miscellaneous knobs and dials. / *Boeing 55703-B*

Bottom right: Contrast this combat cockpit that has, literally, been through the war with the pristine production cockpit shown in Boeing photo P-38536. This one has signs of wear, chipped paint, taped-on calibrations, instructions and warnings, including one not to exceed 300mph indicated airspeed. Radio call is 69760, indicating the aircraft is a Wichita-built B-29-60-BW (serial 44-69760). / *Dr Lyman C. Perkins*

Below: Aircraft commander (left) and pilot (right) of a Superfortress had excellent forward and upward visibility through the greenhouse nose of the B-29. The then super-secret Norden bombsight can be seen, uncovered, forward of the gap between the two flight instrument panels. / *Boeing P-38536*

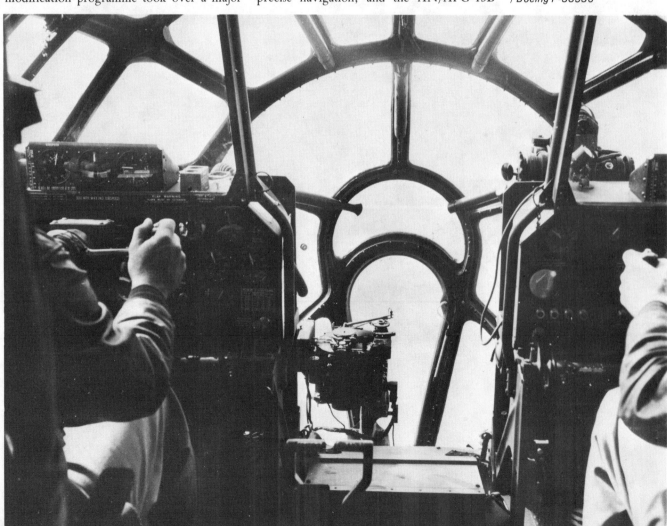

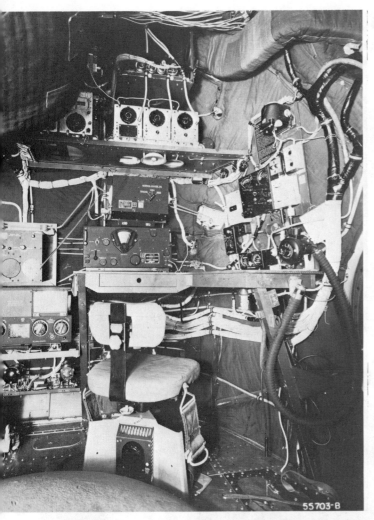

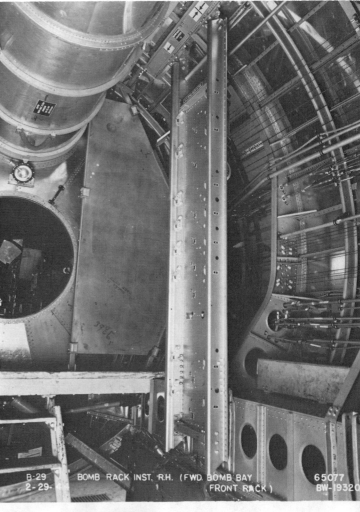

B-29
2-29-4   BOMB RACK INST. R.H. (FWD. BOMB BAY   65077
FRONT RACK)   BW-19320

55703-B

Above: The Superfortress bomb-bay structure was forthright: Horizontal beams fore and aft to carry the loads across the gaps of the bays, and vertical bomb racks from which to sling the shackles that held the various combinations of bomb loads. But this photograph also shows the vulnerability of the B-29 at this section: Note the hydraulic lines (11 of them), electrical wiring bundles (3) and control cables (20) running along the side of the fuselage. The forward pressure bulkhead is at the left; its centre is pierced with an access door to the bomb bay. Above it is the long cylindrical pressurised tunnel connecting the forward and aft pressure cabins.
/ *Boeing BW-19320*

181

Right: Early models of the B-29 had provisions for crew bunks for relief, as well as provisions for troop carrying. These features soon were abandoned, as the fuselage space was taken over by radar operators and 'Ravens' who ran the complicated electronic countermeasures equipment. / *Boeing X-711*

radar for night sighting of the tail guns. Its fuel capacity was the same as standard B-29s.

The powerplant of the B-29 was a quartette of R-3350 engines — the number refers to the total displacement in cubic inches — a team of powerful, untried engines developed by the Wright Aeronautical Corporation. They were twin-row radials, with 18 cylinders, and their exhaust was directed through ducting to drive a pair of General Electric Co B-11 turbosuperchargers for improved high-altitude performance. The turbos were automatically regulated by a Minneapolis-Honeywell electronic system. Under the engine were slung two oil coolers and the intercooler for the turbosupercharger operation.

Engines were rated at sea level at 2,200 brake horsepower for takeoff, and at 2,000bhp for maximum continuous operation. The superchargers held the sea-level power rating up to an altitude of 33,000 feet.

The Wright engines were called everything from the Wrong engines to flamethrowers. They ran hot on the ground, and required redesign of the cylinder baffling and reworked cowl flaps before they would even approach reasonable cylinder head temperatures. They also were prone to swallow valves. In later years, the engines became reliable and much less troublesome. But in World War 2, they were nothing but trouble. Ask any pilot, any flight engineer, any mechanic.

'Engine fires were one hell of a problem. When the magnesium caught, there was no stopping them. One night we had a crash at Pratt during training, and the fire tender came up and poured on a whole load of foam. I swear it didn't change the intensity of the fire one bit.

'We were sitting on Saipan one night, looking across the water watching the 313th and the 58th take off from Tinian. Five B-29s caught fire, either on the runway or over the water between Tinian and Saipan.

'There's a story that the very last plane off Saipan, after the war had long since ended, just got into the air and the number four engine burst into flames.' — *H. W. Douglas, 869 Bomb Sqn, 497 Bomb Group*

The XB-29s were powered by the R-3350-13 model, and the YB-29s got -21 engines. Production B-29 aircraft had the R-3350-23 engines installed, and the B-29A got -57 engines.

They turned three-bladed, 17-foot diameter propellers on the experimental ships, and four-bladed props with a diameter of 16 feet 7 inches on the production airplanes. They were Hamilton Standard Hydromatic propellers, with constant-speed governors and hydraulic operation for pitch change and feathering. The engine gear ratio was 0.35, which meant that the propeller turned a little more than one-third of the engine revolutions per minute. At takeoff, with 2,800 engine rpm, the prop was turning at 980rpm, and at minimum cruise setting of 1,400 engine rpm, it was just ticking over at 490rpm.

Toward the end of the war, some B-29s particularly those acquired by the 509th Composite Group, were equipped with Curtiss electric propellers, which had reversible pitch for added braking effect. They also were fitted with blade cuffs near the root of each blade, to increase the airflow

Above: Boeing's Wichita plant turned out B-29s by the dozen. In this spectacular rainy night shot, there are 24 B-29s — the -45-BW version — complete or nearly so. Three huge bays of this plant each had two parallel production lines, and each of them had four final assembly positions, judging by this photograph. / *Boeing BW-23991*

Bottom left: B-29 wings built at Wichita, and at all sub-contractors' plants, had a continuous centre section, with the wing roots meeting on the airplane centreline and the fuselage half-shells bolted on top and bottom. The B-29A models built at Boeing's Renton plant had a short cylindrical fuselage centre section with stub wing attachments, plus two outer panel sections to make up a five-piece wing. Here B-29 wing centre sections are being produced at Wichita, at aft stations on the production line. / *Boeing BW-23591*

Above: The last Renton-built Superfortress off the line (serial 44-62327) shows a couple of late-model changes to the airplane. Curtiss reversible-pitch electric propellers have replaced the Hamilton Standard Hydromatic units, and a streamlined, four-gun turret housing has replaced the earlier flattened hemispherical shape. / *Gordon S. Williams*

Right: The 'wing' underneath this B-29's belly is the radome of the AN/APQ-7 'Eagle' radar, a precision bombing radar system. It was installed on B-29B models only in service, and is here shown in an experimental installation on a standard Boeing B-29 identified as a Martin-built aircraft. / *Gordon S. Williams*

184

in that area and drive it through the engine cowling for improved cooling.

The B-29 sported a variety of new electronic equipment. As tactics evolved, additional pieces of radio and radar gear were developed to aid detection, or evasion, of enemy defences. Other equipment was designed to improve the performance of the B-29's bombing systems, or to enable the navigators to plot positions and find targets more accurately.

Early model B-29s used the AN/APN-4 Loran system, a long-range navigation aid based on the detection of a broadcast 'grid' of Loran lines of known position. Late model aircraft carried the APN-9 equipment. Philco built the -4, and RCA built the -9 Loran equipment.

The major radar bombing-navigational aid was the AN/APQ-13 equipment, developed by the Bell Telephone Laboratories and the Massachusetts Institute of Technology Radiation Laboratory. It used a 30-inch radar antenna mounted in a hemispherical radome installed between the bomb bays. It was often retouched out of photos released during the war, but it was standard equipment on B-29s in the Marianas.

The AN/APQ-7 Eagle bombing-navigation radar was developed at MIT's Radiation Lab and at Bell Telephone, and built — as was the APQ-13 — by Western Electric Co. It saw service on the B-29s of the

315th Bombardment Wing (VH) in their campaign of precision attacks on radar-located targets at night.

The Eagle radar was installed in a wing-shaped housing slung underneath the belly of the B-29s. It spanned 17 feet, had a 31-inch chord, and was just under eight inches thick. As built, the forward section was a white plastic radome and the aft section was conventional aluminium alloy. As used in the field, the entire unit was painted black along with the rest of the B-29 belly area.

Late in the war, and too late to have any real operational significance, a gun-laying radar was installed on the B-29s of the 315th BW. Built by General Electric, this radar solved the relatively simple problems of tail gunnery: No lead angle, point-blank range, straight-in attack. It was mounted in a ball-shaped radome below and completely outside the tail turret.

The SCR-729 radar interrogator system had paired antenna, one a double dipole type and the other a whip, mounted on each side of the B-29 nose near the navigator's and flight engineer's positions. This Philco system was used to determine the range and bearing of any aircraft it interrogated by radar.

The SCR-718C radio altimeter, built by RCA, was used primarily to determine the absolute altitude above the ground for the bomb run. Its output could be used with data

One anticipated problem — ditching a B-29 in the open seas — was investigated in a number of model tests in a towing tank operated by the then National Advisory Committee for Aeronautics at its Langley Memorial Laboratory, Langley Field, Virginia. Scaled, dynamically similar models were suspended on the instrumented carriage shown, which moved above the surface near scale stalling speed and released the model to strike the surface in a simulation of the actual full-scale ditching. / *NACA LMAL 46809*

from the drift meter to get an indication of ground speed and track.

The B-29 carried the usual complement of radio equipment for communications with ground stations and other aircraft. The state of the art of those days produced radios with tubes, and the sets were bulky, heavy, fragile, unreliable and limited in capability. And, since it was before the days of jet speeds, the B-29s carried a number of external antennas, including a long single wire that stretched from the fuselage to the vertical tail.

'When we took delivery of our new B-29, she wasn't complete in every detail, as we had expected. Some fairings and small trim items were missing. But we scrounged the parts and put a beautiful ship together. The guys even waxed the leading edge.

'I fitted a picture of my wife behind the plastic piece in the centre of the wheel, under the impression B-29. (I still have this piece today; it flew every hour with me.)

'When I first went up to the cockpit, I had to remove the bill of sale from the pilot's seat before I could sit down. The bill was from Boeing to the US Army, for one each B-29 aircraft, price $1,000,203.50.

'We flew it out to Guam, and immediately upon landing our airplane was confiscated for another crew to fly a mission that night. The next day we were waiting for them to bring our bird back, and we spotted this lame B-29 in the pattern, shot full of holes, bomb-bay doors flapping. Right; it was ours. We never flew that machine again.

'I had been in the Air Force since 1941, and had flown a lot of different aircraft, but none was more exciting or challenging than the

B-29. I hated it and I loved it. We had great admiration for its advanced — and untested — technology, its speed, comfort, defensive weapons. She was extremely rugged, but always unpredictable. Every flight or mission had its problems. Forced landings were common occurrences. Sometimes we wondered whether the battle was with the Japanese or the B-29.

'People have this stereotyped image of the heavy bomber pilot; you know, the dogmatic, by-the-book, straight-and-level type. But we were flying the greatest fighter plane in the air at the time. We had the manoeuvrability when we were light, and my gunners and their equipment were so good they could make a Japanese fighter pilot change his mind and his course 1,200 yards off.

'We flew tight formation when we had to, and we flew straight and level over the target. I never left the formation on the run in, of course, but it was frustrating not to be able to break loose and tangle with a Japanese fighter.

'When we were on individual missions, operating independently of any formation — say on a 'porcupine' mission — we'd fly to the target as briefed. We were flying on what we called 'government time'. Coming off the target, we said we were on our own time, and that's when you'd see some fast and fancy flying, even some aerobatics.

'Let me tell you, she could fly like a fighter. When we were light, we could go fast on the level and very fast downhill. We saw a couple of Navy Grumman Hellcats once when we were light and on a test flight, and we bounced them. I must have surprised the

hell out of them when they saw this big four-engined bird do a wingover and roar past them. She did beautiful wingovers for such a giant airplane, and everything stayed right in place inside.' *Charles B. Hawks, Jr, aircraft commander, 43rd BS, 29th BG*

When the crews trained on the B-29s, they learned all the limitations the airplane had. They learned that the power settings were not to be exceeded, that landing weight limitations were to be taken seriously, and that speed and manoeuvrability parameters were to be respected.

When they got to war with the airplanes, they learned differently. B-29s that weren't supposed to be thrown around by their pilots were thrown around violently by turbulence in the thick of fire raids. Engine power was pushed to the utmost, and airframes were asked to take strains that would have made the Boeing designers shudder. But the B-29 had the ability to do more than the designers had intended, and her rugged airframe got the crews back home, time after time. It also enabled the pilots to do things with the airplane that they had learned not to do in training.

'Soon after the B-29s had left, one was back in the pattern. The pilot — who was a Lieutenant Colonel, and I wish I knew his name — made a beautiful landing, and taxied over to the hardstand area. He called the crew chief over and asked him to fix some item on the airplane, right away. When the crew chief asked him why right now, the Colonel said that he wanted to take off again and catch up with the group.

'The crew chief said, well, Colonel, you know we'll have to refuel and reload the bombs, and that's going to take some time to do all that. "It's all still in the plane," said the Colonel.

'Damned if he hadn't landed a fully loaded B-29!' *H. W. Douglas*

'Major Joe Kramp, who always followed his signature with three letters — WGA, for World's Greatest Aviator — may have been just that. He flew a stretch of five missions in three days with green crews each time, which could not have been a picnic.

'The pilots all took advantage of the height of the cliff at Saipan to gain a little extra airspeed. They'd lift off just before the cliff and then put the nose down to gain a bit on the speed. Kramp used to use every foot of that height, and once he cut it so close that the plane actually skipped off the water, like you'd skip a stone across a pond. The waist gunners reported that water came into their compartment. The impact cleaned off the radome, bent the bomb bay doors and the tips of the two inboard props.

'That didn't stop Major Joe Kramp, the World's Greatest Aviator. He flew the mission, 3,000 miles round trip, and in his post-flight report he said the airplane felt a little rough.' *Don Miller, tail gunner, 874 BS, 498 BG*

'I rode along on a test flight to check out the APQ-13 radar, and I sat in the CFC (Central Fire Control) gunner's seat for a while. We were bounced by four camouflaged P-47s, and they got pretty close. Our pilot waved them off, but they continued to buzz us. So

Engine-out performance was critical on the B-29s, and a combat situation was very different from this controlled test flight done over the friendlier environment of the Arizona desert. Here, only the number one engine is running; two, three and four have been shut down and their props feathered. The airplane is a B-29-35-MO (44-27274), built by Martin at Omaha. In combat, you could get back on three engines, and occasionally on two. But on one... unheard of.
/ Boeing X-1241

our pilot got fed up, put the nose down a little and asked for full power. We left the first two fighters behind fairly soon, then the third and finally the fourth. We were in a shallow dive, with full power, down to about 22,000 feet.

'The pilot asked the navigator for the maximum speed during the dive, and the navigator said we were doing 475 miles per hour.' *H. W. Douglas*

Defensive Armament

Range and pressurisation dictated development of the remotely controlled defensive gunnery system on the B-29s. The great range of the aircraft eliminated all-the-way fighter escort and created a need for an effective defence with heavy firepower. Its pressurisation meant that men could not ride in the turrets as they did in other bombers.

A remote system, however, would allow the gunners to sit inside the pressurised fuselage of the B-29, and the turret assembly could be sealed in an enclosure to maintain the pressurisation integrity of the aircraft.

Bendix, General Electric, Sperry and Westinghouse competed for the defensive system, and Sperry won the initial contracts. The first three prototype XB-29s had the Sperry system, with retractable turrets and periscope sights, but all production aircraft were armed by the General Electric system.

There were five gun positions — upper forward, upper aft, lower forward, lower aft, and tail — and five gunnery positions, manned by four gunners and the bombardier. On early model B-29s, the upper and lower turrets mounted a pair of .50-calibre machine guns. The tail turret had the same pair, plus a 20mm cannon. But combat experience — the Japanese made head-on attacks on B-29 formations — caused a change to a four-gun upper forward turret, and the removal of the 20mm cannon because of problems with the feed mechanism and because its shells

followed a different trajectory from that of the .50-cal machine gun bullets.

Originally, the Air Forces decided to produce the system without a computer for solving the ballistics equations, hoping that the gunners would be able to solve them by visually compensating for lead, lag and windage. That was asking a bit much, because if a gunner were to have control of two turrets simultaneously, as was the plan, two different sets of ballistic equations would have to be solved visually, and even the most expert gunners could not handle that.

So the B-29 system ended as a computerised and flexible system that gave control of the turrets to more than one gunner, in case another gunner was wounded and could not handle his primary assignment.

The key man in the system was the Central Fire Control (CFC) gunner, who perched on an elevated seat known sometimes as the barber's chair under a transparent sighting blister just forward of the upper aft turret. He controlled the master gunnery panel, which assigned turrets to each gunner. The upper forward turret was primarily for the bombardier, and secondarily for the CFC gunner. The upper aft turret was primarily for the CFC gunner. The lower forward and lower aft turrets were assigned to the side gunners, and either could fire one or both turrets to meet attacks from his side. The lower forward turret could be taken over by the bombardier as a secondary assignment. The tail turret was primarily the tail gunner's responsibility; but it also could be fired by either of the side gunners.

The gun sights included a dead-man's switch; if a gunner were knocked out of action, his turret automatically was assigned to the gunner with secondary control. It was a reflector sight, with the optics focussed on infinity so that the gunner could use it with both eyes open. What they saw in the sight was a circle of orange dots around a central pip. They selected a wingspan dimension, and adjusted the sight manually to that number. When an enemy fighter came into view, the

trick was to set the orange circle with the right-hand range knob on the sight, so that the circle just enclosed the wingspan. Then the gunner had to continue to change the diameter of the orange circle while the fighter bored in, holding the pip on him at the same time, and firing the guns with thumb triggers when the aim and range permitted.

Computation of all the geometry and the ballistics involved was done electro-mechanically by analog computers in 'black boxes' under the cabin floor, protected by armour.

'By World War 2 standards, the B-29 had an extremely sophisticated self-defence system. And I recall the horror in the eyes of an Air Forces general when he learned that each gun turret had six vacuum tubes, and failure of any one would cause the loss of that turret's protection.

Above: Twin .50-cal machine guns point skyward under the control of the top gunner, whose head can be seen in the upper sighting blister, partially hidden by his gunsight. / *Boeing X-379*

Right: The tail turret guns — one 20mm cannon and a pair of .50-cal machine guns — are protected by covers while this B-29A-1-BN (42-93838) stands in the open on the ramp at Boeing's Renton, Washington, plant. The tail gunner's escape hatch is just above the small fairing between the inboard end of the elevators and the fuselage. / *Boeing X-258*

190

'The decision was made to rush into production of the analog computers roughly 12 to 18 months after the production decision on the turret system itself. So the first computers were installed at a modification centre at Birmingham, Alabama, and I was GE tech rep there.

'When the Air Forces were rushing to get the first wing of B-29s off to India, it was pretty apparent that a lot of the systems were in bad shape. So General K. B. Wolfe called the president of each company involved, at 3.00am as I recall, to emphasise the gravity of the situation, and asked them to send out a team of experts to get their particular systems in shape to go overseas.

'I was sent from Birmingham in a chilling ride in a B-24 when the pilot got lost and descended to read the name of a town off a sign on the post office. Teams were sent to four towns in Kansas where the B-29s stood at nearby airfields.

Above: The initial armament of the B-29 tail turret was the trio shown: One 20mm cannon, two .50-cal machine guns. But the unmatched trajectories of the two types of projectiles, and problems with the feed mechanism for the cannon, led to its removal in war zones, and reliance on the paired machine guns for defending the tail. / *Boeing X-385*

Right: The 'barber's chair' was the position of the top, or CFC (Central Fire Control) gunner. The seat was directly opposite the entrance to the pressurised tunnel between the forward and aft cabins of the B-29. The top gunner operated the switching system that allocated specific turrets to specific gunners, and additionally operated his own gun sight controlling the upper aft turret as a primary responsibility. / *Boeing X-321*

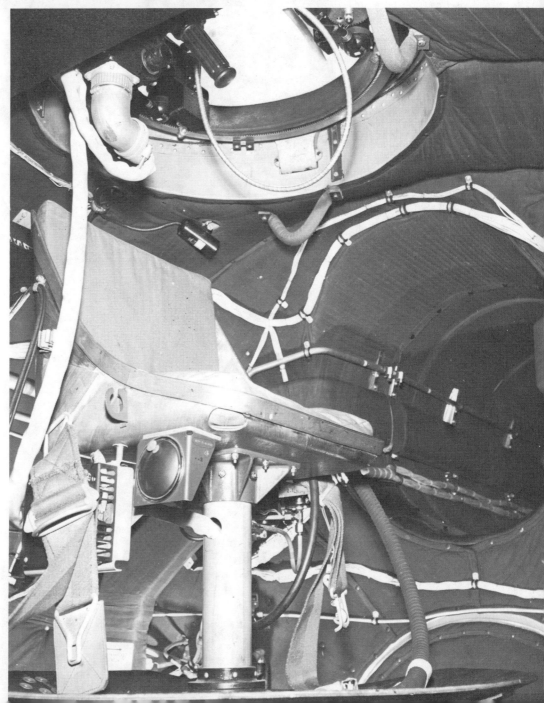

Alternate armament schemes were devised and even tested on the B-29, and this combination of Emerson, Martin and Sperry turrets was one such programme. The nose installation was a pair of Emerson barbette turrets, remotely controlled, each mounting a single .50-cal machine gun. The General Electric turrets were replaced by Martin manned turrets on the upper fuselage, forward and aft, and by Sperry ball turrets on the lower fuselage, fore and aft. Additionally, the side gunners' sighting blisters were replaced with installations for a single flexible mount .50-cal machine gun. These installations were made on the 72nd production B-29 off the line at Wichita, a B-29-29-BW model, serial 42-24441. The photographs were taken on 7 October 1944. / Boeing

192

Right: 'Hey, don't watch me! Watch what you're doing!' And what they are doing is loading the four .50-cal guns of the upper forward turret on *Thumper*, a Wichita-built B-29-41-BW (42-24623). The protective fairing has been removed for the job, and — with the guns fully loaded — is now about to be replaced. / A. F. Migliaccio Collection

Below: Technicians check the mechanisms of the tail guns and load the 20mm cannon feed drum on this B-29 operated by the 500th BG on Saipan / Ingram T. Hermanson Collection

'We worked 16-hour, sometimes 24-hour shifts. When we got too tired to carry on, we would return to the tiny hotel, wake up our replacement, and climb into the still warm bed.

'It was freezing cold at the time with blizzards and high winds. I recall sitting in the tail of a B-29, trying to resolder a bad connection, and having to cup the soldering iron in my gloved hands to get it warm enough to do the job. Aircraft sat out in the open, heated by external engine-driven gas heaters and with the power supply coming from a separate engine-driven generator. One or the other was always running out of fuel, halting our operations until we could hike a half-mile to get more gas.

'The condition of the GE system was pretty horrible, and I assume that was true for many others. Wires interconnecting aircraft cables made by newly trained workers sometimes ran to the wrong pins on connectors. Whoever stripped the insulation off sometimes nicked four or five of the seven strands of wire, and left the connection hanging by only a couple. There were blobs of solder shorting out adjacent pins or sockets in the connectors. We did the best we could to assure that the turret system was operable, but we lacked the time to inspect every wire and every connector, and we could only hope they would hang together.

'In late 1944, after the B-29 was already operational, Eglin Field started its "operational suitability" tests, and I was sent down there when we got reports that the system was doing badly in the tests. When I arrived at Eglin, I discovered two reasons why the system was doing so badly. First, Eglin was short of competent engineers to run the test on the GE system, so our competitor thoughtfully volunteered to supply one of their engineers, already

193

stationed there, to supervise the tests on the GE system at no cost. Second, nobody had bothered to check out the GE equipment before tests to see if it was in operating condition. I discovered that a rat had built a nest in one of the computers.' *Philip J. Klass, technical representative, General Electric Company*

'We got a specialised briefing, just for gunners, after the main briefing. They told us the usual thing: how many and how good the fighters were going to be, what their tactics might be like, things like that. Then we'd go and clean and load our own guns and check the ammo. The ammo came out from ordnance in belts and boxes, and we'd lay them out and check them for rounds that were out of alignment in the belts.

'When it came time to board the airplane, I'd go in the aft entrance door, crawl through the tail section and into the tail turret, close the door and adjust the seat. You had to sit up straight, there was no relaxing back there. Not that you'd want to, anyway . . .

'We gunners used a lap belt only, wore soft helmets with oxygen masks, a flak helmet over that, and a full suit of flak armour. The chest chute was stowed on the floor, and you generally hooked it on at the start of combat. If you had to bail out, you were supposed to take the flak suit off first, over the chute and over your shoulders. There was a rip cord on the flak suit that unfastened the thing, supposedly.

'It was cramped, but there was sufficient space for the job. I first flew the tail turret when there were three guns: one 20mm cannon and two .50-cal machine guns. But we could only get about 20 rounds out of the cannon before it jammed, and there was so much trouble with the feed mechanism that they removed the cannon. We carried 120 rounds for the cannon and 1,200 round per machine gun. We came home empty.

'Some time after takeoff we'd test-fire the guns by triggering a couple of short bursts. If we had minor troubles, there was a pretty good chance we could fix them in the air on the way to the target and before we had to pressurise the airplane for the climb to altitude. We kept the gun heaters on all the time and we did not lubricate the guns with oil, because the oil would freeze at the high altitudes we flew.

'The tail guns would cover a volume of plus or minus 30 degrees in both azimuth and elevation. The sight was the same as the side gunners' sights. The left hand gripped a deadman's switch, which you had to hold down in order to fire. The right hand you used to work the ranging control. It was the job of the flight engineer to set the airplane altitude, airspeed and temperature to get true air data

Left: Sgts William F. Dawson (left) and W. R. Lambert load the four .50-cal machine guns of the forward upper turret on their B-29 during the Korean war. / *William F. Dawson Collection*

Below left: The tail gunner had adequate, although somewhat cramped space. 'There wasn't room to spread out back there', said one of them. Isolated from the rest of the crew during combat, he was lonely as well as apprehensive. His guns, gunsight and bullet-proof glass windshield protected him in front; he leaned against a piece of armour plate to shield his back. / *Boeing Wichita BW-24594*

Right: The side gunners worked in large hemispherical blisters that blew out from time to time, adding some uncertainties to their combat experience. On the bulkhead to his right are oxygen and electrically heated suit controls; above and to his left is the rotating switch for the intercom system. / *Boeing Wichita*

Below: Among the four .50-cal machine guns of the forward upper turret is the cam follower, a simple mechanical insurance policy to keep gunners from shooting off parts of the aircraft. / *Boeing Wichita BW-29382*

out of the computers for all the gunners. All we had to do was to sight, adjust the ranging control for the wingspan of the fighters, and thumb the triggers.

'You could hear your own guns when you fired them, of course. And you felt the shock, the recoil, of the other guns when they were fired, even though you couldn't hear them. The belt links and spent cases from the tail turret and the two lower turrets were ejected overboard; the rest of the cases and links fell into the fuselage. Our first bombing formation was a diamond, and the tail-end plane flew above the lead, high enough to clear his wake and still low enough to see the tip of the tail of the lead aircraft. They did that to avoid getting the links and cases of the airplane ahead through their own windshield. There was one crew that got a little too low in the formation, and got a face full of links and cases. When they got back, the pilot and co-pilot were ordered to change the windshield glass themselves, to remind them not to get too low in the formation the next time.

'After we got back to base, we cleared all the guns before we left the airplane, swabbed them with gun oil, and went to the debriefing.' — *Don Miller*

Eleven Men

The crew complement standardised for early operations of the B-29 consisted of 11 men. Five were officers: the aircraft commander, pilot, bombardier, navigator, and flight engineer. Six were enlisted men: radio operator, radar operator, central fire control gunner, left and right gunners, and the tail gunner.

Later in the war, one or two additional officers, known as 'Ravens', flew with the crews to operate the highly specialised and highly classified electronic countermeasures equipment.

By mid-1944, the flight engineer ranks had been opened to enlisted men, and they took over that position toward the end of the war and subsequently.

The crew concept was the cornerstone of the B-29 operations. Crews were selected to be a permanent team, to be changed only in the event of the wounding or the death of one or more members. They trained together, after completing the individual specialist trainings that each crewman received. That required some juggling of the standardised cirricula and schedules that were then in existence.

Training programmes were fluid during the war, in response to the changing needs and the demands of new tactics and new equipment. Pilots at first spent nine weeks in each stage of their training — primary, basic and advanced — and later the course was lengthened to ten weeks per phase. Navigators started with 15-week courses, later increased to 18 and then to 20. Gunners took a 12-week course that later shrank to six weeks. Bombardiers also took a course in flexible gunnery — non-turreted machine guns — either before or after their specialist courses.

The first of the B-29 crews were drawn from among combat crews with previous experience on four-engined aircraft. One nucleus came from anti-submarine operations in Europe and North Africa, and had flown Consolidated B-24 bombers. Other pilots were taken from among the instructors in multi-engine flight schools. Then, as the war progressed, raw aviation cadets were moved through primary, basic and advanced to transition training and the co-pilot's seat of a B-29.

Training Command had the responsibility for all the specialist training courses for aircrew classes. But all B-29 crew training and unit training was the responsibility of the Second Air Force.

The B-29 was a special airplane, and it required a new approach to training. It was, of course, bigger than the standard heavy bombers. Further, the intended B-29 operations emphasised high-altitude, long-range navigation and the use of radar for both navigation and bombing. It demanded much closer integration of the crew, whose functions overlapped and became interdependent during the flight.

The aircraft commander, pilot and flight engineer were one such team. Their ability to think and to react as a single individual was most important during critical portions of the flight, such as the takeoff, where a slight hesitation in recognising the problem and taking corrective action could mean a fiery and sudden death.

The bomb run tied together the efforts of the aircraft commander, the navigator, the bombardier, and the radar operator. Navigation also required the assistance of the radar operator and the pilots as well as the work of the navigator himself. The left and right gunners also were scanners of the airplane, whose duties included watching the engines for signs of trouble, calling out flap deflections and the condition of the landing gear. By reporting attacks, the gunners often gave indirect steering information to the pilots.

For five weeks prior to their crew assignments, the pilots, co-pilots and flight engineers went through a special course designed to emphasise the teamwork they would need in operations. Then they were assigned to the Second Air Force units that would give them their full crew training.

This specialised training plan, modified specifically for the requirements of B-29 operations, began in the fall of 1943, and turned out a total of 2,350 crews before the end of the war.

'The available flying time in the B-29 was very limited in training; there was a shortage of aircraft. Most of the early crew training was done in B-17s. I had come to B-29s from a tour with an anti-submarine squadron in England and I had 450 hours in B-24s. I was one of two pilots with combat experience in the squadron.

'My first flight in the B-29 was on 18 May 1944. I logged six hours, 20 minutes, and shot 14 landings in that time period. I didn't fly a B-29 again until 7 June, when I made 10 landings on a five hour 20 minute flight. On 11 June I was checked out as pilot of B-29s, with a final flight of one hour 40 minutes with three landings.

'Co-pilots of B-29s seldom made landings; yet the co-pilots of later replacement crews arriving on Saipan had more landings than I had recorded in the B-29s, and bear in mind that we were an original combat crew out there and a lead crew as well, which meant that we could fly extra training flights.

'My last B-29 training flight was a simulated group combat mission that lasted 14 hours 25 minutes. By then we had 20 trained crews — two per airplane — and we moved to a staging area at Kearney, Nebraska, to wait for 10 B-29s to come off the production line so that we could deploy to Saipan. I had a grand total of 105 hours in the B-29 at that point.' *Ferd J. Curtis, aircraft commander, 881st BS, 500th BG*

Havana, Cuba, was the target for the first long-range missions many of the B-29 crews ever flew. It was, of course, a training flight. The distance was representative of the trip to Japan from the Marianas, and the approach to Havana was over water, similar to the approaches to Japan.

The missions began in late August 1944. The B-29s would lift off training fields in Kansas, and head generally southeast for Cuba. They landed all over the southeastern United States, out of fuel. Crews still hadn't learned the secrets of cruise control on the B-29.

It was a serious situation. The B-29s were expected to start striking the home islands of Japan from Saipan in November 1944, and — with only three months to go — they weren't able to be flown on an equivalent mission without bomb loads, with good communications and meteorological information, and with no enemy fighters or flak.

Training began to tighten. Flight engineers quickly learned about cruise control. The secret was simple: run the manifold pressure way up, and keep the rpm low. Down went the fuel consumption.

'The 58th Bomb Wing had taken just about all the serviceable B-29s with them when they left for the CBI theatre, and we were left with some very tired B-17s for training. It seemed that every one of these planes had some part that didn't work. It's a tribute to the long-suffering ground crews that they were able to fly at all. We had to scratch training missions because of some malfunction, time after time.

'Finally we began to get some B-29s. What a giant of an airplane this 50-ton machine seemed to be! I was awed by the power they represented, and remained so throughout my service in them.

'The first phases of training accelerated after the big birds became available. We shot endless takeoffs and landings, flew bomb runs over three local ranges dropping flour bombs. We gunners had to learn to adapt from the Sperry manned turrets we had trained in to the more complicated General Electric remote control types on the B-29. Malfunctions were commonplace. Guns would jam, overheated barrels would "cook-off" rounds, electrical systems would burn out. But as time passed, these irritations were overcome.

'On gunnery-training missions, we kept busy in simulated attacks made against us by fighter aircraft. The next day, we'd view the gun-camera films to see which crew had the best score. One time the fighter — we trained against one, coming from one angle, but the Japanese had other procedures — failed to show. We didn't want to scrub the mission, so the B-29s took turns making passes at each other. The films next day caused some lifted eyebrows, because they showed four-engined bombers flying in on tight pursuit curves!

'Kansas thunderstorms are legendary, and we had our share, which complicated the training missions. One time we were coming back from a long-range bombing mission in the Gulf of Mexico near Galveston, and we were caught in a severe storm. We were tossed around like a feather, and finally spit out clear of the clouds, upside down. Another time we had turned on final and had just broken out of the overcast when a B-29 broke through the same overcast just ahead of us on a collision course. If his wheels had been down, as ours were, he would have hit us. Never did find out who he was.

'These training programmes, however dangerous, were taken as a matter of course as the programme rolled along. Personally, I always felt safer in the air than I did in the buses that served the base.

'As more B-29s became available, they had us in the air sometimes for two missions per day, which played hell with our love life in town. Missions became longer with bomb runs on Gulf targets, and non-stop missions to Florida and back. We always took a Class A uniform along on those flights just in case we had engine trouble over Florida. Several times we did have such trouble, however

suspect. It turned out that those missions were approximately the same length as those we would later fly from Saipan. And let's not forget the "booze runs" to Chicago and Peoria, to pick up a cargo rack filled with the snakebite medicine that couldn't be bought in dry Kansas!' *George S. Gray, CFC gunner, 883rd BS, 500th BG*

Candidates for flight engineer training were expected to be officer graduates of maintenance engineering courses or, later, experienced mechanics. They were to become much more than throttle jockeys. They were expected to know all about the airplane and its systems, and their tasks ran the gamut from providing and setting input data for the central fire control system to adjusting the pressurising in the cabin. In emergencies, they were expected to repair these systems, if necessary.

Their training began with the standard pre-flight aircrew school. It was followed by 19 weeks in a study of first- and second-echelon maintenance of the B-29s. For their advanced training, engineer candidates spent ten weeks in a three-phased course geared to the many real problems of the B-29s. First, they learned how to be excellent mechanics, so that they could handle in-flight malfunctions and emergencies. Second, they learned the operation of the powerplants for best cruise control. Third, they had four weeks of flight training. Most of that time was flown in B-24 bombers that had been modified to carry several flight engineers at separate stations. It wasn't exactly like the B-29, but it was the best that could be done under the circumstances. It was well into 1944 before the very first B-29 became available for ground instruction of flight engineers.

By the time of the Korean war, the B-29s had settled down a bit. Being a flight engineer was no easier then than it had been five years and more earlier, but at least by then, almost everything that might happen had happened, and the proper preventive or corrective actions were fairly well defined. But there was always the unexpected:

'B-29 combat crew training for the Korean war was rough on young teenage engineers, and on retread pilots who didn't want to be there in the first place. And it didn't help matters to know that after the training at Randolph (AFB, Texas), there was Korea waiting. Check rides, standboard exams, and flight checks were things to be despised, but we all knew the best thing to do was pass and get the hell out of Randolph anyway.

'On one particular day our crew was getting a check ride from a major who occupied the co-pilot's seat for the flight. He was a stickler for detail, and he demanded instant response and perfection from the crew. After minor skirmishes on pre-flight, takeoff and climb-out, we settled down for the rest of the routine.

'Our aircraft commander was a retread captain who didn't give a damn for anybody or anything, and his nickname was "Tex". We were sitting there, flying straight and level with everything working like a well-oiled watch, when the major yanked number four throttle back to idle, slumped over the control column and yelled, "You just lost number four and I'm dead! What are you going to do about it, Captain?"

'Old Tex punched the mike button, and in a cool, couldn't-care-less tone said, "Engineer! Come up here and drag this dead bastard out and help me fly this son-of-a-bitchin' airplane!"

'We passed the check ride.' *Eugene L. Davis, flight engineer, 370th BS, 307th BW, Korea*

And training never stopped. Even after flight crews were flying combat missions on a regular basis, there were often special training flights to accomplish.

'Would you believe flying a 3,000-mile mission only to land, refuel and then practice formation flying? We did. Our CO was unhappy with our daylight bombing patterns, because he believed — and he was probably right — that the Japanese fighter defence picked on loose formations. And let me tell you, tight formation flying in the B-29 — the only kind our CO would allow — took lots of muscle and sweat.

'During our next daylight raid we flew so tight that one flak burst nearly took out two aircraft. We got punctured, and our wing man got punctured.' *Charles B. Hawks*

'Our crew was designated as a lead crew and it was regarded by some as a dubious honour, because the attrition rate of lead crews was high. The Japanese fighters had found that their most effective attack was a direct frontal approach, because from more conventional fighter approaches the B-29 had very effective defensive firepower. B-29 formations were staggered vertically to make full use of that firepower.

'The Japanese fighters would attack from the front of the formation and, rather than break away within our firing range, they would continue right on through the formation and be in position to attack the next formation in trail behind. The lead aircraft was the prime target for this type of attack.

'Initial selection of lead crews was from the three flight leaders in each squadron, and that was based on rank. We lost our initial flight leaders rapidly. Major Bob Goldsworthy was shot down by fighters over Tokyo in December 1944. The deputy flight leader on that mission, Captain Joe Irvin, had to ditch on the way back with a damaged B-29, and didn't survive. Captain Hod Hatch replaced the operations officer in January, which left only Captain Bob Fitzgerald as a flight leader and he was shot down over Nagoya later.

'The selection of my crew for lead training was not by my rank or record, because I was a junior captain and had not led a single mission. I think that greater consideration was given about then to the performance of the crew as a whole. My navigator, bombardier and radar operator had worked with good co-ordination since our early training. I had done an earlier combat tour, in an anti-submarine squadron based in England, flying Consolidated B-24s, and that was a factor. Anyway, my crew was selected as a lead crew in January 1945.

'That meant additional training, and it had not been anticipated that there would be any need for training in the theatre. There was no bombing range. Later, replacement crews bombed the island of Truk for shakedown purposes, but that practice was discarded because of the poor ratio of aircraft flight time to the training time over the target on the bomb run. So we used nearby islands for simulated, dry-run bombing.

'A typical training mission would start with a crew briefing given by the squadron staff including a flight plan and a target bomb plan. We followed standard combat procedures except for the bomb and ammunition loading. A shortened low-level flight was made to the point where we began the climb to bombing altitude. We reached that height just prior to the departure point for the run. A radar run was made to the initial point (IP) where the bombardier took over and made a visual bombsight run on the primary target. We continued to follow the flight plan with a complete radar run to another departure point, initial point and the secondary target. Return to base was normal and the debriefing was done by the squadron staff.' *Ferd J. Curtis*

In retrospect, the training time available for B-29 crews was terribly limited. Crews were sent into combat with a minimum of time in the very weapon they were expected to use well. It was a situation that held throughout the war, because of the shortage of B-29s for training, because of the accelerating needs for combat crews in the Pacific, and — ultimately — because wars are like that.

Bombardier Del Shaffer arrived at his combat crew training squadron at Clovis Army Air Field, New Mexico, with 186 hours and five minutes of flying time,

most of it in training for his specific crew task. It was September 1944, and the war had less than one year to go, although nobody really thought it would be over that soon.

There was no flying time for him during September, but in October he logged three flights. One of them was a 12 hour 55 minute training flight in a B-17G, the workhorse for the early phases of B-29 combat crew training. His first two B-29 flights were made that month, one of seven hours and the other of seven hours 25 minutes.

In November Shaffer flew on six B-29 training missions, five of them a series of short flights, and the sixth a simulated combat mission lasting 11 hours 40 minutes. In December, he flew five times, four of them in B-29s for about seven hours each, and one in a B-17G lasting a little more than three hours. During the first half of January 1945, Shaffer trained on two B-29 and two B-17 flights, and then he was transferred with the rest of his crew to Kearney, Nebraska, for the staging procedure that would eventually send him to Saipan.

He then had a total of 268 hours 25 minutes in airplanes, and less than ten hours of that time was flown at night. He did no flying at Kearney in January. On 12 February he was on his way to Saipan and a slot in the 874th Bombardment Squadron, 498th Bombardment Group, of the 73rd Bombardment Wing (Very Heavy).

On 16 and 17 February he made two flights out of Saipan in the B-29. The first lasted two hours, 20 minutes; the second took six hours 35 minutes. On 25 February, Del Shaffer went on his first combat mission, a daylight raid on Tokyo. The mission lasted 15 hours 30 minutes, and included nine hours in instrument conditions and three hours of night flying.

The night incendiary raids began in March and, by the end of that month, Shaffer had spent nearly 44 combat hours under night conditions. That was more than four times as much night flying time as he had acquired in five months of training.

All of the pre-deployment training was done at a network of bases scattered around the midwestern and southwestern United States, where the weather was generally more co-operative than it was along the eastern seaboard or around the Great Lakes region. Many of the young airmen were married, and their wives — if they weren't working — made the trek from base to base to be with their husbands. Their constant moves from station to station, their need to find temporary housing near the base, their youth and inexperience and often their naivete, made them vulnerable. That they put up with so much, and that so many marriages survived it all, is remarkable.

'Tom graduated in the pilot class of 42-F at Phoenix, Arizona, and we were married the day he pinned on his wings. He was ordered to Salt Lake City, Utah, for assignment, so we boarded a troop train in the June heat. It was probably 110 degrees, but Tom proudly sweltered in his brand-new Second Lieutenant's uniform, the "greens and pinks". We rode all the way to Salt Lake City via Los Angeles and rode right back again. Tom's orders were for Tucson, Arizona, which may be 100 miles or so from where we started out. We must have spent a week on trains.

'Tom was a B-24 instructor pilot there, but after a couple of months changed to crew training and we were moved to El Paso, Texas, where the crews had to live on base under simulated combat conditions. That meant I lived in the YWCA in town, and got to see Tom on his one day off each week.

'Juarez, Mexico, was right across the river, just a short streetcar ride away, and every crew member who wanted to get liquor would come to the YWCA, ask for me, and take me to Juarez where I would get "my" allotment and carry it back for the crew. One day Tom got an extra day off and came in for me, but I had already headed for Juarez with the officer who was the best man at our wedding. We had a rather prim lady at the YWCA desk, and when Tom asked for me, she told him that Mrs Isley had left. Tom asked where, and she said, "I don't know; but she had pants on!" Tom's retort: "Well, I certainly hope so!" Women didn't wear slacks as much in public those days. I had been in the fashion business, and in Hollywood at that, so I was probably a little far out for my fellow YWCA inhabitants.

'When we were ordered to Salina, Kansas, the people there were willing to make sacrifices, saying they wanted to take good care of "their boys". We, along with another couple, were able to rent a bedroom apiece in a Salina home. One of us paid $40 and the other $50 per month rent. Our landlords slept in the basement. (Note: For comparison, a three-room luxury garden apartment in the New York suburban area was renting for as much as $60 per month at that time.)

'One night they invited us for dinner at a local restaurant. Fine; we thought we'd earned that. So we all went out, and the husband picked up the check while giving us the "everything-for-the-boys" routine. The next day the lady of the house came to us girls and said, "Well, we don't know how it is where you come from, but when we go out to dinner, we always share the check, so would you please pay for your dinners?" And, of course, we forked over the money.

'After Tom had served a year in North Africa and England in an anti-submarine outfit, he came home and went into B-29 transition training at Clovis (New Mexico), and we were house-hunting again. Clovis was full, but we finally located a backyard shack in a neighbouring town. It was about 12 feet by 12 feet, made into a living-bedroom, kitchen and bath. The outside was painted purple and it was trimmed in orange. I forget what we paid, but I know it was a horrendous amount for a brightly coloured shack out back.

'In Great Bend (Kansas), we couldn't find a place there either, and again settled in a neighbouring town where some people rented us their basement. Our shower facilities were a water pipe with a nozzle at the end, suspended over a storm drain. No lavatory, but a kitchen-type sink in the corner that we shared with a congress of cockroaches. It was Tom's duty the first thing every morning to wash them down the drain before I'd put my feet to the floor — one time into six inches of water, I well remember.

'We were young, we were in love, and it was wartime. We kept saying that, and thinking that, like a litany, perhaps to avoid the thought that we were being used, that "nothing's too good for our boys" usually carried a hefty price tag and wasn't too good anyway.' *Mrs Thomas Isley*

Capt James J. Garrity was the Adjutant of the 883rd Bomb Squadron, 500th Bomb Group, 73rd Bomb Wing when that unit moved to Saipan to begin the aerial assault against the Japanese home islands with other units of the 73rd Wing. He put together a photo album which included these pictures (*right*) of the first crews to fly with the 883rd, and added his own personal comments about each crew. They constitute a remarkable documentation of one group of men at one stage in time, and they are presented here exactly as Garrity showed them in his album.

LT. COL. WILLIAM L. McDOWELL

LT. COL WILLIAM L. McDOWELL (COMMANDING)
WEST POINT CLASS OF 1939
SECOND TOUR OF DUTY OVER SEAS AFTER SUB-PATROL IN CARRIBEAN
SQUADRON "COS" REQUIRED TO FLY ABOUT 8 MISSIONS, COL MAC
FLEW ABOUT 20+. A REGULAR "JOE" AND "A MANS MAN".

REQUIESCANT IN PACE

LT COOPER'S CREW CRASHED INTO FARM HOUSE AND WHEAT
BARN IN COPELAND, KAN. DURING TRAINING, ALL MEMBERS, EXCEPT
THE OFFICER IN CENTER (HANK) WERE KILLED, HE WAS ON THE FLIGHT
BUT THEY LANDED BECAUSE HE WAS SICK, AND CRASHED ½ HR LATER.

201

351 HANSEN ('B' FLIGHT LEADER)
REQUIESCANT IN PACE

MAJ. HANSENS CREW DEPARTED SAIPAN ON THEIR FIRST
MISSION, AT NIGHT, ON NUISANCE RAID OF ONE EVERY HALF HOUR. JOE AMOS (SEE LATER)
AND I WERE ON THE END OF RUNWAY AND WERE LAST TO SEE THE PLANE AIR BORNE.
TO THIS DAY THERE IS NO REPORT. THEY JUST VANISHED.

363 AMOS
REQUIESCANT IN PACE

JOE'S PLANE WAS CRIPPLED OVER THE TARGET AND HE NURSED IT BACK TO THE
JIMA ISLANDS (NIP HELD). LANDED AT SEA AND TOOK TO DINGHIES. OUR GANG FOUND HIM
AND NURSED A U.S. SUB. UP TO ABOUT 2 MILES. THE SUB DID NOT GET THEM, AND CONTACT
WAS LOST AT DUSK. NO FURTHER REPORTS.

357 CHARTERS
REQUIESCANT IN PACE

THIS WAS CHARTERS 2ND TOUR AGAINST THE NIPS. HE FLEW WITH THE OLD 19th BOMB GP. THEY LANDED AT SEA, AFTER DAMAGE OVER TARGET. HIS "BUDDY" PLANE TOOK HIM DOWN, BUT CONTACT WAS MADE AT NIGHT. NO FURTHER INFORMATION.

"RESTRICTED"

354 HOLMES
REQUIESCANT IN PACE.

THIS WAS HOLMES 2ND TOUR AFTER ONE AGAINST GERMANY. THEY LANDED AT SEA ABOUT 200 MI. FROM SAIPAN NEAR A U.S. DESTROYER, MAJ. GAY, OPERATIONS OFF. AND LT. SPARKS WERE BURIED AT SAIPAN. THE PERSONNEL, INDICATED WENT DOWN WITH THE PLANE. OTHER PERSONNEL CAME BACK ON THE DESTROYER WITH SEVERE FRACTURES, LT. POPE AND SGT. COLLINS RECEIVED MINOR SHOCK AND REMAINED IN THE COMMAND.

"RESTRICTED"

343 ASHLEY ("A" FLIGHT LEADER)

CAPT. ASHLEY, AIR LINE PILOT, WAS SUCCEDED BY LT. BARRON. AFTER 5 MISSIONS. THEIR PLANE WAS NAMED "THE BARRONESS". THEY FLEW 35 MISSIONS, ALL WERE RETURNED SAFE TO THE U.S.

SGT. DIETZ A TOP TAIL GUNNER IN EACH THEATRE. →

← THIS LT. DID NOT COME WITH US. HIS BROTHER WAS SHOT DOWN A WEEK BEFORE THEY DEPARTED.

The Crew of "Supine Sue"

344 MORELAND

ONE OF THE BEST B.29 CREWS IN COMBAT. OUR "LEAD CREW" AND EVENTUALLY ONE OF THE LEAD CREWS FOR THE AIRFORCE. COL. MAC FLEW THIS CREW OUT FROM 20 TO 30 MISSIONS. MORELAND WAS ORDERED TO U.S. TO SET UP "LEAD CREW" SCHOOL AT MUROC.

346 SETTERICH

SGT. DALEY
RADIO OPERATOR
HELPED CONTACT
THE SUB.

A SCRAPPY CREW OF THE FIRST ORDER. THIS WAS THE CREW FOUND (AMOS)
AND FLEW COVER TO GET THE SUB IN FOR A PICK UP. THEY POWER DIVED ON, AND
SHOT DOWN, A NIP SEA PLANE WHICH WAS SNOOPING AROUND. THEY FINISHED ALL
MISSIONS SAFELY.

"RESTRICTED"

347 RYAN

RYAN FLEW THEM ALL AND THE CREW CAME BACK O.K. OVER THE TARGET
ON ONE MISSION THE FUEL CONTROL CABLES, FOR TWO ENGINES, WERE SEVERED. LT. LOGAN, HELD
THE ENDS OF THE CABLES AND FED GAS, BY DIRECTION, ON THE RETURN 7 HR TRIP TO
SAIPAN HE WAS AWARDED THE D.S.C. THEY SELDOM STAY AIR BORNE WITH TWO OUT ON
THE SAME SIDE.

"RESTRICTED"

348 CHENEY

BILL FLEW A SNOOPER MISSION ON THE ISLAND OF TRUK, MAST HIGH.
THE AIRPLANE LOOKED LIKE A SIEVE WHEN HE RETURNED. A GOOD CREW
AND THEY FINISHED ALL MISSIONS.

THIS CREW
HELPED ME
CONSTRUCT THE
E.M. CLUB-HOUSE

(3RD FROM RIGHT)
SGT. GLOCKNER
2ND TOUR 81
TOTAL MISSIONS.
AND TIED AS TOP
GUNNER IN OUR
AIR FORCE.

350 CLINKSCALES

THE SCRAPPING GAME-COCK FROM SO. CAROLINA. ONE OF THE ROUGHEST
CREWS IN THE SQUADRON. MAN FOR MAN "CLINK" FINISHED THEM ALL AND WAS
MOTHER TO THE FIGHTERS FROM IWO, FOR NAVIGATING THEM HOME.

"RESTRICTED"

352 ▮

A DAM GOOD CROWD OF FELLOWS, BUT THE ORIGINAL (CAPT) AIRPLANE COMMANDER DOES NOT DESERVE TO BE EXHIBITED IN THIS COMPANY.

← SGT. RENNER
2ND FROM RIGHT.

353 McCLANAHAN

MAC STARTED WITH THE R.C.A.F. IN EUROPE AND HE HAD A SCRAPPY CREW. HE RETURNED ONE NIGHT WITHOUT SGT. RENNER, OUR FIRST CASUALTY. A GUNNERS GLASS BLISTER BLEW OVER TOKIO AND RENNER PLUMMETED INTO SPACE. MAC DOVE THE PLANE TO SAVE THE CREW IN REAR. ALSO, HE SAT ON BRADENS BACK (SEE LATER) WHEN THE FORMERS GUNS WENT OUT AND FOUGHT THE NIPS OFF FOR SEVERAL MINUTES. THEY ALL CAME HOME EXCEPT RENNER

Towards Command and Control

One of the key figures in Superfortress operations was Brig Gen Haywood S. Hansell, Jr, an outstanding pilot, combat commander and brilliant planner. Hansell was the first commander of the XXI Bomber Command when it deployed to the Marianas. He has drawn on that experience, and his earlier planning studies, to summarise the background of the organisation that eventually commanded and controlled the B-29 operations.

'The grand strategy of World War 2 called for the defeat of Hitler first. To help in that battle, the B-29s were planned for deployment first against Germany, with 12 groups to be based in Northern Ireland and 12 near Cairo, Egypt. When the time had come when we were sure that the defeat of Hitler could be accomplished, we would turn to the offensive in the Pacific. And that time came in August 1943 at the Quadrant meeting of the United Nations in Quebec.

'At that time, the strategy for the offensive operations in the Pacific was laid down. The Joint Plans Committee strategy called for a surface operation across the Central Pacific, terminating somewhere on the east coast of China, and another one coming up through the southwest Pacific with the same objective. For the final victory over Japan, there was to be an invasion. There was no mention of any air offensive or of any strategic air warfare in these plans.

'At the conclusion of the meeting, Gen H. H. Arnold tabled a plan for airpower operations. He was determined that the B-29s should be used directly against Japan, rather than in support of a surface invasion by surface commanders. It was very difficult to rationalise, however, because we didn't have the bases. There was no way of getting to the Japanese islands at that time.

'Arnold proposed basing B-29s in India, and at advanced bases in China, and of attacking the Japanese homeland from those bases. The plan was immediately thrown out by the Joint Plans Committee and the Joint Logistics Committee as being completely infeasible. And it was a horrendous plan, but it was the only plan that would permit the use of the B-29s against Japan.

'It was brought up again at the Cairo Conference in December. Chiang Kai-Shek

Marpi Point, the northern tip of Saipan, was the site of a Japanese fighter strip, Banadaru field. It was converted, as were the other Japanese airfields on the island, into an operational strip for US aircraft.
/ Dr Lyman C. Perkins

Left: Kobler Field, a fighter strip adjacent to the B-29 base at Isley Field, was at the southwestern tip of Saipan. Isley is out of the picture on the right. The prominent mountain (left centre) is Mount Topatchau. Magicienne Bay and Kagman Point lie beyond the runway. Saipan was blocked on the West by an almost continuous reef, which can be seen in this picture. Anchored ships lie outside the reef. Saipan was, and remains, a beautiful island, with a moderate temperature range, and glistening white beaches behind the reefs. / *Dr Lyman C. Perkins*

Below: The operations shack on Isley Field was converted from the Japanese operations building at the field. The B-29 base was named after Navy Commander Robert H. Isely — the correct spelling — who was shot down during an attack on Aslito field. Somewhere along the line, his name went into the official records as Isley, and that's the spelling that was used. Notice the sign. It originally spelled the name correctly, and later the letters 'E' and 'L' were reversed. / *A. F. Migliaccio Collection*

was at the conference and he agreed to build the bases. The President approved it; we had abrogated a number of agreements with China, and this looked like an opportunity to do something that would recognise the importance of China. It was approved in spite of its very bad logistics.

'There were three very important things accomplished at Cairo, from our point of view. One of them was the recognition of a strategic air offensive. The plans from Cairo on recognised the strategic air operation as one of the vital elements of the overall strategy. The second thing was the approval of the bases in China, and the agreement of the British that they would build bases in India, in order to launch the B-29 operations. The third was the agreement of the Joint Chiefs of Staff (JCS) to capture the Marianas islands as bases for B-29 operations, and that of course was a basic strategic step.

'When we got back from Cairo, we began to run into an extremely difficult command and control problem. The B-29s that were operating in the China-Burma-India (CBI) theatre would be under the control of Lt Gen Joseph W. Stilwell. This was also a political agreement of Quebec. There had been a lot of argument about American forces being commanded by British commanders, and the American position had insisted that all forces in the CBI theatre be under an American commander, who was Gen. Stilwell.

Above: The control tower at Isley Field performed only a secondary function in regulating the flow of aircraft on and off the field. Radio silence was maintained for all strikes, and so aircraft took off on a timetable, with flagmen to send each aircraft on its way. / *Collection of Mrs Thomas Isley*

Left: The roads on Saipan required some care in driving. Good safety practices demanded some reminders to drivers, and this billboard — one of many done around a similar theme — was one of the more striking eyecatchers. / *Dr Lyman C. Perkins*

CURVES ON ME MAY LOOK SWELL....... BUT ON THIS ROAD THEY CAN BE HELL—

DRIVE CAREFULLY—

Left: Over the tail of V-45 is the panorama of the hardstand area of the 499th Bomb Group, 73rd Bomb Wing, at Isley Field on Saipan. Quonset huts and tents dot the spaces between the aircraft. The aircraft are standing quietly now, waiting for the crowds of armourers, mechanics, technicians and ground crews to arrive and prepare them for the next mission.
/ *AAF Pacific via Boeing-Wichita*

Below: Later in the war, the hardstand area of the 497th Bomb Group, 73rd Bomb Wing, looked like this. Same planes, same tents and Quonsets, same feeling of quiet waiting. Only the tail markings have changed, the A above the 73rd Wing's square symbol was replaced by the single large A on the vertical tail.
/ *Dr Lyman C. Perkins*

'But Stilwell had ideas of his own about using the B-29s, and for using them in Southeast Asia. The Marianas, when we got them would be in Admiral Chester W. Nimitz' command area; he naturally assumed that he would have control of all forces in the area. Gen Douglas A. MacArthur was screaming to high heaven for B-29s for the Southwest Pacific, prompted by Lt Gen George C. Kenney. Kenney had been in on the inception of the B-29s at the Materiel Division. He had a great desire to get them. Gen MacArthur had a great deal of influence, and great pressure was brought to bear to get the B-29s to the Southwest Pacific. In addition, if we built a base in the Aleutian chain as once suggested, that base would be under still another commander.

'What we needed was centralised control at the target, not the base area, but it's very difficult to do that properly. We found a way, however, through — of all the people in the world — Admiral Ernest J. King, Chief of Naval Operations (CNO). With Gen Arnold's agreement I went to him and told him that we had a problem very much like the Navy problem. Their fleets were based at various bases in many theatres of operation, but the control of these forces was retained through Navy channels all the way up to Admiral King. The theatre commanders who controlled the bases had no control over Admiral King's forces.

'We had a similar problem. We had strategic air forces based in many separate theatres, but the critical issue was to control them at the target area: Japan. This was going to require centralised control similar to that

exercised by the Navy, and actually similar to that exercised by Admiral King. He was not only CNO and Navy member of the JCS, he was also Commander in Chief, US Fleets, and he commanded and controlled Naval fleet units wherever they might be.

'We suggested to him that a similar arrangement might be appropriate for the B-29 strategic air forces, and that Gen Arnold might occupy a similar position on the JCS, exercising control over the B-29s wherever they might be. Admiral King agreed to this, Gen George C. Marshall went along with it, and on the basis of this we got the Twentieth Air Force (20 AF) established.' *Haywood S. Hansell, commander, 73rd BW*

Setting Sun to Matterhorn

The debate on the best employment of the B-29 force was not settled until after the first B-29s had arrived in India, ready to fly combat missions. It had started with an ambitious plan called Setting Sun, which was modified into one called Twilight, which was further modified into a plan called Matterhorn which was argued, changed, augmented, reduced, simplified, complicated, reconsidered and finally informally approved by the JCS in April 1944. In its final form, Matterhorn assigned the first operational unit — the 58th Bombardment Wing (Very Heavy) — to India and advance bases in China, and assigned the second and subsequent wings to the Marianas. Logistics support of the 58th in China was to be by air, using the B-29s themselves.

It took a year to approve Matterhorn from the time that Gen Arnold had named Brig Gen Kenneth B. Wolfe to organise, equip and train B-29 units. The 58th Bomb Wing was activated 1 June 1943, established at Marietta (Georgia) Army Air Field (AAFld) 15 June and Gen Wolfe moved in as commander 21 June. Training, it had been decided, would be done in the area near Wichita, Kansas, where Boeing had built a new factory to turn out the B-29s. The Second Air Force was given the task, and set up on four fields: Smoky Hill AAFld near Salina; Pratt AAFld, at Pratt; Great Bend AAFld, at Great Bend; and Walker AAFld, near Victoria, Kansas.

Wolfe moved his headquarters to Smoky Hill in mid-September, and took over 27 November as commander of the newly organised XX Bomber Command, which included the 58th Bomb Wing and the newly activated 73rd Bomb Wing, later to be assigned elsewhere.

'I'd been at Langley Field, Virginia, with a Signal Heavy Construction Battalion and was transferred, on 11 August 1943, to Marietta Army Air Field, to be assistant communications officer in the newly formed 58th Bomb Wing. The problem, of course, was to get the 58th ready for deployment overseas and combat in what was no time at all.

'The first B-29 any of us had ever seen arrived during the month and promptly went into the shop for rework. About a week later, it was rolled out on the ramp, ready to go. Somehow, the main landing gear switch was activated, and the B-29 collapsed on the ramp with a great crunch. People were working

Above: Inside the Quonset hut you had a bunk, a dresser made of bomb crate wood salvaged from the dump, and a clothesline that served to hang your extensive wardrobe and your laundry. TSgt Anthony F. Migliaccio, CFC gunner on *Thumper*, lived here, his 'room' labelled by the stencil on the side of his B-4 bag at the head of his bunk. His helmet hangs from the left side of the foot of the bunk. / *A. F. Migliaccio Collection*

Top left: And this was your home away from home, if you were a combat crew member of the 73rd Wing on Saipan: Standard Quonset huts, with corrugated sheet metal sides and roof to warm in the sun, and some semblance of ventilation from hinged side panels and the roof vent. The hut with the picture-window front was the squadron mess hall. / *Ferd J. Curtis Collection*

Bottom left: Let's be frank; the accommodation on Saipan was not de luxe. Sgt Don Hetrick (left) and his buddy stand in front of their living quarters, and the name explains itself. / *Don C. Hetrick Collection*

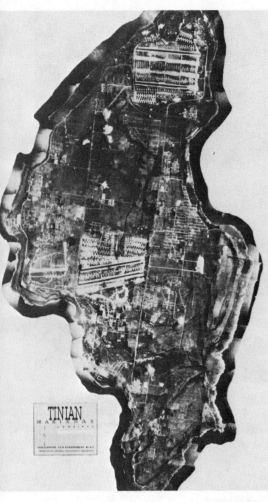

around it at the time, but the only casualty was a civilian engineer who had been standing on a ladder in the rear bomb bay when the gear folded. The medical report was that he had not been touched by any part of the airplane, but had a heart attack and died from that.

'Less than a month after arriving at Marietta, I was transferred to Smoky Hill AAFld for duty with the 58th Bomb Wing Development Detachment, an advance headquarters for the wing until it could be moved from Marietta.

'We were supposed to be ready to fly combat missions in May 1944, and we had yet to see more than one B-29. We had to select four training bases, create bomb groups, find the men to fill the tables of organisation, get the equipment, and complete accelerated service tests on the aircraft. And while we were doing this, thousands of Chinese and Indian labourers were building four fields in China and four in India.

'Well, the service tests were very limited. We wanted to make sure some of the radios worked in the air, and they did.' *Francis B. Morgan, ass't communications officer, 58th BW*

The tables of organisation called for a bomb wing of four groups, each with four squadrons, with seven aircraft per squadron. Eleven-man crews were assigned to the squadrons, two for each airplane. On paper,

Right: Parts of three of Tinian's North Field runways can be seen in this picture, taken from about 2,000 feet almost directly over one runway. At left centre, one B-29 picks her way along the taxiway, headed out of her hardstand and toward takeoff. */ Dr Lyman C. Perkins*

Above: This overhead photo mosaic of Tinian shows the two major airfields used by American units after the island was captured. North Field, with its four parallel runways, is — logically — at the North end of the island. It was home for the 313th Bomb Wing and later added another tenant: The 509th Composite Group. About midway along the island is West Field, home of B-24 units. */ 313th Wing Photographic Laboratory*

Right: North Field on Tinian was the world's biggest bomber base, and probably still holds that record. Four parallel runways, each nearly two miles long, handled the movements of the 313th Bomb Wing and the 509th Composite Group. In this picture, B-29s are rolling on three of the runways, and at least 200 more can be counted. */ Dr Lyman C. Perkins*

Top right: Northwest Field on Guam was home base for the 315th Bomb Wing and its turretless B-29Bs. Here, aircraft 73 of the 501st Bomb Group shows its clean upper and lower fuselage decking, unbroken by turrets. / *Murray Singer*

Centre right: Nine mechanics — and maybe one or two more hidden by the huge nacelles — swarm over the number one and two engines of this 500th Bomb Group B-29. This may show an engine change on number one; the support underneath the nacelle looks like a jacking unit rather than a standard wheeled maintenance stand. Two cowl panels, containing a section of the ducting to carry air to the engine, lie on the ground near the camera.
/ *James J. Garrity Collection*

Below: The designers didn't intend that the engine cowling would serve as steps and a perch, but that's the way it turned out in practice. The number four engine of this B-29 gets detailed attention from a trio of mechanics.
/ *Mike Janosko Collection*

it looked good; but the facts were different for aircraft availability and crew experience.

There was only one B-29 available to every 12 crews in training. By the end of 1943, only 67 first pilots had been checked out in the Superfortresses, crews had logged an average of only 18 hours in the planes, and only a half-hour of formation flying in that time. In fact, only one B-29 had even flown a long-range mission.

The 58th was due to ship out, and was nowhere ready to do so. By the end of January 1944, the training programme should have been completed; but less than half had been accomplished. There were three major reasons for shortfalls in the crew training programme. First, delays had occurred in both airframe and engine production. Second, modification programmes were essential to make production aircraft suitable for combat. Third, trained mechanics were lacking, so an abnormally high percentage of Superfortresses were unfit to fly.

Things had gotten critical by the end of February, and Arnold sent out a special team from Washington to break those three bottlenecks. The team had a simple directive: Get the B-29s to India, ready for combat.

One result was the 'Kansas blitz' or 'The Battle of Kansas', as it later became known. Military and civilian employees from the

Army Air Forces, from Boeing and Wright and subcontractors all over, worked on rows of B-29s parked outside in one of the worst Kansas winters in memory. Howling winds could carry a heavy piece of engine cowling a hundred yards along the icy ramp. Snow fell, driven horizontally by frigid blasts, reducing visibility and making working and walking hazardous. Frostbite was a very real danger. Working hours were stretched until people were at the breaking point. Some critical parts were delivered by ambulance.

But when it was over, the B-29s had gone on their way with their crews, late to be sure, and with a whole new job of learning ahead of them.

Building the Bases

An existing network of B-24 bases in India, on the plains west of Calcutta, was the starting point for B-29 base construction. They had existing runways, concrete and 6,000 feet long, which could be strengthened and lengthened.

Wolfe set up headquarters at Kharagpur, about 65 miles from Calcutta by rail, and selected four other bases at Dudhkundi, Piardoba, Kalaikunda and Chakulia. The work force included about 6,000 US troops from Engineer Aviation units, augmented by 27,000 Indian civilians. Work began in late

November 1943; they installed a fuel pipeline from Calcutta to the bases, added concrete to strengthen the runways and lengthened them to 7,500 feet.

The schedule was tough, and wasn't met. A British base at Charra, taken over by the US by agreement, received the first B-29s in April 1944.

'Charra was originally a British base for medium bombers and fighters. It consisted of two runways; one 6,000 feet long and the other approximately 4,000 feet long at right angles. The runways sloped with the lay of the land. The land didn't lay too well. When landing, if the back slope or the top c. one of the ridges was overshot, half of the runway was automatically unused. We attribute our lack of runway trouble to the conservative statement: we had the best pilots in the Air Force.

'The months spent at Charra were the hot months of the year. The hottest month was June, just before the summer monsoon rains. The sky was generally clear and the scorching wind was from the India desert to the northwest. The only precipitation came from the afternoon thunderstorms and line squalls . . . preceded and accompanied by thick blowing dust and strong gusty winds. The normal maximum temperature was 115

The cowl panels of the B-29 nacelles were held in place by Dzus fasteners, a patented quarter-turn screw with a spring retainer. They were a loose fit in the hole, but could be drawn up very tightly, to secure the cowling even after it had been bent out of shape by continual removal and re-attachment. The mechanic has just begun the task of opening up the engine nacelle preparatory to doing any of a number of things to its complex interior. / Mrs Thomas Isley Collection

degrees and the normal minimum at night was 85 degrees. Due to the heat the working hours were from 0700 to 1500.

'Because of the decreased lift due to heat and an increasing number of engine fires on takeoff, the times of flying were set at a maximum of 105 degrees, which meant no flying between 0900 and 1700 each day.'
444th Bomb Group unit history

Charra was used until July 1944, and the other bases were not completed until September. Kalaikunda became a transport base; the others handled B-29s.

The advance bases in China were built near Chengtu and the villages of Kwanghan, Kiunglai, Hsinching and Pengshan. Local farmers were conscripted for the work, with village quotas being 50 workers per 100 households. By the end of January 1944, about 200,000 had turned out. They started draining the rice paddies on 24 January. Exactly three months later, on 24 April, the first B-29 landed at the first available field, Kwanghan. By 1 May, all four fields were open for traffic, and some of the fields were operationally ready. It was a remarkable task, done by hand by thousands of Chinese labourers.

'On 4 February 1944, I was moved from Smoky Hill to Washington on TDY. The orders were secret, because I had been designated as security officer for a couple of plane loads of cryptographic material. From Washington I went to Miami Beach on the first leg of a long flight via Marrakech, Morocco, and Karachi to Kharagpur, India, Headquarters of XX Bomber Command. I arrived on 1 March with the crypto material and at the end of the month was moved to Hsinching. The base was designated A-1 to distinguish it from three other bases exactly alike and in the same area. A-1, A-2, A-3 and A-4 together formed the forward bases for the four groups of the 58th Wing.

'I was promoted to major and was assigned duty as Communications Officer of Advance Headquarters. That was on 7 April, and A-1 was the advance headquarters of the 40th Bomb Group, but in name only. I arrived there before the base was finished and obviously before any of the B-29s arrived.

'The bases had been rice paddies. They were drained and then excavated to a solid base of earth, and then painstakingly built up to a level about six feet above the surrounding paddies. It was all hand work, done with shovels, wheelbarrows, shoulder-yokes carrying baskets of rocks, and thousands upon thousands of Chinese. There would be up to 90,000 working on any one runway at one time. The final layer of small stones was topped with a slurry of mud —

probably a fairly stiff clay mix — and compacted with huge rollers pulled by dozens of labourers. The runways were 8,500 feet long, and the altitude was about 2,000 feet above sea level at those bases. It would have helped if the runways had been concrete, but you can't have everything.'
Francis B. Morgan

The complex of bases in India and China would bring much of Japan's steel industry into target range. But the rich oil fields of Sumatra, a Japanese-held prize, were out of reach. The only way seen to hit them was by staging the B-29s through Ceylon.

The British had developed airfields on that large island, and discussions and negotiations finally settled on one of them, China Bay on the northeast coast. It was expanded to handle two B-29 groups with a total of 56 airplanes. The runway was extended to 7,200 feet, and additional hardstands and a fuel distribution and storage system were completed by mid-July 1944. The field was officially operational on 10 August, when the first mission to use the base staged through there. It was also the only B-29 mission ever to use the China Bay field.

Preparing for Combat

The 58th Wing flew its air echelons out to India by way of Gander, Marrakech, Cairo and Karachi. They settled in, with the 58th Headquarters and its 40th Bomb Group taking the base at Chakulia, the 444th Group operating temporarily out of Charra, the 462nd out of Piardoba, and the 468th sharing the field at Kharagpur with the headquarters operations of XX Bomber Command.

Then began a massive effort to move fuel and other supplies to the Chinese bases in quantity, to meet planned dates for combat sorties. Some Consolidated C-87 cargo aircraft were attached to the Command, and they were to be augmented by the B-29s themselves. Some of the bombers had been stripped of all armament except the tail guns, and could lift about seven tons of fuel in auxiliary tanks as against their usual complement of three tons. Air Transport Command also assigned aircraft to the supply task, and flights over the Hump began. They left their bases near Calcutta, flew northeasterly over the Brahmaputra River valley, and turned east at Likiang or Hsichang in China to head for the advance bases. It was a dangerous route, with bad and sudden changes of weather, poor communications, and the danger of interception by Japanese fighters. It counted as combat time for the B-29 crews.

The hauling started early in 1944; it was July before the B-29 operation approached a self-sufficient basis. That month, the

Superfortresses transported about 3,000 tons of supplies, just enough to support the 115 combat sorties they flew during July. But that was the best rate they achieved as cargo craft, and it was less than half of the combat effort they were expected to make.

Under the best conditions, it took two gallons of fuel burned by the B-29s to deliver one gallon to an advance base. Under the worst conditions, it took twelve gallons.

Events were soon to make these advance bases an unneeded asset. A policy shift had resulted in plans to capture the Marianas islands as bases for the B-29s, and that day was near. Further, the operations out of China were so inefficient that Gen Arnold already was weighing alternatives. It was a hopeless cause, and the B-29 effort was redirected to the Marianas.

The Island Bases

The Mariana Islands stretch 500 miles along a gentle arc parallel to the Mariana Trench, a deep cleft in the Pacific Ocean that includes the world's deepest spot, sounded 36,198 feet down. They lie between latitudes of 13 and 21 degrees North, and if you fly north-northwest out of Saipan, Tinian, or Guam, you will fly over the home islands of Japan, about 1,800 miles distant.

That distance made the Marianas very important to the B-29 offensive. No other prospective base area offered available flat land at a reasonable remove from the target area, land that could be seized and held against an enemy that was beginning to feel the effects of its over-extended supply lines. And so the Marianas were marked for invasion and capture by American forces. Amphibious units moved into the area, preceded and supported by heavy bombing and shelling by Air Forces and Navy aircraft and Navy battleships.

The first blow was struck against Saipan on 15 June 1944, the same day that B-29s first bombed Japan from bases in China. The Marine 2nd and 4th Divisions hit the beaches at Saipan; by afternoon of the next day they had secured enough of a beachhead for a landing by the Army's 27th Infantry Division. Aslito airfield was captured by the evening of 18 June, and four days later Republic P-47 fighters of the 19th Fighter Squadron were in action, operating from the field against the remaining pockets of resistance on the island. Mopping up continued until the end of the war, but the island was secured for all practical purposes by 9 July.

Guam was next; its capture began 21 July, with a landing by the Marines' 3rd Division and 1st Provisional Brigade, augmented by the 305th Regimental Combat Team of the 77th Infantry Division. By 10 August they had taken the island and organised resistance had ceased.

Tinian was invaded 24 July by the Marine 4th Division, rested a bit after helping to take Saipan. The island was secured by 1 August.

The dust had hardly settled on the coral before the Seabees took over. Seabees — the word was a short way of referring to Naval Construction Brigades, abbreviated NCB or simply CB — filled the bomb craters, regraded the airfields, repaired or replaced buildings, laid out streets, blasted latrines and made the islands not only useful, but habitable, to a greater or lesser degree. In some cases, the schedules were impossible to keep. Saipan's Isley Field — renamed from Aslito when the ownership changed hands — was not really ready for B-29 operations when the first aircraft arrived 12 October 1944.

The Seabees had a little more than 90 days to convert Aslito, a small, bomb-cratered single coral strip, into Isley Field, a huge complex capable of handling the 73rd Bomb Wing: Four bomb groups, 12 bomb squadrons, 240 B-29s and supporting units by the dozens. That they didn't meet the schedule was hardly a surprise; that they came close was a miracle.

The largest bomber base ever built was the one on Tinian, the responsibility of the 6th Naval Construction Brigade (several Seabee battalions made up one brigade). North Field, which handled the 313th Bomb Wing and the 509th Composite Group, had four parallel, paved 8,500-foot long runways, plus their attendant taxiways, hardstands, fuel and bomb dumps, warehouses, shops, housing, roads, sanitation . . . the list is almost endless. The Seabees also built West Field on Tinian for the 58th Bomb Wing, with two parallel 8,500-foot runways.

On Guam, the 5th Naval Construction Brigade built North Field for the 314th Bomb Wing, and Northwest Field for the 315th. On Iwo Jima, the 9th Naval Construction Brigade finished a single, 9,800-foot paved runway, completing it in stages as control of the island gradually passed from the dogged Japanese defenders to the Americans.

Other bases were planned for, and partially constructed, on Okinawa and Ie Shima, as part of the overall concept of basing 20 B-29 groups on those islands.

The Seabees became a legend in their own time, for their brave work under fire. And, in spite of the inter-service rivalry, the airmen respected the Seabees and appreciated what they were doing. They recognised the contribution in a unique way: At least three B-29s were named after Seabee units: The 9th, 18th and 110th Naval Construction Battalions.

Right: The most common battle damage done to the B-29s was from anti-aircraft bursts nearby. The shrapnel would riddle the aircraft, making dozens, sometimes hundreds of small to medium-sized holes, all needing repair. This pair of photographs shows typical flak damage to a B-29 of the 500th Bomb Group. / *James J. Garrity Collection*

Bottom right and below: The Spirit of F.D.R., a B-29 from the 504th Bomb Group, 313th Bomb Wing, staggered back to Tinian with most of her vertical tail shot away. Now the engineering officers and staff take over; how much has to be replaced? How soon can she be back in action? Can we patch the tail or does it all have to come off? / *313th BW*

220

Keeping Them Flying

There were very detailed plans for maintenance and support of the B-29s in their combat environment, looking fine on paper, but lacking something when applied to the real world.

Guam Air Depot was to be set up to provide primary support for all B-29s in the Marianas. It was not even organised when the Superfortresses flew their first attack against Japan from Saipan on 24 November 1944, and was not ready to supply fourth-echelon maintenance for the B-29s until February 1945. Some of its facilities, particularly the floating units, didn't arrive until April 1945.

This meant that the service groups attached to XXI Bomber Command units had to perform work that had never been contemplated for them to do. In November 1944, Gen Hansell said, in effect, enough of this, and changed the supply and maintenance procedures to match the needs of the war.

Centralisation was the answer; all supply and maintenance functions came under a deputy chief of staff at Hansell's headquarters. Maintenance at the Group level, which had been the standard procedure planned, was replaced by a pooled operation under the wing maintenance controller. Centralised shops were established and production techniques were adapted quickly. The new system was much more flexible, much more responsive to the conditions of war.

'We were getting about 200 to 250 hours of operation out of an engine initially, before it was time to replace it with another. That meant maybe 15 missions average, assuming the engine wasn't hit by flak or fighters, and that there were no operational problems. Later in the war — by about June 1945 — we got that figure up to 750 hours per engine, which wasn't bad, considering the conditions under which those engines had to perform. One of the reasons was that some of our men figured out a way to add some cooling area to the rear cylinder bank; we fabricated the baffles there, installed them, and dropped the rear cylinder head temperatures by 45C. That change was incorporated in later production engines.

'We made wheeled engine stands for easy handling and the wheels were bogies from the scrapped amphibious landing craft that had littered the beaches at Saipan. We made extra ones for the squadrons, and they could pull an engine, hang it on the stand, and haul it over to our shop for a replacement engine. They got so they could do the whole cycle — pull the old engine, put on a new one — in five and one-half hours. We didn't overhaul engines on the islands; we just weren't equipped for that. They had to go back to the States for overhaul.

'Incoming B-29s brought new engines in for inventory; they could carry a spare R-3350 in the bomb bay. We had to do the engine build-up, because the engines arrived crated with unmounted accessories and carburettors, and we had to install them and build up the complete powerplant with hose connections, coolers, and such. We had an engine build-up line going in the big canvas-

topped warehouse we used as a shop. We could handle 275 engines at one time.

'Engine generators were our worst single problem in maintenance, and most of the trouble centred on the brushes. Another trouble area was in the control system for the Hamilton Standard props. It was susceptible to fungus, and the fungus would spread, short out the controls, and the prop would run away in flight.

'Tyres took a hell of a beating, and we got maybe ten to 15 landings per set.

'One of the first problems we had to face was what to do to clear the runway if the gear collapsed on a B-29 during takeoff, for example. It was critical to keep that runway open and handling departures. We didn't want to ruin the airplane completely, as we would if we just bulldozed it off the runway. There was always a shortage of spares and we could repair or cannibalise a ship that wasn't badly damaged. But we did have to consider getting a more-or-less whole B-29 off the runway fast.

'We finally settled on a pair of big "cats" (tractors) with cables that could be slung over each wing root and attached to each "cat". We knew that combination would drag a fully-loaded B-29 off the runway if necessary. Happily, we never had to do that particular job, but the twin "cats" were always on standby near the runway during takeoffs.'
Alberto R. Pearson, commander, 52nd Eng'g Sqdn, 330th Service Grp

The statistics bear out the effectiveness of pooled wing maintenance. The abort rate for mechanical failures was almost twentythree

per cent in January 1945, before the wing maintenance concept was in full operation. It dropped to about seventeen per cent in February, ten per cent in March through June, less than seven per cent in July and seven and one-half per cent in August.

There was never any critical problem with parts supplies, even during the maximum-effort raids of March 1945, although there was a chronic shortage of B-29 spare parts until the end of the war. The supply bins and shelves did get very empty at times.

All the parts in the world can be available, and be useless unless they are installed by superior technicians. The B-29 ground crews never got much recognition — although late in the war their names were added to the sides of some B-29s — and few decorations. But the B-29 combat record would have been a sorry one indeed if it had not been for the endless, fatiguing, dirty, often painful work done and done well and continually by the ground crews that truly kept the B-29s flying.

'Before Iwo was taken, the Japanese used to fly over from Iwo and raid Saipan, shoot up the place and drop a few bombs. They'd come in low, part of the time.

'We had some ground crew guys on the airplanes, getting them ready for the first mission to Tokyo. Our lights were on for working around the ships. And here they came — we saw red streaks by the runway and nobody had to tell us it was the Japanese coming in low and trying to knock out our B-29s, and us too. There was one guy working on top of the fuselage, around one of the top turrets. He saw the Japanese, jumped off the top of that airplane, hit the ground and kept running. And that's a hell of a drop!

'The Betties (Mitsubishi G4M2 bombers) used to come over almost every night we were there, before Iwo was taken.' *Gerald Coke, CFC specialist, 869th BS, 497th BG*

There was a story in *Brief*, the official publication of the Army Air Forces in the Pacific Ocean Area, that told it well. It may be a legend, it may not even be about a B-29, but it has a universal ring of truth and it applies.

The latest report the ground crew had was that their plane had feathered number three engine and number two was throwing oil. The hydraulic system had been shot out, and the engineer had spliced the control cables running to the horizontal and vertical surfaces, hoping they'd hold for the trip back. All equipment had been ditched, and she was managing to hold 3,000 feet altitude.

Then they saw her, one feathered, smoke pouring out of another engine, on final approach. She landed, taxied to the hardstand. The crew chief saw a hole in one cowling, skin rips and tears in the belly. Hydraulic fluid was dribbling down a prop blade. He saw a flak hole just outside an oil line under the cowling of number two engine. Inside, he checked the spliced cables.

The pilot came up to him and said, "Guess she's ready for the graveyard, huh?"

The crew chief looked him straight in the eyes and said, "No, sir! Not *MY* plane!"

Sometimes they just ran off the runway and into the ditch, as did this B-29 of the 505th Bomb Group, 313th Bomb Wing. The props seem to be in low pitch and the partially deflected flaps indicate that the accident probably happened during takeoff. The recovery cranes are already on the job, and will move the stricken aircraft out of the ditch for analysis, repair or the scrap pile. / *313th Bomb Wing*

Thunder out of China

The first combat mission flown by B-29 Superfortresses in World War 2 was sent against the Makasan railroad shops in Bangkok, Thailand, on 5 June 1944. The big bombers flew from Kharagpur on a round trip of about 2,000 miles. The Japanese defences were expected to be light. It was to be a shakedown mission, but yet one with enough difficulty to introduce the crews and their aircraft to real combat.

In an early morning take-off, 98 B-29s got into the air; 14 of them aborted later. They were supposed to fly in four-plane diamonds, but the weather posed some problems and the formation never solidified. The target was overcast; the formations, such as they were, broke into loose gaggles of single and paired aircraft. Individual planes made their runs over the target, some bombing by radar, some visually, from altitudes between 17,000 and 27,000 feet. The mission had been briefed to drop between 23,000 and 25,000 feet. Seventy-seven planes bombed the target, 48 of them by radar through the overcast.

The trip back was just as disorganised. Five B-29s were lost on the return, 12 landed at B-29 bases not their own, and 30 landed at bases outside the Command. Reconnaissance photos taken a few days later showed that 16 to 18 bombs had fallen in the target area. It was not a great start.

The second strike — a night raid — got off the ground on 15 June, with 68 Superforts headed for the Imperial Iron and Steel Works, in Yawata, Japan. Forty-seven bombed the target, 15 visually and 32 by radar. There was one combat loss, six non-combat losses of aircraft, and a total of 55 crewmen killed or missing. The post-strike photos showed a single hit in the target area, on a powerhouse three-quarters of a mile from the aiming point.

It looked like an impossible situation for the XX Bomber Command. Its resources were strained to the breaking point; the logistics of supplying the advance bases posed nearly insolvable problems. The first two combat missions had done little to impress observers. Wolfe was relieved on 4 July, and sent back to the States with a promotion.

Brig Gen LaVerne G. Saunders was left in temporary command and he continued to order missions against enemy targets. One of them, 10 August, sent 54 Superfortresses agains the oil storage and refinery at Palembang, staging through Ceylon on the trip to and from the distant target. The only damage was done to one small building, and Ceylon was never used again by the B-29s.

On 29 August Maj Gen Curtis E. LeMay arrived to take over the XX Bomber Command. He rode the 8 September strike

Cowl flaps opened wide for maximum available — never enough — cooling on the ground, all four of the big Wright R 3350 engines powering the *Eddie Allen* roar in a full-power run-up. Based at Chakulia, India, *Eddie Allen* carries the four horizontal tail stripes and tip identifying the 40th Bomb Group. The stripes were yellow, the squadron colour of the 45th Bomb Squadron of the 40th BG. *Eddie Allen* was a B-29-40-BW, serial number 42-24579. / *Boeing 88806*

against Anshan, Manchuria, as an observer, and what he learned resulted in an operational revision for the Command. LeMay replaced the four-plane diamond with the 12-plane formation he had used with great success in Europe. He decided to concentrate on daylight precision attacks, and to subordinate night strikes. He suggested that both radar operator and bombardier follow the bomb run, and drop the bombs depending on who had the target in sight at the last critical moment before the triggering. Finally, he asked each group to designate six lead crews, and set up a school to train lead bombardiers.

On 20 September, the Command was streamlined. The 58th Wing was disbanded, along with 16 maintenance squadrons and four B-29 squadrons. Their personnel and aircraft were redistributed in an organisation which had three squadrons of ten airplanes

Top right: Rows of fuel drums, jacketed mechanics and the desolate appearance of the place seem to mark this as a forward base in China. The aircraft is from the 40th Bomb Group, possibly from the 25th Bomb Squadron (red tail stripes and tip).
/ *Ron E. Witt Collection*

Centre right: The huge roller in the foreground was used by the Chinese who built this forward base to compact the crushed rock foundations for the runways. The Superfortress with the neatly aligned props carries the yellow tail stripes and tip of the 45th Bomb Squadron.
/ *Ron E. Witt Collection*

Below: This line of Superfortresses, pristine and devoid of any markings except for serial numbers and manufacturer's hull numbers, is parked at a forward base in China waiting to be fuelled and armed for the raid of 15 June 1944, against Yawata and the Imperial Iron and Steel Works. It was to be the second combat mission for the B-29s, and was to produce a single hit on a powerhouse almost one mile from the aiming point.
/ *USAF 52819 A.C. via Boeing-Wichita*

each, per group, instead of the former complement of four squadrons with seven B-29s each. Maintenance squadrons were merged with bomber squadrons, so that ground personnel increased in number for each squadron.

'Mission by mission the Superfort was proving itself, and the men who flew her had become acquainted with her every whim and foible. These men were now thoroughly indoctrinated in the harsh school of combat and they accomplished their mission with cool precision and deadly "know how". Squadrons hit the target and withdrew in tight defensive formation bristling with cooly manned and accurately fired 50-calibre gun turrets. Flight engineers calculated their gas consumption and established power settings which returned them to base within 50 gallons of the expected 150 gallon reserve. Navigators felt their way across the uncharted and ever changing vastness of China with obscure landmarks and exacting celestial navigation, and terminated their 1,200 mile trip by splitting the home airfield. Letdowns into the mountain-walled Chengtu valley were effected by pilots feeling, timing and guessing their way in the heavy soup and often severe icing on multi-split bent radio-range legs through passes, over low ranges, and within the 20,000 foot west wall until successful contact was accomplished — sometimes a bare 50 feet above the ground. The men of the 20th considered these extreme operational conditions — but continued to carry on.' *444th Bomb Group unit history*

By that time, Arnold was considering the transfer of the XX Bomber Command to a better location. The move was stayed for a few months while the B-29s went after the targets they could reach.

There was a second strike against Anshan on 26 September, staged again through the forward bases near Chengtu, and almost 100 planes bombed the target. But the results were poor.

In October, the Command flew three missions in support of the invasion of Leyte in the Philippines, to hit targets on Formosa that were supplying the major share of aircraft to the Japanese defenders. The 14 October strike, against an aircraft assembly and overhaul plant at Okayama, Formosa, was the first punishing attack the B-29s flew. It had taken them ten missions to learn some of the tricks of the trade. They were to fly less effective missions during the rest of October, all of November and into December.

But in mid-December, they hit Hankow, China, in a raid that has since caused some controversy. Hankow was a major supply base for the Japanese forces in China, storing and moving a large portion of the logistical support for the occupying armies. Maj Gen Claire L. Chennault, commanding the 14th Strike Force in China, had argued loud and long for an air strike against Hankow by the B-29s, but had been denied each request. He had been told that such a raid would dilute the effectiveness of the strategic air war conducted by the B-29s, and that the job was properly the responsibility of the 14th Air Force.

The Japanese kicked off an attack in November that looked as if it were headed straight for Kunming. That city was one end of the strategic air routes over the Hump of the Himalayas, and its loss would have been

Beter 'n' Nutin tells an interesting and full combat life story in mission markers and nose art. She was a B-29-36-BW, serial 42-24538, assigned to the 676th BS, 444th BG, 58th BW. When photographed, she had completed 24 Hump flights, 25 bombing missions, acquired eight Purple Hearts for her crew, and shot down one Japanese fighter. In the left background is the tail of aircraft 17, a B-29-35-BW (42-24524) of the 444th BG, 58th BW. / *Ron E. Witt Collection*

critical to a lot of operations in China. This time, Chennault's pleas were heard and acted upon, and LeMay was directed to strike Hankow.

It was to be a joint attack with the 14th Air Force. The B-29s were targeted to strike the docks and warehouses along the Yangtze River by daylight, using loads of incendiary bombs; the heavy bombers from the 14th Air Force were to hit the Japanese-used airfields.

Ninety-four B-29s lifted off the advance bases in China on 18 December, and 84 of them fire-bombed Hankow. The plan had called for a carefully timed sequence of formation flights and drops over the target, but the timing was off and smoke from the fires started by the first formations hampered accurate bombing by the later groups. No matter; the bombs that hit the target burned out about half of the designated area, and ended Hankow's value as a major supply base.

For some time afterward, this single fire raid was cited as 'the reason' for LeMay's later decision to make the fire-bombing of Japan a primary B-29 mission. But such strikes against Japanese cities had been in mind even before Hankow was hit, and before the B-29s had even been committed to combat. Careful and extensive studies had been made at various planning levels. At least two prototype sections of towns, built according to the best intelligence information on Japanese architecture and construction,

Left: On the high road, this formation of B-29s from the 44th Bomb Group shows the diamond markings identifying the group. In the centre of the picture is a camouflaged B-29-1-BW, serial number 42-6251, the 37th production aircraft off the line at Wichita. / *Ron E. Witt Collection*

Below: Made up attractively and posed prettily, *American Beauty* shows off the slim lines of the Queen of the Skies. She was born in Wichita, a B-29-45-BW, and christened with a number: 42-24703. Her rudder and cowl panels carry her colours, probably the yellow of the 794th BS. The two diagonal stripes on the rudder marked aircraft of the 468th Bomb Group. Names of Group aircraft were painted in the streamer, coming off the nose like the tail of a comet. The radome for the AN/APQ-13 bomb-nav radar juts down between the bomb bays. / *Ron E. Witt Collection*

Right: The light-coloured dots forming a figure eight above the cowl flaps of the nacelle in the foreground are bombs dropped from the high Superfortress at the right. Another bomb cluster is obscured by the whirling propeller blades at left. The planes are from the 58th Bomb Wing, and it is early in their war against the Japanese.
/ Ron E. Witt Collection

Above: It is 3 November 1944, and above the winding and sluggish river and low cumulus clouds flies the *Eddie Allen* from the 40th Bomb Group of the 58th Bomb Wing, headed out on a strike against Rangoon.
/ USAF 57217 A.C. via Ron E. Witt

were erected at bombing ranges and fire-bombed to check the conclusions of the studies. USAAF Headquarters and XX Bomber Command Headquarters had both, independently, considered stripping the B-29s and sending them in low against the Japanese cities, armed with heavy loads of incendiary bombs.

The 18 December raid was further evidence that the concept was sound, and was considered as a 'test' strike. It must have carried some weight in LeMay's mind. But it was not 'the reason' that he made the decision later. That resulted from a much more detailed consideration of the advantages and the disadvantages of B-29 operations against the home islands of Japan.

On 15 January 1945, the B-29s flew their last mission from the advance Chinese bases. It was against Shinchiku, on Formosa, and it was one of several that month sent out to support another invasion of the Philippines, this one against Luzon. Three days later, LeMay was transferred to the Marianas as chief of the XXI Bomber Command.

The B-29s of the XX Bomber Command, now operating only out of their Indian bases, continued to fly against targets in Burma, French Indo-China, Malaya, Singapore and Thailand, but they were generally small shows of force against tactical targets suggested by theatre commanders. In February, the 58th Bomb Wing was deactivated, and the deployment of its forces to the Marianas began.

The last strike by Superfortresses in the China-Burma-India theatre was flown on 29 March 1945. It was a low-level assault against oil storage facilities on the island of Bukum, Singapore. By then, the first air echelons of the 58th Wing had left for the Marianas, and within days, the rest of the B-29s had loaded and flown away.

The XX Bomber Command flew only 49 missions in ten months, putting 3,058 aircraft sorties into the air and dropping 11,477 tons of bombs. It was a poor record: only about two combat sorties per aircraft per month. And of these missions, only a small fraction of them went against Japan.

They did score some notable successes, against Okayama and Hankow, in support of the invasions of Leyte and Luzon, and in their mining of the Shanghai area and its great river mouth, the Yangtze. That experience paid off later in the Marianas.

As a strategic bombing operation, the experience of the XX Bomber Command was of little value. But as a strategic bombing training and shakedown operation, it was of inestimable value. It had taken the B-29 from its fledgling status as an untried weapon of war and had shown the crews and the planners how to operate with it, how to attack with it, and how to cope with many of its technical and operational problems.

San Antonio and Beyond

The first B-29 combat strike from the Marianas against Japan was scheduled for November 1944. As is so often the case, that decision was made at a very high level of command, motivated by many political and strategic factors, and it was then up to the lower levels of command to carry out the operation. There were many pressures, of time, equipment, training, intelligence, and the availability and capability of the island bases themselves.

Gen Haywood S. Hansell, Jr, describes the background to that first mission:

'The JCS set up the 20th Air Force with Gen Arnold in command, acting as their executive agent, and they issued a directive for operations in the Pacific under the XXI Bomber Command. The first objective was listed as the undermining and defeat of the Japanese air forces through the destruction of engine and aircraft factories.

'It made pretty good sense. But it had some very extensive repercussions. In the first place, we didn't know where any of those engine and aircraft factories were. We knew there were some in the vicinity of Tokyo, some in Nagoya, but there were no photographs, no detailed maps, no target folders. Obviously, we were going to have to find them ourselves.

'In the second place, they were precision targets. We couldn't hit them by night operations, or by radar. So we would have to use daylight optical bombing to do that job. We would have to operate in formation with no fighter escort and against heavy opposition, and operating in formation would cut down the range of our aircraft very seriously.

'So we had to go into an almost convulsive change of tactical operations. In August 1944 we suddenly reversed the whole field of tactics on which the 73rd Wing had been training, abandoned the radar bombing approach, and adopted a new programme for optical bombing. This involved a drastic change, not only in bombing and formation flying, but also in gunnery. We had to learn to use the fire control system, which was very complex, and to select and adopt a bombing formation suitable to the firepower and flying characteristics of the B-29. The effect was to disrupt the whole training programme.

'I got a call to report to Washington just before Jack Catton (Commander, 873rd BS, 498th BG) and I were to go out to Saipan, and I had an interview with Gen Marshall in early October 1944. He said that the joint strategy for the Pacific campaigns had been laid out, and the bombing of Japan was part of that national strategy. He said that the first attack on Tokyo would be a joint operation with the Navy. The Navy would undertake to send a carrier task force up into the Japanese area to divert some of the defending fighters and to provide us with some fighter protection. The idea certainly was welcome from our point of view.

'Gen Marshall wanted to know whether we could carry out our part, which involved an attack on Japan in the month of November, a very short time from then, and he wanted a commitment on that. Obviously I couldn't very well tell him that we couldn't do it, so I told him yes, we could. And I said we not only could, but would. It would involve an attack from bases which were 6,000 miles away, which we had never seen but hoped were ready, against targets whose location we did not know.

'Two days later Jack Catton and I were heading for Saipan. We alternated flying on his airplane, which was called "Joltin' Josie, the Pacific Pioneer" (T Sq 5, 42-24614) and we arrived on Saipan on the twelfth of October after calling on Admiral Nimitz in Honolulu.' *Haywood S. Hansell, Jr*

At this point, let Catton interrupt the story:

'When Gen Hansell and I took the first B-29 out to the Marianas, it was still a classified airplane. So everywhere we went, we created quite a fuss. Would you believe that at Hickam, in Honolulu, we had a white-glove inspection of the airplane by Admiral Nimitz, Commander in Chief, Pacific? And thanks to Master Sergeant Quentin Hancock, my airplane could stand a white-glove inspection.

'When we went through Kwajalein, the island had just been taken in a very severe fight. A lot of blood had been shed to get that stepping-stone for us. We no sooner landed the airplane than a whole bunch of guards cordoned it off, put ropes around it. The folks were a bit upset, and properly so; they wanted to see this new, big airplane, and the Marines had it guarded and nobody could get near it.

'The next day when we came down to take off, there was a B-24 of the 7th Air Force parked next to us. They had a couple of officers standing by a big sign out in front of it, and the sign read, "This is a B-24, a combat airplane. Everybody welcome".' *Jack Catton, commander, 873rd BS, 498th BG*

Hansell, Catton and crew were met by cheering crowds, literally. Thousands of soldiers, sailors, and marines lined the runway, surged after the airplane as it taxied toward a hardstand. Hansell was asked to say a few words, and he did. 'The advance air element of the 73rd Bomb Wing has arrived on Saipan', he stated. 'When we've done some fighting, we'll do some talking'.

A difficult job lay ahead, as Hansell says: 'The situation was pretty bad. We thought we had two bases, with four paved runways, each 8,500 feet long, with shops, warehouses, and storage facilities available. Well, one of the bases couldn't handle B-29s at all because of a hill near one end of the runway. The other base was half-finished, with only one runway, and it was paved for only 6,000 feet. Its second runway was not finished at all.

'Instead of 100 hardstands for each base, we had about 40 all told, and no facilities: no shops, no warehouses, nothing but gasoline

storage and a bomb dump. We had to complete and organise a base, bring in 120 B-29s, and launch an operation in 35 days, and that was going to be very difficult to do.

'We hadn't been there but a short time when we got a big break. Captain Ralph D. Steakley (3rd Photo Reconnaissance Squadron) came in with a photo-recon B-29. He and his crew had been flying constantly, stopping only for refuelling, all the way from Kansas, and he insisted on going at once to Tokyo to get pictures. I tried to discourage him. I even thought of forbidding him, because they were exhausted. But they never faltered, and thank the Lord I did not forbid them, because the next day they fell on one of those rare occasions when the skies were absolutely clear over Japan, and they flew over Honshu for almost three hours and got magnificent pictures. They had pictures of all the aircraft and engine factories that we needed for our first objective. It was a tremendous break.

'But then things began to get a little bad. On 24 October the Japanese fleet started its operations against MacArthur's landings at Leyte Gulf in the Philippines, and there was a major naval engagement. The confusion threw the Navy command in the Pacific into complete disarray. We had only about 20 B-29s on Saipan by then, but I had them armed with 2,000lb bombs and declared our readiness to support the Navy to the best of

The 494th Bomb Group visits Japan and flies past one of its most spectacular tourist attractions. They are about 60 miles out of Tokyo, and all hell is about to break loose in the air and on the ground. Aircraft in the group include T-Square-21, *Lassie Come Home* (left foreground); T-Square-27, *Torchy* (lower right); and T-Square-22 *Bedroom Eyes* (above *Torchy*). / *XXI Bomber Command via Boeing-Wichita*

our abilities. Admiral Nimitz called off the Tokyo operation for the Navy, requested the JCS to stop the B-29s, and recommended that they ground us until such time as the Navy was able to give us the planned support.

'On top of this setback, Gen Kenney sent a most disturbing letter to Gen Arnold, with a very persuasive argument that we couldn't do the Tokyo operation from Saipan. He contended that we didn't have the range, and couldn't do the mission, and he said the Japanese would shoot us all out of the air anyway.

'The questions of range and defensive firepower were very sensitive. The Air Transport Command had refused to let us fly from California to Hawaii (2,400 miles) in squadron formation, without bomb loads, on the grounds that the airplanes lacked the necessary range. Yet almost immediately after arrival we would have to fly a 3,200-mile mission, with bomb loads, in the face of bitter Japanese fighter defences.

'Gen Arnold forwarded a copy of the letter to me and said that all his senior air commanders agreed with Kenney and that he was inclined to agree with him too. But he concluded, "If you still think you can carry out the mission, good luck."

'Almost at the same time I got a message to the effect that Admiral Nimitz had requested that the entire B-29 operations be devoted to aerial mining. Aerial mining is a fine idea; but the idea of shifting the entire aerial offensive against Japan to support the Navy's attack on the Japanese transportation system didn't sit very well with us.

'And then "Rosey" O'Donnell (Brig Gen Emmett O'Donnell, commander, 73rd Bomb Wing) came to me with a handwritten letter. We met in privacy, sitting on a log near my headquarters shack. He said frankly he didn't think the 73rd Bomb Wing was in any position to carry out the mission, and he proposed that we change it to a night operation.

'I said, "Rosey", I couldn't agree with you more. A night operation would be much safer, we could pull it much more easily, there is much less risk involved, but the catch is we can't do our job that way. If we have to tell the JCS that on our first mission we have had to give up the job, it will be very serious indeed. It will jeopardise not only the 20th Air Force and the strategic air war against Japan, but the whole future of the Air Force.

'These were the issues that were facing us just before that first operation:

'If we followed the Navy's first request, if we grounded ourselves until the Navy was ready to come along, we would be admitting that we couldn't operate without the support of the Navy, and we didn't want to put ourselves in that position.

'If we changed to the aerial mining operation, as requested by Admiral Nimitz, using the entire XXI Bomber Command, we would be abandoning the air war against the Japanese homeland and devoting ourselves to support of the Navy. This would destroy the basic reasoning for direct command by the JCS and hence would destroy the need for the 20th Air Force.

'If we went to night operations, we would have to abandon the primary target objectives which we had been given. This would also undermine confidence in the 20th Air Force, and raise questions about the need for it.

'If we tried to carry out our daylight attacks on the aircraft factories at Tokyo and failed, we would probably lose the Command as well as a lot of fine people.

'If we tried the daylight attack and succeeded, then the whole future was open to us.

'So at that time and under those conditions, the entire weight of the future was resting on the 73rd Wing: the air offensive against Japan, the future of the 20th Air Force and of air power in the Pacific, and the future of the United States Air Force.

'I took a deep breath and decided to go with the daylight mission as planned. I issued the orders for Mission San Antonio I. You know what happened from then on. It was successful. It did open the way. It did lead to victory over Japan by air power.' *Haywood S. Hansell, Jr*

Mission from the Marianas

V-Square-30 rumbles by, her radome protruding like a half-laid egg from her belly. Loaded and low on her wheels, she heads for the runway and a takeoff into her proper element, the air.
/ *AAF Pacific 1039-7 via Boeing-Wichita*

San Antonio I was directed against Tokyo, and specifically against the Musashino plant of the Nakajima Aircraft Co, Ltd, later to be known as the durable, infamous Target 357. The strike was planned to drop a mix of incendiary and 500lb general-purpose bombs, and was scheduled for 17 November.

Bad weather delayed the attack, first for a single 24-hour postponement, then through successive ones. Rain fell on Saipan, and the wind — so necessary as an aid to takeoff of the heavily loaded B-29s — swung around so that the preferred runway direction had to be reversed. Isley Field ran uphill in that direction, and it was obvious that the B-29s would be dangerously marginal in such a situation.

Finally the weather pattern broke, and the morning of 24 November was clear. 'Rosey' O'Donnell climbed aboard the lead B-29, *Dauntless Dotty*. Carrying the tail marking

A Sq 1, the aircraft was normally flown by Maj Robert K. Morgan, commander of the 869th Bomb Squadron, but 'Rosey' bumped him to co-pilot for this mission. At 0615 *Dauntless Dotty* began to roll. One after the other, 111 B-29s took off that morning. Several Boeing F-13As (reconnaissance versions of the B-29) from the 3rd Photo Reconnaissance Sqdn, also left Saipan to feint at Tokyo from the southeast, to drop 'rope' to decoy the Japanese radars, and to photograph the strike results.

The weather over Tokyo was miserable. There was a high-altitude wind of about 120 knots — later to be identified as the jet stream — which nudged the Superfortresses' ground speed toward the 450mph mark. An undercast almost hid the target. Already, 17 aircraft had aborted the mission, and six more were not able to bomb because of malfunctions.

The force that hit the primary target was 24 B-29s; the other 64 dropped on the urban areas and docks. Almost half of the striking planes had to bomb by radar. There was a single combat loss, when a B-29 was apparently intentionally rammed by a Japanese fighter and fell, out of control, into the water.

Photo coverage also was hampered by the weather. The post-strike photos showed that 48 bombs had hit in the factory area. Postwar studies showed how little damage had been done and that the casualties were 57 killed, 75 injured. Two B-29s had been lost, one to the fighter, and one when its fuel ran out and it had to be ditched. Eight Superforts were damaged by the enemy, and three by B-29 gunners who got carried away in the heat of their first engagement. One man was killed, a whole crew of 11 was missing and presumed dead, and four were wounded.

But the real value of that first raid lay in two intangibles. First, the B-29s had hit a very important and very heavily defended target area in bad weather and had come through their trial almost unscathed. Second, the attack served the first notice to the Japanese population that their home islands were no longer safe from direct attack.

The strike was typical of the attacks to follow over the next three months. Hansell's basic plan was to make maximum-effort attacks against high-priority targets in good weather with an available force of at least 60 Superforts. Secondary targets were to be attacked when the weather was not good enough for visual bombing and when the available force was smaller. And every night, a combined weather and strike mission was to go.

Top right: 'Throw your oxygen mask away, General LeMay is here to stay!' And that's the General himself, aircraft commander of this B-29 just touching down on a new runway in the Marianas. Wartime secrecy being what it was, not even the island is identified further. / *XXI Bomber Command via Boeing-Wichita*

Centre right: With bombs and guns loaded and props aligned, this B-29 waits for her crew on the hardstand at Saipan. / *Mrs Thomas Isley Collection*

Below: It's April 1945, and some of the 500th BG's B-29s have been marked with the big Z on the vertical tail while others still retain the smaller Z, the square of the 73rd Wing and the aircraft number as their identification. For the moment, this aircraft is alone on the hardstand, surrounded by jacks, maintenance stands, boxes, and oil drums that help to keep her in the air. / *Mike Janosko Collection*

'My first mission to Tokyo was a very eventful one. I hadn't flown in combat before; I'd been an instructor pilot for three years before I got my chance. I recall vividly flying in a formation some 1,600 miles up to the island of Honshu, and approaching our IP, which was Mount Fuji. Over Fuji we go, head into the bomb run, and we have what is now known as the jet stream. But back then, nobody had heard about jet streams.

'We're at 35,000 feet and we're doing about 500 miles per hour ground speed. Things were really happening fast. We were told that the flak wouldn't reach us at that altitude. It did. We went through, and just about the time we passed out of the flak, the fighters hit us. We had also been told that the fighters couldn't get to 35,000 feet either.

They were there, and they pressed their attacks very aggressively.

'We stayed in formation, nine B-29s of the 873rd Bomb Squadron, and we flew on to the target, released our bombs, and flew off the target together. I looked out to the left, and I looked out to the right, and I saw those gorgeous machines tucked in close and I thought, the Japanese haven't a chance. We're going to whip them. No question about it'. *Jack Catton.*

On 27 November, the 73rd Wing flew a second mission against the Nakajima plant at Musashino. No damage was done to the target, but back at Isley Field, ten to 15 Japanese raiders came in fast and low and destroyed three B-29s while the mission was over the home islands. Earlier that day, two twin-engined Japanese bombers had run in from Iwo Jima and had blown up one Superfortress.

The B-29s flew a night radar-bombing raid against Tokyo on 29 November, and on 3 December went back to Musashino and Target 357 for another try. Six of the Superforts were lost on that mission, and still the Nakajima plant continued to turn out engines for the defending Japanese who were beginning to take the measure of the big bombers both over Japan and back on Saipan.

On 7 December, Japanese planes attacked Isley Field again, and blew up three Superforts and damaged 23. These raids were becoming a serious threat to the B-29 operations and it was said, only half-jokingly, that it was safer to be over Japan in a B-29 than on the ground at Saipan. Before the raids ended, the Japanese attackers had destroyed 11 Superfortresses, had done major damage to eight more, and minor damage to 35. Airplanes could be replaced, at a cost; but the 45 dead airmen left in the wake of the raids could not. Additionally, more than 200 were wounded in the attacks.

To counter them, a major strike was planned against the Japanese airfields on Iwo Jima, co-ordinated with an attack by B-24 bombers from the 7th AF. On 8 December they flew the 600-mile trip; 62 Superforts dropped 620 tons of bombs and 102 B-24s dropped 192 tons. It was a deterrent; the Japanese strikes stopped for a while.

So far, it had been downhill all the way for the B-29s. They were accomplishing little, losing many. But the next attack reversed their fortunes, at least temporarily. It was a daylight raid against the Mitsubishi Heavy Industries Co, Ltd engine plant at Nagoya, a major source of powerplants for defending Japanese fighters. The Superfortresses made 13 December a lucky day. Ninety bombers took off for the attack; 16 of them aborted and three dropped on other targets. But the

It's time to go, and the ground crew begins its treadmill, turning the giant prop blades through a few times by hand before the starter is called into play by the flight engineer.
/ *Ingram T. Hermanson Collection*

Above: Led by *Fancy Detail*, Z-Square-50, of the 500th Bomb Group, the long line of Superfortresses trundles along the taxiways towards takeoff and the flight to Japan.
/ *Mike Janosko Collection*

Centre right: T-Square-9, *Devil's Darling* (42-24629), from the 498th Bomb Group, lifts off the runway at Saipan on a mission against Japan. On her 23rd mission, she was hit hard by fighters and her airplane commander was killed. With two engines out, she ran out of fuel and ditched 20 miles off Saipan. All the crew, except for the commander, were rescued.
/ *Mrs Thomas Isley Collection*

Bottom right: The ground crews watched them go and waited for them to come back. This is Saipan, and the B-29 is from the 500th Bomb Group.
/ *Ingram T. Hermanson Collection*

main force of 71 dropped 500lb general-purpose bombs and incendiary clusters and destroyed almost 18 per cent of the roofed-over plant area, according to post-strike photos. But the pictures failed to reveal the true extent of the damage. It was so severe that machining of parts was halted at Plant 4 in the target array, and engine production from then on depended on the inventory of parts at 13 December, augmented by parts from outside suppliers. Further, the attack initiated a programme of factory dispersal to underground sites, but it was done so poorly that no engine production ever came from the dispersed sites.

It was a short-lived success. The big bombers made two return trips to Nagoya, on 18 December against the Mitsubishi aircraft plant there, and on 22 December against the engine factory again. Neither raid did much damage. The 22 December strike was a daylight incendiary raid, with the bombers carrying only fire bombs. It was in response to pressures from USAAF Headquarters, based on the success of the 18 December raid by XX Bomber Command against Hankow, China. It was regarded as a test of the fire raid concept, and it was supposed to be flown with a force of 100 B-29s. But the strike on 22 December dispatched 78 bombers and did very little damage.

On 24 December the Superforts struck Iwo Jima again, hammering the airfields in another tactical diversion from the strategic air offensive. It was Musashino again on 27 December, and once again the attack failed to do any substantial damage to Target 357.

The 3 January mission against Nagoya was more nearly the test fire raid that had been suggested by Arnold's Headquarters. At take-off, 97 Superfortresses left the runway at Saipan, each carrying 4,900lb of incendiary clusters and one 420lb fragmentation bomb. It was another bad run; only 57 bombed the primary target, starting some fires. The test was inconclusive.

Target 357 was hit again — or perhaps missed is the more accurate term — 9 January. One warehouse was destroyed; it

A mixed formation of Superfortresses from the 497th and 498th Bomb Groups soars serenely above cumulus on the way to the home islands of Japan. Left to right: T-Square-44, *Patches* (42-24624); T-Square-51, *Houston Honey* (42-63475); T-Square-50, *Forbidden Fruit* (42-24607); T-Square-?; A-Square-44, *Ponderous Peg* (42-63431); A-Square-?; A-Square-?; A-Square-11; unmarked; A-Square-9. / *AAF Pacific 1233-11 via Boeing-Wichita*

cost six B-29s. On 15 January the bombers flew against Nagoya and Mitsubishi's aircraft factory, dropping four bombs in the target area out of the loads carried by 40 B-29s.

XXI Bomber Command broke its losing streak on 19 January with an assault on the main aircraft and engine plant of Kawasaki Aircraft Engineering Co, Ltd, at Akashi, 12 miles west of Kobe on Japan's Inland Sea. The plant was a major one, producing twin-engined fighters, and engines for single-engined fighters. The raid was a rousing success; 62 B-29s out of the 77 dispatched bombed the factory and knocked it out of the war. The company closed the plant, moved the machine tools to another site, and used what was left for very limited assembly.

It was Hansell's swansong as commander of the XXI Bomber Command. The next day, LeMay was moved from XX Bomber Command to take over Hansell's command, and Hansell was on his way back to the United States to work in the B-29 training programme.

Hansell said later that there were four major problems with the early B-29 operations. First, he had to convince the 73rd Bomb Wing that precision bombing was better than radar night bombing. Second, the bombing accuracy was very poor. Third, the abort rate was much too high, almost one out of every four sorties never getting to the target area. Fourth, losses due to ditching were too high and air-sea rescue operations needed to be improved.

The mission pattern stayed much the same after LeMay's takeover. Strikes against the top-priority targets — aircraft engine plants — dominated the list, and Target 357 was assigned its share. LeMay tried his luck 27 January, sending 76 bombers against Musashino. But the weather protected the area; 56 of the bombers dropped on their secondary targets and six bombed the alternate targets. Nine Superforts were lost, and one almost didn't make it back. It was *Pride of the Yankees*, Z Sq 24, from the 500th Bomb Group, and its commander was Lieutenant Frank A. Carrico. This was his debriefing report:

'When we hit the coastline, we picked up our first fighter, which came up, got our altitude, and followed us in and out of the target. Just before the IP, we picked up a twin-engined Irving (Nakajima J1N1 'Gekko'), nine o'clock level, which stuck out there for a few minutes throwing bursts at us from his turret, then he made an attack on our ship and the boys got him.

'We were jumped good and hard before we got our bomb doors open. All guns were blazing away and just as we let the bombs go, a Tony (Kawasaki Ki-62 "Hien") got a good burst in our number two engine. Lt (Morris M.) Robinson was flying because we were on the left side of the formation, and I told him to stay on the controls and stay in formation.

'I tried to feather the damned prop and naturally it won't feather. It's burning good by this time, and I yell to Lt (Albert E.) Woodward, my engineer, to cut it off and pull the extinguisher. He'd already cut it off and when he pulled the fire extinguisher, the whole installation came out of his panel.

'Just about that time, the prop ran away and blew the fire completely out. Our speed dropped, and we lost the formation. In the meantime we had another attack on the nose which shot out two of the large glass panels and put a bullet through the side, under my instrument panel and between my feet. My bombardier was wounded in the legs, and that left our nose unprotected. After we dropped out of formation, we received nine concentrated attacks on the nose.

'Our astrodome was blown out when we lost pressurisation, and we had a wind blowing through the nose compartment which I thought would surely freeze Lt Robinson and myself; it was 40 below zero Centigrade outside. We had on jackets, gloves and boots, but our legs were freezing, so we gathered flak suits, maps and anything else we could find to wrap around them. One man would fly for a few minutes and then start shivering so much he couldn't stay on the controls. The crew in the meantime had gotten ready to bail out, because I didn't want them to ride the burning plane down from 25,000 feet.

'I told Lt Robinson to fly until the prop came off so I could watch and see where it

Top left: Three different Superfortresses carried the T-1 designator from the 498th Bomb Group; two were lost after enemy action, and the crew of one of those was rescued. Here one of them drops a string of 14 500lb bombs from both bomb bays. */ Donald L. Miller Collection*

Bottom left: Danny Mite, T-Square-28 (46-69777), starts dropping a train of 500-pounders by invervalometer. She was lost on Mission 72 on 24 May 1945, after she lost two engines over the target. She was last heard reporting that they were headed toward the ocean. */ Donald L. Miller Collection*

Below: Ponderous Peg, a Marietta-built B-29-16-BA (42-63431) and A-Square-44 in the 497th Bomb Group, is coming home with numbers three and four dead and feathered. Major F. L. Trickey is at the controls, nursing A-44 back to Saipan, one of the first times a B-29 has come home 1,500 miles on two engines. Low cruise power and rpm makes it appear that all four props have stopped. */ A. F. Migliaccio Collection*

went. By this time, I had all the men in their ditching positions. At 1625hrs, the prop came off, but it hadn't read the SOP (Standing Operating Procedures) on how props were to come off. The metal of the nose section melted on the inboard side and the prop peeled off to the left in flat pitch. It held there an instant and then went hurtling into the number one engine. It broke the two bottom mount braces and bent the upper two; at the same time all four blades on the number one prop bent almost double. The prop would not feather and the vibration was terrific.

'The left wing was vibrating through an arc of about 20 feet, and I had the crew ready to bail out again and was just pressing the mike switch to give the order when the damn prop feathered. Capt (Horace E.) Hatch came up then and asked what our condition was, so we got an accurate position report from him and worked out an ETA (Estimated Time of Arrival) to our base. We didn't have enough gas to make it.

'I asked Capt Hatch to stick close, as all our navigation aids were out and all we had to navigate with was a map and a pencil. We flew until dark and the moon was very bright, so I decided to keep going and make a moonlight ditching. After dark I found my instrument lights were out, and the moon was bright enough to counteract the fluorescent paint glow from my instruments, so Lt Robinson flew until 2100.

'At that time we ran into instrument conditions and it took both of us to hold the ship. We both flew from his panel; he kept the wings level and I held altitude.

242

'We figured a very accurate ETA to the base and we were ten minutes short of gas. I called Capt Hatch and told him we would fly until 15 minutes remained and then we would ditch under the overcast. I got the crew in ditching positions again, and then my engineer called to say he'd found 75 more gallons of gas in the centre tank. We came on in.

'When we got to the base, we had to make the normal right-hand traffic pattern because I couldn't turn the plane into the dead wing. We held 2,000 feet of altitude, and when I got on base leg, we took out all the trim and let down the wheels. I flew the approach at 1,500 feet until I knew we could get down, power off. We chopped all power and stuck the nose down and still lost too much speed because when we got below 140 miles per hour we lost aileron control.

'But when we levelled off, we picked up our aileron control and she landed good. Our landing was strictly a two-man job also. Everyone was okay with the exception of the bombardier and myself; we both picked up a little flak in our legs.' *Frank A. Carrico*

Carrico's return was one of the first times that a B-29 had been flown back from a mission on two engines. It was a difficult, tiring, and risky condition for a fresh crew; it was doubly difficult, tiring and risky for a crew that had flown to Japan and fought its way to the target. Not many B-29s with two engines out made it back.

One of the nine B-29s that didn't come back carried tail gunner Sergeant Olinto F. Lodovici. He described his experience on that mission against Target 357:

'Our regular crew was changed; we got a new aircraft commander, a new engineer and a new navigator, and we were assigned to a strike against Target 357 on 27 January 1945. That was the tough target and they were waiting for us when we arrived. The first pass by a fighter got our pilot, co-pilot and bombardier. We heard the pilot ask the co-pilot for a hand, because he'd been hit bad in the chest, and the co-pilot told him that he couldn't help much because he'd been hit in the head.

'Our number one and number two engines were burning, and when I realised how bad it was, I tried to call somebody up front and got no answer. So I got out of my seat and looked through the glass toward the aft section of the ship. The aircraft was burning pretty bad inside, so I knew I had to get out of there. And that's a hell of a decision to make because you think maybe they'll make it back and leave you dangling on a chute over Japan. And I couldn't communicate with anybody up there. But I knew it was just a question of time before she blew.

'Besides, I didn't have any more ammunition. It was no sense trying to bluff them out, because I couldn't see out of my window. They'd blown my guns to hell and the window looked like spiderwebs.

'So I released the escape hatch, grabbed my chest pack off the floor, hooked it on one side of the harness — because I knew I couldn't get out of the hatch with the thing all hooked up — and I pushed myself out. I pulled the

That's Sgt James B. Krantz hanging outside the port gunner's blister of A-Square-7, *American Maid*, of the 869th Bomb Squadron, 497th Bomb Group. The Superfortress was at 29,000 feet when his blister let go, and Krantz was sucked outside to dangle over Tokyo on a harness he made himself. The aircraft commander Lt J. D. Bartlett, dove the plane to a much lower altitude to save Krantz and the gunners in the rear, and — after 15 minutes — Krantz was hauled back inside through the combined efforts and muscles of four crewmen. Krantz was severely frostbitten from the extreme cold at altitude, and injured by the buffeting from the slipstream that hammered him against the side of the fuselage. But he lived to tell the tale, one of the most remarkable in a war that was full of remarkable experiences.
/ *Donald L. Miller Collection*

Above: There are two out and feathered on the port side, and T-Square-10, 498th Bomb Group, is headed back toward Saipan and down toward the Pacific simultaneously. At least six B-29s bore the T-10 designator with the 498th. One was destroyed on the ground by Japanese bombers in an early hit-and-run raid. A second was missing after a raid on 3 December 1944. A third ditched in the ocean after running out of fuel on 27 January 1945. The fourth was named *Homer's Roamers*, and nothing further is known about her. The fifth was destroyed in an emergency landing, which the crew survived, on 6 April 1945. The sixth was named *Lucky Strikes*, and nothing further is known of her history, either. / *Donald L. Miller Collection*

Top right: And that's what it looks like from inside, when one of those Wright engines packs up and the engineer shuts down the engine and the pilot feathers the prop and a buddy comes up alongside to stick with you while you're in trouble. / *A. F. Migliaccio Collection*

Bottom right: Now the long mission is over, and we're set up on final approach over Magicienne Bay, coming in to Isley and rest. The flaps are all the way down, the gear is down and locked, and we're going to squeak down just past the threshold and roll out along the runway with one more mission gone and that much closer to going home. It's a beautiful sky, and a pretty island, and a hell of a long and hard trip out and back. / *Donald L. Miller Collection*

chute through after me, and I sat on the little fairing of the left stabiliser. I took my chute and finished hooking it on and checked it, sitting back there, and believe it or not, the slipstream just didn't move me for some reason.

'I sat there for a while, enjoying it, and then I started to push myself away from the aeroplane. But my damn boot — I had them open and forgot to lace them — hung up in the cleat of the hatch. So I'm hanging down alongside the fuselage with one foot hung up on the aeroplane. I just kept pushing and pushing and finally broke loose. As I was free-falling, the airplane blew.

'I delayed opening the chute, because I had my bailout bottle on, and I waited until I could see Mount Fuji sticking up above the clouds, sort of at eye level. Then I popped the chute. Some fighter made three or four passes at me and I was swinging the chute, trying to make myself hard to hit, and I damn near collapsed it. He gave up and I landed just off shore in Tokyo Bay.

'I was captured immediately by civilians and they beat me up pretty bad until two home guards came up and protected me and then turned me over to a Japanese officer who came riding up on a horse. The civilians were still trying to get at me, and this soldier finally took his sword in the scabbard and laid around with it, to convince the people that they should clear out and let me go with him quietly. That's the guy that saved my ass.

'I was worried there; civilians captured some of our guys and just pulled them apart. Well, our people would have done the same thing, I guess. It's a hell of a thing to have bombers over your homeland.' *Olinto F. Lodovici, tail gunner, 870th BS, 497th BG*

Between attacks on the Japanese aircraft industry, LeMay's bombers worked over the islands of Iwo Jima, Moen and Dublon, softening their offensive and defensive capabilities in preparation for the planned invasion of Iwo.

There was another 'test' incendiary raid, this time against Kobe on 4 February. It was the first strike flown by two wings; the 313th, now operational, joined the 73rd in the attack. They dropped 160 tons of incendiaries and 14 tons of fragmentation bombs from high altitudes with substantial effect. They wiped out fabric and synthetic rubber production, halved the capacity of one shipyard, and generally raised a small amount of hell.

But the B-29s stayed with their basic doctrine of precision bombing of single targets, sending a heavy strike on 10 February against Ota and its Nakajima aircraft factory that was producing the Ki-84 (Frank) fighter. Eighty-four B-29s bombed the primary target, damaged some buildings and ruined 74 of the fighters. It cost 12 B-29s, the highest loss so far.

The results of the 4 February fire raid continued to absorb the staff at Arnold's headquarters. On 19 February they issued a new target directive, redefining priorities. The top priority targets continued to be aircraft engine factories, but incendiary attacks on urban areas was the first of two secondary target policies specified, and the second was aircraft assembly plants. That directive marked the change in policy that elevated fire raids to a second level of priority. That day the XXI Bomber

Command went out in force against Target 357 again, dispatching 150 aircraft. But the target was completely closed in by weather, so 119 bombed the secondary target and 12 hit the target of last resort. Six B-29s were lost, and Musashino continued to stand firm.

The conclusive test of fire bombing came on 25 February. It was the biggest strike to date, involving aircraft from three wings then active in the Marianas: the 73rd, 313th and the recently arrived 314th Bombardment Wing (Very Heavy). They flew to the Tokyo urban area, and 172 Superfortresses bombed the primary target. Only 30 hit the alternates. When the smoke had cleared, 28,000 of Tokyo's buildings were in ashes. About one square mile had been levelled.

There was one more attempt to knock out Target 357 by precison bombing. On 4 March, the XXI Bomber Command sent a strong force of Superfortresses to bomb Musashino; weather defeated them again and 159 aircraft had to be content with bombing the secondary target. It was the end of precision high-altitude visual daylight bombing in the Pacific theatre, although nobody said so very loudly at the time.

Eight times the B-29s had flown against Target 357 in a total of 835 bombing sorties. They had destroyed less than four per cent of the factory area. Worse, a single attack on 17 February by Navy carrier-based aircraft had done more damage than any single assault by the powerful B-29 forces. It was high time to examine the whole traditional doctrine of bombing and to find out why it wasn't working in the Pacific.

245

All she wore was a great big friendly smile

Nose art! Where would books like this be without at least a half-dozen well-chosen pictures of nearly nude women, painted in provocative poses along the length of the forward fuselage?

Nose art is almost as old as the airplane itself; its definitive history awaits the dedicated researcher. But by the late days of World War 2, the art form had reached a very high level, and it graced at least one of every type the military forces flew.

The long fuselage nose of the B-29 was a natural canvas for the imaginative, or the copying, artist. There were sign painters in the military, some good and some very good, who turned their spare-time talents to the decoration of aircraft. The going price, it is said, was from $60 to $100, depending on size, complexity, and other factors, such as what the traffic might bear. A good artist, with the blank aluminium sides of a squadron's ships beckoning, could make $1,000 or more in a few hours of his spare time. And that was when $1,000 *was* $1,000.

As long as the images were kept reasonably decent, or had minimal clothing, the upper echelons of command went along with nose art, officially not seeing anything at all on those fuselage sides. Official pictures for release back in the States were taken generally from the right side of the airplane, because the nose art was almost invariably confined to the left side.

'In the 314th Bomb Wing, we reserved the starboard side of the fuselage for the formal name. Each aircraft was officially and formally named the *"City of Someplace"*. Ours was the *City of Arcadia;* we figured we might get a crate of oranges out of it. We didn't. Each flight station was labelled with the name of a wife or girl friend. On the port side, we had the customary nose art, or the unofficial name. Ours was *No Balls Atoll.'* Charles B. Hawks

'Our aircraft was T–42, *Sweet Sue.* When the word came down that we could add the names of our wives or girl friends at our positions, we jumped at the chance. I figured that our daughter was born just about the time we were over the target at Ichinomiya, so I painted her name, Ellen Dorothy, just outside the side window of my tail turret.' *Mike Janosko, tail gunner, 875 BS, 498 BG*

The B-29 ladies got a little barer, and the captions got a little bolder, and one day the chaplains had enough. Perhaps we shouldn't blame the chaplains; it may have been a

There were probably a dozen or more B-29s that were named *American Beauty*. Most of them featured a lovely girl; one featured a monstrous caricature. But this one featured a bottle of fine bourbon, an 'American Beauty' indeed. She was assigned to the 444th Bomb Group. / *Ron E. Witt Collection*

morally outraged general officer. Anyway, late in the war, the girls had to go. The voluptuous virgins were erased, and replaced by a simple chaste symbol and a neatly lettered and innocuous name. Just who was being corrupted by these lovely ladies, reminders of home, mother and girl friends, is hard to say. But morality, legislated or commanded, works in strange ways.

That's why you could have seen a 73rd Bomb Wing B-29 with its yellow streamer labelled *Kansas Farmer.* You just know that in an earlier day the plane would have been named *The Farmer's Daughter,* and the decorative theme would have been a young, concupiscent blonde in very short shorts, lots of leg, low-cut blouse only half on . . .

Nose art in the Korean war has been largely undiscovered. Few collections of photos of the lovelies exist. The left side of many B-29s had been pre-empted by Strategic Air Command insignia, and SAC took itself and its insignia very seriously indeed. But the right side of the fuselage was bare, and soon so were the beauties who suddenly appeared on the B-29s once they had been deployed to Japan or Okinawa where few could see and complain.

Some of the titles or names found in the nose art of that war are a bit difficult to understand, unless one remembers contemporary American slang, or can translate Japanese expressions — many of the artists were Japanese employed on or near the base — not normally used between diplomats. Miss Minooky, for example, does not memorialise a small town in the state of Minnesota. And Miss Megook manages to offend Koreans, women, and Korean women simultaneously.

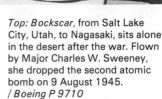

Top: Bockscar, from Salt Lake City, Utah, to Nagasaki, sits alone in the desert after the war. Flown by Major Charles W. Sweeney, she dropped the second atomic bomb on 9 August 1945.
/ *Boeing P 9710*

Above: A close-up of the nose art on *Eddie Allen*, a B-29-40-BW of the 45th BS, 40th BG, after the crew had completed seven flights over the Hump and six bombing missions.
/ *Boeing 88802*

Left: Miss Megook, lovely in her long blonde lines, probably has little in common with the Korean ('gook') woman on the mind of the guy who chose the name.
/ *Thomas H. Brewer Collection*

247

In both wars, the themes for nose art were predominantly sexual, with a name or title that was often double entendre: King Size, Cream of the Crop, Over Exposed. There were comic-strip characters, taken from the pages of hometown newspapers: Sad Sac, Lonesome Polecat. There were caricatures of the crew with humorous overtones: The Herd of Bald Goats, The Honeybucket Honshos.

Sometimes there were more involved stories behind the nose art, and here is one example from the Korean war:

'One of the B-29s in the 92nd Wing was named *The Wanderer*, and there's a story there. We had a Lieutenant Colonel named Ralph M. Wanderer, commanding the 325th Bomb Squadron of the 92nd, and he was pushing for full colonel at the time. Nothing wrong with that; we understood. Captain Norman B. Hemingway was the aircraft commander of a new B-29 that needed a name and he chose *The Wanderer*. The nose picture showed a tramp, with a butterfly net, chasing a couple of little — well, they looked like butterflies at first glance. But if you looked real close, you saw that they were little silver eagles, the insignia of a colonel.

'So that B-29 immortalised Lt Col Wanderer's chase for his colonel's eagles, and how Norman B. Hemingway had the guts to do that I'll never know. He got away with it.' *Vern Piotter, navigator, 92 BW, Korea*

Nose art has disappeared again from contemporary aircraft, replaced by supergraphic colour schemes. All that is left now are the pictures of the works of the forgotten great masters of the time. Some of them have been reproduced here as a tribute to the brave crews that, like medieval knights, carried their ladies' favours into battle.

Top right: When the nose art came off, the luscious ladies were replaced — at least on the 73rd Bomb Wing aircraft — by this black winged device, the black globe, and the yellow streamer carrying the aircraft name in black letters. This aircraft is *Kansas Farmer*, with the name superimposed on the streamer, in turn superimposed on what has been described as a headless chicken carrying a bowling ball. *Kansas Farmer* was aircraft 47 in the 73rd Wing; she flew 50 combat missions, and her crew downed six Japanese fighters. */Weber*

Below: This B-29 of the 313th BW, based on North Field, Tinian, honoured the Navy's 'Seabees'. */313th BW*

A Litany of Some B-29 Names in Alphabetical Order

Adam's Eve and Andy's Dandy,
American Beauty, American Maid,
Booze Hound, Bock's Car, Bengal Lancer,
Battlin' Betty, Bedroom Eyes,
City of Pittsburg, Constant Nymph,
The Challenger and the Coral Queen,
Dragon Lady, The Devil's Delight,
Dauntless Dotty and Destiny's Tots,
Esso Express and Eddie Allen,
Forbidden Fruit, Filthy Fay,
Fire Belle, Fever from the South,
Gunga Din and Gertrude C.
Gravel Gertie, Geisha Gertie,
Heavenly Body, Homer's Roamers,
Hell on Wings, Honshu Hawk,
Inspiration, Island Princess,
Jokers Wild and Jumpin' Stud,
The Kayo Kid and Kickapoo Lou,
Limber Dugan, Lady Be Good,
Lethal Lady, Little Jo,
Miss Lace, Miss Hap, Miss-Leading Lady,
Mary K. and Mustn't Touch!
Noah Borshuns, Next Objective,
O'Reilly's Daughter, Oregon Express,
Pride of the Yankees, Pocahontas,
Party Girl, Patches, Ponderous Peg,
Ramblin Roscoe, Raidin' Maiden,
Rodger the Lodger, Rabbit Punch,
Stripped for Action and Supine Sue,
Sure Thing, Sweet Thing, Super Wabbit,
Tanaka Termite, Terrible Terry,
Tokyo Twister and Thunderbird,
Uncle Tom's Cabin, The Uninvited,
Victory Girl and Vanishing Rae.
Wichita Witch and Windy City,
Winnie II and Willie Mae.

Above: The Japanese horse-drawn cart that serviced the latrines was the inspiration for the name of *Honeybucket Honshos*. / *William F. Dawson*

Centre left: Lonesome Polecat runs along the side of this B-29, a long way from Dogpatch and Al Capp's 'Li'l Abner' comic strip. / *William F. Dawson*

Bottom left: The ultimate plunging neckline does little to conceal the fine figure of the young woman on this 98th Bomb Wing B-29. And the French expression lends sort of a classic touch, doesn't it ? / *William F. Dawson*

Fire in the Islands

Above: A 505th Bomb Group B-29, doors open for the drop, skirts the boiling smoke clouds billowing upward over the burning target. Flak is bursting ahead and at ten o'clock. / 313th BW

Right: The 14 May 1945 raid against Nagoya was the first of the four-wing missions, flown by B-29s from the 58th, 73rd, 313th and 314th Bomb Wings. They put 472 bombers over the target, and here we are in the nose of one of them from the 497th Bomb Group, 73rd Bomb Wing, while the bombardier sights the target, and smoke from the burning city boils up ahead. / A. F. Migliaccio Collection

Left: Hundreds of incendiary bombs cascade from the bellies of B-29s of the 500th Bomb Group in a daylight raid on Yokohama, 29 May 1945. The lead crew for this raid was commanded by Capt Ferd J. Curtis, flying Z-12, and it was the left gunner, Sgt Howard J. Clos who took this photograph. It was widely reproduced, and was later used as the heading photo for a propaganda leaflet dropped on named Japanese cities to warn them in advance of a fire raid.
/ Ingram T. Hermanson Collection

Weather was the worst enemy of daylight, high-altitude precision bombing. It affected the results far more than the best defences the Japanese could mount. And worst of the weather phenomena was the jet stream.

It was — and still is — a shallow, roaring rapids of wind, strongest at the latitudes and altitudes where the B-29s were working, and worst during the winter months above Japan. It howled out of the west on a twisting course, bowling along at speeds that routinely reached above 200mph and occasionally touched 300mph.

It was a new realm; aircraft had not penetrated the jet stream before the raids on Japan. Navigators checked their mathematics and their plots; radar operators recalibrated their sets, twisted the knobs again, changed the scales. The figures showed ground speeds of less than 100mph on headings generally toward the West; when the bombers made their runs on Tokyo from an initial point near Mount Fuji, southwest of the city, the ground speed jumped to 400, 450 and 500mph as the big B-29s were swept along in the raging torrent of the jet stream.

The ballistics data books, compiled so carefully for each of the bomb types carried, were useless. The range of ground speeds just did not extend as high as 500mph or as low as 20 or 30. (Or even zero, as one crew found to its shock. They suddenly were standing stock-still over Japan, hanging there like a balloon in the sky, with the big Wright R-3350 engines roaring and propellers flailing, and the wind blowing them backwards as fast as the airplane was flying forward in the moving air mass.)

Some of the effects of high winds can be cancelled or at least reduced by flying cross-wind. But these winds were too fast to use that strategem; the bomb ballistics and the bomb sight never could have handled the amount of drift.

252

About the only advantage of a downwind approach was that you got in and out of the target defences very fast. But you left your bombs scattered all over the countryside below. Upwind, you hung there, drifting slowly while every anti-aircraft battery on the ground had time to boresight you and fire a string of bursts.

This problem was certainly a major factor that led to a shift in bombing tactics, away from the concept of the high-altitude precision strike by daylight to the low-altitude sweep by night with incendiaries.

There were other advantages to going in low over the targets. The winds at the lower levels were down to 25 to 35 knots, which could be handled within the normal range of bomb ballistics data and the capabilities of the bomb sights that were used. It would not be necessary to limit the direction of the approach, either; a bombing strike at low level could be mounted from any direction of the compass.

Clouds, the major drawback to visual bombing, were almost ever-present, but they were less numerous and thinner at low altitudes.

The radars, relatively primitive at that stage of their development, were able to 'see' better at low altitudes, and the scope pictures were of better definition.

Flying at lower altitudes was an easier task for the engines, stressing them less and burning less fuel. The fuel saved could be traded for bomb load, and the lessened strain on the engines translated to a simplification of the engine maintenance problem. Improving maintenance meant that a higher number of B-29s would be available for missions at any given time, and that meant in turn that there was a higher number of B-29s over the target with more bombs.

Since precision bombing was not going to be required with the new approach, the attacks could be flown at night. Formation flying, developed to give the maximum defensive firepower massing, would not be necessary at night, nor even desirable, and that meant lower fuel consumption on a mission to the home islands of Japan. Formation flying involved a lot of jockeying of throttles to maintain position, and it burned extra fuel.

If maximum defensive firepower was not a pre-requisite, then the ammunition load for the turrets could be reduced, again trading the weight saving for fuel or bombs or both.

The crews were experienced in night navigation, because they returned home in darkness after many of their long missions to Japan.

And finally, the intelligence assessment was that the Japanese were not believed capable of putting up an effective night-fighter defence, a supposition that was proven in the months to come. Automatic weapons fire was expected to be largely ineffective above 5,000 feet, and the accuracy of the radar-directed heavier flak deterioriated badly below 10,000 feet altitude.

For all of these reasons, the low-altitude fire raids were planned for altitudes between 5,000 and 8,000 feet. The B-29s would be stripped of excess weight, including guns and ammunition. Originally, only the tail gunner had any ammunition on these flights. The bomb load was entirely incendiaries on most of the missions, with an occasional mixed loading of high-explosives and incendiaries to attack specific target complexes.

The bombers were to attack individually, in a bomber stream of the type pioneered by the Royal Air Force in its night-time bombings over Europe. They were to drop on fires set by a small, highly trained and daring pathfinder force, again taking a leaf from the RAF's book.

Above: Hang on, because it's gonna get rough! B-29s of the 498th Bomb Group, their vertical tails emblazoned with the large T identifier, fly over turbulent and boiling masses of smoke from the burning Japanese city below. Aircraft at the left carries a black lead crew flash on its fin.
/ *Donald L. Miller Collection*

Bottom left: The incendiary clusters fall away and the lightened Superfortresses heave buoyantly into the air. This group, from the 497th BG, are dropping through scattered clouds and a thin undercast of stratus in a fire raid after April 1945.
/ *Mrs Thomas Isley Collection*

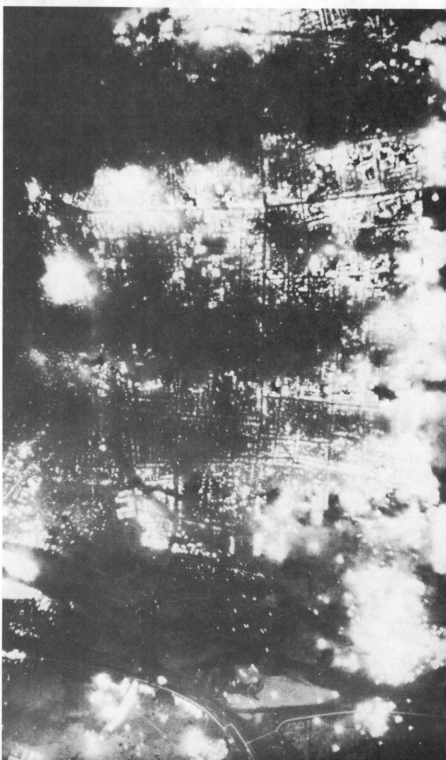

The first mission in the experiment was scheduled to leave on 9 March 1945. The time was fixed to get the best weather over the target. The main force, following the pathfinder strikes, was to make radar approaches to the targets, using visual corrections if possible for the actual drop.

The concept, and the decision to carry it through, came from Gen LeMay. It was a daring approach, and a fateful decision. LeMay made it, the B-29s carried it out, and they burned most of Japan's industrial cities to the ground.

'The 881st Squadron started operations on Saipan with only ten of our authorised 20 aircraft, and early losses in combat reduced this number further. I flew only two combat missions in December 1944, and one of them was a weather reconnaissance flight on Christmas Eve.

'Replacement aircraft started arriving in January, and the second one was assigned to my crew and designated Z Sq 12. At the same time, we were designated a lead crew.

'Our bombing accuracy in the early missions left much to be desired. The formation — nine to twelve aircraft — dropped bombs on the lead aircraft signal to insure the planned impact pattern. By designating a lead crew and allowing them special training flights, we improved bombing accuracy.

'Our crew was given scarce B-29 time for four such training flights in January and again in February, and we were assigned to combat missions only as the lead or the deputy lead crew. We continued in that assignment, and flew more training flights on 3, 5 and 7 March. On 8 March a very unusual Wing meeting of all staff personnel, and including all lead crew aircraft commanders, was called. Gen LeMay outlined the concept of the low-level incendiary strike against heavily defended Tokyo. Since this was going to be a maximum effort, my precision-trained lead crew was going to be part of this mass strike.

'My initial impression was of a B-29 traffic jam with the air filled with bombs and machine-gun rounds; it was a frightening thought. But as the details of the strike unfolded, we began to see the safeguards that had been planned to reduce the chance of self-inflicted losses.

'Ammunition was removed from all but the tail guns. Several routes were used to the target area to avoid congestion en route. Indicated airspeeds for cruise and the bomb run itself were assigned, as were staggered altitudes over about a 4,000-foot spread to provide controlled bomb waves over different aiming points.

'The big unknown was what kind of a reception we'd get. I've forgotten what we were told in the intelligence briefing about their defence capabilities, but as we approached our bomb run it looked like all hell was breaking loose ahead of us, and I wasn't sure if that was good or bad.

'As it turned out, it was good for us; Tokyo was burning.' *Ferd J. Curtis*

The B-29s were loaded with about six tons of bombs in each plane. Each lead aircraft carried 180 M47 napalm bombs, and each of the main force aircraft carried 24 of the 500lb M69 incendiary clusters. One by one, they surged down the runways on Guam, Saipan and Tinian, 334 Superforts from the 73rd, 313th and 314th Bomb Wings, headed for Tokyo on the night of 9 March 1945.

'On the long trip to the target, I found it hard to believe that such a serene and tranquil sky could, at any moment, become filled with so much violence and destruction. And in the face of that beauty, the thing that bound us all together in a common bond was that we were scared to death.

'My first fire-bombing mission was also my first night mission. The fire from earlier drops was so bright we could see it from miles away as we approached the target. We were without guns — to save weight for fuel and bombs — and carried only two gunners on the trip as scanners. We went in on the target individually, because it was too dangerous to fly formation at night. I never liked those night raids. It felt too much like you were alone. Just the sight of other planes helped.' *George S. Gray*

It was the first of the great fire raids. The planes went in low, in an area attack on a section of about 12 square miles of Tokyo. They dropped from altitudes between 4,900 and 9,200 feet. The fires were spread by the wind, and blown to other parts of the city. They raced through the wood and bamboo and plaster houses and small factories, leaped

roads and fire breaks, blended into an enormous fire storm.

'She was a very tough lady. The low-altitude runs took us close to target fires sometimes. What turbulence! Worse than any Texas thunderstorm I'd ever experienced. The smoke was filled with the litter and the smells of a burning and dying city.

'One one occasion we were tossed upside down in the smoke and survived a 90-degree split-S recovery made on instruments. The 90-degree turn was to miss a mountain ahead. All of us had some injury; I chipped my front teeth on the control column. And the flak suits were going up when we were going down and vice versa, flailing at our faces. From that time on, most of us sat on them.' *Charles B. Hawks*

The target is urban Nagoya, the date is 14 May 1945, and the time is 0955 hours as these clusters of small incendiary bombs drop away from our B-29. The steel bands holding the shells together will separate at lower altitude, and each of these clusters will break into dozens of six-pound bombs of gelled gasoline, and magnesium powder. And that will take care of Nagoya. / *Del Shaffer Collection*

When it was over, it was to stand as the most destructive air attack of the war, over-shadowing even Hiroshima and Nagasaki. One-quarter of all Tokyo's buildings were destroyed; a million people were homeless; almost 84,000 had been killed and 41,000 were injured. Fourteen B-29s were lost.

Ernie Tyler was then a 19-year-old Staff Sergeant and right gunner in a B-29 of the 40th Bomb Squadron, 6th Bomb Group, 313th Bomb Wing on Tinian. He kept a diary and recorded these impressions of his second mission to Tokyo on the night of 9 March 1945, in *Grand Slam*

'Mission No 2
'Night bombing

Primary:	Tokyo
Results:	Excellent
Takeoff:	1910
Target:	0230 Alt 5,200ft
Landed:	1030
Total time	15:20

'The night of the 9th and the morning of the 10th we hit Tokyo again. Our second mission — scared the blue blazes out of us. This time we were to carry 32 bombs but we only got 24 loaded before it was time to go. The trip up was very turbulent. We hit the mainland at 0230. All the lights were out. 300 planes going in, in rat-tail fashion and bombing from 5,000 to 6,000 feet. We were at 5,000 feet. We got a little flak and auto fire. Saw fires started by planes ahead of us from about 70 miles away. Over the target the turbulence caused from the heat of the fires was beyond belief. We could smell the smoke and the sky was red from the glow. We dropped our bombs . . . immediately afterward we hit a huge smoke cloud which caused everything loose in the ship to hit the ceiling. Everything was tossed around and we all thought we were going down. Then the pilot said, She's OK, men, take it easy — we'll get out of here in a minute, just as calm as if he was talking to a Sunday School class.

'The whole city seemed to be on fire. The long trip home was okay and then on the final approach all hell broke loose. We started the putt-putt (auxiliary power unit) and it caught fire. The battery blew up. The interphone amp burned up. Both inverters burned. Voltage regulators burned out. The whole electrical system went out next. Number three engine feathered itself and we hit the runway for a beautiful landing, all electrical power gone. Right landing gear collapsed and we eventually came to a stop. No one was hurt, thanks to our pilot, Lt Charles Neal. It sure was good to walk around on the ground again, but I sure hated to see our airplane ruined. There'll never be another one like *Grand Slam.*' E. L. Tyler, *right gunner, 40th BS, 6th BG*

'We were usually met at our hardstand after a combat mission by the crew chief and his crew ready to start on the long task of mending and maintaining the aircraft for the next mission. The morning after the first night incendiary strike on Tokyo we landed, taxied up to the hardstand, and saw bomb loading trailers. The new tactic had proven highly successful, and we were going back for an encore the next night. As it turned out, our aircraft — Z Sq 12 — stayed in commission and we flew all five of the fire raids against Japan during nine days.' *Ferd J. Curtis*

On 11 March, 285 B-29s hit Nagoya. On 13 March 274 Superforts bombed Osaka. On 16 March, they hit Kobe:

'We made an emergency landing on Iwo coming back from one of the fire raids. The fight for the island was still going on, and the Japanese still held the area around one end of the runway. We landed downwind and downhill to avoid them.

'Down at the other end, we were visited by some GIs and Marines, who had fought for that island for days and had gone without sleep or baths or shaves and had worn their uniforms for days. And we were sitting in the B-29 wearing clean T-shirts and cutoff pants for shorts, and eating well.

'So they said to us, hey, you guys been over Japan? And we said, yeah, that's where we were coming from. And one of them said, Jesus, I wouldn't trade jobs with you guys for anything! And he meant it. They were really impressed that we had actually flown over Japan and had been shot at by flak and attacked by fighters.

'Before we took off, we gave them whatever food we had left, including some fresh bread. And when we were getting ready to leave, some Marines wanted to give us hand grenades to chuck at the Japanese when we took off. They were real disappointed that we couldn't use them.' *E. L. Tyler*

On 19 March, the B-29s hit Nagoya again, because the first strike had not been completely effective. And that raid brought an end to the March fire blitz. LeMay's forces had run out of bombs. Four cities had been burned out. B-29 losses were light. Morale was very high, compensating for the long and hard work done by maintenance crews and for the fatigued pilots and airmen.

There was a hiatus in the fire-bombing campaign while the Superfortresses were diverted to support the invasion of Okinawa, and while the bomb dumps were resupplied from off-shore ammunition ships. On 14 May the bombers went out again, this time against Nagoya with the first of the four-wing raids.

The 58th, 73rd, 313th and 314th put 472 B-29s over the northern urban area of Nagoya and burned out major portions of it. A few nights later they were back to burn the southern urban section, with 457 Superforts that dropped for almost three hours over the ill-starred city.

The largest single mission of the B-29's war was sent against Tokyo's urban industrial area on the night of 23 May. A force of 562 aircraft left Saipan, Tinian and Guam for the strike; 510 of them bombed the city. Two days later they went back, with 464 Superforts, dropping incendiaries on the areas they had not hit on previous strikes. It was a costly raid; 26 B-29s fell to the enemy. But Tokyo was finished as a factor in the Japanese war plans.

'Different tactics were evolved as the war progressed, to reduce our losses over specific targets. One of them was the pathfinder mission, pioneered by the Royal Air Force in night bombings of Germany. I don't believe it was widely used against Japan, and our lead crew only flew one such mission. I don't know how we were selected; it was the 500th Bomb Group's turn to furnish the Wing Task Force Commander for the mission, and the Deputy Group Commander, Lt Col Harry S. Brandon, flew with my crew. That may have influenced our selection.

'Some targets weren't very good aiming points for a radar bomb run; their return characteristics were pretty bad or could be confusing. There was one good one in the Tokyo area, a fine radar target, but it had to be approached across the heavy flak defences of that city. It was a command decision to make the pathfinder runs on the target from that approach, and we expected to get heavy flak.

'On the way up we had better winds than forecast, and I decided to hold to the time schedule for the strike, so I killed some time to compensate for the wind. The others didn't

A trio of 504th BG Superfortresses bounce skyward as they drop their loads of fire bombs over a Japanese city. Low haze partially screens the target, and smoke at the left indicates the city is already burning briskly. The dark bursts are flak, and it's close, and — if this picture is any indication — heavy. / 313th BW

wait; they dropped when they got there, and they alerted the defences, who were sitting there waiting for us when we sailed in toward the target. It was my roughest mission. We wound up with flak holes in all four engine cowlings, and more skin damage than on any other mission we'd flown.' *Ferd J. Curtis*

'Pathfinder missions against Tokyo seemed suicidal. Maybe 12 aircraft would draw that mission, with very specific target points they had to hit with incendiaries to mark the area for bombing by the main force.

'We'd fly in, fast and low, always in searchlights with every gun in the city banging at us. Only the rugged speed and manoeuvrability of the B-29 — plus some fancy flying — allowed us to survive.' *Charles B. Hawks*

'We came back from one of those Tokyo nights in *Torchy*. It was 1,500 miles to go, with no electrical controls or instruments for anything in or on the left wing, and the rear spar of that wing was shot through. When we began the letdown, our number one and two propellers were fixed in high pitch at low rpm and at cruise power. We had to shut them down by feathering as soon as we touched down.

'When *Torchy* rolled to a stop, the left wing drooped until it had no dihedral at all.

They counted the machine gun and cannon holes in the plane and quit when they got to 800 holes.' *Donald L. Miller*

'The number two engine on our plane, *Sweet Sue,* always ran hot and the ground crew never could find anything wrong with it. On our last mission to Tokyo, we had a hot number two again, and so we started the usual routine of babying it for the trip back home. When we came off the target, we were supposed to head south, but we saw what looked like a lot of action down there and the pilot decided it might be better to go east for a while. Besides, the smoke from the fires was blowing that way, and it was up at our altitude, and he thought we might be able to get behind it and use it for cover.

'We got hit by flak in the dark, and the airplane was running rough, so we decided to land at Iwo. But Iwo was socked in by weather, and we flew around for a while hoping it would clear. After three hours, the pilot called in for a decision, and the crew decided that we'd rather bail out than ditch anytime.

'So the ground gave us a heading for Mt Suribachi, where we were supposed to bail out. I was back in the aft pressurised compartment by then, because I always left my tail gun position empty until 100 miles before landfall and then left it 100 miles after

Sakai was burned early in the morning of 10 July 1945, and this is what the strike looked like from one of the B-29s in that raid.
/ Mrs Thomas Isley Collection

we left the coast. We bailed out of the main hatch, and I counted to five real fast, then a slower five and pulled the rip cord. Prettiest sight I ever saw. I drifted down and landed on a soft field being graded by a Seabee running a bulldozer.

'Everybody else got out all right, and we stayed on Iwo for two days. We heard small arms fire every night; the Japanese weren't really through defending the island.

'Anyway, when we got back, the other crews that had flown in that airplane came around on the quiet and thanked us for losing the plane.

'It was an expensive way to fix a hot engine.' *Mike Janosko*

Yokohama went on 29 May, victim of 454 B-29s. Osaka was hit 1 June by 458 aircraft; Kobe on 5 June by 473. It was Osaka's turn again on 7 June, when 409 B-29s attacked with fire bombs and left the city in ruins. More than 55,000 buildings were destroyed. It was hit once again on 15 June by 444 aircraft, and that strike concluded a month of concentrated and devastating fire raids. The first phase of the planned destruction of Japanese urban areas had been completed. The top six industrial centres — Tokyo, Nagoya, Kobe, Osaka, Yokohama and Kawasaki — had been levelled.

There had been a total of 17 attacks, with 6,960 sorties dispatched, or an average of more than 400 Superforts on each strike. They had dropped 41,592 tons of bombs and had lost 136 of their number to the Japanese defences.

With the major industrial cities off the target lists, the XXI Bomber Command planners looked to the smaller cities. These held many industrial plants and transportation centres, so they were legitimate strategic targets. They also were congested, and typically Japanese cities, so they would burn well.

Beginning on 17 June 1945, these cities were systematically fire-bombed in night attacks, with radar bombing techniques.

The first four to be hit were assigned, one each, to the four combat wings of Superfortresses in action. The 58th struck Omuta; the 73rd flew against Hamamatsu; the 313th attacked Yokkaichi, and the 314th hit Kagoshima. More than 450 B-29s headed out on the strike, and the results were highly successful. The pattern of the attack was to become standard for the rest of the war.

Whenever there was a B-29 force ready to go, and whenever the weather conditions indicated that radar bombing was the technique of choice, they were dispatched against the cities on the target list. Usually four cities were chosen, one for each wing. Once in a while, one target would seem to require the attention of two wings, so that only three targets would be assigned for that raid.

Sixteen of these raids left Saipan, Guam and Tinian, on an average of about twice each week until the end of the war. They met increasingly less opposition; the defence systems around these smaller cities had been neglected by the Japanese in favour of concentration of effort at the major cities.

LeMay took another chance in late July. It seemed like a bold gesture, and it was; but it also was a very shrewd appraisal of the Japanese psyche at the time. LeMay had a leaflet printed in Japanese, warning that some of the 11 cities listed would be hit the following night in a bombing raid, and urging the residents to leave those cities for their own safety. Six B-29s roared over the eleven cities on the night of 27 July and dropped 660,000 leaflets. The following night, the first six cities on the list were hit hard. Fighter opposition, even with the advance warning of 24 hours, was weak. LeMay's psychological gamble had worked, and he used it again on 1 and 4 August. Those leaflets convinced thousands of Japanese civilians that the war was lost, and that their government had been lying to them for months about the strength of the defences of the home islands and the power of their military forces.

The fire raids against the smaller cities were generally as successful as those against the six major cities. These secondary raids hit 57 cities, three of them twice. They burned out an average of forty-three per cent of their areas, with the most destruction being wrought at Toyama, which was 99.5 per cent destroyed.

The momentum built in those last terrible days of the war, as city after city crumbled into ashes. The strength of each attack increased as LeMay's forces grew in number and ability. A force of 300, 400, 500, even 600 B-29s was not unreachable.

On 1 August 627 Superfortresses hit four cities with incendiaries; it was one part of the day's effort — its largest — by XXI Bomber Command. In addition to the fire raid, 120 B-29s went after an oil depot at Kawasaki, and late that afternoon 37 B-29s were sent to mine the Shimonoseki Strait and six other sites. A total of 836 Superforts was dispatched from the island bases; 784 bombed their primary targets.

It was a massive effort, recalling the day-and-night, 1,000-plane raids over Europe a few months earlier. But even these powerful assaults were to be erased from memory by the effects, short- and long-term, of two strikes yet to come.

One Damned Mission after Another

And it seemed that way. Load up, make the long flight to the target, drop your bombs, fight your way home, debrief, hit the sack. Then get up and do it again.

That was the other guy's mission. Yours was always different, remember? You came back on three engines, or you ditched and got rescued by a submarine, sent your way by a circling Superdumbo. It was your B-29 that a Japanese fighter rammed and took off a chunk of the tail; you got back, but that sure as hell wasn't a routine mission. Remember getting turned over when you hit that cloud of smoke in a fire raid? How about the time you watched in horror as your bombs neatly spaced themselves to miss the wing and tail of another B-29 that had slipped beneath you at that moment?

But underneath all the exceptions, there was the routine, the established Army way, the SOP of a combat strike.

'We completed our crew training at MacDill Field, Tampa, Florida, and it was time to head out to the Pacific and a combat assignment. Our shiny-new B-29 was waiting for us at the staging area in Kearney, Nebraska.

'She was elegant. She had all the brand-new smells of upholstery, fibreglass, miles of rubber-insulated wiring, dozens of little and big motors throughout her frame, new aluminium, hydraulic fluid, and that exclusive smell of high-octane aviation gasoline that no longer exists. It's a shame that these long-gone smells couldn't have been recorded, like a Glenn Miller tune, to be played back later for reminiscing. She even had good-luck messages pencilled on her framework by an anonymous Rosie the Riveter at Marietta.

'The more we checked this new bird out, the more we liked her and the prouder we became of her, especially because the Wright engines didn't even once catch fire when we took off on check flights, unlike some of the ships in which we had trained. How could we lose with such a fine piece of machinery?

'When everything checked out OK, we took off for Mather Field, Sacramento, California, found a place in Air Transport Command's pipeline that cleared us out over the wide Pacific, and headed for Guam via Honolulu and Kwajalein. We saw our first enemy flak when we flew too close to Japanese-held Motji on the approach to Kwajalein. But we really remember

The bombs are loaded on Z-51 of the 500th Bomb Group. She carries 34 mission markers and three Japanese flags on her starboard nose; at 35, her crew goes home.
/ Dr Lyman C. Perkins

Kwajalein because that's where somebody stole our case of Scotch.

'We landed at Guam, unloaded a bomb-bay full of mail and spare parts, and picked up orders assigning us to the 6th Bomb Group, 313th Wing, on Tinian. That station was about 25 minutes' flying time north of Guam, and on the way up we saw our very first enemy fighter. It was a dead-duck Zero, sitting broken in the middle of the knocked-out Japanese airstrip on the island of Rota, bypassed in the campaigns to take the Marianas.

'We landed at Tinian, and taxied in past more B-29s than I had ever seen, a crew-of-the-week from MacDill, red hot and hot to trot. After the "Follow Me" jeep had parked us on a coral hardstand, we loaded a 6 × 6 truck that took us several miles away to a Quonset hut marked, "Headquarters, 39th Squadron, 6th Bomb Group (VH)". Our pilot, who was a major and a veteran of 100 missions over Europe in B-24s, went inside to report that the crew that would win the war had arrived.

'In fifteen minutes he came back out, mad as hell, to report that our crew had been broken up for replacements and that our shiny new B-29 had been taken away and assigned to another bomb group. What kind of a war was this? How could we ever beat the Japanese this way?

'As luck would have it, I was the first one to be reassigned to another crew. The crew of Capt Catts was short a top CFC gunner; he had been severely wounded and two other

crewmen had been killed by a direct flak hit on a mission over Osaka. They had just returned from R&R (Rest and Recuperation) in Hawaii, and I am sure they were delighted to get a new, green top gunner. As it turned out, they were a great team and never showed me anything but help and friendship.' *J. R. Pritchard, Jr, CFC gunner, 39th BS, 6th BG*

'Aircraft availability was the key to crew selection for a strike mission. Almost all of the major strikes through March 1945 called for a maximum effort, that is, every combat-ready airplane was assigned to the mission. That pretty much selected the crews automatically; the crew or alternate crew primarily assigned to each aircraft was selected.

'The final target was chosen — by Wing prior to 25 February 1945, and then by XXI Bomber Command — after the strike was ordered, based on target priorities and weather forecasts.

'The responsibility for crew selection at squadron level for heavily defended targets was eliminated by this procedure, even though it had not been developed for that purpose.

'Every effort was made to keep a crew together for their entire combat tour. The concept of flying a crew only in their own aircraft on any major strike was really beneficial to the abort rate. The big psychological factor was the pride and confidence you had in your own aircraft. If your own was not available, you might be

assigned to another if it was going to be a relatively "easy" mission.' *Ferd J. Curtis*

The men walk into the hot Quonset hut, make their way through the crowded benches and sit, facing an elevated stage and a podium. A large sign above the stage tells them, 'Stand up when you talk. Hand up if you can't hear.' At the edge of the stage is another sign, propped against the panels. It reads, 'Do not walk or stand on benches.'

Captain Marmion begins the briefing. Behind him are huge charts with the plan of attack, the course from Saipan to the target, the call signs and radio frequencies.

A blackboard at the left of the stage lists the altitudes for the mission. It assigns the 73rd Wing to route altitudes between 3,000 and 3,500 feet, and attack altitudes between 7,000 and 7,800 feet. The 313th Wing will fly between 4,000 and 4,500 feet to the target, and attack from altitudes between 6,000 and 6,800 feet. The 314th will be the low wing, cruising between 3,000 and 3,300 feet, and attacking from 5,000 to 5,800 feet.

In large letters the blackboard shows the name of the force commander: Col Dougherty. Below his name, the timetable: Stations at 1730K time, start engines 1825K, takeoff 1840K. Radio silence requires a timed operation.

The room is filled. Captain Marmion continues to describe the mission, and the men take notes, quietly. An occasional question, a request to repeat a number comes from a crewman. To many, it's a familiar

Above: Boarding ladder in place, this B-29 waits quietly for the action to begin.
/ Dr Lyman C. Perkins

Top left: Censored, aircraft 11 of the 39th Bomb Group, 314th Bomb Wing, taxies out of the hardstand area at North Field, Guam. It's late afternoon; the shadows have begun to lengthen and the clouds have built up.
/ via Boeing

Bottom left: This well-known picture of a B-29 of the 504th BG over Osaka is shown once again to correct the impression earlier users had that the number three engine was losing oil. That was not unusual for the B-29 engines, but in this case, the dark area behind the number three engine is the shadow of the B-29 fuselage from which this picture is being taken, and the shadow of the upper aircraft's number two engine nacelle can be seen on the upper fuselage of the plane in the picture. Regardless of details, Osaka is burning, and the moated palace on the right has been untouched by bombs.
/ 313th BW

Above: Four little friends — P-51 Mustangs from the fighter base on Iwo Jima — fly escort to B-29s of the 498th Bomb Group. The fighters were escorted, in turn, by the big bombers because most of the P-51s were very poorly equipped for long-range navigation. One B-29 generally shepherded the fighters to and from Iwo on long strikes. */ Mrs Thomas Isley Collection*

Top right: Shiny, late-model B-29s of the 29th Bomb Group, 314th Bomb Wing, fly a tight combat formation on the approach to the target. */ Charles B. Hawks Collection*

Bottom right: It's April 1945, and the powers that be have decreed that the old identifiers be removed and gigantic single letters replace them for group identification. So it's up on the ladder and clean off the T and the Square and the number, and paint the big T of the 498th Bomb Group on the rudder. */ Mrs Thomas Isley Collection*

run; they've been to that target before, hit it a number of times. But the factories continue to produce engine parts for the Japanese fighters. This time, they think, we'll get 'em.

Other briefers take the stage, describe the weather, the target, the air-sea rescue services, alternate fields. And then the general briefing is over, and the crews file out, breaking into smaller groups headed for specialist briefings: Navigators over here, radar operators there, bombardiers in that building, gunners down by your aircraft.

The machinery of the mission has begun to turn. It will build momentum and maintain it for the next 24 hours or so, until each of the strike aircraft has returned or is accounted for.

'My first mission ever was a night incendiary raid on a fuel storage and refinery area in Nagoaka, across Honshu island northwest of Tokyo on the Sea of Japan. It was a mere 1,800 miles from Tinian, a 3,600-mile round trip.

'We were briefed for an afternoon takeoff which would put us over the target around midnight. The ground crews did ninety-nine per cent of the work preparing each plane for its mission, but our crew went down to the flight line anyway to pre-flight the B-29. The gunners helped the armourers load the .50-calibre ammunition into the turret cans. We did all this in the afternoon before takeoff.

'Our crew had lost its aircraft to the junkpile on Iwo Jima after staggering in there on the proverbial "wing and a prayer" following their sad and terrible experience over Osaka. So we were assigned a combat veteran B-29 named *Irish Lullaby* that had belonged to a crew of the 24th Squadron who had completed their missions and had gone home.

'She was resplendent with the "Pirate" insignia of the 6th Bomb Group on the nose, yellow Pirate, blue triangle, white, red-edged "wing" painted back toward the leading edge. *Irish Lullaby* was painted in black script, shaded in green. And of course, she had the red cowl panels and rudder top common to all aircraft of the 6th Bomb Group.

'With all its twelve turreted .50-calibre machine guns loaded and pointed up or down for safety, its ten tons of thermite incendiary bombs that could burn through two inches of steel plate, and some 12,000 gallons of gasoline on board, she was a formidable war machine. But parked just a few hundred yards across the field was another B-29 named *Enola Gay*, and within a few more days, our tough *Irish Lullaby* would look like a pussycat by comparison.' *J. R. Pritchard, Jr*

The B-29 stands fuelled, bombed and loaded with ammunition, on the coral floor of the hardstand. Its guns are stowed off the horizontal, a sure sign they are loaded and

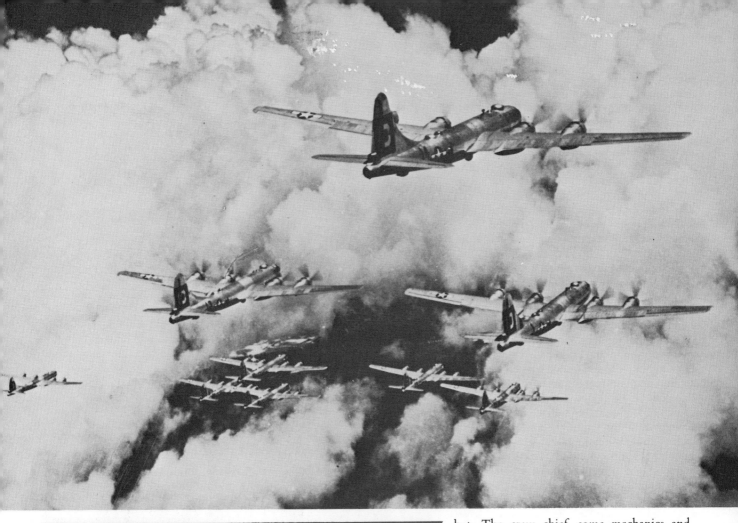

hot. The crew chief, some mechanics and armourers, a radio technician stand and wait, their tasks done for the moment.

'I used to ride around to the hardstands just before mission time, just to hang around and talk a bit with the crews, maybe ease their tensions. One night, coming toward Z Sq 42, Capt Moreland's plane, I heard a lot of fuss and saw a couple of guys sliding down the props. Now we had a notice on the bulletin boards that they were not to slide down the props; it was hard enough keeping those things working without having guys knocking them out of line or whatever by using them as a quick way down from the wing.

'Anyway, somebody spotted me and there was the usual type of covering talk, the kind that anybody who's ever been in the service knows is just trying to divert attention. So I said, okay, men, what's the problem? Well, there was some fidgeting and then one sergeant said, "Sir, we have a mouse on board Captain Moreland's plane and we check before every mission to make sure he's there and ready to go, too."

'They took me into the bomb shelter, where they kept a running score of missions for the crew and probably some other stuff, and there was a board with the crew's names and at the bottom was the twelfth crew

265

member, Mister Mouse, credited with five missions.

'That mouse had been along in the B-29 for five rides over Japan and — the last I knew — he had completed 14 missions and was expected to stay on the crew for the rest of its tour.' *James J. Garrity, adjutant, 883rd BS, 500th BG*

The truck brakes to a stop by the hardstand, and the crew jump off. They unload their personal gear, chutes and manuals, flak suits and dinghies and life vests. The pilot and flight engineer start a walkaround inspection; the rest of the crew tosses equipment aboard the B-29, stows the food, jokes with the ground crew. The pilot gives the order to board, and the crew enters.

Soon, the auxiliary power unit starts, its rhythmic stutter the reason for its nickname of putt-putt. The tail gunner, whose job was to start the putt-putt, moves to his station. 'Interphone check', says the pilot, and the crew calls back, co-pilot, bombardier, navigator, flight engineer, top gunner, left gunner, right gunner, radar operator, and tail gunner. In similar rotation, the crew makes a check of the control surfaces, reporting on their condition, and a station check of equipment ready to go.

Outside the airplane, the armourers have pulled the safety wires on the bombs in the bomb bays and are standing clear of the ship. The pilot acknowledges their task.

'We bombed our own hardstand once, and that was a thrill. I was CFC gunner in the crew of *Dragon Lady* on a night mission to Nagoya, with the Group Commander aboard. We were loaded with 500lb demolition bombs, and we got in the airplane as usual. The procedure was that after everybody got in, and when we were ready to start the engines, the right gunner turned out the light in the bomb bay.

'What he didn't know, and what the ground crew had neglected to tell us, was that they had just completed a modification changing the position of two switches. One was the bomb bay dome light; the other was the emergency bomb salvo switch. You can guess the rest.

'The right gunner felt around where he thought the dome light switch was, and found it safetied. So he got his pliers, cut the safety wire, and flipped the switch. And the sickening rumble of those bombs dropping out on to the hardstand I will remember forever. From my perch I could look through a plexiglass window into the bomb bay and I could watch those bombs go. We left the plane hurriedly.

'The Colonel was cool; he asked for an explanation and got it, then called for the

armourers to reload and we went off on the mission.' *Robert B. Hill, CFC gunner, 871st BS, 497th BG*

Inside, the flight engineer gets his orders to start the engines, and he energises the starter switch on number three engine. The blades swing through their huge arcs to the whine of the starter motor. Six, seven blades go through the vertical and 'Eight!' yells the fireguard watching number three. The engineer flips the ignition switch. The Wright R-3350 wheezes, coughs, chugs a few times, spews clouds of exhaust, and the prop changes from individual blades to a blur. The engine roars its power. It is time to roll.

All four engines are noisily idling; the throttles are advanced, the big bomber begins to bounce, to lighten on her gear; then she is free of friction's grasp and starts to roll away from the revetment.

The gunners call in that the landing gear and tyres look okay. The flaps whine down all the way, then retract to 25 degrees for takeoff, monitored by the side gunners.

The B-29 reaches the end of the runway. The pilot calls for one more crew check and they respond, in the same order again, ending with, 'Tail gunner, sir'. The engines go to full power, howling their strength into the afternoon quiet.

Ponderously, the Superfortress starts its takeoff roll. It accelerates smoothly, wheels rumbling over the hard-packed runway surface. Pilot, co-pilot and engineer work easily, their persuasive movements easing on power, feeling for control reactions,

'Hey, Lieutenant, I got this great idea for a publicity shot! We'll get a crew down by the airplane — I think they're B-29s or something like that — and we'll have them loading bombs and bullets and they'll be painting things like "Screw you, Tojo" on the bombs and...' That's what seems to have happened to this unwitting B-29 from the 500th Bomb Group, as ground crews swarm over her with 'busy' work for the camera. Painting insults on bombs, yes. Sitting on the prop, sure. But did any of the armourers out there ever, ever load the top fifties that way ? */ XXI Bomber Command via Boeing-Wichita*

watching the runway ahead, sensing the great
surging power of the engines. Their practised
actions conceal the tension below the surface,
the knowledge that every second of this
takeoff run is critical, that if anything
happens they have a split second to react and
to make the correct judgment and take the
correct action. Miss the fleeting opportunity,
and they are all dead.

The wing seizes the air, deflects it
downward and begins to lift the weight off
the landing gear. The shock absorbers stretch,
showing more of their chrome-plated struts.
Back pressure on the controls, now. The nose
wheel lifts off the runway; the nose rises. And
then the main wheels also rise, slowly. The
landing gear starts to ease into the wheel
wells.

Watching, you see the great bird hurtle
down the runway, hell-bent on a suicidal
jump off the cliff at the end. She begins to
rotate before the edge, she eases into the air at
the very end of the runway, and almost
immediately drops from view as the pilot lets
her down to the level of the waves pounding
against the base of the cliff. She accelerates
slowly in this heat and with that load, and he
uses gravity to help him gain a few extra feet
per second of flight speed.

You watch, while a second and a third B-
29 move down the same runway, make the
same jump off the edge, disappear below the
lip. And then you see the first one, coming
into your line of sight miles offshore,
climbing slowly toward Japan.

The island shakes to the sound and the
echoes of the engines, full-throated howling

in quartettes, three airplanes on the runway at
once, one holding, one rolling, one lifting,
twelve engines screaming out their full
power.

'The early B-29s, operating from Saipan, had
cooling problems. Saipan was hot, which
didn't help. We just couldn't make an engine
run-up and an ignition check at any
reasonable power on the ground, standing still.
So we did those tasks during takeoff. There
was a marker along the runway at a critical
distance; if you reached it and everything was
running smoothly, you continued. If things
were troubled, you cut the engines at that
point and refused takeoff.' *Haywood S.
Hansell, Jr*

'We had a two-mile runway at Guam,
downhill the first half and uphill the second,
with a 500-foot drop off a cliff at the end. I
learned to get her out of the starting gate fast.
If you lost anything during the second mile of
the run, you'd had it. The way we were
loaded, it did no good at all to try to raise the
nosewheel off the runway at anything less
than 210mph.

'We aborted takeoffs twice, and the first
time was a beauty. We lost an engine just at
the halfway point. We made all the drag we
could: dropped the flaps, opened the bomb
bay doors — and a couple of bombs shook
loose, just to add to the fun — and we
burned out our brakes. We drove off the
runway and over the rough coral shoulder
separating the strip from the jungle. We bent
the props and blew a tyre. Then, we had just

enough speed to get back on the runway, so we taxied down and across traffic to get on to the nearest taxiway. It was all in a midnight blackout, and with other aircraft taking off at thirty-second intervals from the same runway, we didn't have much time to clear the strip.

'Within minutes I reported, by request, to General LeMay who was in the tower during this takeoff. Actually, he did all the talking, and I agreed with everything he said!' *Charles B. Hawks*

'We did a night takeoff I'll remember. In our ship, the bombardier — that was me — called off the airspeed for the pilot and co-pilot. They liked it that way.

'Anyway, we were rolling and I had just called off our decision speed where we had to keep flying or abort, and a waist gunner called that there was fire in number four engine. The flight engineer called that number four was losing oil pressure. Our load was a gasoline tank in one bomb bay and bombs in the other, and we sure wanted to fly rather than ditch off the end of the runway.

'We went off the end, over the cliff and headed for the water to pick up speed. The pilot feathered the engine and asked me to jettison the load. I figured we were too low and told him so, and he came back and *ordered* me to jettison the load. So I dumped both bays.

'The airplane was so close to the water that the gas tank couldn't drop clear. It hit the rear bulkhead of the bomb bay and bent the doors. I swear I could have stuck my foot out and dragged it in the water. And after that,

268

we had to fly until the rest of the strike force was launched before we could go back in there and land.

'The worst part was when there would be somebody burning on the water underneath you as you took off.' *Del Shaffer, bombardier, 874th BS, 498th BG*

'The photo lab reported that there were salt deposits on the films they got from our camera. The camera installation was just aft of the exit door, and we used it to take pictures of the target after we dropped. It was a convenient hatch, and the first thought was that the guys in the back were using it as a urinal.

'That wasn't it at all. The real problem was that we got pretty close to the water right after takeoff, trying to pick up some extra speed. And what we were doing was kicking up spray off the ocean with our props. It was seeping into the camera hatch and depositing on the film, the camera and the whole installation.' *Robert B. Hill*

'T Square 5, *Jolting' Josie*, was Major Catton's plane, but she was being flown by another crew when she crashed on takeoff. I had been at the living quarters and got a call to the flight line to service some of the aircraft. I got a lift from a GI driving a weapons carrier, and as we came around the northeast end of the runway, he stopped to watch a couple of the takeoffs, and he stopped right at the end of the runway.

'There was a wind blowing, maybe 20 or 25 miles per hour, and the B-29s were taking off as usual. *Joltin' Josie* had just reached the

end of the runway by the cliff where they usually started to fly, and the wind just stopped. Dead. Flat calm. And T Square 5 just kept on going down to the water and hit. Nobody got out.' *H. W. Douglas*

And then the noise fades. The last of the Superforts has disappeared over the lip of the cliff. You watch, see it rise once again, and climb to join the rest of the formation, now only distant specks on the horizon.

The island is suddenly quiet. It will stay that way for more than twelve hours, while the planes go to Japan and come back. You walk back, in twos and threes, already starting to sweat out your ship.

'To keep the statistical people happy, we had to increase our bomb tonnage dropped. This meant lighter fuel loads, and the only way we could do this was to stay at low altitude for the flight to the target. We did it on the deck, skimming the sea at maximum cruise power, dodging small tea-growing islands in the moonlight.

'We flew through or below the usual two weather fronts on our trip north, and over and through the same fronts on our return. Those trips almost always included a sunrise and a sunset. The variations in light and colour in the Pacific were fantastically beautiful. They softened our own strain and anxieties over the war'. *Charles B. Hawks*

'Basically, we navigated by dead reckoning and by shooting the stars at night. The astrodome was in the tunnel between the two pressurised compartments and I had to crawl

Above: Jumbo II, aircraft A-50 of the 497th Bomb Group, carries 53 tiny bomb mission markers plus three that can't be identified in this photo. She also has 13 Japanese flags stencilled on her nose above the numerals 50. A tough airplane, and it seems as if she had a fighting crew as well. / *James J. Garrity Collection*

Top left: Ponderous Peg, sure of her identity, carries both the large A identifiers of post-April 1945, and the earlier A-Square-44, which can be seen under the large A on the tail. / *Mike Janosko Collection*

Centre left: Neatly lined up in Isley Field revetments, these 500th Bomb Group Superfortresses sun themselves in the mid-day brightness of the tropics. / *Mrs Thomas Isley Collection*

Bottom left: It did indeed rain on Saipan, and these B-29s of the 497th Bomb Group are reflected in the shallow puddles under the leaden skies. / *James J. Garrity Collection*

Aircraft 62 of the 444th Bomb Group coasts in for a landing on West Field, Tinian, as another B-29, engines idling and flaps partially down for takeoff, waits to take over one of the two 8,500 foot parallel runways. / Ron E. Witt Collection

into the tunnel with my sextant, climb up in the astrodome and shoot the stars.

'Later, we got some Loran stations on Iwo, and in the Marcus and Philippine Islands, so that we could get a good set of Loran lines for navigation between Saipan and Japan.

'Then toward the end of the war, the crew complement began to change. We got commissioned, rated navigators as radar operators, replacing the sergeants we'd had earlier. The sergeants were okay, but they hadn't been trained well. About all they could do was to turn the set on and off, and trouble-shoot it a little. That was important, but it didn't help navigating that much.

'The APQ-13 got to be reliable after some initial problems. It had a full 360-degree presentation, so it was good for navigation and only secondarily a bombing radar. The APQ-7, on the other hand, was designed to scan a 45-degree segment directly in front of the airplane, so it wasn't too great for navigation. But it was some bombing radar. We bombed from 25,000 feet in training using that system, and we often dropped within 100 feet or so of the target from that altitude.' *Vern Piotter*

'Before we got to the islands, we put on our flak suits. They were some protection, but they were heavy and cumbersome. This was long before nylon armour, and the suits were made with small metal plates sewed individually into pockets. We were supposed to wear them, but most of us sat on them to protect the family jewels.

'The B-29 had some internal armour plating to protect various crew stations. It was weight that we thought we could use to better purpose, and so our crew voted to remove all of it except for one piece. That was the piece that was forward of the tail gunner. We wanted to feel that we wouldn't shoot off our own tail, or kill the gunner by accident, or by a round that cooked off in a gun.' *Robert B. Hill*

'The APQ-13 was called a bomb-nav radar, but most everybody used it primarily as a navigation aid. It was, by today's standards, very primitive and it worked part of the time most of the time. We used it a lot to define landfall, because it did a good job of defining a coastline and separating land from water, so you knew when you were coming over the coast. We didn't bomb with radar that much unless we really couldn't see the target.

'The way we bombed was standard procedure. When we got to the IP, the bombardier directed the turn on to the target heading, based on his maps and the pre-flight briefings. The pilot actually made the turn, and then levelled the plane to align it on course for the target.

'If we were bombing by radar, which the navigator operated for the bomb run, he would give me corrections during the run, based on what he saw on the scope.

'Then the bombardier took over for the bomb run, synchronised the bomb sight, and held the airplane heading while the pilots controlled and held airspeed and altitude. We had to have all three steady and constant during the run. It made for better bombing, but it also simplified the computations for enemy anti-aircraft.' *Del Shaffer*

'Our bombing got better as the war went on. You have to remember that we were really doing on-the-job training, because back in the States we had been hampered by not having enough B-29s to train in and even fly.

Right: Three P-51 Mustangs from Iwo Jima stick close to a B-29 during a flight over cloud cover. The escort fighters are carrying long-range auxiliary fuel tanks, and they are outbound to Japan.
/ *Donald L. Miller Collection*

Below: Dead centre in the picture, a Nakajima J1N 'Gekko' ('Irving' in Pacific name codes) is photographed by the strike camera on one of the 500th BG B-29s. Target is unidentified, but it is a heavily settled urban area with a major railroad line running through the centre and feeding a large complex of factory buildings or warehouses at the lower right of the picture.
/ *Elmer Huhta Collection*

So it was natural that we started out with some pretty poor bombing accuracies.

'Our best effort came on a daylight mission to Osaka, with Hitachi as a secondary target. The wing put up 12 squadrons. We took off from the parallel runways at North Field (Saipan) with a launch every 25 seconds. Normally, each ship flew toward the rendezvous area alone, or maybe in a very loose formation with one or two others. We usually set a rendezvous point about 150 miles off Japan. The pilot of the lead ship would lower the nose gear to identify himself as lead, and the rest of us would form on him. He'd circle for 20 minutes or so until the rest of the squadron joined in and established the formation. This was at maybe 1,500 feet to 3,000 feet altitude.

'Then we'd start the climb to bombing altitude as a formation. I've forgotten if that was our exact procedure on this particular mission, but it was typical. Our primary target was cloud-covered, so the Hitachi Engineering Works became the target. The sky was clear as we flew our bomb run at 19,000 feet. We had a good run, and all the planes dropped on the signals from their lead bombardiers, and all dropped within 20 minutes as successive formations came over the target.

'The post-strike photos showed that we had gotten 98.5 per cent of our bombs within the predicted CEP (Circular Error Probable), and I believe it was the most accurate of all bombing raids in all theatres during the war.'
Bernard J. Mulloy, aircraft commander, 869th BS, 497th BG

'There's total darkness everyplace, you can't see anything — anything — around you, and all of a sudden, right underneath you or right

271

Above: B-29s of the 444th Bomb Group fly over their home base of West Field, Tinian. / *Ron E. Witt Collection*

Top right: Z-41, of the 500th Bomb Group, at bombs away. Aircraft at upper right still carries the old identifier of Z-Square-number, and so this picture must have been taken early in April 1945, the month the markings change took effect. / *Don C. Hetrick Collection*

Bottom right: Bombs dropping from this 6th BG Superfortress form a figure-eight in midair. / *313th BW*

over you, there goes a B-29. And the searchlights are continually, frantically searching for you. You see an airplane in front and the lights have caught him and they follow him for miles. Once they catch him, they'll keep the light on him all the way. Sometimes the beam would flash past your window and the light would be so bright that you just couldn't see anything for a while after that. If you were ever caught, and followed a while, they'd get you, almost certainly.' *Del Shaffer*

Through the searchlights on the bomb run, holding a steady course while flak blazed underneath, or fighters bored in from ahead, then the relief of 'Bombs away!' and almost immediately, 'Let's get the hell out of here!', and the B-29 turning, diving maybe, working its way through the smoke or the lights and the flak. Head for the coast, navigator. The run over enemy territory, sometimes free, sometimes chased by determined fighter pilots pushing their light aircraft to the limit. Cross the coast, take up a heading for Saipan. The fighters stay for a while, throwing a last defiant burst, and then break away. You're safe, so far, and now all you have to worry about is getting the airplane back in one piece.

'We used to take one can of beer per crewman — we were rationed to three cans per week on Saipan — along on a mission. We wrapped them in rags and paper to keep them from freezing, and stowed them in the unpressurised tail compartment between the aft pressurised compartment and the tail gunner's position. After we were clear of the target area and the defences, the tail gunner

would bring the cold beer forward, and we'd open it and wash down our cold Spam sandwiches with a very cold beer.' *Robert B. Hill*

'There was always an informal competition to get home first, and there was a practical reason, too. It was a lot less congested in the traffic pattern if you got there first and early. We seldom flew in formation after leaving the target, and it was every man for himself after leaving the Japanese mainland.

'We had problems with the jet stream going up and over the target, and one day it hit me that maybe we could use the jet stream to get back home faster. So I worked the natigational problem, and learned to take advantage of the pattern of the jet stream going home. We'd head out from the target as if we were going to cross the Pacific, and we'd drift with the changing direction of the jet stream. The object was to fly a constant heading from "coast out" to home base.

'Once I gave the pilot a heading on leaving the Japanese coast, which he held constant all the way home. We arrived over Isley and split the field on course. Boy, was I proud of that navigational job! We were actually pioneering the practical use of "pressure pattern" navigation which in later years became a SAC training requirement.

'We were especially in keen competition with the crew commanded by Capt Thomas P. Hanley. They were a replacement crew and flew a brand-new, late-model, Renton-built ship. It gave us a special satisfaction to arrive home in our old, war-weary *Coral Queen* (A Sq 17) ahead of Hanley's new model.' *Vern Piotter*

'It was a long trip back, because our mission times varied from nine to as much as 25 hours in the air. I'm almost certain that some B-29s just fell into the sea with everybody aboard asleep.

'Just short of Guam once, we tried to rouse one; we watched him peel off course in a descending turn and dive straight into the sea. Even bennies (benzedrine) and coffee had their limits.

'The total mission time — from briefing through de-briefing — must have averaged about 24 hours during the time I was flying.

'My first experience sleeping was also the last time I ever shut my eyes in a B-29. I had dozed off, and when I woke, I found the entire crew asleep and the ship ghosting along on autopilot. So I took to mixing a little pure oxygen with the "Voice of America" and Tokyo Rose, and managed to stay awake on the rest of the missions.

'A six- to eight-hour return flight over the peace and quiet of the Pacific gave us time to settle our nerves, and even the big lady seemed pleased to have her load lightened. Her props turned over slow and easy, flying a gradual descent from maybe 20,000 feet to touchdown over 1,500 miles of water.'
Charles B. Hawks

'As bad as the weather was, it didn't produce icing conditions very often. In fact, icing was so rare that we took the de-icing boots off the airplanes for combat. We figured we could use the drag saving, because every little bit helped.

'So naturally we did pick up ice on one mission, and it was bad. We knew we

273

couldn't make it back to Saipan, so we headed for Iwo and landed there. Believe me, if Iwo hadn't been there, the wing would have been wiped out. There must have been 100 B-29s on the ground at Iwo that day.'
Bernard J. Mulloy

'We must have set some kind of a record for most forced landings per hour of flying time in the B-29. On our very first mission over Japan, we ran out of fuel and were lucky to make a safe landing on another strip just five miles short of home. It would have saved a lot of sweat if Iwo Jima had been available for that one.

'Once we were coming back from Japan on two and one-half engines, and we had to go into Iwo before they were really ready to handle us. The battle for the island was still going on, and the Marines wanted to keep the small Japanese fighter strip clear, after they'd gone to so much trouble to take it. They were going to push our B-29 into the sea to clear the strip, but my crew would have none of that. They argued down the Marines, took five days to repair the ship, and flew one rescued airplane and crew back to Guam.

'One night, during a violent tropical storm, we had to choose between ditching or trying to get into Iwo. We elected for the landing, on a small, muddy strip with an unperfected GCA system. We made it, but we never saw the ground until the next day after spending the night stuck in the mud.

'Twice we ran out of fuel on final after a long mission, and landed dead stick on auxiliary strips a stone's throw from home base on Guam. In the approach attitude, small amounts of gas were trapped in the wing cells and were unusable, even though they read as fuel on the gauges. So you'd come in, thinking you had just enough to make it, and trim her for final approach. Suddenly, you have a very quiet airplane as the engines quit.' *Charles B. Hawks*

If you had fuel, and if you had no trouble with the airplane as a result of combat, and if it was a nice day and you felt like it, you could have some fun on the way back with the B-29, strictly unofficially, of course. The Air Force and Navy pilots in the area maintained the usual inter-service rivalry. Navy fighters would bounce the B-29s on test flights; Air Force pilots would pit their Mustangs against the Grumman Hellcats the Navy flew. And the B-29s waited for a chance to strike back with a gesture of their own.

'One of our B-29 pilots was returning from a mission with a light airplane, feeling pretty good, and he spotted a Navy carrier miles ahead. He feathered one engine, and set up the B-29 on a long glide toward the carrier. He entered the pattern on the downwind leg, turned on to base, lowered the flaps and landing gear and set up a final approach just as if he were going to land on the damned carrier.

'You should have seen the waving from the signal officer. They had deck crews out there waving their arms, their jackets, their hats, anything. And the old B-29 kept coming down the groove. At the last minute, the pilot cleaned up the airplane, poured on the coal, and roared down the length of the carrier, turning away as he did so.

'In all the fuss, nobody bothered to get his tail number or identification, which was just as well. The next day the Navy issued a notice that unidentified aircraft in the landing pattern would be fired upon, and that ended the buzzing of carriers. We figured the Navy was not being a very good sport about it all.'
H. W. Douglas

'Once we were committed on final approach, and we did not have enough fuel to make a go-around. That's when the landing gear chose not to extend and lock. There are two-man hand cranks for this particular emergency, and they are fine when you have plenty of time, because they take about 400 turns to extend the gear and lock it. The manual says it takes twelve minutes to do that.

'The navigator checked the manual and told me that the gear did have to be fully extended to support the weight of the B-29. My co-pilot told the tower that we were probably going to crash.

'We touched down while the gunners were still turning the cranks, and rolled to a stop. No crash. I firmly believe that the tough gunners I had in the crew just held that gear down with the hand cranks and muscle-power.' *Charles B. Hawks*

Now, climb out of the seat, stretching the legs that were riding the rudder pedals until a couple of minutes ago. Down through the hatch by the nose wheel, away from the B-29 after signing the form and turning the ship over to the crew chief.

Sorry, Sergeant, we got some holes in her. That's okay, sir, we'll fix 'em.

Climb in the truck, head for the debriefing, tell the intelligence officer about the new fighter squadron we saw on the way in. Diagonal yellow strip around the fuselage back of the cockpit. Aggressive; they jumped is in pairs, and they came in much too close. We got hit, but our gunners got three, they think, and a couple of probables.

I'm tired; Christ, am I tired!

Back to quarters, stumble into the hut, fall on the bed, kick the boots off . . . sleep . . .

Special Missions, Special Planes

Just in case the atomic bombs didn't work, there were a few alternate ideas that were evaluated and tested. One was to increase the size of the bombs carried by the B-29s by slinging them on underwing external racks, thus avoiding the limiting dimensions of the bomb bay structure. A Wichita-built B-29-75-BW, serial number 44-70060, was converted to a test bed for these wing-rack experiments. Each of the underwing racks could carry one 22,000lb British 'Grand Slam' bomb, or one 12,000lb British 'Tall Boy' bomb, or a pair of M56 4,000lb light case demolition bombs. These latter bombs were carried inside the B-29s in combat; but it was a tight, tricky installation and required special loading equipment. The biggest bombs were to be turned against Yokohama. That city is sited on a coastal shelf with a well-defined fault line behind it. In theory, 'Grand Slam' bombs — they were also nicknamed 'earthquake' bombs — could be dropped so as to trigger the failure of the shelf along the fault line and dump Yokohama into the ocean. In this picture, the test B-29 is loaded with a pair of sand-filled dummy 'Grand Slam' bombs, checking the flying qualities of the aircraft on a flight out of Wichita on 29 June 1945./ *Boeing*

As the war progressed, the Superfortresses were assigned to changing missions. They had started with the expectation of doing the traditional job of precision daylight bombing from high altitudes. Weather, primarily, forced a change from that tactic, and the B-29s went on to score their greatest successes in area night raids, dropping fire bombs from low or medium altitude. They shifted then to a mix of high-altitude precision strikes when weather permitted, and low-level fire raids when the weather did not permit. Since the latter case was the predominant one for Japan, more fire raids were flown than precision strikes.

The Navy never gave up its fight to get the B-29s assigned to the mining of Japanese home waters. They, and the Army Air Forces, knew it was a job that had to be done, that it would pay off strategically, and that only the B-29s had the range and load capabilities to do it properly.

Finally and grudgingly, the USAAF gave in. LeMay designated the 313th Bombardment Wing (VH), based at North Field, Tinian, to do the job. The decision was made late in January 1945, and the wing began training for the special assignment the following month. They flew four to eight practice flights per crew, with five radar approaches to a target on each flight.

The basic tactics were to be night attacks by individual aircraft, dropping on radar scope presentations. To get maximum load and best performance, the crews assigned to those missions lightened their aircraft by removing all the .50-calibre ammunition and by leaving two crewmen home. Further stripping of the Superforts would have hampered their speedy transition to other missions flown alternately with the night mining efforts.

The problem had simplified itself by early 1945. Japanese shipping lanes had been lost, one after another, to Allied forces that controlled the area. Only a few remained, and the most important of these was a single eastern approach to the Inland Sea, a nearly landlocked body of water that lies south of Honshu Island. There are two southern approaches to the sea, but they were so open to enemy attack that the Japanese had stopped using them by 1945. Most of Japan's shipping cleared the Shimonoseki Strait at the eastern end of the Inland Sea.

It was a narrow approach, ideal for mining, and on 27 March 1945, 92 B-29s from the 313th Wing dropped a mix of 1,000 and 2,000lb acoustic and magnetic mines in the strait. Three nights later, 85 aircraft finished the job, closing the strait and all approaches to it. The Japanese, caught by the suprise attack, could only recover with hasty and often suicidal minesweeping operations.

The demand for B-29 support of the Okinawa invasion halted mining activities for a while as all available aircraft turned to tactical support of the campaign, but the results were still coming in after only two strikes against the strait. No large warships were able to get out of the strait after 27 March. Some destroyers tried it during the Okinawa battle; they were desperately needed by the Japanese forces defending the island. But at least four of them were sunk by mines. And by 27 April, 18 Japanese ships lay on the bottom, or had been permanently disabled in the Shimonoseki Strait.

LeMay knew better than to argue with success, and ordered the 313th to keep one group assigned to the mining task whenever it wasn't called to the top-priority mission of hammering the home islands of Japan. The 505th Bombardment Group (VH) was the chosen unit, and they started with a flurry of 14 missions between 7 June and 3 July 1945. They put up 404 B-29 sorties, dropped 3,542 mines in ten major shipping lanes in the Inland Sea and the Sea of Japan.

The mining mission produced some of the longest flights of the war and one in particular, to the Korean port of Rashin, set a record. On 11 July 1945, one of the 6th Bomb Group's B-29s flew from its base on Tinian to Rashin, 2,362 miles away, dropped its mines, and returned non-stop logging a total of 4,724 miles on the journey. It was in the air for 19 hours and 40 minutes.

Most of the aircraft flying this route, or going to the other Korean ports they mined, did stop at Iwo Jima for fuel either on the way out or the way back. Bombardiers started their runs at the initial point 60 miles south of Vladivostok, Siberia, after spending three hours flying across Japan. After the drop, they turned and crossed Japan again on the way home.

It was a superb effort, and it effectively bottled up what was left of the Japanese merchant fleet, the Empire's lifeline. The last missions of the 313th were leaflet drops, propaganda messages urging the Japanese to surrender as the only alternative to starvation. It was a very real possibility, because the mining, coupled with the destruction of stored rice in the devastating fire raids, had reduced the Japanese diets to a near-starvation level.

In the short time that the B-29s had been mining Japanese waters, their efforts accounted for more than ten per cent of all the merchant shipping lost to Japan. They dropped more than 12,000 mines and, as a contemporary note, many of those mines remained unswept for years after the war. As recently as 1975, the Japanese began construction of new minesweepers which, when completed, were to be assigned to

With four M56 4,000-pounders slung under its wings, this test Superfortress is flying in an experimental programme to evaluate the changes caused by the underwing bombs. / *Boeing*

locating and destroying the mines remaining from those raids of the 313th Wing in 1945.

Supporting an Invasion

Okinawa is an island in the Ryukyu group, about 300 miles from the nearest Japanese home island, Kyushu. In the island-hopping strategy of the Pacific theatre, the importance of Okinawa loomed large. It was intended to be a base for 20 additional B-29 groups, which would be used to pound Japan in preparation for the planned invasion by ground forces.

The Japanese defended Okinawa vigorously; they knew its value and the effect its loss would have on the outcome of the war. In that defence, they unleashed a relatively new weapon: the kamikaze aircraft. First used against naval forces in the Battle of Leyte Gulf, the suicide sortie became almost co-equal with conventional air attacks by the Japanese.

The invasion campaign got off to a conventional start, with a pair of supporting strikes by the B-29s against Japanese airfields on Kyushu island. But a few days after the invasion, the Japanese counter-attacked by air, mixing kamikaze and conventional strikes to send two destroyers, two ammunition ships, a minesweeper and a landing ship to the bottom. About 700 combat sorties were made by the Japanese from Kyushu, about half kamikaze, half conventional.

The Superfortresses went back to the home airfields on Kyushu and hit them, or secondary targets, in two strikes during April

1945. The Japanese struck back even harder, and began a series of ten major assaults that included almost 2,000 kamikaze sorties. During this time, they sank 25 ships and damaged scores of others.

The seriousness of the situation called for a major shift in B-29 bombing activities. Beginning in mid-April, the Superfortresses struck against the Japanese airfields on Kyushu, or against secondary targets nearby, with the aim of denying use of the airfields to the Japanese fighter and kamikaze units, and keeping at home those that did get off the ground.

About three-quarters of the B-29 combat sorties during the period between 17 April and 11 May were flown to support the Okinawa campaign by diverting the attacking Japanese aircraft. The big bombers flew more than 2,100 sorties against airfields, hitting some of them several times. The Japanese defenders kept their fields in action a large part of the time by rapid repair of the cratered runways, and there is recorded evidence that most of the Japanese fighter attacks were flown on the same day that their bases had been hit by B-29s.

The B-29 was not a tactical bomber, even though it was flown well in the hands of pilots who made bomb runs at low altitudes and walked their bombs neatly across runways. That was asking the B-29s to fly interdiction missions like fighter-bombers did, and the crews responded.

Nobody can identify the plane or the crew involved in one specific incident, and there's

a chance that it is an apocryphal story anyway, but it's in character with the B-29's capabilities and the proclivities of some of her pilots.

One of the aircraft commanders in the strike force against a kamikaze base in Kyushu had never gotten over the idea that he had been born to be a fighter pilot. He took his B-29 right down to the ground after his bomb run, swung it around in a long pattern and went roaring down the main runway of the Japanese field, belly close to the ground and all guns blazing. The gunners went wild, and shot up the parked aircraft as if they had been sitting ducks.

Several B-29 pilots mentioned this story, and there are guarded references to it in official histories. It's a good story and probably happened. But wouldn't a photograph of that run be great?

By 11 May 1945, the island of Okinawa had its own defence force, US fighters operating from airfields at Kadena and Yontan, and from an auxiliary strip on the island of Ie Shima. The B-29s were released to go back to their primary tasks.

Blasting the Oil Supplies

Near the end of the war, specialised precision bombing attacks were assigned to the newly arrived 315th Bombardment Wing (VH), which had reached Northwest Field, Guam, in May and June of 1945. The 315th had done its unit training as a night radar-bombing outfit, at the expense of learning about visual bombing and daylight formation flying.

Their aircraft were B-29B models built by Bell at Marietta. They were equipped with

90.17-116/12
MITSUBISHI OIL
HAYAMA PETROL
'BEFORE' 315ᵗʰ BOMB

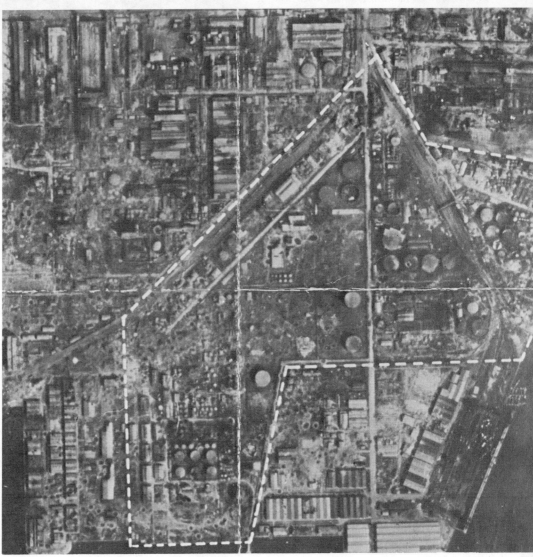

Left: The Mitsubishi Oil
Refinery and the Hayama Oil
Refinery were located on a
peninsula of reclaimed land,
roughly rectangular in shape and
clearly defined by the APQ-7
radar capabilities. Before the
315th Bomb Wing struck it, this
was its appearance from the air.
/ *315th BW via Murray Singer*

Right: On the night of
1-2 August, the 315th BW
raided the two petroleum
refineries, levelling a major
portion of the target area.
/ *315th BW via Murray Singer*

the new AN/APQ-7 Eagle radar housed in a small wing slung below the fuselage on two struts. The 315th B-29s lacked any turrets except for the tail gun position, and their bellies were painted glossy black as a protection against searchlight detection.

One characteristic of early radar was its relatively good performance against ground patterns that were clearly defined, such as a coastal area where water and land met. Logically then, the best targets for the 315th would have to be fairly large and located on the Japanese coast. Oil refineries and storage depots filled that requirement, and accordingly the 315th was sent out to strike Japan's oil industry.

Their first attack was mounted against the Utsube Oil Refinery at Yokkaichi on the night of 26 June. Between that first strike and the end of the war, the 315th flew 15 missions against ten targets. The Superfortresses dropped 9,084 tons of bombs — the 500lb general purpose type — in 1,095 sorties. Because of the lack of armament, extra weight was available for bomb load, and the B-29s of the 315th started by carrying an average of 15,000lb per airplane. On their last mission, the planes were lifting close to 21,000lb each, and might have gone to even higher bomb loads had the war lasted.

They lost four aircraft to enemy action, and 66 of the B-29s were damaged by flak. It was a very low price to pay for the work done.

Typically, a 315th mission would begin in the late afternoon with takeoffs at 45-second intervals from Guam. The first group of bombers would climb to 8,000 feet and the second to 10,000 feet for the cruise to the target. As they neared the coast of Japan, they would climb to the bombing altitudes of 15,000 feet.

At the initial point, the groups established three converging tracks to the target, separated horizontally by about ten miles at the IP. Bombing was done by individual aircraft, rather than by the formation, flying in a stream with a 200-foot altitude separation of the converging streams.

Ideal bombing weather for the 315th was solid cloud cover, with a minimum of turbulence. When cloud cover was not available at the target area, the B-29s faced the ever-present radar-controlled searchlights of the Japanese forces. Aluminium foil 'rope' was used to decoy the radars; as soon as a searchlight locked on a bomber, the countermeasures operators ejected some 'rope'. Generally the resulting target strength caused the Japanese radar to lock on to the aluminium foil cloud and leave the B-29. If the response was slow, other searchlights

TARGET 90.32 - 1841
UBE COAL LIQUEFACTION CO
BEFORE 315TH BOMB. WING STRIKE
5-6 AUG 1945

would join the first to catch the B-29 in its beam. In that case, the B-29 pilot would try to evade the flak that would surely follow by going to full power and top speed.

The use of the APQ-7 radar modified the usual bomb run procedure. The radar was synchronised electrically with the optical bombsight in the nose of the B-29. The radar bombardier and his scope were further aft, in the navigator's compartment. He tracked the target, aligning it with a reticle on the radar scope. This information was fed to the optical bombsight and resulted in a display of the track to fly, presented on an indicator in the cockpit. The radar data also gave ground speed and time for release for the optical bombsight.

The pilot set the plane on automatic pilot, turned to the track displayed on the PDI (Pilot's Direction Indicator), and held that course to the target. He also stabilised the airplane speed and altitude, so that the pilot himself was controlling all three parameters of the bomb run. In the usual approach to optical bombing, the pilots only controlled speed and altitude; the bombardier held the course.

The Ube Coal Liquefaction plant was another well-placed target for radar bombing, with its characteristic geometry set off by surrounding water. It was targeted for the 315th Bomb Wing late in the war.
/ *315th BW via Murray Singer*

280

TARGET # 9032 - 1841
UBE COAL LIQUEFACTION CO.
"DESTROYED AND SUNK" BY
315TH BOMB. WING 5-6 AUG 45

(315 PL)(286 X 8-5-45 X C•PY X CONF)

After the strike by the 315th BW, the Ube Coal Liquefaction Company's plant was not only destroyed, but it was sunk, a unique experience for a land-based target. The B-29s battered the terrain so heavily that they breached the dike separating the plant from the waters outside, and the area flooded after the raid.
/ *315th BW via Murray Singer*

'Down in the nose the bombsight indicators come together, my red light comes on, bomb doors have snapped open. Bombs away! The aircraft lifts as the forty 500-pounders leave us in a minimum train stick. I break away right and down since we're the lowest aircraft in the stack. My co-pilot, Major Greg Hathaway, is on the inside of the turn and has the best view of the tremendous explosions which even light up the clouds above us. We've hit pay dirt! We were all decorated for that mission; the target (Maruzen Oil Refinery) was ninety-five per cent destroyed.' *Boyd Hubbard, Jr, commander, 501st BG*

But strategically, the 315th missions — however well executed — had only small significance. By then, the blockade and the losses of Japanese shipping had dried up most of the country's oil resources. Domestic production had never been very important; the bulk of Japanese crude oil came in from overseas, which was the overriding reason behind their early drive south to take the Netherlands East Indies, source of tremendous crude oil reserves.

In another setting, the record of the 315th against the Japanese oil industry would have been hailed as outstanding. But in the context of Japan's last days, it has to be judged as of limited strategic value.

Ravens and Porcupines

At night, the heavy Japanese defence around the major industrial cities relied on radar to direct searchlights and anti-aircraft artillery. The Japanese radar, unlike the German types in the European theatre, operated at a relatively low frequency. 'Chaff', or 'window' as the Royal Air Force called it, worked well in the European air war decoying German radars. But the narrow, short strips of aluminium foil were almost useless in the Pacific theatre.

'Rope' was developed instead. It also was aluminium foil, but the pieces were one inch wide and were from 100 to 400 feet long. By the end of the war, B-29s were carrying a load of 600lb of 'Rope' on night missions against Japan.

Gun-laying radar was a different problem. Some of the Japanese equipment had been developed from British units that had been

Yokohama Yo-Yo was an F-13A-40-BW (42-24621) converted from a standard B-29 to the reconnaissance role and assigned to the 73rd Bomb Wing on detachment. Here she shows 11 photo mission markers.
/ *Donald L. Miller Collection*

captured in the fall of Singapore, and their characteristics were available to US radar experts for the development of counter-measures. They developed a jamming system and verified it in 'ferret' flights.

Special equipment, operated by trained officers called 'Ravens', was installed in the B-29s to meet the threat. It could intercept and analyse Japanese radar signals so that appropriate jamming signals could be sent out.

Initially, there was a severe shortage of the 'Raven' operators. On the early raids against the home islands, only a few planes in each major formation carried the operators. Late in the war, they were carried on many more aircraft, often on all the planes in the formation.

Night raids were a different and more difficult problem for solution, because of the bomber stream tactics, with individual aircraft making separated runs over the target. Each airplane would be the focus of a number of Japanese radar sets, operating at a number of different frequencies, and it was too much for one or two 'Ravens' aboard to handle.

One solution was to modify a batch of B-29s for radar countermeasures (RCM) work. These planes carried as many as 18 sets of intercept, analysis and jamming equipment.

'We had a "porcupine" mission one night; they were named for the aircraft, which had many antennas protruding in all directions from the fuselage. It was intended as a super radar-jamming platform, and we interfered with their searchlights, their flak, their radios, everything.

'The "porcupine" had to arrive at the target first and leave last. About an hour of circling and dodging the searchlights and flak was fun, with the crew dropping rope, playing jamming records, and the like, and me in the lightweight B-29 making like a fighter pilot. Sometimes we carried intelligence people along to plot flak positions and to observe the bombing results. They had a grandstand seat for what was then the greatest show on earth!

'Our waist gunners were identical twins, and they carried letters from General Arnold advising that they never were to be separated in combat assignments. They saw their 21st birthday in on a "porcupine" mission over Tokyo.' *Charles B. Hawks*

These early RCM aircraft were very effective, given the state of the radar art of their day, and they were the basis for further development that continued after the war. Between World War 2 and the Korean conflict, special RB-29s based on the 'porcupine' aircraft of the Pacific campaigns flew dangerous and unpublicised missions around the edges of the Soviet Union and other countries. Operating as weather reconnaissance squadrons in Alaska, or as detachments from a weather squadron, these RB-29s monitored Russian radar developments and deployments until a later generation of RCM aircraft and equipment replaced them on station.

Photographic Reconnaissance

The availability of the Superfortress with its very long range changed the reconnaissance situation in the Pacific. When the B-29s first went into action, there was no reconnaissance aircraft that could make the post-strike photos of the target that are so necessary to the analysis of bomb damage. With reasonable haste, some B-29s were field - modified to be used for the task.

Normally, all B-29s carried a single camera on their missions and used it to record the initial bomb drop — the lead plane in the formation held his bomb run for 45 seconds after the drop to get photos — and possibly to catch the early hits of other planes in the formation. Once the target began to burn or crumble, there was little chance to see it until the smoke and dust cleared away, some hours or days later.

The modified B-29s were so successful at their new mission that Air Forces reconnaissance specialists at Wright Field initiated a special modification programme to produce the F-13, a photo-reconnaissance version of the basic B-29.

The F-13A aircraft that saw service from the Marianas held a number of K-18 and K-22 camera installations for both vertical and oblique coverage. Its bomb bays held long-range fuel tanks.

A small number of F-13As made up the 3rd Photo Reconnaissance Squadron, detached for duty on Saipan. One of them, *Tokyo Rose,* flown by Capt Ralph D. Steakley, was the first American aircraft to fly over Tokyo after the Doolittle raids of 1942. Steakley's crew photographed the urban areas around Tokyo on 1 November 1944, from 32,000 feet, and brought back pictures of Japanese targets that had not been photographed before then. The single mission produced more than 7,000 photos of the area, a reconnaissance bonanza.

F-13 crews from then on flew over the home islands of the Japanese Empire on a frequent basis. Flying singly, they would make the run at high altitude to escape fighter interception. The Japanese tried; on a number of occasions they scrambled large numbers of fighters, vectored to intercept the F-13s. But the fighters did not have the performance to get to altitude and stay there while closing and manoeuvring for firing.

It was a very different situation for the RB-29s (redesignated from F-13) in the Korean war. Russian-built MiGs made the skies very inhospitable for all reconnaissance aircraft, and particularly the RB-29s. They were slow, outmoded, and belonged to another war, another age. Yet their crews made the maximum effort. After one disastrous engagement, the RB-29s were ordered not to go to the Yalu River again.

Yet in spite of this setback, the RB-29s continued to fly reconnaissance missions. The 91st Strategic Reconnaissance Squadron moved to Yokota, Japan, in November 1950, five months after the war began, and started flying routine missions against target areas. The first MiG-15 to fall to the guns of any B-29, bomber or recon version, was shot down by one of the gunners from the 91st SRS.

Les's Best, an F-13A operating out of Saipan on photo-reconnaissance missions, has 20 mission markers emblazoned on her nose. The officer in the cockpit is Capt James Garrity, adjutant of the 883rd Bomb Squadron, 500th Bomb Group. / *James J. Garrity Collection*

470119

From where I sit, I can see one dead engine, and that's bad. But I can also see a Superdumbo, and that's good. This Superdumbo — more properly, an SB-29 — was converted from a Wichita-built B-29-80-BW, serial 44-70119. More radio, better radar, more observers, and much more rescue equipment, including a lifeboat slung under the belly, outside what was the bomb-bay area, made the SB-29 a very useful and versatile search and rescue aircraft. Still it was, at best, a stop-gap measure and was replaced by later and better aircraft. This photo is a late wartime — possible post-war — shot, and the B-29 with the dead engine is a late model with Curtiss reversible-pitch props and cooling cuffs at the roots.
/ Boeing 148125

Rescued by a Big Elephant

There are many miles of open water between the home islands of Japan and the Marianas. A pilot of a B-29 in trouble had only one place to set down on route before Iwo Jima was captured: the Pacific Ocean. And it was a wild ocean, with violent storms, rain squalls, whitecaps, and heavy waves.

Ditching a B-29 — landing it on the open sea — was not an enjoyable prospect or experience. Procedures had been worked out in model tests by the National Advisory Committee for Aeronautics at its Langley Memorial Laboratory, and in one full-scale test ditching in calm and sheltered waters.

But even under ideal conditions, the B-29 was an inconsistent performer in a ditching. A few, skilfully or luckily landed, did float; one B-29 ditched in the Bay of Bengal floated for more than 24 hours and drifted ashore. But most of them broke in two and sank fairly rapidly. Getting out, getting life rafts deployed and emergency equipment from its storage places required more time than often was available. And if the crew did get out, the prospects for rescue depended on an earnest, but disorganised, search and rescue effort involving Navy submarines and patrol planes, joined later by Army amphibians of a special rescue squadron.

The best answer lay in the B-29 itself, converted to a search and rescue aircraft, the SB-29A 'Superdumbo'. For some reason, rescue aircraft had been dubbed 'Dumbo', after the Disney flying elephant, and the B-29, being super-everything, became the 'Superdumbo'.

It carried extra crewmen, extra emergency gear and provisions, and a lifeboat slung below its belly. Working as part of a developing search and rescue team, the Superdumbo was able to stay on station for as long as 14 hours, scanning thousands of square miles of ocean in search missions. They retained their armament as well, and were able to fight off enemy aircraft or ships that attempted to interfere with the rescue operations.

Mission time in the 'Superdumbo' counted as combat time, because the search and rescue patrol was dangerous. Often the planes orbited just out of fighter range off the coast of Japan, but if needed, they closed to the coastal waters. They coordinated pickups in the Inland Sea, a land-locked body of water heavily defended and surrounded by Japan.

The capability for search and rescue increased as the war went on, and on the very last B-29 mission from the Marianas, the strike force was supported by an air-sea rescue team that included 14 Navy submarines, 21 Navy seaplanes, nine SB-29A 'Superdumbo' aircraft, and five surface ships. More surface ships were stationed on the waters off the ends of active runways, and Navy patrol planes circled those areas. More rescue aircraft were on standby at the bomber bases. For every three B-29 crewmen on that mission, there was one man on the surface ready to help rescue downed crews.

When the final statistics were in, they showed that an airman had about a fifty per cent chance of surviving if he were forced down at sea. Ditching was to be preferred to crashing or bailing out, obviously, but all of them offered far better chances of survival than being captured did.

Rescued by Mao's Guerrillas

From the Miami (Florida) *Daily News,* 11 November 1944 (Saturday):
'WASHINGTON, 11 Nov. — (AP) — B-29's Saturday hit three vitally important targets — Nanking and Shanghai in Japanese-occupied China and Omura on the Japanese home island of Kyushu.

On the basis of preliminary reports, one of the B-29's is missing, the 20th Air Force said in a communique.'

One man aboard that missing B-29 was not a regular member of its combat crew. As a group communications officer, his assignment normally kept him on the ground. But the circumstances for this trip were different, and the result was an adventure that few B-29 crewmen had. Francis B. Morgan, then a Major in the Signal Corps and 40th Bomb Group Communications Officer, tells his story:
'We were having troubles in mission communications. The radio operators didn't have much to do, because they kept radio silence on the way to the target and through the bomb drop. When they crossed the Yellow River on the way back, they sent a single code word, repeated three times, to indicate they had completed the drop and were on the way home.

'They were supposed to monitor the radio, through, for the entire mission. But twelve hours is a long time to wear a headset. I wanted to find out if we could do anything to ease the situation and so I arranged to fly on a mission as an observer.

'On 11 November 1944, I boarded *Sir Trofrepus* (42-6237) — the name is Superfortress backward and slightly changed — and we took off from A-1 at Hsinching to bomb Omura. Just after liftoff, a scanner noted we were siphoning gas out of one wing and the pilot decided to abort the mission. When he turned to go back, the siphoning stopped, and so he decided to go on to the rendezvous. We usually flew east to a

Rescuers and rescued pose for a picture in the winter sunlight of a Chinese village. Seated, left to right, are Commissar Deng, 4th Div, New Fourth Army; 1st Lt W. G. Warburton, flight engineer; Major F. B. Morgan, observer; General Chang, 4th Div Commander, New Fourth Army. In the rear row, same order: Unknown; Leo Young, New Fourth Army interpreter; S/Sgt Dwight E. Collins, radio operator; 1st Lt Felix O. Sinicrope, navigator; Sgt George R. Schuchardt, tail gunner; Major Wu, New Fourth Army, Commander of Cavalry. / Francis B. Morgan Collection

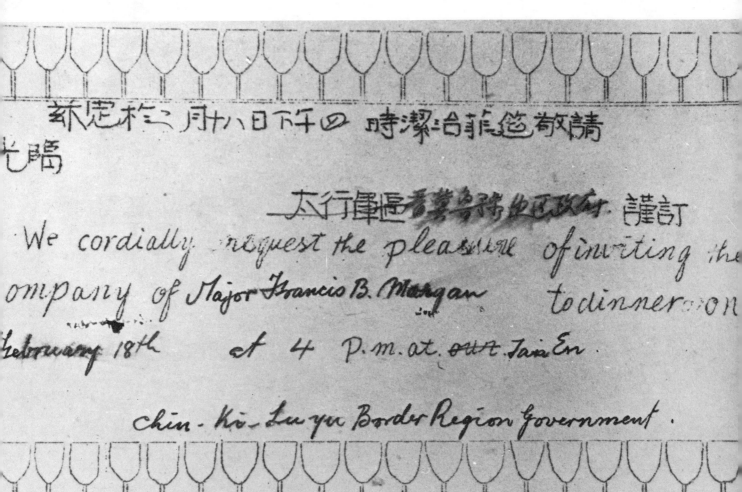

Above: This formal invitation requests the company of Major Morgan at dinner on 18 February at 4pm. The invitation came from the Chin-Ki-Luyu Border Region Government, and was one of many examples of the hospitality shown to the rescued B-29 crewmen by their Chinese hosts and rescuers. / *Francis B. Morgan Collection*

Left: Major F. B. Morgan (front centre) and seven other American fliers pose with General Chang, commanding the 4th Division, New Fourth Army, on their way out of China to American bases in India. / *Francis B. Morgan Collection*

287

rendezvous over a lake about 800 miles away, formed the group and headed to the target. The problem with the siphoning delayed us about ten minutes or so, just long enough to arrive late at the rendezvous. The group had formed and gone on ahead, so we continued in their wake. Over the Yellow Sea, our radio operator received a mission abort signal because Omura was solidly covered with cloud. Our secondary target was Shanghai.

'We were circling alone, over the Yellow Sea, and by the time we got the message decoded, the formation had changed its course and backtracked toward Shanghai and passed us below and about 15 miles away. We swung in behind them, still way behind, and the formation bombed Shanghai. For some reason, our pilot — 1st Lt Richard Vickery — decided to bomb Nanking, and we went in alone over that target.

'The flak briefing had indicated weak to moderate intensity, inaccurate to fairly accurate, with a maximum ceiling of 20,000 feet. We flew at 22,000 feet and due south at bombing speed. We were carrying bombs in the rear bay only, and gas in the front bay. The doors cranked open for the bomb run and just at "Bombs away!" we felt a thump. We thought it was a bomb hung up in the bay, and we saw the bombs hit our target of warehouses on the river.

'But the thump had been a near-miss flak burst. It set the number four engine on fire and also ignited the fuel transfer system in the rear bomb bay. The rear bomb bay was in flames. The flight engineer called the CFC gunner and asked him if he could put out the fire. "Shit, no!" said the CFC gunner. "We gotta get out!"'

'Vickery decided to stay with the airplane as long as possible, because we wanted to get as far from Japanese-occupied Nanking as we could. After all, Tokyo Rose had said that captured B-29 crews would be executed.

'We believe the gunners in the waist jumped then and didn't wait, because Vickery gave the bail-out order about ten or fifteen minutes after we were hit and got no response from the waist. The tail gunner acknowledged the order. Our nose wheel was down so we could bail out the wheel well. The radio operator and I tied down the key so that base could get a DF fix on us, and got ready to destroy our code books and other crypto material. The navigator bailed out first, then the flight engineer, and the tail gunner had gone as soon as he heard the order. The aircraft rolled to the right suddenly and I was flung into the flight engineer's compartment. I was standing on the window, trying to reach the wheel well and that's the last I remember until I came to, free-falling through the air. I could see people on the ground, and I must have fallen 19 or 20,000 feet.

'I pulled the D-ring but nothing happened because my right hand was lacerated and I couldn't pull hard enough. So I pushed on the ring with my left hand, the chute popped, I swung two or three times and hit in a rice paddy, the only one with water in it for miles around. I tried to push the chute under water to hide it, not too successfully. I looked up and saw pieces of the airplane still falling, one wing with an engine attached still several thousand feet in the air. I saw three chutes and walked about a quarter of a mile to meet them. It was the tail gunner, the flight engineer and the radio operator.

'We had been briefed about Chinese guerrillas in the area, and we talked about it after we landed. Warburton (1st Lt William G. Warburton, flight engineer) had a first-aid kit in the leg of his flying suit, and he bandaged my hand. Warburton and (Sgt George R.) Schuchardt, our tail gunner, had bailed out in the usual way. (S/Sgt Dwight E.) Collins, the radio operator, and I were blown out of the B-29 when it exploded. The four of us were standing there deciding what to do when we were fired upon by unknown Chinese in peasant dress. We hit the dirt, heard more shooting, and then five Chinese came running up, gestured to us to run with them, and with them leading and covering us, we headed for the hills. They were from Mao's New Fourth Army (N4A), there to harass the Japanese and help the US forces. We moved five or six miles real fast.

'We had been shot down around nine or ten in the morning; it was dark when we reached a place to rest more than 15 miles away. Later that night we moved another 20 miles or so on donkeys with pack saddles. The next day, we rested in a small village part of the day, and walked to another one where we rested and ate. That night we travelled another 20 miles on donkeys to another tiny village where we met Sinicrope (1st Lt Felix O. Sinicrope, navigator). Up to that point, we had been escorted by two men and two women guerrillas. In the village we were taken over by Lee Kong, from the N4A.

'Next day we were told we were waiting for Comrade Yu, who was coming in from N4A headquarters with horses. They arrived on 14 November, and the following morning we mounted up at 0730 and rode until 1300 with one stop for lunch. We arrived at a small house near a village, and it had begun to rain so hard that we couldn't travel, so we rested there overnight. In the morning we set out again at 0800 and arrived at the N4A headquarters at 1500 to be greeted by officials there. We radioed the American delegation at Yenan, told them our names and serial

Above and right: On 7 February 1945, another B-29 crew led by Captain Varoff (initials unknown) was picked up by an American B-25 at Li-Cheng and flown out to India. Morgan's Chinese hosts gave him these pictures of that event, which would be duplicated later when a B-25 arrived for Morgan's party.
/ Francis B. Morgan Collection

numbers, said we were alive and well, and requested transportation out of the area.

'For the next few days we loafed, bathed, shaved, were visited by doctors, were given clean clothes, read some books — all Upton Sinclair novels — made a checker board, sent another message to Yenan, celebrated Thanksgiving, and generally enjoyed the care and hospitality of our hosts. They got together a special Thanksgiving dinner for our benefit; they were wonderful people.

'Finally on 3 December we got word back from Yenan that our delegation would make arrangements with the Central Government in Chungking and would notify us of the results. On the 12th, a month and a day after we were shot down, we got the message from XX Bomber Command making four points. First, Col Savoie (an earlier escapee) had arrived back at the Command and had given talks about escape and evasion at all the bases. Second, he had been returned to the US. Third, the Central Government (under Chiang Kai-Shek) refused to accept any more rescued fliers from the N4A. Fourth, could we go to Yenan? Apparently, Savoie had been too laudatory in his remarks about the Red Army units that had rescued and returned him, and the Central Government was displeased.

'It had begun to freeze at night, and we were getting snow, and so the N4A officials recommended that we wait until March to try to get to Yenan. We really didn't want to, and they understood, so they worked out a coordinated plan with the Eighth Route Army (8RA) to leave the day after Christmas.

'On 24 December we were invited to General Chen's place for dinner. We had cold meats, year-old eggs and wine; then fish, chicken, duck, and "lion's head" (steamed chopped meat). Then vegetables with more wine, and little meat balls inside pastry. Then sweets — lily seeds in syrup — then mutton soup and then mushroom soup, more wine and finally coffee. The most I've ever eaten in my life! We then adjourned to a hall of sorts which had two Christmas trees, a painted Santa Claus and other decorations. There we had plates of peanut brittle, sesame seed brittle, peanuts, pears and candies. While we tried to nibble, Liu Young, who was our assigned interpreter, introduced dancers, singers and musicians. Bill sang a solo and when General Chen had sung one at my request, he demanded that I sing in return. Later we all sang carols together, got Christmas cards from others and a bottle of wine and a can of honey from Loh Tsei.

'It was our turn the next day, and we entertained the officers from Headquarters and the doctors at Christmas dinner, with their food, of course. The next morning

Commissar Yao, Dr Wei, General Chen, General Chiang, General Lai, and Doctors Chiang and Gung came over for breakfast and brought more maps to add to the ones we had received earlier from them. Then our pictures were taken and we started off on horseback.

'The weather held us up unpleasantly, and hospitality delayed us pleasantly. We were handed along from unit to unit, greeted, wined and dined all along the route, picked up a fifth rescued airman, a P-51 pilot named Walter Krywy, heard and saw B-29s overhead on a number of missions, picked up three more airmen: Lt Al Fisher, Sgt Pat Patterson, and Sgt Pete Kouzes, pilot, flight engineer and radio operator of a C-46 that got hit. We inspected troops, described our basic training methods, our manual of arms and bayonet drill, received presents of Japanese swords, aluminium chopsticks, souvenirs, new tailor-made uniforms, winter clothing, and padded shoes.

'The Chinese were very considerate, very thoughtful. We were fed when others either did without or got less, and this was in some areas where there was so little food that the people ate leaves off the trees.

'On 15 February we sent a message to Yenan asking that a plane be sent out to a rendezvous point to pick us up. On the 25th we got an affirmative answer and headed for the strip to wait. On 3 March, at 1445, the prettiest B-25 I ever saw came in with a pair of fighters for an escort, and took us off. We got back to A-1 at 1745, were debriefed, fed and placed under a heavy armed guard. The reason was that the Central Government's secret police, the Dai Li, were expected to make an attempt to kill us because of the unkind things they thought we were going to say about the Central Government.

'We left the next morning from Kharagpur, and I stopped off on the way to leave some intelligence information the N4A and 8RA people had given me. They thought it would be helpful in what was expected to be an invasion landing on the Chinese coast. That evening I was back in India, and within a few days I was on my way home to the US.

'It was quite a trip. We covered 850 miles in 30 travel days, much of it through Japanese-controlled areas. I'm glad I knew how to handle and ride horses. We rode typical cavalry style; we'd trot one-third of the time, walk the horses one-third of the time, and then dismount and lead the horses for the remaining third of the time.

'And I can't say enough about the Chinese who rescued us and cared for us. They all went out of their way to do things for us, and to make us feel comfortable in what they knew were unfamiliar and strained conditions for us.'

One B-29, One Bomb

What the Japanese radio announcer was saying was perfectly credible, given the usual nature of information about B-29 raids released to his intended audience. But it was perfectly incredible, given what had happened.

A small number of B-29s, he said, penetrated into Hiroshima city just after eight o'clock yesterday morning and dropped a small number of bombs. As a result, he added, a considerable number of homes were reduced to ashes and fires broke out in various parts of the city.

It was 7 August 1945, and the morning before, a single B-29 had dropped the first complete model of an atomic bomb, and it had worked. In a millisecond, Hiroshima was nearly obliterated.

In one mission, one B-29 and one bomb had changed the course of warfare forever.

The B-29 had been singled out for the job more than two years earlier. In June 1943, the only feasible atomic bomb seemed to be one based on a plutonium gun design. It was a long device, literally a gun, in which two subcritical masses of plutonium were driven together in a long barrel by explosive charges, and thereupon immediately went critical and exploded. The gun was something like 17 feet long, and it could be carried only in a specially modified B-29 whose two bomb bays would have to be joined into a single long bay for the weapon.

Underwing installations had been considered and rejected. The outstanding British heavy bomber, the Avro Lancaster, had been studied as a possible carrier, but also was rejected on the grounds that it could not be fitted into the existing logistics and maintenance pipelines.

So a test B-29, which was very hard to get even for such a high-priority project as the atomic bomb development, was modified and used for drop tests of the long gun weapon mockup, by then called the 'Thin Man', and for the implosion plutonium bomb of a different design and shape, by then called 'Fat Man'. Test drops of both weapon mockups had been made at the Muroc Dry Lake Bombing Range beginning in March 1944, and the last of a series damaged the carrier B-29, laying it up for repairs and delaying the tests. By June, when the bomber was ready to

fly again, the gun design had been shortened considerably, the bomb was renamed 'Little Boy', and it could fit in one bomb bay of a standard B-29.

By September 1944, the external bomb shapes — which had been changing as the designs were revised — were frozen, as were the aircraft requirements. By the next month, the first of a special lot of 15 B-29s was beginning to be used in drop tests of mock-up bomb shapes over the Wendover Bombing Range, 125 miles west out of Salt Lake City, Utah.

These were B-29s that had been modified for the atomic bomb delivery, not by combining the bomb bays as first planned, but by installing stronger bomb racks — each atomic weapon was going to weigh about five tons — and mounting the new fuel-injection R-3350 engines, with reversible-pitch electrically controlled Curtiss propellers with root cuffs to aid the cooling of the ever-hot Wright engines. Only the tail guns had been installed; all other armament was removed. The bomb bay doors used pneumatic actuators, a feature that was introduced late in the production of the B-29s, to snap the doors open and closed in a fraction of a second.

The operating organisation was a unique one. It was designated the 509th Composite Group, and it included most of everything it would need to be a completely self-contained outfit. It would be equipped with 15 B-29 bombers, assigned to the 393rd Bombardment Squadron, and five Douglas C-54 transports, assigned to the 320th Troop Carrier Squadron, and nicknamed the 'Green Hornet Line'. It would also include the 390th Air Service Group, the 1395th Military Police Company (Aviation), and the 1st Ordnance Squadron, Special (Aviation). The total authorised strength of the 509th was 225 officers and 1,542 enlisted men.

The unit was constituted on 9 December 1944, and activated on 17 December 1944, the 41st anniversary of the Wright brothers' first flight. The 509th was first based at Wendover Field, Utah, where they practised strange flight profiles with single bombs carried to and dropped from great heights.

Parallel to the training of the 509th, several series of test drops were made for

NAGASAKI STRIKE PHOTO

development of the atomic weapons. The fuses were to be set for air bursts, and there was some problem getting a reliable proximity fuse that would do the trick. Then somebody noted that the Radio Corporation of America was developing a tail-warning radar, the AN/APS-13, whose characteristic ability was detecting an object at a fixed, preset distance, and then triggering a relay to actuate a warning aboard the aircraft. The APS-13 was adapted for the atomic bomb fusing, and tested in a number of drops made over the Salton Sea, a range facility that offered an overwater approach and a drop to an altitude just about at sea level, something not available at either the Wendover or the Muroc bombing ranges.

California Institute of Technology's Camel Project was charged with the responsibility of solving the problems of the bomb assembly mechanism, and of the combat delivery of the weapons. They produced a number of 'pumpkin' bombs, for tests, built within the casings of the 'Fat Man' implosion bomb, but without the nuclear materials installed. These were dropped at the Navy's Inyokern rocket range, and later by the 509th at Wendover and over Japan, where the 'pumpkin' cores contained high explosives.

By the spring of 1945, the first batch of B-29s assigned to the 509th had revealed a lot of weaknesses, so a second batch of new airplanes was acquired. And about the same time, the 509th started its move to Tinian. The official date of departure from Wendover was 26 April 1945; the advance air echelon had arrived at Tinian's North Field on 18 May. The ground echelons began to arrive on 29 May, and the combat crews flew their aircraft in beginning 11 June.

By 30 June, the 509th was ready to start its combat flight training. They began with a half-dozen practice missions, which typically included a navigational flight to Iwo Jima

294

Above: Hiroshima, minutes after. / James J. Garrity Collection

Top left: Enola Gay, a B-29-45-MO built by Martin at Omaha (serial 44-86292), lifts off the runway at Wendover Field on a training flight. / Boeing 109360

Centre left: Bearing the markings of the 6th Bomb Group, 313rd Bomb Wing, for deception, Enola Gay comes in for a landing at Tinian after dropping the first atomic bomb. / Boeing 151200

Bottom left: At rest, the Enola Gay shows her cleaned-up and developed airframe. No turrets break the upper or lower fuselage lines; only the APQ-13 radome protrudes from the belly. Curtiss reversible-pitch props, with blade root cuffs for extra cooling of the engine, were installed on the planes of the 509th Composite Group. The arrow in the circle is the official Group designator. The aircraft number — 82 — was on the nose and fuselage behind the US insignia at the latter site. / Boeing 2B1855

with a bomb drop on Rota, the bypassed and beaten island, on the way back; perhaps another pair of short bombing missions to Rota, and a long run to Truk for a drop on that punchboard island. These missions were flown by two to nine aircraft.

It still wasn't certain that an atomic bomb would work. The 509th had gotten this far on the strength of calculations and some very limited experiments. But on 16 July, the Trinity test explosion lit up the pre-dawn sky around Alamogordo, New Mexico, and the scientists knew that their calculations had been verified.

On 20 July, the 509th began flying combat missions against carefully selected targets in Japan, cities that had been hit earlier, or that were near ones that had been bombed, and which additionally were in the general area of those cities on the short list for later atomic attacks. There were 12 of these strikes, flown on 20, 24, 26 and 29 July, involving formations of two to six aircraft, each dropping a single 'pumpkin' bomb. It was hoped that the Japanese wouldn't be disturbed by the strange sight of small formations, after seeing some of them over the islands, dropping single 'blockbuster' bombs.

The first atomic bomb, 'Little Boy', was ready on 31 July, seventeen days after the first — and only — test of a nuclear weapon.

The War Department, Office of the Chief of Staff, sent a special secret order on the afternoon of 24 July, direct to Gen Carl Spaatz, the Commanding General of the United States Strategic Air Forces. It told him that the 509th Composite Group would deliver its first special bomb, as soon as weather would permit visual bombing after about 3 August, on any one of four targets: Hiroshima, Kokura, Niigata, or Nagasaki.

On 5 August the forecast predicted good visual bombing weather over the target areas for the following day. Gen LeMay confirmed 6 August mission date, and the typewriters began to pound out the words of the orders for Special Bombing Mission No 13. The primary target was to be the urban industrial area of Hiroshima. The secondary was the arsenal and city at Kokura. The third alternate was the urban area of Nagasaki. Only visual bombing would be permitted; the target had to be observed personally by both pilot and bombardier, and they had to agree that what they saw was indeed the target city. The mission was to bomb from an altitude of 28,000 to 30,000 feet at a speed of 200mph.

And so at midnight the crews went to their briefing. At 0137, Tinian time, three B-29s roared down three parallel runways on North Field, headed for Japan and three separate weather reconnaissance flights over the three target cities. Major Claude R. Eatherly's Straight Flush headed for Hiroshima. Major Ralph R. Taylor, in Full House set course for Nagasaki, and Major John A. Wilson steered Jabbit III toward Kokura.

At 0245, Lt Col Paul W. Tibbets released the brakes of the Enola Gay; as she began her take-off run, two more B-29s carrying instruments and observers rolled into position for take-off. Major Charles W. Sweeney was at the controls of The Great Artiste, and Capt George W. Marquardt was commander of an unnamed B-29 marked only with the fuselage number 91. One after the other, the three aircraft lifted off the runways at Tinian, hauled up their landing gear, and headed into history.

At 0605 they crossed over Iwo Jima, and turned toward the target area. 'Little Boy' was armed, by hand, by Navy Commander Frederick L. Ashworth, working in the cramped and crowded bomb bay. Tibbets started the climb to bombing altitude at 0741, levelled off at 32,700 feet at 0838. The target was spotted at 0909, they made the bomb run and dropped 'Little Boy' at 0915:17 Tinian time.

Forty-three seconds later, Hiroshima ceased to exist as a city.

The second strike, planned against Kokura, was plagued by problems, large and small. Maj Sweeney traded planes with Capt Frederick C. Bock; Sweeney flew Bock's Car and Bock flew The Great Artiste. They hit bad weather, lost contact with one of the two observing aircraft, made three bomb runs without seeing the target. They decided to bomb their secondary target, found it covered by cloud, and were running dangerously low on fuel. A hole opened in the clouds, the bomb was dropped visually, and it destroyed Nagasaki two minutes before noon on 9 August 1945.

295

The Last Days

What can be added to the simple eloquence of the chalked message? The war is, indeed, over, and the long, arduous and hellish journey that began for the world in September 1939 has ended in August 1945. The Superfortresses had been in action for 14 months out of the 72 that the conflict raged. Now the dignitaries were to sign the armistice in Tokyo Bay, and there would be time for a few sightseeing flights, a show of force over the Bay, and then the island hopping eastward over the Pacific, back to the Golden Gate and San Antonio and Oconomowoc and Burlington and the Bronx. The war is over. / *George S. Gray Collection*

While the Japanese agonised over whether or not to surrender and under what terms, the XXI Bomber Command stayed with its mission of convincing them beyond all doubt. The day after the Hiroshima atomic attack, 124 B-29s struck the naval arsenal at Toyokawa, and 29 Superforts mined the waters of the Inland Sea. On 8 August, Yawata was fired by 221 B-29s; about 60 others bombed an aircraft plant and an arsenal in Tokyo, and 91 dropped incendiaries on Fukuyama. Nagasaki was hit by the second atomic bomb on 9 August; on the same day, 95 B-29s hammered Amagasaki's Nippon Oil refinery. On 10 August, the Superforts went back to Tokyo and pounded the arsenal with a force of 70 aircraft. That night 31 B-29s mined the Shimonoseki Strait and shipping lanes in the Inland Sea.

The last raids of the war were heavy. With a fighter escort, a force of 302 Superfortresses bombed a naval arsenal at Hikari and an army arsenal at Osaka; another unit of B-29s hammered the railroad yards at Marifu, with 108 bombing the primary target. During the night, more than 160 bombers showered Kumagaya and Isezaki with incendiaries.

The longest nonstop combat strike of the war occurred that night also, when 132 Superforts took off on a planned 3,650-mile round trip to bomb a refinery of the Nippon Oil Company. Still another group of B-29s — 39 of them — mined the Shimonoseki Strait and the Inland Sea.

'... as we taxied out, the *"Fleet Admiral Nimitz"* showed a 200-rpm magneto drop on one of two mags on one engine. When we reached the runway, a jeep drove up in front and an officer signalled "Cut engines". He climbed in and said, "Admiral Nimitz says the war is over." He had departed and I had just finished chiding my crew chief for the only time the *Nimitz* was short of perfection when another jeep arrived with, "Get going! LeMay hasn't received word that the war is over." We cranked up and took the runway knowing that if we didn't get a good power

Above: But the war was not over for prisoners in Japanese hands. Often their captors refused to believe the facts of surrender, refused to open the gates, refused to increase rations or add medical attention. The last great missions of the B-29s were errands of mercy, dropping food and medical supplies and clothing to prisoners of war in camps in China and Korea and Japan. Hundreds of B-29s lined up on the fields, nose to tail, to load for these flights. On Isley Field alone, this picture shows more than 117 B-29s lined up on one of Isley's two runways, waiting to be despatched to a drop at a prison camp site. / *Prescott Martin Collection*

Left: B-29s of the 58th Bomb Wing lined up to load for prisoner-of-war drops. Each airplane carried large letters under each wing, reading P. W. SUPPLIES. / *Ron E. Witt Collection*

check and runway speed and had to chop throttles and abort, most probably all aircraft would follow us back to the ramp, thinking that the mission was scrubbed. Thankfully, the *Nimitz* performed and we lifted off greatly relieved.

'President Truman announced the surrender during our return to Guam after dropping a full bomb load on the oil refinery at Akita on northwest Honshu the night of 14-15 August. This was the longest combat strike, 3,740 miles. We met over 300 B-29s and passed through them as they departed Tokyo leaving an inferno. All aircraft had landing lights on and (were) flying at assigned altitudes, but even so it was a bit unnerving.' *Boyd Hubbard, Jr*

The war was over, but the B-29s still had some more missions to fly. This time they dropped supplies — food, medicine, clothing — to prisoners of war in camps in China, Japan and Korea. First of the drops was made on a camp near Peking, China, on 27 August, and about 900 sorties followed during a one-month period. Long lines of B-29s, their wings marked on the undersides with large letters reading, P. W. SUPPLIES, parked on the runways for loading of palletised crates of supplies.

One of the B-29s, Z-28 from the 882nd Bomb Sqdn, 500th Bomb Grp, was on a mission to a POW camp near Konan, Korea, but the crew couldn't locate the camp after arriving in the general area. They were circling and looking when Russian Yak fighters came up and flew formation with them.

The Russian pilots appeared to be waving greetings, so the American crew waved back and continued orbiting. One of the Russian pilots pointed toward the ground and the co-pilot, Lt Robert S. Rainey, thought they had located the camp and were pointing it out. But the Russians had led the B-29 to a very small airfield, and the crew concluded that the Russians wanted them to land there. The field was too small, and there were no orders covering what to do, so they turned away and continued their search for the camp.

'At this point,' said Lt Rainey in his post-mission statement, 'The Russian fighter pilots were becoming very angry and were making all sorts of gestures with their hands, also they were raising and lowering their landing gear.'

The pilot turned the B-29 and headed for the ocean and home, and one of the fighters fired a burst ahead of the B-29's nose. The airplane commander kept his course, figuring that the Russians would leave them when they realised the B-29 was heading home. Instead, the fighter off the left wing angled in, and fired a burst into the number one

engine, starting a fire in the accessory section and the oil tank.

The airplane commander turned back toward land and ordered the crew to bail out. Six of them went, and then one of the gunners reported that the fire seemed to be dying out. The crew were ordered to stop bailing out, and to take their positions for a crash landing. The pilots set the B-29 down on the small airfield the Russians had led them to earlier.

After three days of minor difficulties and some tense moments, the crew and the airplane were released by the Russians. They later supplied a statement, written by the senior officers at Konan, dated 6 September 1945. The translation of that report identified the two as Commander of the 14th Fighter-Bomber Regiment Major Savchenko, and Assistant Commander of Operations Department of the 88th Infantry Corps Senior Lieutenant Churvin. They wrote:
'On 28 August 1945 at about 1430 Korean time, there appeared in the vicinity of the Red Army Airfield at Konan an unrecognised B-29 without signalling to the Russian aerodrome. Commanding Officer and Staff of the Red Army did not know in advance about the appearance of this B-29 in the Konan area and the fighting with the Japanese had not ceased. Due to the fact that during the war with Germany there had been American-type planes flown by German pilots that still had American markings on them, the Russians were not sure who was flying the B-29. In accordance with the above, the Commander of the 14th Fighter-Bomber Regiment ordered all measures be taken to land the B-29. Four fighters were sent aloft to land the B-29. The fighters signalled to the B-29 and pointed out the airport. The B-29 did not land, so the Russian fighters opened fire and as a result the B-29 returned to the airport at Konan and landed. All 13 men of the B-29 crew are now being quartered with a company of English soldiers at Konan. All supplies in the B-29 were received by this company of English soldiers.'

There were 154 camps known to Air Force intelligence, confining more than 63,000 prisoners. The supply effort was a necessary one, not just a gesture; the prisoners had been neglected by their captors, and only after the Japanese finally came to personal terms with the surrender did the prisoners begin to get the minimum food ration and the medical attention they so desperately needed.

And that was it. The war was over, the long process of going home began, and the B-29s began to leave the islands, one by one, heading for home, the scrapyard, the desert storage areas, or later service with a new

Right: An hour or so before the estimated time of arrival of the B-29s with supplies, these leaflets were dropped over the Japanese prison camps by other B-29s. They detailed the supplies to come, with items and quantities specified for packages for 50 and 500 men. And the caution: Do not overeat or overmedicate.
/ Elmer Huhta Collection

レンゴウグンホリョヘ
ALLIED PRISONERS

The JAPANESE Government has surrendered. You will be evacuated by ALLIED NATIONS forces as soon as possible.

Until that time your present supplies will be augmented by air-drop of U.S. food, clothing and medicines. The first drop of these items will arrive within one (1) or two (2) hours.

Clothing will be dropped in standard packs for units of 50 or 500 men. Bundle markings, contents and allowances per man are as follows:

BUNDLE MARKINGS				BUNDLE MARKINGS			
50 MAN PACK	500 MAN PACK	CONTENTS	ALLOWANCES PER MAN	50 MAN PACK	500 MAN PACK	CONTENTS	ALLOWANCES PER MAN
A	3	Drawers	2	B	10	Laces, shoe	1
A	1-2	Undershirt	2	A	11	Kit, sewing	1
B	22	Socks (pr)	2	C	31	Soap, toilet	1
A	4-6	Shirt	1	C	4-6	Razor	1
A	7-9	Trousers	1	C	4-6	Blades, razor	10
C	23-30	Jacket, field	1	C	10	Brush, tooth	1
A	10	Belt, web, waist	1	C	31	Paste, tooth	1
A	11	Capt, H.B.T.	1	C	10	Comb	1
B	12-21	Shoes (pr)	1	B	32	Shaving cream	1
A	1-2	Handkerchiefs	3	C	12-21	Powder(insecticide)	1
C	32-34	Towel	1				

There will be instructions with the food and medicine for their use and distribution.

C A U T I O N

DO NOT OVEREAT OR OVERMEDICATE   FOLLOW DIRECTIONS

INSTRUCTIONS FOR FEEDING 100 MEN

To feed 100 men for the first three (3) days, the following blocks (individual bundles dropped) will be assembled:

3 Blocks No. 1
(Each Contains)

2 Cases, Soup, Can
1 Cases Fruit Juice
1 Case Accessory Pack

1 Block No. 5
(Each Contains)

1 Case Soup, Dehd
1 Case Veg Puree
1 Case Bouillon
1 Case Hosp Supplies
1 Case Vitamin Tablets

1 Block No. 3
(Each Contains)

1 Case Candy
1 Case Gum
1 Case Cigarettes
1 Case Matches

3 Blocks No. 2
(Each Contains)

3 Cases "C" Rations
1 Case Hosp Supplies
2 Cases Fruit

1 Block No. 7
(Each Contains)

1 Case Nescafe
1 Sack Sugar
1 Case Milk
1 Case Cocoa

1 Block No. 10
(Each Contains)

3 Cases Fruit
2 Cases Juice

This reconnaissance photo is typical of many that were taken to provide some target identification for the B-29s dropping supplies. These photos were part of the briefing folder and went with the crews aboard the planes. Marked by intelligence officers to show the camp locations, these photos became the target identifiers for drops. / *Del Shaffer Collection*

force structure then being built: Strategic Air Command.

When the war ended, 40 B-29 groups were in being and 21 of them were on station in the Pacific. Japan had surrendered, unconditionally, with about two million men still under arms, countless citizens prepared to defend suicidally every inch of their homeland, and several thousands of kamikaze airplanes held for a final strike.

Two atomic bombs, coming on top of months of fire raids and precision bombing attacks by endless streams of B-29s, had done the job. Whether or not Japan would have surrendered if the two nuclear weapons had not been dropped is an argument that will continue as long as military strategy and history are subjects for discussions and dissertations.

The fact is there. The war was over, and its end was hastened, certainly, and brought about, probably, by the bombing offensive conducted by the B-29s of the 20th Air Force.

That offensive must have seemed a long way off to the men of the 58th Bomb Wing who pioneered the introduction of a new airplane, new engines and a new armament system in combat. The experience was eloquently summarised in the 444th unit history by an anonymous writer:

'. . . only those who readied this plane and flew it can fully know the harsh pains of its birth and dangerously rapid development . . . of explosive decompression at altitude, of engine temperatures soaring above 300C, of props that refused to feather, of remote controlled turrets "cooking off" and spraying wildly, of multiplied stresses from unprecedented loads . . .

'To the men who flew these early planes they were, at the least, serious (troubles) and often fatally dangerous. They meant engine fires, perhaps consuming a wing before men could bail out, gunners "cannon-balled" from the cabin when their blister blew, planes shuddering and mushing off the runway and hugging the ground until they disappeared in the distance in their pitiful attempt to gain speed and engine cooling, ships in formation riddling each other or themselves with .50-calibre bullets . . .

'. . . at that time, the solution of these difficulties was of life and death concern to the pilots and crews who flew these planes with soaring cylinder temperatures, runaway props on takeoff, flaming and disintegrating engines with props that refused to feather in flight. During the first few months the record time before change was 100 hours, average takeoff cylinder temperatures were 290C, and four forced landings because of fire were accomplished on one day. At the end of four months in India, the ironic boast was that now it was a proven fact that a B-29 could be raised from the ground twice in one week without the aid of jacks.' *444th Bomb Group unit history*

Operating from its bases in India and advance bases in China, and in the face of formidable logistics and operational problems, the 58th Bomb Wing struck targets in Manchuria, Korea and the home islands of Japan itself. They dropped about 800 tons of bombs on Japan, a small amount in the light of the weight of the later offensive, but a substantial accomplishment considering the circumstances. As it turned out, these bombings did not seriously disrupt the Japanese war economy. But they served notice that more was to come, and they made some Japanese realise that the war was going to be lost.

The bulk of the bomber offensive started late in November 1944, with Mission San Antonio I against the Musashino plant of the Nakajima Aircraft Co. The first phase of the offensive continued through early March, and was built around the traditional concept of daylight, high-altitude precision bombing, using visual approaches, and targeted against the Japanese aircraft industry, particularly engine plants. The results were moderately successful. As one direct effect, the Japanese began a programme of plant dispersal, but never carried it out as well as they might have done., From November 1944 on, Japanese fighter production began to decrease, and the production curves skidded downward at an ever-increasing rate.

The low-level fire raids began on 9 March 1945, and in ten days destroyed four of Japan's largest cities. The B-29s flew 1,595 sorties, dropped 9,373 tons of bombs, most of them incendiaries, and destroyed — the word applies well — 31 square miles of industrial and urban area.

They shifted to a tactical support role during April and early May, 1945, to support the invasion and the subsequent fighting to capture Okinawa. Their job was to bomb tactical military objectives, often under control of Army ground forces, and including the fighter fields on Kyushu Island that were sending defending aircraft and devastating kamikaze strikes against the invasion forces.

In May the Superfortresses went back to their task of pounding Japan, flying both low-altitude fire raids and higher-altitude precision attacks, depending on the chosen targets. During May and June, they finished off the six largest cities and began going through the list of secondary targets. By 9 August, 66 urban centres had been struck, and 178 square miles of industry and urban area lay desolated.

Parallel to the last few months of these strikes against larger areas were campaigns of attacks on point targets such as oil refineries, and mine-laying in the waters and shipping lanes that served Japan. More than 12,000 mines were dropped in the Inland Sea and in well-travelled shipping lanes, and they sank almost ten per cent of all the merchant shipping tonnage lost to Japan. It was a truly remarkable accomplishment done in a very short time.

When the totals were added, the B-29s had dropped more than ninety-one per cent of all the bombs delivered against targets in the home islands of Japan: 147,000 tons out of the total of 160,800 tons dropped by all Army and Navy aircraft.

The damage done to Japan was about the same as that done to Germany, in terms of its effect on the ability of the country to continue the war. But because of the differences between Japanese and German city and factory construction, layout, protection and defences, it required only about one-ninth of the bomb tonnage dropped on Germany to do equivalent damage.

The B-29 losses were light, militarily speaking, and amounted to 1.38 per cent of all combat sorties. The B-29s flew a total of about 33,000 sorties, so that meant that more than 450 aircraft were lost, with all or part of their crews.

Japanese fighter attacks, although pressed home with determination, were light compared to the strength of the German fighter assaults by day and night against USAAF and RAF bombers over Europe. Only 11,026 fighter attacks were reported over Japan, or one for about every three sorties. Averages, of course, don't convey the real picture. Japanese fighter defences were heavy against the early raids and tapered off later in the war, so that some raids went in and out of the target area completely unopposed except by some sporadic flak.

B-29 gunners claimed 714 Japanese fighters destroyed, 456 probably destroyed, and 770 damaged. These numbers are considerably lower than the claims made in the European theatre and reflect the lighter Japanese defences.

At the end, the Japanese said it beat them. Prince Konoye, of the Japanese Royal Family, said, 'Fundamentally, the thing that brought about the determination to make peace was the prolonged bombing by the B-29s.' And Premier Suzuki said, 'I myself, on the basis of the B-29 raids, felt that the cause was hopeless.'

It was.

Sunday Surprise

Another Sunday, another surprise attack. At dawn, 25 June 1950, the North Koreans struck across the 38th parallel. Ground forces resisted the brunt of the attack, held briefly and broke before the North Korean momentum. The call went out for immediate help, and among those that answered were the 22 Boeing B-29 Superfortresses in the Far East. They had been sitting in revetments at Anderson AFB, Guam, leftovers from World War 2, nearing the end of their service lives. Now reclassified as 'medium' bombers, they made up the strategic force within 'Far East Air Forces (FEAF).

'Korea was the swan song for the B-29s, and they were really too old for that war. Our worst enemy was the engine, and after that those old World War 2 airplanes. We lost more in training than we did in combat.

'We lost them in collisions. The problem was that a lot of our aircraft commanders were wartime co-pilots who had been recalled. All of a sudden, this kid finds himself flying a four-engined aircraft, and he has trouble hacking it. Weather flying was rough on them; they hadn't had much experience, and they'd lose control in turbulence.

'The problems of maintenance were also tougher. The airplanes were older, the flight crews didn't baby them, and the ground crews had to work on them in open docks, out in the heat and rain and all the extremes of Okinawan weather. The ground crews lived in tents, and so they didn't have much opportunity for relief from the weather during their off-duty hours.

'The maintenance crews were great, though, and they did one hell of a great job.'
Robert F. Goldsworthy, deputy commander, 307th Bomb Wing, 2nd Air Force

There was one other B-29 unit in the theatre, the 31st Photo Reconnaissance Squadron (Very Long Range), equipped with six RB-29s and based at Kadena Air Base, Okinawa. There were 24 weather reconnaissance WB-29s in FEAF, and four 'Super-dumbo' search and rescue SB-29 aircraft.

The 19th Bomb Group moved from Guam to Kadena, ordered by 20th Air Force Headquarters to strike against targets of opportunity such as assemblies of tanks, artillery, or troops. On 28 June, four B-29s flew their first combat mission of the Korean war. Two searched the parallel rail and road lines between Seoul and Kapyong, and the other two scanned the line between Seoul and Uijongbu. They dropped bombs on anything that seemed to be a worthwhile target.

The next day nine Superforts bombed Kimpo airfield, dropping 260lb fragmentation bombs from altitudes as low as

'Somewhere over Korea' says the official caption in the usual vague identification of wartime photos. She's an RB-29A-45-BN, serial 44-61727, operating with what was then the 31st Strategic Reconnaissance Squadron, later redesignated the 91st SRS, of the 15th Air Force. She carries at least 45 photo mission markers on her nose. / USAF 82168 A.C.

3,000 feet. They were jumped by three Red fighters; the B-29 gunners shot down one, damaged another. Two other B-29s bombed the main railroad station at Seoul.

Fifteen bombers hit enemy troops and landing craft on the north bank of the Han River on 30 June. Ten B-29s struck Yonpo airfield on 2 July, after reports of a heavy concentration of aircraft at that enemy-held base had been received. Loaded with fragmentation bombs, the Superforts roared over Yonpo, counted 16 airplanes, dropped, and destroyed none at all.

The next day, Gen Hoyt S. Vandenberg, USAF Chief of Staff, moved the 22nd and 92nd Bomb Wings (Medium) from Strategic Air Command to temporary duty with FEAF. And on 8 July, FEAF organised its own Bomber Command (Provisional), headed by Maj Gen Emmett O'Donnell, Jr, a long-time bomber commander and leader of the 73rd Bomb Wing in the Marianas during World War 2. 'Rosey' got his orders: work in the area north of the Han River, and destroy North Korean industry. It was the standard strategic bombing mission and one that O'Donnell and the B-29s were best able to handle.

But the ground forces were in desperate straits, and the B-29s were first thrown into the battle to support them. They dropped on targets of opportunity around the battlefield area and behind the lines, doing what fighter-bombers would probably do better. They stood it for about nine days, and on 18 July, Lt Gen George C. Stratemeyer, who was Gen Douglas MacArthur's top air commander in the Far East, told MacArthur that it was not the way to run a strategic bombing effort, and no way to use the B-29s.

MacArthur agreed, and issued orders for the B-29s to concentrate in the area between the bombline and the 38th parallel, with the idea of isolating the battlefield. The target list they were given was terrible; some of the targets

Aircraft 9894, carrying the Circle H and the insignia of the 98th Bomb Wing, and the insignia of the 343rd Bomb Squadron, stands in its parking area at Yokota Air Base, Japan. / *William F. Dawson*

didn't exist, and others were misnamed or mislocated. It was World War 2 and Japan all over again, complained one bomber commander.

MacArthur had, in effect, only changed the task of the B-29s from one of close support to one of interdiction. FEAF wanted to get on with the campaign of strategic bombing. The exigencies of the Korean War demanded that both be done simultaneously.

So Gen Vandenberg offered to send two more B-29s groups to the war, if they would be used solely against strategic targets. MacArthur agreed, and the 98th and 307th Bomb Groups were ordered to make the move.

There was only a handful of strategic targets in North Korea. Five major industrial areas were identified, with a few others of secondary importance. One was ruled off-limits for political reasons; it was too near the Manchurian border, and dropping on the wrong side might kick off a war.

By 27 September the strategic campaign was completed. Any target worth hitting had been pounded into ruins. It had taken just over a month, and 'Rosey' O'Donnell could report to FEAF that Bomber Command had run out of targets to destroy.

The Superfortresses had flown 3,159 sorties against the strategic Korean targets. The 18 available specific targets had been hammered into ruins. One Superfortress had been lost during the campaign.

'Our first mission to Korea was disastrous. At the assembly point over the Sea of Japan, our flight commander got a call that one of the aircraft had lost an engine. The commander told him to leave the formation and head back, and to jettison his bombs after leaving the formation.

'The pilot acknowledged, and said he was dropping them in train. In a few seconds he reported that some of the bombs had hung up, and they were going to try again for release using the intervalometer (for automatic timed release in succession). They were still hung up after he tried that, and so he called again to say that he would hit the salvo switch. (Salvo means to drop the entire load of bombs simultaneously.)

'As the bombs left the bay, two of them hit together, detonated, and blew up the airplane.

'We were still using bombs left over from World War 2, and the RDX explosive was unstable after five years. Nobody bothered to tell us, and we lost a fine crew that way.'
Vern Piotter, navigator, 92nd Bomb Wing

But the interdiction campaign never stopped. One of its major features was bridge-busting, certainly a tough mission to fly successfully. Bridges are long, narrow targets and are hard to hit. The North Koreans repaired them within hours after they were hit, or built another one upstream or down, or ran a ferry across instead.

Many of the Korean bridges had been built to modern standards from steel and concrete by the Japanese during their long occupation of the country. They had built them with solid footings and abutments that resisted near misses.

The B-29s evolved a simple tactical approach. They formed a bomber stream at about 10,000 feet, and flew toward the bridge at a 40-degree angle to its span. Each B-29 triggered off four bombs on a single run. There was little or no opposition; they had all the time in the world to get stabilised on the bomb run. No fighters hassled them during this early stage of the war.

Later statistics showed that it took more than 13 runs to destroy each bridge, using 500lb bombs that were the accepted standard for the job. Heavier bombs should have been used, but the bombing problem was complicated by the fact that the crews had to

A trio of B-29s from the 98th Bomb Wing, photographed from the gunner's blister of a fourth, fly formation into North Korea on a combat strike. / *William F. Dawson*

load their own bombs and never knew quite what missions they would be flying in time to plan a load. Further, not all the B-29s had bomb racks for the heavier bombs. Only the 19th Bomb Group was equipped to load and carry the 2,000lb bombs that would have made an impression on any bridge.

Even so, by the end of the first interdiction campaign, O'Donnell reported that the B-29s had destroyed 37 of the 44 bridges they had been assigned as targets only a month earlier. The remaining seven were useless for carrying heavy traffic.

'Itazuki, Japan, has the best hot baths in the world. There's an auxiliary strip there and if you got into trouble in Korea, you would declare an emergency and go into Itazuki.

'One time I was coming back from a bridge-busting mission at Sinan-ju and I had an engine fire. Well, I thought of that old saying, "In 30 seconds, either it goes out or I do!" But we were over North Korea, and I had been a prisoner of war once in Japan and I didn't really want to do that again. So I stayed with it, encouraged because I could see the battle lines ahead.

'That fire in number four kept burning, and I couldn't feather the prop and I'd already pulled the fire extinguisher to no effect, and we were still over enemy territory. So I sweated that one out and — believe me — just as we crossed the battle line into our own area the fire went out, all by itself. The prop was windmilling, and so I called Itazuki, declared an emergency and we made the strip on three engines.

'And we all needed those hot baths that night!' *Robert F. Goldsworthy*

'Those of us who were based on Okinawa envied the 98th Bomb Wing. They were stationed at Itazuki, Japan, and that was the lap of luxury. They had fresh milk, fresh eggs, fresh women. So when we were coming back from a mission, we'd think of any excuse we could to put in at Itazuki — engine trouble, radio trouble, whatever — just to get some decent food like fresh eggs and bacon.

'Old Tex would get on the intercom and say, "Engineer! We're thirty minutes out of Itazuki; time to feather number four!" So I'd feather an engine, and he'd call Itazuki to report engine trouble. We'd go in, land, have a great breakfast, and then fly back to Okinawa, where the food was lousy'. *E. L. Davis*

The 19th Bomb Group, with its capability to carry 2,000lb bombs, was assigned a steel railway bridge on the line at Seoul. For almost one month, the 19th mounted strike after strike against the bridge, using 1,000- and 2,000lb bombs, and even in desperation some 4,000lb bombs. The decking was blown to bits time and time again, but the bridge still stood.

The Japanese firm that built the bridge furnished its original drawings to try to help solve the problem. The 19th changed fuse settings, hoping to damage the superstructure if they couldn't knock out the footings. Still the bridge stood.

Gen MacArthur said he'd commend any air crew that knocked it out, and Gen Stratemeyer quietly promised a case of Scotch to the crew that did the job.

On 19 August, the 'elastic bridge' finally met its doom. The 19th sent in nine of its bombers, carrying six tons each of 1,000lb bombs. They dropped them from their trail formation, and reported hits. 'We'll finish it off tomorrow', they promised. Soon after,

B-361, a B-29 from the
98th Bomb Wing.
/ William F. Dawson

Navy pilots from Task Force 77 came in on the bridge with a mix of 37 Vought Corsairs and Douglas Skyraiders. They dive-bombed the bridge, scoring eight times. After the attack, one Navy plane peeled off, and roared along the bridge to check it for damage. He reported that it was still standing, but useless for some time to come.

On 20 August the 19th Bomb Group returned to the target, thinking to finish it off. They were surprised to see that two spans of the bridge were in the water, evidently having fallen during the night. But they bombed the bridge anyway, and had the satisfaction of seeing a third span drop into the river.

The 19th Bomb Group and the Navy's Air Group 11 both received a trophy from Gen MacArthur, and Gen Stratemeyer bought two cases of Scotch instead of one.

By September, the fortunes of the United Nations forces in Korea had changed for the better. They were driving the North Koreans north faster than the Reds had advanced south. Some of the crack NK units were at the edge of panic in their headlong retreat.

There were no more strategic targets; there was little point in maintaining the total strength of Bomber Command. Near the end of October 1950, the 22nd and 92nd Bomb Groups were sent home. On the 27th of the month, FEAF disbanded Bomber Command.

And for three days, things were quiet. Then it was like 25 June all over again as the Chinese volunteers boiled up out of their airfields on 1 November, flying their MiGs out of the privileged areas on their side of the Yalu, and following these strikes with a major ground assault on the night of 2 November.

The mood changed abruptly at Bomber Command. It was a new contest, and the old rules were no longer in use. The political restrictions that had banned the use of incendiary bombs in earlier strikes at strategic targets were rescinded. Bomber Command's B-29s were loaded with fire bombs, just as they had been six years earlier, and they headed north. They flew almost continuously for two weeks, burning the heart out of North Korean cities. MacArthur told them to start at the Yalu and work south, and to bomb anything that even resembled a strategic objective. They obeyed the orders.

'Mission day was a big day at Kadena. It was like the day of the big game when I was playing high-school football; there was excitement in the air, and it never changed the whole time I was there. It was hard to eat breakfast.

'Our wing — the 307th — flew every third day, in a mission rotation with the other wings out there. We had three squadrons, and we'd put up a total of 15 to 20 aircraft from all three squadrons. We flew mostly night missions, leaving Okinawa to arrive over the target at moonrise or moonset for visual bombing. It was sometimes a six-hour ride, sometimes a ten-hour haul. We never flew straight to the target, always went on a diversionary approach.

'With a late evening take-off, the day started early in the morning for the ground crews. They had to load the fuel, bombs and ammo, check the systems, and all that. Assuming we had an 1800 take-off, I'd get to the airplane about 1500. The bombs were loaded by then, and there were only radio people and probably ordnance people around.

'We were parked on hardstands in revetments, and I'd go to the airplane with the crew chief, crank up the external power

unit, and plug it in. Then we'd do a walkround. It was a standing gag that the B-29 was the only airplane in the Air Force with externally lubricated engines, and the only thing we worried about on the walkround was that we wanted to make sure the oil wasn't pouring out on the ground. Anything less was acceptable.

'Then I'd get into the airplane, with a mechanic or somebody to help run the checks. The inside smelled like a locker room; it was hot on Okinawa and humid besides, and the planes were closed up between missions. They got kind of gamy after a while. So I'd get into the flight engineer's seat and get out the check lists. The mechanic would sit in the pilot's seat and hold pressure on the wheel brakes.

'He'd keep an eye outside and yell, "Clear three!" and I'd engage the starter switch. We turned the engine over with the starter, and the guys standing fire guard on the ground would count the blades as they went through. When the count got to eight, I'd hit the ignition switch, shove the mixture control up over the hump, and open the throttle. The engine would catch as the throttle came up to idle.

'Then I'd wait for the oil pressure and cylinder head temperatures to come up and stabilise, and when we'd gotten all four engines started and idling in a stable condition, we'd do a prop check on all four props, running them into low blade angle. That had to be done by the guy in the pilot's seat, because I had no prop controls at my position. We checked the rpm drop with the blade angle change, reported the prop check at 2,100rpm, checked the feathering, again from the cockpit rather than from my position. After a mag check at 2,750rpm, I'd run all four engines up to full power, and the old B-29 would be sitting there jumping, with the nose gear bouncing, just wanting to go.

'After the briefings, we'd all go down to the aircraft, lay our flight gear on a canvas mat and stand an inspection by the aircraft commander. Both the pilot and I would follow that with a final walkaround of the airplane, and then we'd climb aboard. The armourers would come out to the plane, pull all the arming wires on the bombs, and we'd close the bomb bay doors, ready to go. The pilot would make an interphone check of all the crew positions, and we'd start the engines.

'We got individual taxi clearances from the tower, and we'd lumber out toward the runway, holding nose-to-tail while we were waiting for take-off. We were cleared for take-off at 30-second intervals, and we'd have three aircraft on the runway at once, one flying, one rolling, one holding.

'We'd have a final crew check at the end of the runway, and run her up to full power. The B-29 was just roaring and stomping and grunting and groaning, and the pilot would release the brakes and we'd go charging off into the sunset. I don't remember the length of the runway at Okinawa, but I do remember that I never thought it was long enough.

'There was just one runway at Kadena; one end ran straight into some mountains and the other was straight into the ocean. Every combat mission took off toward the ocean, because a loaded B-29 never stood a chance of making it the other direction. Our normal combat load was forty 500lb bombs, full fuel, all the gun turrets loaded with ammo, and nine or ten crew members loaded with flak vests, flak helmets, and as many flak curtains as we could scrounge.

'We taxied out one evening bound for North Korea with a brand-new 1st Lieutenant co-pilot. It was a hot night, and

Above: Engine start on a B-29 of the 370th Bomb Squadron, 307th Bomb Wing. / *E. L. Davis Collection*

Above right: 'With all four engines running up to power, the old B-29 would just bounce and buck and shake, like she had to move'. This B-29 of the 370th BS, 307th BW, is getting a power check well before the scheduled departure of a mission. Her bomb load has been stacked at the edge of the hardstand. / *E. L. Davis Collection*

Right: Salvoing both bomb bay loads at once, this B-29 of the 98th Bomb Wing drops demolition bombs on a North Korean target during a mission on 13 July 1951. / *USAF 80340 A.C.*

we were going to use every inch of runway and more getting off. The co-pilot's job on take-off consisted of handling the radios, holding the control column forward, and calling out airspeeds. With the turbosuperchargers on, and the old R-3350 throttles to the firewall, we might — if we were lucky — be able to pull 60 inches manifold pressure on the roll.

'When the brakes released on the old bird, it was like pulling your foot out of a gluepot. The running joke was, "Everybody stand up; it'll make it lighter!" Down the runway we go with the airspeed indicator moving like the hour hand on a Mickey Mouse watch. When we got to the point where we had better think pretty seriously about flying, our co-pilot comes on the interphone with, "The manifold pressure on number three is dropping! Abort! Abort!"

'Not another word was said. I had the throttles locked forward to the firewall with my feet. Well, we managed to get off, as I knew we would, because nobody was looking forward to a swim in the China Sea. After we got the gear up and the climb established, the pilot, ol' Tex, tossed his headset back to me and said, "Engineer! Get me another headset, will you? I can't hear a damned thing out of that one!"

'At climb power it took more than an hour to get to cruise altitude, depending on the load, and so we were off to North Korea and the flak and the MiGs. If we had loaded 2,000lb bombs, we knew that it was going to be a rough, sweaty mission because we were after something big.

'I was scared to death, but I relished it, thought about it, enjoyed it, because I thought we were accomplishing something. I felt pride, fellowship; it made me feel good to do it. But I was scared.' *E. L. Davis, flight engineer, 307th Bomb Wing*

Air superiority in the north was held by the Chinese MiGs and they proved the point time and time again. The B-29 missions were flown with fighter escort. When the big and little friends missed connections, disaster resulted. The 98th Bomb Group arrived late one day for a rendezvous, and their 18 B-29s had to make the run unescorted. Nine MiGs bounced them, damaging ten of the 18 bombers severely, three so badly that they had to make emergency landings at Taegu, in Korea, instead of making the trip back to base.

On 12 April, 1951, 39 B-29s struck the bridges at Sinui-ju on the Yalu, under an escort of high cover and screening fighters. No matter; the MiGs boiled through the formation, fought through the screen, shot down two of the B-29s and hammered six badly. That did it. Those losses were prohibitive, and the B-29 strikes in that area were called off.

'Day raids were discouraging in Korea. The MiGs got eight out of nine B-29s from the 307th Wing on what was to be their last daytime raid. After that, it was night time work, and — other than worrying about intense flak — you just hoped the airplane kept on running. That was your biggest danger.

'We went in on the target in a bomber stream, with the planes about two minutes apart. After a couple of these, the North Koreans started vectoring MiGs up towards us, and they'd get in trail with us and sit there. We could see them more easily than they could see us, because their jet exhaust was a lot brighter than the piston-engine exhaust on the B-29s.

'Anyway, gunners would call in and say, "I've got one right in my sights! Can I fire?", and we'd have to say that they couldn't. The worst thing we could have done was to fire on a MiG at night, because that would reveal our position as well as if we'd turned on the lights. With a pair of them out there, they were hoping that one would draw our fire and the other could then shoot us down. So we had a lot of frustrated gunners who never shot at anything.

'The jet stream was the big problem in Japan during World War 2, but it wasn't a problem in Korea because we were bombing between 18,000 and 25,000 feet, well below the jet stream effective altitudes. What we did have to contend with was the contrail problem. The North Koreans — or whoever it was fighting with them — would pick up our contrails at night with their searchlights. It was easy; all they did was aim the lights generally upwards and they were bound to pick up some contrails. They they traced them back to the airplane, and vectored fighters in using the contrails as telltales.

'The command level dictated the bombing altitudes to try to avoid contrails, based on forecasts from Tokyo weather central. We also got some information from weather soundings in Russia'. *Robert F. Goldsworthy*

'Those missions were long. We were doing maybe 12-hour missions in Korea. We used a lot of benzedrine, taking it just after take-off which was generally just before dark. Then we'd fly all night, come back in the morning, get our mission whisky, and take a sleeping pill. That was it, alternating benzedrine and benadryl. Sometimes I'd sleep all day and into the night, and right through the night into the next day. Luckily, we didn't fly every day.' *Vern Piotter*

Change was constant in the Korean war, and the USAF F-86 Sabres began to shoulder the fighter load. They swept into combat and seized control of the sky from the MiGs. The B-29s came out of their revetments and

headed north again, and in April pounded all the North Korean airfields, denying their use to enemy MiGs for forward operations.

Bridge-busting continued to get tougher as the war dragged on. Red flak and fighters combined to limit the bombers to a single run at altitudes above 20,000 feet. Bomber Command changed its tactics, and struck the bridges from a formation of four B-29s, coming in at an angle less than the 40-degree standard set earlier in the war. Both the 98th and 307th Bomb Group's B-29s were retrofitted with the racks that could handle 2,000lb bombs.

But their real hope was the radio-controlled bomb. The 19th Bomb Group had experimented with Razon bomb (Range and AZimuth ONly) in the summer of 1950. It was a weapon left over from the closing days of World War 2. Controlled by a direct radio link, the bomb could be corrected in range and azimuth by the bombardier.

The 19th Bomb Group knocked out about 15 bridges that way, but they really wanted the newer and bigger — and supposedly better — Tarzon bombs.

'We had three B-29s that had been modified and equipped to drop Tarzon bombs. They were 12,000lb bombs that had a special fin assembly with control surfaces that could be actuated from the drop plane. The bombardier was supposed to be able to track the bomb after the drop by a burning flare in the tail section, and to steer it in azimuth and range to correct for any ballistic problems.

'The modified B-29s had the bomb bays cut away partially, and they carried the bomb so that two-thirds of it was housed in the airplane, and about one-third stuck outside. The bomb reduced the ground clearance considerably, and so the planes were loaded in a special revetment that had a pit to increase the clearance for convenience in loading and adjusting.

'The whole effort was classified Top Secret, we were told. There was a special weapons loading team that was the only crew allowed to approach the airplane during the loading phase, and it seemed like they took days to get the airplane ready for a drop. They went through a long ritual of levelling the aircraft before they slung the bomb in place. They used special bomb dollies, and they raised the bomb into position, rather than hoisting it in as was done with the smaller conventional bombs.

'A lot of the details have faded, and so have some of the names. But I can't forget the name of Payne Jennings, Colonel, United States Air Force, Strategic Air Command. He was, in many ways, a very likeable guy, but he was also very gung-ho, and gave the impression that he was out to win the war single-handed.

'One of his pet projects was the Tarzon bomb, and he flew several missions with crews on Tarzon drops. We had an aircraft commander in my squadron who was very professional, and very good, and Payne Jennings elected to ride with him on a Tarzon mission.

'They took off and were well along toward Korea when they radioed back that they were having some trouble with an engine. Now the rule was that if an engine gave you trouble with Tarzon aboard, you jettisoned the bomb and came back home. If you didn't, you wouldn't get home. You were carrying a 12,000lb bomb, and that was not a job for three engines.

'Well, they lost the engine, but they radioed that Colonel Jennings had ordered that they press on to the target and that's what they were doing. A short time later they lost a second engine, probably because they had to increase power to stay in the air

B-29s from the 92nd Bomb Wing drop on targets in Korea. The Circle W was the wing identification for the 505th BW in World War 2. That Group was de-activated in June 1946, and its letter became available for use with the 92nd at a later date and in another war.
/ USAF via Boeing

on three, and the second engine couldn't take the stress. But they said they were continuing to Korea, and that's the last word we ever heard from the crew.

'Everybody was convinced that they finally had to ditch — they just ran out of altitude — and that the plane and crew were lost in the ditching. But even at that, some of us believed that Colonel Payne Jennings was somewhere out in the China Sea, astride that Tarzon bomb, paddling like mad for Korea.'
W. B. Leake, armament chief, 93rd Bomb Sqdn, 19th Bomb Group

A similar accident that was observed later, again involving a heavily loaded B-29 with a Tarzon bomb, showed that the bomb could not be jettisoned 'safe'. The tail assembly ripped off on impact with the water, and simultaneously armed and detonated the bomb.

The loss of Col Jennings and the crew was attributed to an attempt to jettison the Tarzon bomb in the last few seconds before ditching, rather than as soon as the trouble developed. The bomb probably blew up on hitting the water, destroying the B-29 and killing the crew.

Tarzon bombing was one attempt to advance the art — or science, for the bombardiers among the readers — of free-fall ballistic bombing. Two other techniques were used in Korea.

One was ground-directed drops, using pre-surveyed radar stations on the ground. These accurately sited points located, tracked and directed the bombers on their bomb runs. It resulted in precision bombing at night, something that the bombing radars of the day could not guarantee. Many of these missions were flown in support of ground troops, because the B-29s were able to saturate a small area with the drop. They used 500lb fragmentation bombs with the fuses set for air bursts, and each bomb covered an area about 150 yards in diameter when it blew. On occasion, the B-29s dropped as close as 400 yards to the UN front lines.

The other technique was the Shoran drop. Shoran — for short-range navigation — had been developed during World War 2, along with Loran — long-range navigation — but both were orginally only navigation techniques. These systems transmitted an electronic grid in the sky, in effect, and equipment on board the B-29s could read the transmissions and compute a position very accurately. The same system could be used to drop bombs, and by mid-1951 the Shoran-guided drop was routine in Korea.

The enemy was hurting, and mid-1951 saw their first attempt to arrange truce talks. By the time the truce talks broke down, in August 1951, the Reds had licked their wounds, devised some new tactics and were ready to sally forth to battle. Their sudden and strong assault gave them control of the air again, and FEAF stopped all fighter-bomber strikes against the Yalu area as too risky.

The Reds took advantage of the truce break to start rehabilitation of their airfields, looking towards their use as forward bases for the MiGs. The B-29s went into action against those bases, getting away cleanly on their first strike on 18 October 1951. But the MiGs were there to meet them the next time, and on the third mission. In one week, Bomber Command lost five B-29s, as many as they had lost in the entire war to date.

Further daylight missions were scrapped as Bomber Command began night raids again. The NK countered with radar-directed searchlights, night fighters and an airborne battle commander, who orbited above the bomber stream and co-ordinated the MiG attacks. Glossy black lacquer was applied to the B-29 bellies to cut down their visibility in the searchlight beams, a trick learned in World War 2 and forgotten or filed. Countermeasures — the 'porcupine' missions of World War 2 — were revived to confuse enemy radars.

On 30 September, a combined force of B-29s and Douglas B-26s struck the Namsan-ni Chemical Plant on the Yalu River. First, three B-29s went in on a flak-suppression strike, bombing known positions with air-burst bombs. Equipped with electronic

countermeasures gear, that trio then continued to fly above the target area and used their ECM to confuse, decoy and jam enemy radars. The B-26s went in low to hit the searchlights, one of their specialised attack routines. The main force of 45 B-29s came in next, made a Shoran drop, and clobbered the factory. That was the end of the last strategic target of any importance in the North.

A ten-day sustained air attack followed the strike at Namsan-ni, using Shoran for most of the drops and proving, as was found out later, that more Shoran training was necessary. New tactics evolved. The bomber stream was compressed to reduce the time gap between successive airplanes to one minute. The 91st Strategic Reconnaissance Squadron (formerly the 31st Photo Reconnaissance Squadron) flew its first 'ferret' missions to locate, monitor and analyse enemy radars. Marine night fighters operated with the B-29s in a barrier screen ahead of the main bomber stream, then added a top cover for the time on the bomb run from initial point to bombs away. Bombing altitudes were chosen carefully to avoid telltale contrail formation. Attacks were scheduled at irregular times and when the moon was dark. USAF Lockheed F-94 night fighters joined the attack, flying the barrier screen and leaving the Marine night fighters free to fly the top cover mission.

Scientific analysis of bombing began about then, and the B-29 missions were studied and restudied. From December 1952 to May 1953, the combat effectiveness of Bomber Command nearly doubled. But the war dragged on only a few more weeks. On 17 July 1953, RB-29s of the 91st SRS flew the last mission for Bomber Command, a drop of psychological warefare leaflets.

The B-29s had fought for 37 months, and had been in action on all but 26 of those days. More than 21,000 bombing sorties were logged, compared to 33,000 in World War 2, and the total bomb weight dropped exceeded 167,000 tons, compared to 147,000 tons dropped on Japan by B-29s in World War 2.

During one period from 13 July to 31 October 1950, which included the strategic bombing campaign, B-29s dropped 30,130 tons of bombs. It was a monthly average tonnage greater than the peak performance of the B-29s in World War 2. And in that earlier war, the planes were new, and maintenance was far simpler.

Bomber Command's authorised strength never exceeded 99 Superfortresses. The combat losses totalled 34: 16 lost to enemy fighters, four to enemy flak, and 14 to 'other causes'.

The B-29s in Korea were flown longer and harder and dropped more bombs, than were the B-29s in World War 2. It was an outstanding performance record for a comparative handful of planes, and it was achieved under some fairly bad conditions. Not all the bases had hot baths.

B-29s of the 92nd Bomb Wing on the high road to a target in North Korea. / *USAF via Boeing*

First Lieutenant Charles A. Stone was aircraft commander of 022, an RB-29 assigned to the 91 Strategic Reconnaissance Squadron and based as Yokota Air Base, Japan. During the Korean war, Lt Stone's crew flew reconnaissance missions above North Korea during a tour of duty that lasted from 23 October 1953 to 18 July 1954.

Stone was a good amateur photographer and he took these pictures — with the one obvious exception — of his crew during one of their missions. They were made available by Jim Cliver, then an Airman First Class and flight engineer on *Old Double Deuce*.

The crew wore baseball-style flight caps, almost covered with markings. Each man has his home state named on the visor of the cap. Over his left temple was the Circle X identifier of the 91st SRS, with the unit written out next to it. Proceeding around the cap, the next item was a red silhouette of a B-29, then his nickname at the back. Next to that was a cutout white silhouette of his home state. His name in Japanese characters was on the right temple. On the top of the hat was the base: Yokota AFB, Japan. And on Jim Cliver's cap, which is lying on the writer's desk at this moment, the top was further emblazoned with his wife's name — Coldine — and his first child, a daughter, Diane. At the front of the cap, above the visor, were the initials FE for his position of flight engineer.

Other crewmen had similar caps with different details.

Above: The aircraft commander, the old man, the skipper, 1st Lt Charles A. Stone, talking, listening, looking ahead and driving the airplane simultaneously.

Far left: 2nd Lt M. N. Hahn digs into canned rations on the long flight from Yokota. He's pilot of *Double Deuce*, flying from the right seat and — sometimes — being allowed to make the landing.

Left: SAC cigar tilted at a jaunty angle, 1st Lt Brackbill, the navigator, studies his charts.

Above left: 2nd Lt J. Jackson, from Louisiana, was radar operator on 022, back in the dark among the scopes, knobs and dials, making sense out of aimless squiggles on screens and weird sounds in the headphones.

Above centre: Airman Second Class Don Barnhart was radio operator, and he's out of uniform; his unadorned flight cap is standard unmodified issue.

Above: Four sets of everything confront the flight engineer, Airman First Class Jim Cliver. Cruise control is only one aspect of his job; he also must know how the pressurising system works, what that funny noise is when the wheels retract, and why isn't this damned thing working?

Far left: Airman Second Class Glowcheski, the left gunner.

Left: 1st Lt Weisburn, the bombardier, doesn't have all that much to do on a reconnaissance flight, so he often stands, hunched over, in the gap between the instrument panels and talks with Stone and Hahn. 'How the hell can you eat that stuff, Hahn?'

Right: Tail gunner Farley, Airman Second Class, is dressed for a long, lonely, cold ride back in the tail of the RB-29.

Far right: 'Hey, Sniker!' And Airman First Class Sniker, CFC gunner for *Double Deuce*, looks toward Lt Stone and the camera.

Below: Suited, chuted and harnessed, right gunner Airman Second Class Kleincuff backs into Korea. He's from Nebraska, and the patchwork farmland below doesn't remind him one little bit of the square-mile farms of his home state. Or of Omaha, either.

Below left: Lt Stone briefs the crew and inspects them before leaving on a mission over Korea. In the background is *Old Double Deuce*, the RB-29 that this crew called home for long hours at a stretch.

On 10 December 1951, Sgt William F. Dawson, then a left gunner in the 343rd Bomb Squadron, 98th Bomb Wing, left the United States aboard a DC-4 transport operated by the Flying Tiger Line. He ended his trip at Yokota Air Base, Japan, after stops at Honolulu and Wake Island. Eight days later, he was aboard *Sad Sac*, a B-29 of the 343rd BS, Capt Anthony H. Carson commanding, and they were dropping propaganda leaflets along the East coast of Korea.

Dawson completed his tour of duty in the Far East in May, 1953. During the period of his combat duty, he spent spare time photographing much of the ground activity that prepared the B-29s for their missions. All the photos shown here are from his collection, most of them taken by Dawson himself.

Above: Well, the first thing we gotta do is open up the accessory section panel. The mechanic on the maintenance stand is doing just that. Flow lines on the propeller blade seem to indicate trouble with the governor mechanism that would produce the leak at the hub.

Centre left: There's just no other way to get at the parts I need to get at! So the tail gunner goes in the turret himself, working on his twin fifties before the mission goes.

Bottom left: If I get a shot at any MiGs, I want to make damn sure these guns are gonna work. Before the missions, gunners load their turrets, check the gun barrels and clean or swab them with gun oil as needed.

Above: 'Sometimes we'd carry an extra pilot, or an ECM operator, or even a passenger who was observing the mission, so that's why you see twelve guys here in the crew lineup. That's Captain Carson in front, and I'm third from the right.'

Above left: 'Before the mission, we'd all line our gear up on a canvas mat spread out near the nose of the ship, so Capt Carson could inspect it all at the same time he inspected us.'

Far left: 'We're about ready to go. That's the flight engineer, figuring out how we're going to do on the fuel he's got aboard. The guns have been loaded; you can tell, because the top turret guns are pointing up in the air and the belly turret guns are pointing straight down at the ground.'

Left: 'That's Dupper — Cpl. H. H. Dupper — and we spent a lot of time together in the back of the B-29, sitting across the fuselage from each other. He was the right gunner and I was the left gunner.'

Right: 'And that's the right side of *Sad Sac*, aircraft 1676, the first one I flew in, in Korea. The 'Couldn't Care Less' on the left side was the insignia of the 343rd Bomb Squadron. I don't think it was ever the official insignia.'

Bibliography

Anderton, David A.; *Strategic Air Command;* Ian Allan Ltd, London; 1975.

Anon; *The Pictorial History of the 444th Bombardment Group;* Newsfoto Publishing Co., San Angelo, Texas.

Anon; *498th Bombardment Group;* Unknown publisher.

Berger, Carl; *B-29: The Superfortress;* Ballantine Books, New York; 1970.

Bowers, Peter M.; *Boeing Aircraft Since 1916;* Putnam and Company, London; 1966.

Brown, Anthony Cave and MacDonald, Charles B.; *The Secret History of the Atomic Bomb;* Dell Publishing Co, Inc, New York; 1977.

Carroll, John M.; *Secrets of Electronic Espionage;* E. P. Dutton & Co, Inc, New York; 1966.

Carter, Kit C. and Mueller, Robert.; *The Army Air Forces in World War II: Combat Chronology, 1941-1945;* Government Printing Office, Washington; 1975.

Collison, Thomas; *The Superfortress is Born;* Duell, Sloan & Pearce, New York; 1945.

Craig, William; *The Fall of Japan;* The Dial Press, New York; 1967.

Craven, Wesley F. and Cate, James L.; *The Army Air Forces in World War II; Volume Five: The Pacific: Matterhorn to Nagasaki;* The University of Chicago Press, Chicago; 1953.

Francillon, R. J.: *Japanese Aircraft of the Pacific War;* Funk & Wagnalls, New York; 1970.

Futrell, Robert F.; *The United States Air Force in Korea, 1950-1953;* Duell, Sloan and Pearce, New York; 1963.

Goforth, Capt. Pat E.; *The Long Haul: The Story of the 497th Bomb Group (VH);* Newsfoto Publishing Co; San Angelo, Texas.

Goldberg, Alfred; *A History of the United States Air Force, 1907-1957;* D. VanNostrand Company, Inc, Princeton, NJ; 1957.

Higham, Robin and Siddall, Abigail; *Flying Combat Aircraft of the USAAF-USAF;* The Iowa State University Press, Ames, Iowa; 1975.

Infield, Glenn B.; *Unarmed and Unafraid;* The MacMillan Company, New York; 1970.

Jackson, Robert; *Air War over Korea;* Charles Scribner's Sons, New York; 1973.

Knebel, Fletcher and Bailey, Charles W., II.; *No High Ground;* Harper & Row, New York; 1960.

Kohn, Gregory C. and Rust, Kenn C.; The 313th Bombardment Wing; *Journal, American Aviation Historical Society,* Vol 9, No 3 (Fall 1964), p 189ff.

LeMay, Gen. Curtis E. with Kantor, MacKinlay; *Mission with LeMay;* Doubleday & Company, Inc, Garden City, NY; 1965.

Maurer, Maurer; *Air Force Combat Units of World War II;* Franklin Watts, Inc, New York; 1963.

Maurer, Maurer; *Combat Squadrons of the Air Force, World War II;* Government Printing Office, Washington; 1969.

McClure, Glenn E.; *An Unofficial Pictorial History of the 500th Bombardment Group;* Rubidoux Printing Company, Riverside, Cal.

Rust, Kenn C.; Bomber Markings of the Twentieth A.F.; *Journal, American Aviation Historical Society,* Vol 7, No 3 (Fall 1962) and Vol 7, No 4 (Winter 1962).

Thomas, Gordon and Witts, Max M.; *Enola Gay;* Stein and Day, New York; 1977.